HISTORICAL STUDIES
OF THE
ENGLISH PARLIAMENT

HISTORICAL STUDIES
OF THE
ENGLISH PARLIAMENT

VOLUME 2
1399-1603

EDITED BY
E. B. FRYDE
Reader in History, University College of Wales, Aberystwyth

AND
EDWARD MILLER
Professor of Medieval History, University of Sheffield

CAMBRIDGE
AT THE UNIVERSITY PRESS
1970

Published by the Syndics of the Cambridge University Press
Bentley House, 200 Euston Road, London, N.W.1
American Branch: 32 East 57th Street, New York, N.Y. 10022
Introduction, notes and this selection © Cambridge University Press 1970
Library of Congress Catalogue Card Number: 78–960 88
Standard Book Number: 521 07733 8 clothbound
521 09611 1 paperback

Reprinted in Great Britain
by Bookprint Limited, Crawley, Sussex

In Memory of
HELEN CAM

CONTENTS

NOTES ON CONTRIBUTORS

A. L. BROWN
Senior Lecturer in History, University of Glasgow.

G. R. ELTON
Professor of History, University of Cambridge.

J. R. LANDER
Associate Professor, Department of History, University of Western Ontario, London (Ontario).

H. MILLER
Lecturer in History, University College of North Wales, Bangor.

SIR JOHN NEALE
Sometime Professor of History, University College, University of London.

J. S. ROSKELL
Professor of History, University of Manchester.

B. P. WOLFFE
Senior Lecturer in History, University of Exeter.

PREFACE

SINCE the times of the Tudors and the Stuarts, the problem of the origins and the early history of the English parliament has engaged the attention of publicists, politicians and historians. The very fact that parliament became the centrepiece of the English constitution, and that it exercised the influence it did upon constitutional development in the British Commonwealth and in lands beyond the British sphere of direct influence, has made its development even in its earliest stages a matter of enquiry, discussion and sometimes political mythology. In this debate it can be argued that the publication in 1893 of F. W. Maitland's discussion of the Lenten Parliament of 1305 represented a watershed. Since that time medieval and Tudor parliaments have been subjected to detailed and systematic scrutiny, often in journals and transactions of learned societies not easily available to students without access to specialized libraries. These volumes, therefore, begin in a chronological sense with Maitland's essay and reproduce certain of the crucial essays published since his time which have shaped the way in which historians of the present day regard the beginnings of English parliamentary history. For one reason and another we have been unable to include everything we should like to have reprinted. In some cases we were unable to obtain the necessary permission to republish and other things had to be excluded because of the limited space at our disposal. Even with these omissions, however, our hope is that what we have reprinted here will provide a convenient compendium of the modern learning about parliamentary history down to the great age of constitutional controversy which opened when a Scottish monarch became an English king.

As editors we have naturally accumulated a variety of obligations. We would wish, first, to acknowledge our gratitude to the authors or their representatives, the journals and the societies which have permitted us to reproduce these essays. The Librarians and library staffs of the University of Sheffield and the University College of Wales, Aberystwyth, have not only provided copies of material but also that constant help which is too often taken for granted by those who use their facilities. We have had every co-operation in our dealings with the Cambridge University Press and wish to thank the editorial staff of the English and American offices. For much labour in preparing material for publication we are grateful to Mrs. Jean Wigfield and Mrs. Pat Holland.

ix

Finally, we dedicate these volumes to the memory of a scholar whose contributions to English Parliamentary history find their appropriate place in this collection. Apart from that, however, Helen Cam inspired others to pursue enquiries in this field as a teacher in the Universities of London, Cambridge and Harvard; and, as President of the International Commission for the History of Representative and Parliamentary Institutions, she was one of those who enlarged the horizons of English parliamentary studies.

EDMUND B. FRYDE.

EDWARD MILLER.

ACKNOWLEDGEMENTS

THE editors wish to thank the auth ᵣₛ and executors and the following publishers and journal editors for permission to reprint the articles in this volume:

Longmans, Green & Co Ltd and the journal editors for chapters 1 and 2 which appeared in the *English Historical Review*, LXXIX (1964) and LXXIII (1958) respectively; Mr. F. H. Hinsley for chapter 3 which appeared in the *Historical Journal*, IV (1961); the Institute of Historical Research for chapter 4 which appeared in the *Bulletin of the Institute of Historical Research*, XXXV (1962); the University of London Press Ltd for chapter 5 which appeared in R. W. Seton-Watson (ed.), *Tudor Studies presented to Albert Frederick Pollard* (London, 1924); the Institute of Historical Research for chapter 6 which appeared in the *Bulletin of the Institute of Historical Research*, XXV (1952); the Royal Historical Society for chapter 7 which appeared in *Transactions of the Royal Historical Society*, 5th series, VI (1956); Longmans, Green & Co Ltd and the journal editors for chapters 8 and 9 which appeared in the *English Historical Review*, LXV (1950) and XXXIX (1924) respectively; the John Rylands Library, Manchester for chapter 10 which appeared in the *Bulletin of the John Rylands Library*, XLVI (1964).

ABBREVIATIONS

A.H.R.   *American Historical Review*

B.I.H.R.   *Bulletin of the Institute of Historical Research*

Econ. H.R.   *Economic History Review*

E.H.R.   *English Historical Review*

L.Q.R.   *Law Quarterly Review*

Rot. Parl.   *Rotuli Parliamentorum*

S.I.C.   *Studies presented to the International Commission for the History of Representative and Parliamentary Institutions.*

T.R.H.S.   *Transactions of the Royal Historical Society*

These are the abbreviations used in the introduction and the end notes; some of the articles follow different conventions.

INTRODUCTION

THE FIFTEENTH CENTURY

IN discussing some of the principal developments in the history of parliament between the usurpation of the crown by Henry IV in 1399 and the death of Henry VII in 1509 we must distinguish as clearly as possible between the trend of political events and the more fundamental changes in the composition and functioning of parliaments.[1] Meetings of parliaments provided the occasion for some of the most important struggles for power and influence; but there is a great danger of dignifying transient expedients of hard-pressed politicians into consistent policies or deliberate 'constitutional' experiments. It will conduce to clarity if we enumerate at the outset some of the episodes when parliament provided a forum for important political developments. Under Henry IV its sessions furnished something of an outlet for the widespread discontent with the shortcomings and the heavy expense of the government. During the minority of his grandson the magnates and prelates sitting in the upper house of parliament claimed that the authority of the crown ought to be vested in them until Henry VI came of age. Between 1449 and 1460 contending factions attempted in turn to use parliaments for the capture or maintenance of power. The Yorkist rulers tried to manage parliament in an effective fashion and Henry VII perfected their methods still further. It will be our task to show how each of these episodes in the political history of parliament left some permanent mark on that institution, but due weight must also be given to more gradual changes brought about by the more normal developments within English society.

In 1924 T. F. T. Plucknett could still speak of 'the commonplace generalization that the fifteenth century witnessed an inordinate growth of parliamentary and constitutional rule',[2] though he went on to expose the wholly anachronistic nature of such views. Stubbs's belief that the Lancastrian period witnessed 'the trial and failure of a great constitutional experiment'[3] was based especially on the evidence derived from the reign of Henry IV. The proceedings in some of Henry's parliaments, especially

---

[1] I am adapting here to parliament the more general comments of S. B. Chrimes, *English Constitutional Ideas in the Fifteenth Century* (Cambridge, 1936), pp. 242–3.
[2] In 'The Lancastrian Constitution', *Tudor Studies presented to A. F. Pollard*, ed. by R. W. Seton-Watson (London, 1924), p. 161.
[3] Quoted by A. L. Brown, *infra*, chapter I, p. 31.

those of 1401, 1404 and 1406, certainly show that the new king was at times in an unusually embarrassed political position. His need for parliamentary grants of taxes forced him to endure criticisms of his household and of his alleged financial mismanagement. For example, a recently discovered report of the happenings at the parliament of 1404 shows the king so discomfited by one such series of exchanges with the commons' speaker, that he altogether absented himself from parliament for five or six days. 'But even when he reappeared the commons resumed their badgering' and when their speaker also demanded explanations from the lords, Henry commanded the upper house to comply with the wishes of the commons.[1] But it does not follow that these incidents led to any lasting changes in the powers of the crown. Stubbs ascribed special importance to the appointment of the royal councillors in the parliaments of 1404 and 1406 and to the fact that these councillors were specially sworn to observe certain conditions imposed by the commons. It is the special merit of Dr. A. L. Brown's article[2] to show that these appointments did not in fact produce any significant changes in the membership of the council and that the commons were not attempting to exercise any control over the council. The sole purpose of the commons was to try to ensure that the grants of money made by them on those particular occasions were spent in such a way as to produce a marked improvement in the king's finances and in the military situation of the kingdom. The commons had apparently no other more far-reaching objectives.

The important part played by the commons in the parliamentary politics of Henry's reign did have some enduring consequences. Some of the accepted official ideas about the position of their assembly were becoming more clearly defined. In 1407 Henry IV expressly reaffirmed the customary right of the speaker to present on behalf of both lords and commons the indenture containing the terms of a money grant.[3] In the same parliament occurred the first recorded recognition in an important official document of the commons' position as 'procurators and attorneys of all the counties, cities and boroughs and of all the people of the realm'.[4] By the fourteen-eighties this would become one of the foundations of the established legal doctrine that no parliamentary statute was valid unless the commons had

[1] C. M. Fraser in *B.I.H.R.* xxxiv (1961), 197–8, conveniently summarized in J. S. Roskell, *The Commons and their Speakers in English Parliaments, 1376–1523* (Manchester, 1965), pp. 47–8.
[2] *Infra*, chapter I.
[3] This promise involved a tacit recognition that the king ought not to make a prior agreement with the lords about the amount of a tax. But as late as 1593 the government was able to do this successfully and thus forced the commons to accept a larger grant than they had originally wished to concede (*infra*, p. 317).
[4] Chrimes, *English Constitutional Ideas*, p. 311.

assented to it.[1] The commons' own views about the history and the rights of their house were undergoing important changes in the early decades of the fifteenth century. A petition of the commons in 1414 contained some very far-reaching claims.[2] It was prompted by the unusually extensive amending of their petitions in the previous parliament of 1413. The king's reply, couched in somewhat ambiguous terms, appeared to promise merely a return to more customary procedures. But the commons used this occasion to assert that 'it has ever been their liberty and freedom that no statute or law be made unless they have given their assent thereto; also it is to be considered that the commons . . . who are and always have been members of your parliament, are both assentors and petitioners'.[3] Henry V ignored in his reply those wider claims, which were quite unjustified historically, but which did correspond in practice to recent developments. Under Henry IV the commons' share in legislation has been effectively increasing and would continue to grow under his son and grandson.

'We may perhaps see the admission of the commons to participate normally in all legislation as one of the most important changes of the first quarter of the fifteenth century.'[4] The only way of reconstructing this story is to combine the official record in the Rolls of Parliament with such original bills, or drafts of bills, as happen to survive and can be precisely dated. Much turns also on the various endorsements entered on these bills, recording their progress through parliament, though, unfortunately, in the early decades of the fifteenth century the makers of these annotations did not adhere to precise rules. Where so much depends on accidental survivals of evidence, there is a considerable likelihood of under-estimating the extent of new developments and of postdating their occurrence.[5]

There were two main types of changes. Private petitions presented at the time of parliament, instead of being normally addressed to the king, began with increasing frequency to be submitted in the first place to the commons in the hope of thus gaining the collective support of the lower house. Under the first two Lancastrian kings a growing number of petitioners came to believe that their adoption of this procedure might materially increase their chances of success. It was seemingly a tribute to the greater political importance of the commons. The same practical reasons probably account for the other main innovation, the most important of all. Proposed

---

[1] *Infra*, p. 12.
[2] What follows is based chiefly on Chrimes, *English Constitutional Ideas*, pp. 159–64.
[3] Quoted from B. Wilkinson, *Constitutional History of England in the Fifteenth Century* (1964), p. 311.
[4] *Ibid.*, p. 280.
[5] The best discussion of the evidence discovered hitherto is in two articles by A. R. Myers in *E.H.R.* LII (1937) and *University of Toronto Law Journal*, III (1939).

legislation, which had already secured the approval of the king's councillors and of the magnates, began to be submitted subsequently to the commons as well, in order to obtain their assent. Most of the earliest instances that can be dated precisely come from the minority of Henry VI, but the origins of this practice may be older. By the middle of the century legislative measures originating with the lords were normally sent later on to the commons for their approval. This may not have been done in the case of some of the exceptional political arrangements of the 'fifties which, anyhow, fell outside all normal rules. If we confine ourselves to the study of the more usual practices, there is no formal record of any proposal originating with the lords being rejected by the lower house during the reign of Henry VI. But two letters preserved among the Paston correspondence show that, in 1454, a bill directed against a particular individual, after passing through the lords, failed to be enacted because the commons were hostile to it.[1] Lastly it must be stressed that in the first half of the fifteenth century the bulk of the more important legislation sprang from petitions sponsored in the first place by the lower house, many of them originating with various sectional interests. 'In the second quarter of the fifteenth century almost every addition to the statute book originated in the commons.'[2] During that period the king's ministers did not regard the introducing of legislation as one of the main tasks of government. Through their lack of interest the initiative in promoting new statutes passed for the first time to the commons.[3] This was merely a passing phase devoid of any 'constitutional significance'. Later on in the century the more purposeful Yorkist and Tudor rulers became again responsible for initiating the bulk of the more important legislation.

In 1455 the royal judges, in the course of criminal proceedings against a certain John Pilkington, demanded from the master of the rolls and the clerk of parliament a statement of the rules observed in amending bills during their progress through the two houses of parliament. The resultant answers convey with great precision some of the changes in the legislative procedure during the first half of the fifteenth century. The commons' share in legislation emerges as almost equal to that of the lords, though there still lingered some remnants of the former more inferior status of 'the common house'. In their testimony these expert witnesses assumed that all statutes normally received the assent of both houses of parliament, irrespective of whether the initial bills had originated with the lords or the commons. In the matter of amendments the position of the commons was

[1] S. B. Chrimes in *E.H.R.* XLIX (1934), 496.
[2] R. L. Storey, *The End of the House of Lancaster* (London, 1966), p. 12.
[3] Cf. Chrimes's remarks, *English Constitutional Ideas*, pp. 241–3.

at that date still somewhat inferior to that of the lords. A commons' bill amended in the upper house had to be resubmitted to the commons only if the lords' amendments extended the scope of the original bill. In the example mentioned in 1455, if the commons granted a tax for two years and the lords extended its duration to four years, such an amendment would need the approval of the lower house. But an amendment introduced by the lords that merely restricted the scope of a measure previously passed by the commons would not require a resubmission to the lower house.[1] A surviving fragment of the lords' journal for the first parliament of Edward IV confirms that these rules were being applied in 1461.[2]

The predominance of the great lords in the royal council formed the most distinctive feature of the English government during the minority of Henry VI. The effect of this episode on the history of the upper house of parliament still awaits a satisfactory study. It may have formed an important stage in what A. F. Pollard described as 'the development or perversion of the king's council in parliament into a hereditary house of lords'.[3] We are particularly concerned here with the gradual change in the status of those councillors who were neither prelates nor important temporal lords, and in order to trace this change we must distinguish clearly between the membership of the king's council outside parliament and the special occasions when the lords temporal and spiritual assembled with other royal advisers in a parliament.

The fluctuations in the composition of the king's council and in the relative importance of the different groups of its members reflected the shifts in the political situation. Under masterful kings like Edward I or Edward III the standing of particular councillors depended mainly on the king's personal estimate of them, and men of non-lordly rank could be as influential as the great magnates. During periods of ineffectual kingship, and particularly during the royal minorities, the council came to consist predominantly or almost entirely of great lords and prelates while other royal officials and the judges were reduced to a politically inferior position. This was particularly the case during the minority of Henry VI, and after he came of age the council continued to be dominated by a particular group of magnates and prelates. The former chief justice, Sir John Fortescue, was presumably remembering his experiences during that period when he remarked 'what lower man was ther sytinge in that counsell, that durste

---

[1] *Ibid.*, pp. 222–4, 231–3. The whole text has been reprinted in W. H. Dunham, *The Fane Fragment of the 1461 Lords' Journal* (New Haven, 1935), pp. 99–102. The most important passages are translated in Wilkinson, *Constitutional History*, p. 312.

[2] Dunham, *op. cit.*, pp. 12, 70, 75–6.

[3] *The Evolution of Parliament* (1st ed., 1920), p. 104.

say ayen the openyon off any off the grete lordis?'[1] When in the later fifteenth century the Yorkist kings and Henry VII re-established an effective personal monarchy they again freely chose some of their most influential councillors outside the group of magnates and prelates.

Originally, in the early fourteenth century, the composition of the council active in parliament corresponded exactly to its membership outside parliamentary sessions. But gradually the membership of the council in parliament began to be permanently affected by the conviction of the magnates that they alone ought to be accepted as the king's main councillors. The long minority of Henry VI may have formed one of the more decisive stages in this obscure process of change, though this is merely a hypothesis. In January 1427 the lords of the council were able, without challenge, to claim that during a king's minority the execution of the king's authority was collectively vested in the whole body of the lords spiritual and temporal and in them alone 'at suche tyme as thei be assembled in parlement or in greet counsail, and ellus hem nought beyng so assembled, unto the lordes chosen and named to be of his continuel Counsail'.[2] These doctrines were again effectively applied during the various political crises of the 'fifties. In Professor Chrimes's words, they had crystallized by then 'into a rather more specifically "peerage" doctrine. When in 1454, York was called upon to assume the Protectorate he did so, he said, only of the due and humble obedience that he owed to the king and to the peerage of the land, to whom by the occasion of the infirmity of the king rested the exercise of his authority.'[3] The ultimate outcome was the emergence of an upper house of parliament confined to the peerage, though the success of the peers in excluding other councillors on these parliamentary occasions was counterbalanced by their failure under Edward IV and Henry VII to monopolize the membership of the council out of parliament.[4]

The non-lordly officers among the royal councillors, and especially the legal officers of the crown, continued to play a vital part in drafting and amending legislation in the upper house. The fragment of the lords' journal for the first parliament of Edward IV mentions the committal of bills to mixed groups of peers, judges and other expert officials.[5] The

[1] C. Plummer (ed.), *The Governance of England* (Oxford, 1885), p. 145.
[2] Quoted from S. B. Chrimes and A. L. Brown, *Select Documents of English Constitutional History, 1307–1485* (London, 1961), pp. 258–9. See also Chrimes, *English Constitutional Ideas*, pp. 147–51.
[3] Chrimes, *English Constitutional Ideas*, p. 151.
[4] Pollard, *op. cit.*, p. 293.
[5] Dunham, *op. cit.*, pp. 19 (Peter Ardern, one of the judges), 25 (the dean of St. Severin at Bordeaux, a master in chancery and an experienced diplomatic negotiator).

reappearance of the lords' journals under Henry VIII shows that in the first years of his reign bills were normally committed in the upper house to the legal officers of the crown.[1] But the distinction between the peers and the non-lordly councillors, who acted as expert assistants of the former, has clearly emerged by that time. Under the Tudor dynasty those councillors who were not peers normally secured election to the house of commons and tried to manage that house in the king's interest.[2]

The fifteenth century was a time of notable changes in the composition of the house of commons. These changes owed their origin chiefly to long-term developments within English society rather than to any particular political events. Some of the most important innovations occurred during the first twenty-five years of the reign of Henry VI (1422–47), 'that is before the time when the government of Henry VI was submitted to those strains and stresses which brought him ultimately to deposition'.[3]

There was a gradual blurring of differences between the types of members who were elected for counties and for boroughs. The origins of this went back to the fourteenth century, but the tempo of change was particularly rapid under the Lancastrian dynasty. In a few cases men who were still actively engaged in trade secured election for counties, though this continued to be rare.[4] But landowners, lawyers,[5] royal and magnate officials began to be returned for boroughs with such frequency that they came to outnumber genuine burgesses. Already in 1422, in the first parliament of Henry VI, 'the gentry in the commons outnumbered the members of the burgess class proper by something like four to three'.[6] The great innovation of the second quarter of the fifteenth century lay in the growing disregard of the legal requirement that members ought to reside in the constituencies that they represented. Under Henry VI a large proportion of the borough representatives ceased to be residents of the localities that sent them to parliament. 'By the middle of the century the non-resident were as numerous as the resident' with the result that the commons became even more markedly dominated by landed gentlemen. In the parliaments of Edward IV they formed at least two thirds of the members.[7]

[1] Pollard, op. cit., pp. 293–4.
[2] Infra, pp. 26–7.
[3] J. S. Roskell, The Commons in the Parliament of 1422 (Manchester, 1954), p. 133. In Chapter VII he provides the most up-to-date account of these changes, based on the pioneer researches of M. McKisack, Parliamentary Representation of English Boroughs in the Middle Ages (Oxford, 1932).
[4] Three men of this sort represented Lincolnshire on six occasions between 1380 and 1439. Cf. Roskell in Nottingham Mediaeval Studies, III (1959).
[5] For the importance of the lawyers later on, see infra, p. 26.
[6] Roskell, The Commons in the Parliament of 1422, p. 131.
[7] Ibid., pp. 129 and 132. See also infra, pp. 25–6.

Men were competing more eagerly for seats in the commons. Some of the smaller towns were 'rapidly acquiring a reputation for accessibility among seat-hunters'. Until the early fifteenth century the number of boroughs represented in the lower house tended to decline, only 74 returning members in 1419. A reverse trend set in under Henry VI. Ten new members were added to the house between 1447 and 1453 through the enfranchisement of five tiny places, all of them pocket-boroughs from the start of their existence. They were created to oblige influential patrons who wished to nominate their representatives.[1] A letter from John Paston to his elder brother, Sir John, written in the middle of a parliamentary election in September 1472, suggests that new constituencies could be created a fortnight before a parliament was due to meet in order to provide places for men who had failed to secure any of the existing seats. In Paston's opinion 'there be a dozen towns in England that choose no burgess which ought to do it' and he advised his brother that 'ye may be set in for one of those towns'.[2]

Another novelty of the first half of the fifteenth century were the statutes regulating parliamentary elections (acts of 1406, 1410, 1413, 1429, 1445). The best remembered of these measures is the act of 1429 which, among other things, authorized the sheriff to question the voters in county elections whether they possessed a minimum property qualification, defined as an annual income of 40 shillings from freehold. This figure was identical with the qualification for service on grand juries, in force since 1293. The power to question voters was to be exercised by sheriffs at their discretion in contested elections, which meant that in the fifteenth century it would only have to be used occasionally, as the outcome of an election was frequently settled in informal ways by the county notables before the shire court actually assembled.[3] The preamble to the statute probably gives a correct clue to its origin when it states that elections of knights of the shire 'have lately been made by a too great and excessive number of people' and expressed the fear that unless these matters were better regulated 'homicides, riots, assaults and divisions amongst the gentlemen and other people of the shire will very likely arise'.[4] Its enactment followed four particularly disgraceful cases of fraud and riot in the elections of 1427 and 1429, three of which became the subject of judicial inquiries.[5]

[1] McKisack, op. cit., pp. 45–6, 114.
[2] The Paston Letters (Everyman ed., 1924), II, pp. 119–21, noted in Mc Kisack, op. cit., p. 46.
[3] Cf. Sir Goronwy Edwards, 'The emergence of majority rule in English parliamentary elections', T.R.H.S., 5th ser., XIV (1964).
[4] Quoted from Wilkinson, op. cit., p. 318.
[5] Roskell, The Commons in the Parliament of 1422, pp. 15–17.

This statute, like the rest of the legislation about elections, tried to impose norms of behaviour which were not easily enforceable. The few known cases of prosecutions of sheriffs in the middle decades of the century all ended inconclusively.[1] The requirement that members should reside in their constituencies was widely ignored by the representatives of boroughs. These statutes are best understood as a symptom of the growing competition for seats which no amount of regulation could contain within orderly bounds.

We cannot attempt here a systematic account of parliamentary history during the Wars of the Roses. Inevitably meetings of parliaments provided the setting for some of the most momentous events of the years 1447–60. The mysterious death of Humphrey, duke of Gloucester, during a parliament at Bury St. Edmunds in 1447 can be perhaps regarded as the beginning of violent upheavals. The parliamentary impeachment of the duke of Suffolk in 1450 started the disintegration of the faction that had ruled England during the 'forties. The first public demand for the recognition of Richard, duke of York, as heir to the crown was voiced in the commons, early in 1451, by Thomas Young, member for Bristol, who was promptly imprisoned in the Tower for this piece of insolence. In 1454 the recognition of York as protector of the kingdom of England took place in parliament, though his election was apparently due solely to the magnates. His second elevation to that dignity in November 1455 came about as the result of pressure by his partisans among both the lords and the commons and in response to reiterated petitions by a pro-Yorkist speaker of the commons.[2] York's first open attempt to secure the crown was staged on 10 October 1460 in the parliament chamber and met with a complete rebuff from the magnates who were surprised by this unexpected claim.[3] Only after protracted negotiations lasting a fortnight did the lords agree to a compromise under which York was recognized as the heir of Henry VI. According to the parliament roll, this agreement had the assent of 'the three estates in this present parlement assembled'.[4]

The lords appear to have played a leading part in many of these transactions. There were some important exceptions. As Dr. B. P. Wolffe's

[1] Cf. for example R. Virgoe, 'Three Suffolk parliamentary elections of the mid-fifteenth century', *B.I.H.R.* XXXIX (1966).
[2] The most recent accounts of York's second protectorate are in J. R. Lander, 'Henry VI and the duke of York's second protectorate, 1455 to 1456', *Bulletin of the John Rylands Library*, XLIII (1960) and in Storey, *op. cit.*, chapter XIII.
[3] The evidence about these events has been recently reconsidered by J. R. Lander in *B.I.H.R.* XXXVI (1963), 126–8.
[4] Quoted from Chrimes and Brown, *op. cit.*, p. 318. See also *Rotuli Parliamentorum*, v, 382.

article clearly shows,[1] the commons consistently took the lead in demanding the resumption by Henry VI of alienated royal properties and revenues. They rightly regarded this as an essential preliminary to financial reform. After an ineffective start in 1450, they were able to procure in the following year a second act of resumption which did produce real improvements. But the most crucial parliamentary decisions of this period were usually made by the lords. They were primarily responsible for the two elections of York to the dignity of protector and for the acceptance of his claim to be recognized as the lawful heir of Henry VI. When, in February 1454, the commons petitioned for the liberation of their speaker Thomas Thorpe, confined to the Fleet prison at the suit of the duke of York, the lords consulted the judges whether the privilege of 'this high court of parlement' covered such a case. The chief justices speaking in the name of all the other judges replied that 'the determinacion and knowlegge of that privilegge belongeth to the lordes of the parlement and not to the justices', and the commons were ultimately bidden by the lords to elect another speaker.[2] The judges were trying, above all, to keep out of trouble, but their answer does bring out the gulf between the position of the commons in the middle of the fifteenth century and a much fuller recognition of their special privileges a hundred years later.

During the turbulent middle years of the fifteenth century parliamentary elections were much affected by the pressure of political factions and there was an increase in the manipulation of local 'connections' from the centre by the government and its opponents alike.[3] The elections in the autumn of 1450 appear to have been successfully influenced by the supporters of York.[4] In 1459 the royal government sent writs of privy seal to sheriffs directing them to return the king's nominees[5] and the resultant parliament carried out a proscription of the Yorkists. One enduring consequence of these practices was the increase in the number of the royal servants sitting in the commons. They consisted mostly of the members of the royal household and of royal officials. At the Bury St. Edmunds parliament of 1447, where the government intended to attack Duke Humphrey of Gloucester, the household group alone made up at least 16 per cent of the lower house. No important royal councillors sat as yet in the commons

---

[1] *Infra*, chapter 2.

[2] Quoted from Chrimes and Brown, *Select Documents*, pp. 295–7. The most recent discussion of this incident is in Roskell, *The Commons and their Speakers*, pp. 253–4.

[3] I am adapting here to the fifteenth century the comments of M. Ransome in *University of Birmingham Historical Journal*, VI (1958), 134.

[4] Roskell, *The Commons and their Speakers*, p. 242.

[5] Cf. the petition of the sheriffs asking for indemnity for their breaches of law on this occasion, *Rotuli Parliamentorum*, V, 367.

because at that period the council consisted very largely of great lords and prelates. In 1447 the household contingent in the commons was led, however, by the controller of the household, Sir Thomas Stanley, who nine years later was himself raised to the peerage. In all the parliaments of Edward IV for which adequate records exist a substantial number of royal servants sat in the commons. There were at least fifty of them in the parliament of 1478, comprising no less than 17 per cent of the lower house.[1] A few royal councillors were now regularly to be found in the commons, especially the successive under-treasurers of the exchequer and the leading household officials. The next decisive change occurred at the start of the reign of Henry VII when several of his principal councillors appeared among the commons and this became the rule in all Henry's parliaments.[2] Perhaps his unwillingness to promote some of his leading advisers to the peerage was due in some part to his desire to use them for the management of the commons. But this is only a tentative suggestion.

'I purpose to lyve uppon my nowne and not to charge my subgettes but in grete and urgent causes' Edward IV told the commons in 1467.[3] His success in building up his income from crown estates and other royal assets increased his independence in dealing with parliaments. After some initial fumbling, Henry VII proved even more successful in achieving the same result.[4] Both Edward and Henry were thus enabled to call parliaments at rarer intervals in the later years of their respective reigns. Government-sponsored legislation again began to form an important feature of parliamentary sessions and there were notable innovations in the drafting of government bills.[5] Acts of attainder designed to confiscate all the property of men deemed to be traitors constituted the largest group of enactments passed by English parliaments between 1459 and 1504. The study of this legislation by Professor J. R. Lander[6] shows that the repealing of attainders was as important a part of statecraft as their imposition. Through procuring attainders and then reversing them kings tried to impose their will on an important section of the aristocracy. Promises to reverse attainders in return for good behaviour provided a

[1] Roskell, *The Commons in the Parliament of 1422*, pp. 134–6.
[2] See the lists of members in J. C. Wedgwood, *History of Parliament, 1439-1509, The Register* (1938). Henry's leading councillors and supporters sitting repeatedly during the first decade of the reign included Sir Reginald Bray, Sir Richard Croft, Sir Richard Guildford, Sir Thomas Lovell, Sir John Risley and Sir Gilbert Talbot.
[3] Quoted from Chrimes and Brown, *Select Documents*, p. 329.
[4] Cf. B. P. Wolffe, 'Henry VII's land revenues and chamber finance', *E.H.R.* LXXIX (1964).
[5] *Infra*, pp. 12-14.
[6] *Infra*, chapter 3. See also G. R. Elton, 'The law of treason in the early Reformation', *Historical Journal*, XI (1968), 211–12.

kind of probation system that proved remarkably effective, especially under Henry VII. In Henry's reign some attainders were inflicted in every parliament save one. In his last parliament of 1504 'more were passed than in any other parliament of his day', involving on this occasion 51 victims. The need for these vengeful measures and for subsequent adjustments of them clearly provided one of the major motives for the holding of parliaments during this period.

By the end of the reign of Edward IV it was the accepted legal doctrine that any legislation passed by the commons was binding on all the king's subjects 'because every man is privy and party to the parliament, for the commons have one or two for each community to bind or unbind the whole community'.[1] This statement was made in 1482 by the counsel for the crown, serjeant Catesby, in a case argued before all the justices. It concerned the powers of the clerical convocation and he used the example of parliament not as something that he was trying to prove but merely as an illustration.[2] He clearly assumed that everybody in his audience would unquestioningly accept the truth of this doctrine. Similar remarks were made on a number of occasions in the reign of Henry VII in the course of other legal pleadings. It was a corollary of these views that no parliamentary statute would be valid unless the commons had consented to it. That this was, in fact, the view of the judges is revealed by an opinion expressed by all the justices in 1488-9. An act of attainder enacted in an earlier parliament was being challenged because, although it was desired by the king and had been passed by the lords, 'no mention was made of the commons. For which reason all the justices clearly maintained that it was not an Act.' The most remarkable feature of this incident was its outcome: Henry VII accepted the ruling of the judges however unwelcome it may have been to him.[3]

During the reigns of the Yorkist kings and of Henry VII an important change occurred in legislative procedures. A type of drafting procedure used by the crown for some of its own proposals began to be adopted for measures originating with the commons or the lords. In 1924 Sir John Neale described it as 'a slow change, too subtle to yield its secret to any but the most careful research'[4] and much of the mystery still remains today. A crown bill of this new type was so worded that it could be

---

[1] Quoted from J. G. Edwards in *Oxford Essays in Medieval History presented to Herbert Edward Salter* (Oxford, 1934), p. 154 (reprinted, *supra*, vol. I, chapter 4).

[2] Plucknett, *loc. cit.* (1924), p. 173. The translation by Sir Goronwy Edwards, referred to in the preceding note, seems preferable to Plucknett's rendering of some of the abbreviated words.

[3] Translated and quoted from Pollard, *op. cit.*, p. 97, n. 3.

[4] *Infra*, chapter 5, p. 155.

enacted as a statute without any alterations. To quote the technical phrase used at the time, 'it contained within itself the form of the act'. It is perhaps no coincidence that the first known case where this procedure is specifically mentioned in the parliament roll should concern the attainder of the late king Henry VI by Edward IV in 1461. The commons are recorded as giving their assent in the following words 'To this *Act* the commons have agreed.'[1] It mattered supremely to Edward that he should determine from the outset the exact wording of this vital enactment.

The adaptation of this royal procedure to bills initiated by the commons or the lords involved several innovations. Hitherto, if such a bill was passed by the two houses and was acceptable to the government, the king would be signifying by his assent only that he agreed with the general purposes of the bill. The exact wording of the final enactment was referred to the judges and other legal experts of the crown who, in altering the bill into a statute, rewrote it in accordance with the king's wishes. But if a bill started on its progress through the two houses in the form of an act its precise wording would be determined entirely by the wishes of the commons and the lords. Any amendments would have to be inserted during its passage through the two houses. Under this new procedure 'parliament considered not merely the general policy but the exact wording of the proposed statute ... Legislation in fact was no longer the government's vague reply to vaguely worded complaints, but rather the deliberate adoption of specific proposals embodied in specific texts.'[2] The detailed report of the members for Colchester to their constituents from the first parliament of Henry VII in 1485 reveals the old and the new procedures coexisting side by side.[3]

After a bill in the form of an act had passed the two houses it was still open to the king to add fresh 'provisos' to it, but only if they limited the scope of the original proposals. Such provisos were appended to bills in the form of additional schedules. Edward IV and Henry VII used this device very freely in modifying acts of resumption of royal property or softening the provisions of attainders. But this usage was virtually abandoned after the early years of Henry VIII, though an isolated instance can be adduced from the reign of Elizabeth.[4] Thereafter if the king wished to accept a bill he would have to ensure that it came up for the royal assent

---

[1] Wilkinson, *op. cit.*, pp. 286 and 313 (document XXV b). The italics are ours.
[2] T. F. T. Plucknett, 'Ellesmere on Statutes', *L.Q.R.* LX (1944), p. 248.
[3] Published in W. G. Benham (ed.), *The Red Paper Book of Colchester* (1902), pp. 61 ff.
[4] Neale, *infra*, chapter 5, p. 166; Pollard, *op. cit.*, p. 274.

in a form entirely agreeable to him. The only way to assure this was to procure the bill's amendment, through proposals moved by the royal councillors acting in either the commons or the lords. The desire to influence legislation in this way may have provided one of the motives for Henry VII's new policy of placing some of his leading councillors in the lower house and it certainly influenced his son after 1529 in choosing for his chief advisers men who sat in the commons and were most skilful in managing that assembly.

THE TUDOR PERIOD: HENRY VIII—ELIZABETH

The historian of parliament under Henry VIII and the later Tudors has at his disposal an abundance of evidence denied to his medievalist colleagues. Some of it comes from the reappearance of older types of records, but there are also new kinds of sources. Though lords' journals were kept in the second half of the fifteenth century, none of them has survived before 1510, apart from a few tiny fragments copied by antiquarians. There are still some gaps in the surviving series for the reign of Henry VIII, but these journals provide one of our most useful sources. We lack information about the membership of the lower house between 1491 and 1529, but fortunately a list of members does survive among Cromwell's papers for the crucial Reformation Parliament of 1529–36. From the fifteen-forties onwards returns of members survive for most of the subsequent parliaments. The state papers of Henry VIII and his children provide a wealth of material about the royal government and its policies that must fill with envy all students of medieval England. Probably we owe to the execution of Thomas Cromwell the survival of his papers as part of this collection. An historian of parliament is even more fortunate in the second half of the sixteenth century. The journals of the house of commons begin in 1547 and become increasingly detailed as we move into the reign of Elizabeth. Several members of Elizabethan parliaments kept private diaries which usefully supplement the official journals and fill the gaps for the periods when those records are missing. And there is also the great storehouse of the Cecil papers at Hatfield. Most of the articles reprinted in this volume could not have been written without the existence of these new collections of sources.

There is no evidence that any of the governments that ruled Tudor England liked holding parliaments. 'All Tudor monarchs behaved as though parliaments were no more than regrettable necessities.'[1] They

[1] J. Hurstfield, 'Was there a Tudor despotism after all?', *T.R.H.S.*, 5th Ser., XVII (1967). p. 102.

differed only in the frequency with which they had to convene these assemblies and in their skill in managing the two houses, and especially the commons. Wolsey was very bad at handling representative bodies and disliked ecclesiastical convocations as much as he resented parliaments. But Henry VIII gradually found out 'that parliamentary institutions could be made the engines of his will'[1] and put this discovery to good uses after 1529. The different regimes that succeeded each other between 1547 and 1558 managed on the whole to impose their wishes on parliaments. But Mary did encounter unusually determined resistance in the commons. Some parliaments had been troubled in the past by the presence of political factions hostile to the government, but it was a new thing to find in the commons an opposition sustained by the strong Protestant convictions of some of its members. Elizabeth had likewise to reckon in several of her parliaments with zealous Protestant critics, but her advisers were almost always able to manage the commons according to her wishes. In her reign the lower house was never allowed to become a genuinely collective opposition to the royal government. As Elizabeth's lord keeper told the lords and the commons in 1593, the queen was 'most loth to call the assembly of her people in Parliament' and 'hath done the same but rarely and only upon most just, weighty and great occasions'.[2] Robert Cecil, Elizabeth's last principal secretary, was expressing the same attitude when he told parliament in 1610 that 'the wisdom of former ages affected not long parliaments; they are neither good for the king nor the people'.[3] There was, therefore, nothing unprecedented in the reluctance of James I to hold parliaments and his dislike of them. Yet his views betray a lack of understanding of the place of parliament in the normal scheme of English government which differentiates him from his Tudor predecessors. Thus, after dissolving the assembly of 1614, he explained his views on parliament to the Spanish ambassador. 'I am surprised that my ancestors should ever have permitted such an institution to come into existence. I am a stranger and found it here when I arrived so that I am obliged to put up with what I cannot get rid of.'[4]

The reign of Henry VIII, and the years 1529–36 in particular, form one of the crucial periods in the history of parliament in the sixteenth century. In the Reformation Parliament, which between November 1529 and April 1536 had eight sessions lasting in aggregate just under eighteen

[1] F. W. Maitland's phrase, quoted *ibid.*, p. 88.
[2] J. E. Neale, *Elizabeth I and her Parliaments, 1584–1601* (London, 1957), II, 246.
[3] Quoted in Hurstfield, *loc. cit.*, pp. 92–3.
[4] S. R. Gardiner, *History of England from the Accession of James I to the Outbreak of the Civil War, 1603–42*, II (1885), 251.

months,[1] Henry could rely for most of the time on the support of a majority in both houses. The spiritual peers outnumbered the lay lords, but some of the heads of the religious houses were invariably absent[2] and, in practice, the secular peers normally formed the majority of those present and voting in the upper house. This was a matter of great practical value to Henry, as some of the bills dealing with ecclesiastical changes are known to have produced a clear cleavage between the spiritual and the temporal lords. According to the report of the Imperial ambassador, Chapuys, the Act for the Conditional Restraint of Annates was passed in the upper house in March 1532 by the votes of some thirty temporal peers. The opposition consisted of all the bishops who were present, together with two abbots and one earl.[3] In the same year the Act of Citations was approved by the lords despite the opposition of all the spiritual peers.[4] The disappearance of the abbots from the upper house after 1539 had much less practical significance than might be assumed on purely theoretical grounds. Henry could also stop peers whom he particularly distrusted from attending parliament. According to Chapuys, in 1534 several prelates and other peers were ordered to absent themselves.[5] Only if a royal proposal aroused widespread and profound unease was it likely to founder in the upper house. This was apparently the case in 1539 with the bill of Proclamations. The original bill was initiated in the lords who gave it an unusually large number of readings and amended it so considerably that it had to be replaced by a second bill, originating with the commons.[6]

Up to 1536 the process of piecemeal creation of new parliamentary boroughs produced only a modest increase in the size of the lower house. The one list of members that survives from the reign of Henry VII for the parliament of 1491–2 ends 'summa totalis 296 men that be in the Comen howse'.[7] By 1529 the membership of the commons had grown to 310.[8] The first really sizeable addition was made by Henry VIII in the last session of the Reformation Parliament in the spring of 1536, when he

[1] A. F. Pollard, 'The Reformation Parliament as a matrimonial agency and its national effects,' *History*, XXI (1937), 220.
[2] J. S. Roskell, 'The Problem of the attendance of the lords in medieval parliaments', *B.I.H.R.* XXIX (1956), 199 and *passim*.
[3] Quoted in J. Enoch Powell and K. Wallis, *The House of Lords in the Middle Ages* (London, 1968), p. 568. See also *infra*, pp. 21–2.
[4] J. Scarisbrick, *Henry VIII* (London, 1968), p. 301, n. 3.
[5] *Ibid.*, p. 329 n. 1; Powell and Wallis, *op. cit.*, p. 571.
[6] Cf. G. R. Elton, 'Henry VIII's Act of Proclamations', *E.H.R.* LXXV (1960). See also *infra*, p 21.
[7] *B.I.H.R.* III (1926), 175.
[8] *Calendar of Letters and Papers, Foreign and Domestic, Henry VIII*, IV, no. 6043 (2).

resorted to the entirely novel device of creating new constituencies by parliamentary statutes. By the two 'Acts of Union with Wales' in 1536 and 1542 Henry introduced 27 new members.[1] Perhaps the desire to extend parliamentary taxation to Wales may have been one of the motives for this innovation. In 1536 and 1543 two other statutes added six more members for Cheshire and Calais. Between 1491 and 1586, when Elizabeth imposed a temporary ban on the multiplication of parliamentary constituencies, 166 new members were added to the house. Because of gaps in evidence it is not always possible to date precisely the appearance of new, additional M.P.s, but Henry VIII was certainly responsible for introducing approximately a quarter of these newcomers.

Neither under Henry VIII nor under his children was the creation of new constituencies part of a design for packing the commons with the supporters of the royal government. There was no need for this, as every Tudor monarch, unlike the first two Stuart kings, could normally rely on loyal backing from a large proportion of members. The northern rebels complained in 1536 that 'most of the House were the king's servants',[2] but the historian Edward Hall, who was himself a member of the Reformation Parliament and was favourably inclined towards the King's policies, said precisely the same thing. In commenting in 1529 on an act freeing the king from the need to repay certain crown debts, Hall remarked that 'the moste parte of the commons were the kynges servauntes and the other were so labored to by other, that the bill was assented to'.[3] This remarkable measure of agreement by men otherwise so opposed to each other suggests that to a large extent they were speaking the truth. Henry must have been satisfied with this particular house of commons, or convinced that he could not get a better one, for otherwise he would not have kept it in being for so long.

The Reformation Parliament is specially remembered for the importance of the statutes sanctioned by it. There was one notable innovation in procedure as well. Much of this legislation originated in measures which were introduced first into the commons. Some of the important government bills, like for example the final version of the Treasons Act of 1534,[4] still continued to be initiated in the lords, but the king's advisers now exercised a novel freedom of choice in this matter. Some of the

[1] W. Rees, 'The Union of England and Wales,' *Transactions of the Honourable Society of Cymmrodorion* for 1937, pp. 77, 97–8 and J. E. Neale, *The Elizabethan House of Commons* (1949), p. 255.
[2] Neale, *The Elizabethan House of Commons*, p. 282.
[3] *The Lives of the Kings: Henry VIII* (ed. C. Whibley, 1904), II, 169.
[4] G. R. Elton, 'The Law of Treason in the Early Reformation', *Historical Journal*, XI (1968), 228, n. 63.

measures originating with the commons continued to be couched in the old form of a petition to the King, but it became more normal to introduce into the lower house bills that could be enacted without any changes in wording, each such bill 'containing in itself the form of the act'.[1] The adoption of this procedure for measures sponsored by the government implied several things. The king's advisers must have reached firm decisions about the exact wording of the proposed enactments. This put a premium on good, clear drafting of government bills. The royal ministers brought these proposals first of all into the lower house because they believed that it was to the king's advantage that the initial process of discussion and of dealing with possible amendments should take place in that house. They were also presumably confident that they could pilot these government measures through all the successive readings of the bills without having to accept any substantial amendments. 'Management of this sort placed the commons on a far higher plane than they might have expected from the power of the king.'[2] Henry VIII, for practical reasons of his own, was considerably enhancing the importance of the commons and stimulating the development of the legislative procedures used by their house. In particular there was now a growing need for committing bills to committees of members. Reference to this practice in the correspondence of M.P.s sitting in the Reformation Parliament suggests that, in the lower house, this was still something of a novelty.[3]

Thomas Cromwell, as a member of the house of commons in the Reformation Parliament and as Henry's principal adviser from 1532 to 1540, was one of the men chiefly responsible for the government's legislative programme in those years. 'He may be claimed as one of the greatest of our parliamentary statesmen,'[4] and it is one of the great merits of G. R. Elton's article on 'The Political Creed of Thomas Cromwell' to have marshalled the evidence for Cromwell's personal attitude to parliament.[5] He had a major share in preparing the bills submitted to parliament during those years on the king's behalf, as can be shown from the drafts that still survive among his papers.[6] 'No aspect of Cromwell's work illustrates to

---

[1] See *supra*, pp. 12–14.

[2] D. H. Willson, *The Privy Councillors in the House of Commons, 1604–29* (Minneapolis, 1940), p. 6.

[3] Pollard in *History* (1937 *cit. supra*), p. 220 and n. 1. A good study of the legislation promoted not by the government but by a group of private sponsors (the corporation of London and other Londoners) and of the procedures used by them is contained in H. Miller's article, *infra*, chapter 4.

[4] A. G. Dickens, *Thomas Cromwell and the English Reformation* (London, 1959), p. 75.

[5] *Infra*, chapter 7.

[6] Some of these drafts are discussed in G. R. Elton's article reprinted below as chapter 6.

better effect his organizing genius, his grasp of detail, his ability to clinch an issue.'[1] At their best these statutes are models of clear and coherent drafting. The Act of Uses, enacted in the final session of the Reformation Parliament in the spring of 1536, has been specially praised by modern historians for this reason. It starts with a clear exposition of general principles, followed by other clauses 'methodically dealing with every possible aspect and detail of its general plan'.[2] The admirable drafting of that bill may have greatly ·assisted the government in getting it passed through parliament with very little change of substance, as can be judged from the two surviving drafts.[3] This high standard could not be uniformly maintained. The 'Act of Union with Wales', passed in the same parliamentary session, was greatly inferior in its draftsmanship.[4] Compared with the Act of Uses it was a much less important measure and it was presumably not likely to attract equally close scrutiny from members of the two houses.

From 1532 onwards Cromwell was very active in seeking the return to parliament of men who were likely to be particularly useful as members. There was nothing new in this, except that Cromwell's activities were organized in an exceptionally systematic and efficient manner. He was not seeking to secure a reliable majority in the House, for there was no need to do so, but he busied himself with placing in the commons several men who might assist him and the other royal councillors in managing that assembly.[5] In 1532 he was concerned with the filling of the vacancies that had arisen since the start of the Reformation Parliament. It is possible that these were the first by-elections ever held in England and that Cromwell may have been the initiator of this practice.[6] His surviving correspondence contains several documents connected with elections of members to the parliaments of 1536 and 1539. What Cromwell was aiming at is shown by his assurances to Henry on 17 March 1539 that 'I and other your dedicate counseillers be aboutes to bring all thinges so to passe that your Maiestie had never more tractable parlement'.[7] He reported in the same letter that he had contrived to place in the commons Richard Morison, a gifted humanist in the government's pay, so that this scholar 'shalbe

---

[1] Dickens, *op. cit.*, p. 52.
[2] Plucknett in *L.Q.R.* 1944 (*cit. supra*), p. 247.
[3] E. W. Ives, 'The Genesis of the Statute of Uses', *E.H.R.* LXXXII (1967), 692–3. See also J. M. W. Bean, *The Decline of English Feudalism, 1215–1540* (Manchester, 1968), pp. 286–92.
[4] Rees, *loc. cit.* The Act of Union is reprinted on pp. 81–100.
[5] Neale, *The Elizabethan House of Commons*, p. 283.
[6] A. F. Pollard, 'Thomas Cromwell's Parliamentary Lists', *B.I.H.R.* IX (1931), 42.
[7] Hurstfield, *loc. cit.*, p. 101.

redy to answer and take up suche as wold crake or face with literature of lernyng'.[1] Cromwell was not trying to build up a personal following in the house, but to assemble a useful group of 'the king's friends' ready to obey the wishes of his royal master. He differed perhaps in this respect from the other royal courtiers and councillors who combined the provision of supporters for the king with the building up of their own clienteles.

It was part of Henry's propaganda that all the revolutionary enactments of the Reformation Parliament should be accepted by his subjects because they had secured the consent of the lords and the commons. This is one of the main themes of his reply to the Lincolnshire rebels in the autumn of 1536. Thus he reminds them that 'the suppression of religious houses . . . is graunted us by all the nobles spirituall and temporall of this oure Realme and by all the commons in the same by acte of Parliament and not set furth by any counsailor or counsaylors upon there mere will and fantasie'.[2] In 1542, in his famous speech delivered before the judges and the delegations from the two houses of parliament, Henry VIII again stressed the importance of parliament 'wherein we as head and you as members are conjoined together in one body politic'.[3] The most explicit expression of this Tudor doctrine that the parliament stood for the whole community is to be found in the *De Republica Anglorum* of Sir Thomas Smith, written in 1565 while he was acting as Queen Elizabeth's ambassador in France. In Smith's words, the legislative sovereignty of parliament was rooted in the fact that 'everie Englishman is entended to bee there present, either in person or by procuration and attornies . . . from the Prince (be he King or Queene) to the lowest person of Englande. And the consent of Parliament is taken to be everie mans consent.'[4]

It is, however, legitimate to ask what realities lay behind this parade of parliamentary consent. Sir Thomas Smith, in the chapter immediately preceding the passage we have just quoted, admitted that the common people, who formed the great majority of the population, 'have no voice nor authoritie in our common wealth, and no account is made of them but onelie to be ruled, not to rule other'.[5] This was an unusually explicit recognition of facts that sixteenth-century Englishmen did not usually even bother to mention, because everyone took them for granted. As for Henry VIII's personal outlook, there are some grounds for thinking that

[1] W. G. Zeeveld, *Foundations of Tudor Policy* (Cambridge, Mass., 1948), p. 230.
[2] Quoted by Edward Hall (ed. Whibley), *cit. supra.*, p. 272.
[3] Quoted in K. Pickthorn, *Early Tudor Government, Henry VIII* (Cambridge, 1934), p. 468. See also *infra*, pp. 22–3.
[4] Ed. L. Alston (Cambridge, 1906), p. 49.
[5] *Ibid.*, p. 46.

he would have liked to depend less on parliamentary legislation. Certainly, Henry was always immensely concerned about acting within the law or, at least, appearing to do so. 'Henry rarely, if ever, broke the law' and he preferred not to do anything that was not lawful or unless it 'could be made lawful'.[1] It may be that, when in 1539 Henry tried to procure an Act of Proclamations different from the measure that was ultimately passed by parliament, he was seeking to diminish in some effective way, which was legally beyond any challenge, his dependence on parliamentary legislation. Historians are now agreed that the Act of Proclamations, based on the second of the two bills introduced by the government, gave Henry no important additional powers.[2] We lack the text of the first, original bill, which had to be abandoned in the face of opposition in the two houses. There will always, therefore, be room for differences of opinion about Henry's real initial intentions. The second bill, which was ultimately passed, may merely have embodied amendments designed to allay fears which, in G. R. Elton's words, 'may well have been exaggerated'.[3] But our own impression is that there may well be some truth behind 'a tradition of great dangers averted' on this occasion 'by a vigilant parliament'.[4] This impression is based on a remark by bishop Gardiner who was an eye-witness, supported by a statement of John Aylmer, the future bishop of London, in a work published in 1559 and, lastly, by a much later comment by James I that 'the King's *seeking* in that point was tyrranical'. James was referring to the strength of the original bill, not the weakness of the final act.[5]

Henry's government was despotic, though in practice it was not quite so powerful as he would have liked, and anybody whose opposition *seriously* contraried the king was in danger of persecution and even loss of life. Even in parliament Henry could enforce his wishes in matters that were of great importance to him by striking fear into peers and commons. According to the reports sent by Chapuys to the Emperor Charles V, the Act for the Conditional Restraint of Annates was passed in 1532 in both houses of parliament in the king's presence. In the commons Henry is alleged to have commanded 'that those among the members that wished for the King's welfare ... should stand on one side of the House and those who opposed the measure on the other. Several of them for fear of the King's

[1] Hurstfield, *loc. cit.*, pp. 88–9, 98, quoting a remark of A. F. Pollard.
[2] Cf. G. R. Elton, 'Henry VIII's Act of Proclamations,' *E.H.R.* LXXV (1960) and J. Hurstfield, *loc. cit.* (1967), pp. 93–9.
[3] Elton, *loc. cit. E.H.R.* (1960), 221.
[4] We are adapting here Elton's words, *ibid.*, p. 220, but our main suggestion differs from
[5] Elton's and agrees with the views of J. Hurstfield.
Hurstfield, *loc. cit.*, pp. 98–9.

indignation went over to the king's side, and in this manner was . . . the bill passed.'[1] If on most other occasions Henry tolerated a certain amount of opposition in parliament this formed part of his deliberate policy of humouring its members in non-essentials, in the expectation of assuring their subservience in all that mattered to him profoundly.

This is the background against which we must view Henry's acceptance in 1523 of the request of the speaker, Sir Thomas More, 'for liberty of speech for the commons in their own deliberations'.[2] The former speakers had always asked only for immunity for themselves. The extension of the claim for freedom of speech to all the members of the lower house was probably one of More's deliberate innovations and his argument that in this way the conduct of the king's affairs in the house could be improved was certainly novel. More's request was repeated by later speakers. By the reign of Elizabeth it came to form the main precedent for the eloquent claims of the commons for a wide freedom of debate. But it is possible to see More's speech not as an attempt to expand the privileges of the commons but rather as 'something of a rearguard action on the commons' part' to protect their customary rights springing from 'a realization of the fragility of custom and long user in face of the ruthless temper informing this new monarchy of Henry VIII's in its attitude to political opponents'.[3]

When, in Elizabeth's reign, the commons had occasion to assert the privileges of their house, most of the important precedents that they were able to invoke went back to the time of Henry VIII. During his reign 'the commons began to assume those new powers which led them to function as a court . . . they assumed them with the acquiescence and probably with the encouragement of the crown'.[4] An Elizabethan writer, Raphael Holinshed, provides a detailed account of one memorable incident, when Henry VIII deliberately supported the claim of the commons to act as an independent court.[5] In a work published in 1587, Holinshed reported it at length 'because this case . . . is commonly alleged as a precedent for the privilege of the parliament'. A member of the commons, George Ferrers, who was also one of Henry's household servants, was detained in a prison

---

[1] Quoted in Sir Goronwy Edwards, 'The emergence of majority rule in the procedure of the House of Commons', *T.R.H.S.*, 5th Ser., xv (1965), 176–7. On Henry's attitude to opposition in the commons see also J. E. Neale, *infra*, chapter 5.

[2] Roskell, *The Commons and their Speakers*, p. 42. For a more detailed discussion see *infra*, chapter 5.

[3] *Ibid.*, p. 51. This represents a more cautious approach than Neale's earlier study, reprinted *infra*, chapter 5, pp. 157–9.

[4] Neale, *infra*, chapter 5, p. 155.

[5] There is a very detailed account reproducing all the relevant sources in Pickthorn, *op. cit.*, pp. 465–77.

of the city of London because he had been a surety for an unpaid debt. The London authorities maltreated a serjeant of the commons who tried to free Ferrers. Instead of following the normal procedure of seeking the help of the king's chancellor, the commons then took the wholly unprecedented action of imprisoning by their own authority the two sheriffs of London and other offending persons. Henry used this occasion to demonstrate publicly, in the presence of all the judges, his support for the commons. It was a gesture typical of him. He went out of his way to please the commons when the new powers that he permitted them to use did not seem to diminish his own authority.

Henry included in his speech a remarkable tribute to the importance of parliament in his scheme of government: 'we be informed by our judges that we at no time stand so highly in our estate royal as in the time of parliament'. He was recognizing that through parliamentary legislation he had been able to achieve certain things that would have been impossible otherwise. Statutes passed by the Reformation Parliament in 1533–4 legitimized the abrogation of the papal authority over England and recognized the king's personal supremacy over the English church. This Henrician legislation for the first time triumphantly demonstrated the omnipotence of parliament to which Lord Burghley, Elizabeth's chief minister, was accustomed to refer by saying that 'hee knew not what an Acte of Parliament could not doe in England'.[1] Some of Henry VIII's opponents, Archbishop Warham and Thomas More among them, were prepared to maintain that there existed certain matters pertaining to divine law and the customary practice of the universal church which no English parliament had a right to alter. Few other Englishmen dared to follow them, but there is some danger of underestimating the confusion that this clash of principles was creating in men's minds. According to William Roper, More's son-in-law, the latter 'declared that this Realme, being but one member and smale parte of the Church, might not make a particuler lawe disagreable with the generall lawe of Christes universall Catholike Churche'.[2] More said this in challenging the rightfulness of his indictment, after the verdict of the jury had already gone against him and he had nothing to lose by making this fundamental denial of parliament's unlimited legislative sovereignty. But it is worth recording that his words caused some embarrassment to the judges who were trying him. Thomas Cromwell, as G. R. Elton has demonstrated, had very clear-cut ideas

[1] Quoted in a speech of James I in the Star Chamber in June 1616. Cf. C. H. McIlwain, *The Political Works of James I* (1918), p. 329.
[2] Quoted in J. D. M. Derrett, 'The Trial of Sir Thomas More', *E.H.R.* LXXIX (1964), 473.

about the unlimited nature of parliament's legislative authority,[1] but perhaps he had firmer convictions about this than some other English lawyers of his time. The judges who tried More in practice did enforce the same idea of parliamentary sovereignty, but their spokesman, Chief Justice Fitz James, expressed their views about it in a remarkably hesitant manner. When Lord Chancellor Audley asked their opinion about the validity of the indictment against More, Fitz James could only answer 'that if thacte of parliament be not unlawfull, then is not the Indictment in my conscience insufficient'.[2] The suggestion that a parliamentary statute might conceivably be *unlawful* does imply a doubt about the unlimited nature of parliament's legislative sovereignty.

Henry's use of parliamentary legislation to settle the succession to the crown and to repudiate the papal authority created precedents that greatly embarrassed his successors.[3] He altered the course of succession three times by parliamentary statutes and the last of those acts also permitted him to make supplementary arrangements in his last will. The order of the succession established by Henry under this parliamentary authority was never successfully set aside for the rest of the Tudor period. The duke of Northumberland, who governed England during the last years of the reign of Edward VI, despaired of securing parliamentary authority to disinherit Henry's daughter in favour of Lady Jane Grey. Under Mary's rule her advisers did not believe that parliament could be induced to change the order of succession in favour of Mary's Catholic cousin, Lady Margaret Lennox.[4] Queen Elizabeth was determined, throughout her reign, not to permit anybody to be designated as her successor, but she found it very difficult to stop her parliaments from trying to legislate on this matter.[5]

The statutes, which in 1533-4 abrogated the papal authority in England and replaced it by the royal supremacy over the English church, form an ambiguous body of legislation.[6] The Act of Supremacy treats the king's supreme power over the church as vested in his regality and purports merely to declare and confirm an authority that Henry derived from God alone. But the other statutes, which try to give practical effect to Henry's newly asserted supremacy, are worded in a way implying that the king in parliament was the sovereign authority for the new ecclesiastical arrange-

[1] *Infra*, chapter 7.
[2] Derrett, *loc. cit.*, pp. 473–4.
[3] The most recent study is M. Levine, *The Early Elizabethan Succession Question*, (Stanford, 1966).
[4] *Ibid.*, p. 126.
[5] *Infra*, chapter 5, pp. 166–70. and chapter 9, pp. 265 ff.
[6] Cf. especially the recent discussion in Scarisbrick, *op. cit.*, pp. 392–8.

ments.[1] After 1534 Henry treated his supreme power over the church as a part of his personal royal prerogatives. Further parliamentary legislation on religious matters could not be avoided entirely, but under Henry nobody dared to contest the king's sole right to initiate such legislation. This was no longer the case under Elizabeth and she had to strive very hard to regain and preserve her father's personal prerogatives in matters of religion.[2]

The repudiation of the papal authority was not followed under Henry VIII by parliamentary enactments imposing upon his subjects radical changes in their religious beliefs. The so-called Act of Six Articles of 1539, which constituted Henry's most important statute dealing with religious creeds, merely reaffirmed penalties for views and conduct which would have been condemned with similar severity by the Catholic church. The first enactments imposing pronounced Protestant beliefs and practice came under Edward VI, culminating in his second Act of Uniformity in 1552. Mary had to secure the repeal of that statute and much of the other Edwardian legislation on religion in order to re-establish Catholicism in her realm. Elizabeth could not avoid using parliament in order to repeal this Marian legislation. But she was determined that, as far as possible, the lords and the commons should not be allowed to meddle with religion on any future occasion. Her experiences in 1559 were bound to strengthen her hatred of parliamentary intrusions into these matters. As Sir John Neale has demonstrated in one of his most masterly articles,[3] Elizabeth was forced at the outset of her reign to accept a religious settlement at variance with her own inclinations. Her own preference was for the restoration of the conditions prevailing at the end of her father's life. But she was compelled in 1559 to accept a statute re-enacting, in substance, the Act of Uniformity of 1552. Her hand was forced by a determined Protestant faction in the commons acting in collaboration with a number of eminent Protestant divines. The latter were not members of parliament but Elizabeth knew that she would have to select her new bishops from among this group and could not afford to alienate them at this juncture.

This house of commons of 1559 was in most important respects typical of all its Elizabethan successors.[4] The great majority of the members

---

[1] Cromwell's contribution to the formulation of the ideas underlying this legislation is discussed in G. R. Elton's article, *infra*, chapter 7. Scarisbrick, *op. cit.*, pp. 395–7, while accepting Elton's conclusions about Cromwell's outlook, suggests that it may have differed significantly from the ideas of Henry VIII.

[2] *Infra*, chapters 5, pp. 167, 173, 8 and 9, pp. 248 ff.　　　　　　　　[3] *Infra*, chapter 8.

[4] There is a good list of its members with biographical details in C. G. Bayne, 'The First House of Commons of Queen Elizabeth', *E.H.R.* XXIII (1908), 648–77. The paragraphs that follow are based mainly on J. E. Neale, *The Elizabethan House of Commons* (London, 1949), especially chapter xv.

belonged to the gentry and some were related to peers. Between 1559 and 1586, when Elizabeth imposed a ban on the addition of new constituencies, she created 31 further parliamentary boroughs. This was done mostly to please influential patrons and thus added still further to the number of landed gentlemen in the lower house. After 1586 the commons contained 460 members, and gentlemen formed at least four-fifths of their assembly. By Elizabeth's time men of this class were able to secure a good legal or university education and often both. Of the 420 members in the 1563 parliament, at least 139 had received a higher education of some kind. By 1593 the total number of members who had been to a university or to one of the London inns of court rose to at least 252, or appreciably more than half the house. There was a parallel improvement in the education of the lay peers. These changes profoundly affected the nature of parliamentary opposition to Elizabeth and the first two Stuart kings. The similarity of their educational background was, in itself, something which increased the solidarity of the commons.

In that age a good education often bred strong Protestant convictions. Elizabeth made sure that the alliance between the upper clergy and the protestant group in the commons, which defeated her in 1559, would never recur. But throughout her reign she continued to encounter in every parliament a prominent group of Puritan-minded gentlemen and lawyers. Peter Wentworth, the most eloquent and courageous of Elizabeth's parliamentary opponents, combined all these qualities.[1] He was a wealthy landowner related to several members of the peerage and privy councillors. He had probably been educated at Lincoln's Inn. He was also one of the leading patrons of the Puritan clergy in the Midlands. 'The inns of court were already beginning to produce the type of Puritan lawyer who would become so important in the struggle between King and Parliament in the next century.'[2] 'The events of 1593 provide one striking illustration of this. When parliament met in February of that year Wentworth tried to concert action with a number of other M.P.s, with a view to organizing a parliamentary campaign on the forbidden subject of the succession to the crown. They held meetings in various inns of court where several of these men had their chambers and for these consultations, held outside parliament and therefore not covered by parliamentary privilege, they were ultimately arrested.[3]

The high quality of the house of commons under Elizabeth was matched by the great ability of her privy councillors, one of whose functions was to

[1] See J. E. Neale's biography of Wentworth, *infra*, chapter 9.
[2] Levine, *op. cit.*, pp. 170–1.
[3] *Infra*, chapter 9, pp. 276–85.

manage parliament on their sovereign's behalf. 'Never before and never again was the privy council so efficient.'[1] By Elizabeth's reign all the councillors who were not peers normally sat in the commons. 'Indeed it may be said that it was looked on as part of the privy councillor's duty to sit in the commons on every possible occasion.'[2] They did carry considerable weight in the house. They invariably sat near the speaker, who was himself always a royal servant in the Tudor period. The speaker and the councillors about him frequently consulted together. At critical moments in the debate the councillors fell to discussion amongst themselves while the house awaited the result.[3] They were members of all the important committees and the clerk of the commons got into the habit of beginning lists of committee members with the words 'all the privy councillors of the House'.[4] It was a sign of deterioration in Elizabeth's government during the last years of her reign that in the parliament of 1601 an unusually ineffective man should have been chosen for speaker and that the privy councillors should have wrangled with each other in public. In the debates about monopolies the speaker and the councillors for a while lost control over the lower house.[5] But the collapse of the Tudor system of effectively managing the commons through the privy councillors occurred only under James I. He hastened this by failing to understand that he must have councillors of ability in the lower house. Thus in the first two sessions of his first parliament he provided only one or two quite mediocre councillors to lead the commons.[6] Largely through his default the initiative in starting proceedings in the commons was allowed to pass to the opposition.[7]

In Elizabeth's eyes Parliament could be both an active source of strength but also a potential source of weakness. All her parliaments save one were held to secure grants of money,[8] though, on occasion, as in 1566, a part of the desired grant had to be sacrificed in order to disarm an inconvenient agitation in the commons. Under Elizabeth the lords were usually more docile than the lower house. In 1593 the government dared to ignore the customary claim of the commons to initiate all money grants and sought from the lords what the commons were unwilling to concede. On this

[1] J. E. Neale, *Essays in Elizabethan History* (London, 1958), p. 36.
[2] E. R. Adair and F. M. G. Evans, 'Writs of Assistance,' *E.H.R.* xxxvi (1921), 369.
[3] A. F. Pollard, 'Haywood Townshend's Journals (1601)', *B.I.H.R.* xv (1937), 2.
[4] Willson, *op. cit.*, p. 9.
[5] Pollard, *loc. cit.*, *B.I.H.R.* (1937).
[6] Willson, *op. cit.*, pp. 56–9.
[7] Cf. W. Notestein, *The Winning of the Initiative by the House of Commons* (London, 1924).
[8] A. G. R. Smith, *The Government of Elizabethan England* (London, 1967), p. 33.

occasion the commons offered two subsidies but Lord Treasurer Burghley managed to procure three subsidies from the upper house. After vain protests the commons had to accept this augmented grant.[1] The government could get away with such sharp practice because Elizabeth's rule was gladly accepted by the great majority of her subjects and because the money was needed for the war against Spain which was supported by the bulk of the commons. Only a government as popular as Elizabeth's could continue to achieve parliamentary successes of this sort.

There were no parliaments in session during 29 out of 44 years of Elizabeth's reign, in marked contrast with a much greater frequency of such assemblies between 1529 and 1558, when there were never more than two consecutive years without a parliament.[2] Elizabeth's reign was a time of efficient conciliar government resorting to parliaments only when this could not be avoided. However these assemblies were usually managed quite successfully through the consummate tact of the queen and the skill of her councillors.

So much depended on sound management of parliaments and especially on the wise handling of the commons because Elizabeth was basically in a much weaker position than her father. In 1566 she herself burst out that the commons would never have dared to treat Henry VIII as they were treating her.[3] Elizabeth had to depend overmuch on the loyalty and the willing co-operation of the commons. Hence she deemed it impolitic to use too often the royal right of vetoing bills that had passed through the two houses, because this was likely to make her too unpopular. This was one of the important reasons for Elizabeth's insistence that matters inconvenient to her should not even be raised in parliament.

The main battles between Elizabeth and her critics in the commons were fought over this issue of initiating legislation.[4] Elizabeth would have preferred to revive an older usage under which, on matters concerning the crown, only the government initiated legislation by bills 'containing within themselves the form of the act', while the commons were expected merely to present humble petitions to their sovereign. But the new practice, of virtually all legislation being introduced in the commons by bills worded in such a way that they could be enacted without any changes, had become very firmly established by Elizabeth's reign and there was no hope of uprooting it. At least the queen insisted that in all matters concerning the

[1] J. S. Roskell, *infra*, chapter 10, p. 317.
[2] R. W. K. Hinton, 'The Decline of parliamentary government under Elizabeth I and the early Stuarts', *Cambridge Hist. J.* XII (1957).
[3] Levine, *op. cit.*, pp. 176-7.
[4] For what follows see J. E. Neale, *infra*, chapter 5, pp. 167 ff.

prerogative neither the commons nor the lords should proceed at all without first petitioning her for permission to do so. In her view the royal prerogative extended for this purpose to all religious matters and to anything connected with the succession to the throne. Attempts to break these rules were dealt with sternly. In 1571 a Puritan enthusiast, William Strickland, for daring to exhibit a bill for the reformation of church ceremonies, was confined to his home and debarred from entering the commons. This proved a false move and, after the matter was raised in the lower house, Strickland had to be restored to his seat in the commons.[1] Thereafter the government proceeded more subtly. In 1587 Sir Anthony Cope was imprisoned with some of his supporters for trying to promote a bill that would impose a Presbyterian church service, but the government successfully justified this punishment by prosecuting these men for matters not covered by parliamentary privilege. They were guilty of holding secret conferences outside parliament.[2] The same tactics were successfully used against Peter Wentworth and his associates in 1593.[3] On more normal occasions the privy councillors were often able to persuade the commons to drop proposals that the queen disliked.[4] In the last resort, opposition might be disarmed by timely promises or concessions, as happened in the stormy debate on monopolies in Elizabeth's last parliament in 1601.[5]

The queen was willing to tolerate freedom of debate on matters introduced by her government or not contrary to her policies.[6] To her critics in the commons unlimited freedom of speech did not matter for its own sake and they came to advocate it only as a means of promoting legislation on the forbidden subjects of the succession to the crown, religion or abuses of the royal administration. Peter Wentworth[7] was perhaps the first man to perceive clearly that, if complete freedom of debate and of initiating legislation could be vindicated for the commons, then the desired reforms in church and state might be promoted with a greater chance of success. For Wentworth freedom of speech in parliament became inseparable from the proper functioning of that institution, a part of a fundamental law that all Englishmen ought to respect. Though his own career ended in

[1] J. E. Neale, *Elizabeth I and her Parliaments, 1559–81* (1953), I, 200–3.
[2] J. E. Neale, *infra*, chapter 9, pp. 261–2 and P. Collinson, 'John Field and Elizabethan Puritanism' in *Elizabethan Government and Society, Essays presented to Sir John Neale* (London, 1961), pp. 158–9.
[3] *Infra*, chapter 9, pp. 276–85.
[4] For some examples see Willson, *op. cit.*, p. 10.
[5] Pollard, *loc. cit. B.I.H.R.* (1937).
[6] J. E. Neale, *infra*, chapter 5, pp. 168 ff.
[7] See his biography, *infra*, chapter 9.

failure and he died a prisoner in the Tower of London, some of his associates played an important part in the opposition to Elizabeth's successors and his belief in the fundamental rights of parliament was destined to become an important tenet of that opposition.

By the end of Elizabeth's reign the commons had evolved into the more important of the two houses of parliament. The lower house was very conscious of its expanding privileges and was jealous in asserting them. The increased size of the house, the great improvements in the education of its members and the considerable developments in its procedures made it into a more distinguished and effective assembly than any of its predecessors in the Middle Ages or the early Tudor period. Under Elizabeth the delicate balance between the requirements of the crown and the aspirations of the commons had been maintained most of the time. Parliament had great potentialities for achieving greater influence and power, but in 1603 the initiative still lay entirely with the crown.[1] James I mismanaged this difficult but, probably, not unsound inheritance. Unlike Elizabeth, he did not realize how he might use parliaments to his best advantage and he lacked her ability to handle wisely these formidable assemblies.

[1] This is one of the main contentions of J. S. Roskell, *infra*, chapter 10.

The Commons and the Council in the Reign of Henry IV[1]*

by A. L. Brown

BISHOP Stubbs's opinion that the Lancastrian period contained 'the trial and failure of a great constitutional experiment; a premature testing of the strength of the parliamentary system ',[2] when kings ruled with the counsel of their subjects and deferred to their parliaments, is little regarded today. 'Lancastrian constitutionalism' savours too much of the nineteenth century to be plausible of the fifteenth, and though it has never been directly assaulted, more recent studies of the later-medieval constitution have driven it piecemeal out of currency. This is not to be regretted, but a certain foundation of fact still remains to support part at least of the theory and requires interpretation. Stubbs's more general arguments can be set aside, for example, that 'the house of Lancaster had risen by advocating constitutional principles' and that these principles were handed on to the new dynasty in 1399,[3] and even he found it difficult to document the theory from the reigns of Henry V and Henry VI. But there remains the reign of Henry IV, and it was from this reign that Stubbs cited most of his evidence. It is undeniable that at the beginning of the reign Henry IV gave a general promise that he would not govern alone but with the advice of wise counsellors.[4] In the circumstances of a usurpation too much weight cannot be attached to this, but the king did meet his magnates in frequent parliaments and great councils, and in particular there were a number of incidents in several parliaments, notably in the first half of the reign, when he undoubtedly behaved in an unusually conciliatory manner towards the Commons. For example, in 1404 the Commons asked the king to remove some members of his household, and he did so; in 1407 he went out of his way to pacify them when they feared that their right to grant taxation was threatened; and there are a number of occasions when he agreed to the appointment of treasurers of wars or the audit of their accounts.

---

[1] I wish to express my debt to Mr. K. B. McFarlane for his advice on many points.
[2] W. Stubbs, *The Constitutional History of England,* 5th edn. (Oxford, 1898), iii. 5.
[3] *Ibid.* iii. 8.**

[4] *Rot(uli) Parl(iamentorum)*, iii. 415 ; S. B. Chrimes and A. L. Brown, *Select Documents of English Constitutional History, 1307-1485* (London, 1961), p. 194.

The king did not always concede what the Commons asked, but these and other actions show that in dealing with them his general behaviour was conciliatory and markedly different from that of his predecessor. These demands and similar ones from the later fourteenth century show also that the Commons were not then mere passive spectators in parliament; they were taking an active interest in affairs and they were not afraid to speak their minds. None of these incidents need, however, mean more than that because of the undoubted financial and political difficulties of the reign the Commons were critical of the conduct of government and demanded reform, and that on occasion they were prepared to try to take advantage of the king's troubles to win changes in procedure; and, on the other hand, that the king, out of weakness or policy, was prepared to listen to their advice and criticism, and sometimes to act on it. There need be nothing 'constitutional' about this. But three incidents can be the test. In 1401, 1404, and 1406 the Commons asked that the king's councillors should be appointed and charged in parliament, and the king agreed to do this. Stubbs knew of the second and third of these cases, and it was these, particularly the third, that he probably considered the best evidence of the constitutional and modern qualities of Lancastrian rule. Here he saw the Commons invading the executive part of government; here, he thought, was ' the real . . . germ of the cabinet ministries of modern times '.[1] Recent writers have been more cautious than their predecessors in accepting this interpretation of these puzzling incidents, but they have never been examined in any detail.[2] This is what this article sets out to do; to establish what happened on these occasions, to see if the Commons claimed or exercised any control over the council, and, if not, what all the fuss was about, and therefore incidentally to determine whether any truth at all remains in the theory of a Lancastrian constitutional experiment.

The first of these incidents took place in the parliament of 1401. It is not mentioned in the parliament roll nor in any chronicle, and almost all that is known about it is contained in three documents on one mutilated piece of paper and one piece of parchment among the records of the council.[3] On the face of the paper is a draft of advice offered to the king about some requests made by the Commons in parliament—I shall refer to this as the ' Advice '; on the back is a

[1] Stubbs, iii. 255. He never formally set out the theory and his views have to be collected from many separated remarks, but the evidence that seems to have impressed him most was of these council nominations. For example, see pp. 8, 73, 255, 257, and 259.

[2] The fullest accounts are still to be found in J. F. Baldwin, *The King's Council in England during the Middle Ages* (Oxford, 1913) and J. H. Wylie, *History of England under Henry the Fourth* (London, 1894–8), and the best commentary is in J. E. A. Jolliffe, *The Constitutional History of Medieval England* (London, 1937).

[3] Exchequer, Treasury of Receipt, Council and Privy Seal, file 28. There is a brief account of these records, *infra.*, p. 37.

letter from ' Voz humbles liges et servantz trestouz de vostre grand conseil ', asking the king to give credence to John Doreward, one of the council, who will explain their views on some important matters. Both these documents are drafts written in the same cursive hand with many deletions and interlineations. The parchment contains another text of the same letter, neatly written in a secretary hand and perhaps at first intended to be sent to the king, but later amended in a more cursive hand, probably the same hand as in the paper.[1] The letters do not mention the ' Advice ' but it is a reasonable inference from all the circumstances that they relate to the same incident. These documents were first noticed by Professor Baldwin who paraphrased them but did not print them.[2] He assigned them to 1404 and to the second of these incidents without discussing the dating, but since then Mr. McFarlane has pointed out that they must refer to an hitherto unknown incident of the same kind in 1401.[3] The letter in its second version leaves no doubt about this. It is dated at London in March with a blank left for the date of the month, and it asks the king to receive Doreward in the presence of the earl of Somerset, the chamberlain, and the earl of Worcester, steward of the household. Doreward was a councillor only during Henry IV's reign; Somerset was chamberlain of England from 1399 until his death in 1410; and Worcester was steward of the household from 1393 until 1399 and again from March 1401 until February 1402, though an earl only from 1397. The letter must have been written in March 1401, and a parliament sat at Westminster from 20 January until 10 March 1401. The dating can be even more precise because the letter refers to a council meeting ' hier le venderdy ', and implies that it was written on a Saturday; the only Saturday in March before the end of parliament was Saturday, 5 March.

The ' Advice ' consists of a heading and the text which can be divided into three parts. The first is a statement though not a copy of some requests made by the Commons in full parliament; this is the part of the text which is mutilated, but it is particularly fortunate that any of it survives because it appears to contain a summary of *all* that the Commons asked in connection with the council though the rest of the ' Advice ' is concerned only with part of it. The Commons appear to have asked, (1) that for his own honour and profit and that of the kingdom the king should ordain his great officers and his council; (2) that these should not be removed before the next parliament; and (3) that before their departure the Commons should be informed of the names and the ' charge ' of those appointed—the word ' charge ' in this case and in 1406 appears to mean the

[1] The ' Advice ' is printed in Chrimes and Brown, pp. 205-6, and the letter is printed from the better text, *infra*, p. 59.* [2] Baldwin, pp. 154-5.
[3] K. B. McFarlane, ' England : The Lancastrian Kings, 1399–1461 ', in *Cambridge Medieval History* (Cambridge, 1936), viii. 369.

obligations that those appointed swore to carry out. This was accompanied by a protest that no derogation was intended to the king's estate, prerogative, or regality. It is curious that all this was written down because by then the first at least of these requests seems to have been granted; this is surely the assumption of the rest of the ' Advice '. In the second part the king is advised on how the officers and councillors should be charged, and the way in which this is phrased and the omission of any advice on whether or not they should be appointed suggests that he had agreed to appoint them. The advice was that they should be charged outside parliament in the king's presence, but, if he wished, in the presence of two or three of the Commons as had been done when the three household officers were charged. Great lords, it was suggested, should take merely the oath they had taken in the past as men who had a right to be members of the council, but if the king did not wish this, let all estates take the oath taken in the past by the others of the council—but with the protest that this was done out of reverence for the king and *not* at the request of the Commons. Finally, in the third part the king was offered advice on matters not mentioned in the statement of the Commons' requests. In view of the large number of prelates, lords, and others ' named and charged ' of the council[1] it would be too costly to pay them wages for constant attendance, and in any case this would be too burdensome for the councillors. It is suggested that after ' aucune bone appointement de governance ' has been made for the estate of the king and the kingdom, arrangements should be made that some councillors can be absent so long as sufficient members of each estate are present.

It is not clear what the ' Advice ' was intended to be; the surviving text is an amended draft, but the original could have been an aide memoire for Doreward, a text to show to the king, or simply a record of the advice offered by the great council—or it could have been all three. The reference to the great council is also puzzling. The term ' great council ' is most frequently applied to the occasional, specially-summoned gatherings of prelates, magnates, and others, which are distinct from the council on the one hand and from parliament on the other.[2] Meetings of this institution are frequent and comparatively well-documented in the fifteenth century, but the letter and the ' Advice ' can hardly have come from it. Parliament was in session and there was no need for another assembly. The reference may be to the ' great council in parliament ', in the sense of a meeting of those individually summoned to parliament, but this

---

[1] This sentence in particular implies that the councillors had already been appointed ; presumably the word ' charged ' refers here not to the semi-public ceremony which has just been recommended, but to their first appointment.

[2] See T. F. T. Plucknett, ' The place of the council in the XVth century ', *Trans. R. Hist. Soc.*, 4th ser., i (1918), and H. G. Richardson and G. O. Sayles, *Parliaments and Great Councils in Medieval England* (London, 1961).

also is unlikely. The most probable explanation is that the phrase is being used to mean simply the council, the body which had a more-or-less continuous existence throughout the year and assisted the king in governing, the body that was being appointed in this parliament. The tone of the letter, the use of Doreward, a frequent attender at the council, as the messenger, and particularly the *ad hoc* meetings at the Friars Preachers, a common meeting-place of the council, suggest this. The same usage is found in connection with other specially-appointed councils, for example in 1386, 1404, and 1406; 'great council' then means the king's council which has been specially, formally appointed.[1] It seems from the 'Advice' that the king had agreed to the appointment of such a body in 1401, and it is possible that it was these newly-appointed councillors who drew up the 'Advice' for the king.

This is all the direct evidence known to exist about the incident, but there is one piece of independent information which appears to confirm that the council was indeed appointed in parliament. This is a privy-seal writ-current to the treasurer and chamberlains of the exchequer dated 19 October 1401 ordering the payment of a fee of hundred marks annually to John Frome, esquire, ordained and assigned to be one of the council in the last parliament at Westminster, to be paid from 10 March 1401.[2] This is the only order of its kind, though there are two payments for attendance at the council, one of wages up to 10 March 1401, the other of wages from 12 March 1401, which may be related to the same incident.[3] The absence of other orders of the same kind is probably of no significance; the 'Advice' had recommmended that wages should not be paid to all the councillors. Another part of the 'Advice', the replacement of the three household officers, can also be confirmed. The earl of Worcester replaced Sir Thomas Rempston as steward about 1 March, and Thomas More replaced Thomas Tutbury as treasurer and Sir Thomas Brownfleet replaced Robert Litton as controller on 9 March.[4] The replacement of all three officers within a few days is most unusual, and the statement in the 'Advice' that the new officers were charged in the presence of two or three of the Commons suggests that it was a change designed to please the

---

[1] Baldwin, p. 109, cites examples of this usage ; and *vide infra,* p. 40, n. 4.

[2] Exchequer of Receipt, Writs and Warrants for Issues, box 17, no. 201. It reads ' come au temps de nostre darrein parlement tenuz a Westmouster eussiens ordenez et assignez nostre bien ame esquier Johan Frome destre un de nostre conseil ' and we have granted him a fee for this, etc. ; ' au temps de ' was translated as ' in parliamento ' on the Issue Roll when a payment was recorded on 26 October 1401.

[3] John Freningham, esquire, received wages for his attendance from 1 Nov. 1399 until 10 Mar. 1401 and is not known to have attended a meeting after this date ; and Sir William Sturmy, who is not known to have attended before this date, was paid for 93 days attendance between 12 March 1401 and 30 July 1402.

[4] R. L. Storey, ' English officers of state, 1399-1485 ', *Bull. Inst. Hist. Res.,* xxxi (1958), 87-90 and Lord Treasurer's Remembrancer, Enrolled Accounts, no. 7, m. 1.

Commons. The chancellor, John Scarle, was also replaced—on 9 March by Edmund Stafford, bishop of Exeter. Scarle, an ex-clerk in chancery who may have been promoted beyond his capacity, was not disgraced and continued to attend the council regularly; Stafford was a protege of Richard II and had been successively keeper of the privy seal and chancellor between 1389 and 1399. He had not been disgraced in 1399 but he had begun for the first time to take an active interest in his diocese; his recall in 1401 and later in 1406 suggests that he had a reputation as a good administrator and seems to have no ' political ' significance. Neither the treasurer nor the keeper of the privy seal were changed at this time, though both were replaced later in the year.

These things suggest that the Commons in parliament were critical of the household and of the conduct of government generally, and that to please them the king changed his household officers and possibly the chancellor also, and formally charged his council in some public or semi-public manner. There is not a word about this on the parliament roll, but a ' crisis ' of this kind would make the roll more understandable. Parliament had been summoned to grant badly-needed taxation but the Commons did not grant it readily. They seem to have been critical from the first; they came before the king a number of times and were told to put any further requests in writing. In the first week of the parliament they asked that the king should not give credence to private reports of their proceedings, and at its close they asked his pardon if they had committed any fault against him. The treasurer came before them to explain financial matters, and it was in this parliament that they asked for answers to their petitions *before* making a grant of taxation. On the roll these are isolated events which require explanation, and they make much better sense if the Commons were critical of the household and government generally and were asking that the officers and the council should be charged to do better. There would be nothing surprising about this. Attacks on the maladministration and wastefulness of the household were a feature of Henry IV's parliaments and a council was formally appointed in at least three more of his parliaments. The parliament of 1401 was probably similar to that of 1404 when the roll records a vigorous attack on the household and the appointment of a council. This is however as far as the evidence will go; it proves that there was a parliamentary ' crisis ' in 1401, but it does not explain why the Commons asked for the appointment of a council nor the significance of the king's concessions. The ' Advice ' suggests however that the Commons' demands were modest, but that, even so, the councillors were suspicious of them and jealous of the king's rights—and of their own.

No list survives from 1401 of those who were appointed to the council, but to some extent this can be deduced by comparing the attendance at council meetings before and after the parliament. This is possible because from 1389-90 the clerks writing for the council had been recording its decisions in a more businesslike manner, noting the date, the attendance, and the decision taken. These things were not however recorded in a register—not regularly in any case; the information was merely recorded on the petitions and draft documents which came before the council or occasionally in a memorandum. The intention was to provide an acceptable warrant to chancery or to the privy-seal office rather than to record the council's business. This limits the evidence in two ways. First, the business recorded is primarily administrative and the purely advisory work of the council is badly represented; for example, the decision to pardon five pounds in a sheriff's account may be recorded, but the advice that the king should campaign in Wales is unlikely to be recorded; no doubt this distorts the evidence of attendance and gives undue prominence to the lesser men. And second, most of these records were sent to the privy-seal office and to chancery; many have been lost, and they are now dispersed in various collections in the Public Record Office; what survives is only a fragment of what must once have existed, quite complete for a few short periods, but incomplete for most. These records do make it possible to compare the attendance at the council in different periods, but these limitations must always be borne in mind. The information for the twelve-month periods before and after the parliaments of 1401, 1404, and 1406 is set out in a table at the end of this article.

The attendance is fully recorded at seventeen council meetings between January and December 1400, and at forty-five between April 1401 and March 1402; this increase probably reflects a genuine increase in conciliar activity after the parliament of 1401 but in view of the chance survival of records it does not prove it. In both periods a small number of councillors attended regularly and a larger number attended more occasionally, and in both the backbone of the council was the three great officers, the chancellor, treasurer, and keeper of the privy seal. But after the parliament attendance increased significantly and became more distinguished. Before, the average attendance was 7.4—or 7 if two meetings at which a group of justices were present are excluded; afterwards, the average rose to 8.7. The figure was even higher immediately afterwards, but gradually declined through 1401, presumably because support for the scheme diminished. This increase reflects a change in the composition of the council, no doubt brought about by the events of March 1401. Three bishops, Richard Young of Bangor, John Trevenant of Hereford, and John Bottlesham of Rochester, who are seldom recorded at the council before, now become frequent attenders. The earl of Northumberland and to a lesser extent the earl of Westmorland, and two esquires, John Frome and John

Curson, also began to attend more frequently. These men with the three great officers and John Doreward, John Prophete, and John Scarle were the regular attenders during the twelve months after the parliament. At the same time at least five men seem to have been released from membership, three London merchants, William Brampton, John Shadworth, and Richard Whittington, and two esquires, Thomas Coggeshall and John Freningham, all of whom were paid wages as councillors from 1 November 1399. Four were paid for one year and Freningham was paid until 10 March 1401; all had attended the council occasionally but none frequently, and none attended afterwards. This probably means that they were not included in the new council, but no great significance is to be attached to their departure, and they may well have asked to be released.[1] The figures of attendance at meetings (and the third part of the ' Advice ') suggest that the council nominated in parliament in 1401 contained as was usual on these occasions a balanced selection of the estates of the realm—probably it included the earls of Northumberland, Westmorland, and Worcester; the three bishops; Lords Berkeley and Lovel; Sir John Cheyne and Sir Hugh Waterton; John Curson, John Doreward, and John Frome; John Prophete and John Scarle; and the three great officers. These are very much the same people as were nominated in 1404, and no great significance can be attached to the names, even to the relative newcomers. Bottlesham is a little-known man, but Trevenant and Young were both lawyers who had attained their bishoprics for their service in the papal administration though they had served the king as diplomats. Their diplomatic experience and their knowledge of Wales was no doubt useful, but that is all that can be said of their appointment. Frome and Curson were already loyal and active servants of the king, and typical of a group of knights and esquires on whom Henry IV relied greatly in the first half of his reign. The most likely explanation of the whole incident is that after the first three months of the reign when attendance was large and aristocratic, the council had become smaller and less substantial during 1400 and the most regular attenders had been clerks, knights, and esquires. The king himself may have seen the danger in this because on 4 January

---

[1] In Council and Privy Seal, file 29, there is a petition presented to the king during a parliament by a group of councillors who said that they had been appointed to the council in the last parliament but now wished to be discharged because they were ' de petitz estatz et meins suffissantz a tiel charge supporter ', and they asked that others ' de greindre estat ' be appointed. From its appearance and provenance this petition belongs to Henry IV's reign but it is difficult to fit it into the circumstances of any of his parliaments. It may have come from these five men in 1401 ; no other group fit it so well. This would of course mean that the council had been appointed in parliament in 1399. There is no record of this on the parliament roll, but seven councillors, these five and John Doreward and Sir Hugh Waterton, were paid wages from 1 November 1399, so it is likely that a council was appointed then—in time of parliament, if not in parliament itself.

1401, before parliament met, fourteen councillors including the earl of Northumberland and the three bishops attended a council meeting.[1] When parliament met the criticism of the Commons no doubt included the unsubstantial council; in 1404 and 1406 there is some evidence that they were suspicious of men of their own estate on the council. The result was certainly the larger and more substantial council of the period after the parliament. The Commons achieved some success in 1401, but they did not achieve a new council, and there is not a scrap of evidence that they wished in any way to control it.

The second of these incidents took place exactly three years later in the first parliament of 1404, and it yields almost precisely the same conclusion. On this occasion it is mentioned on the parliament roll;[2] one paragraph states merely that

> ' au fyn qe bone et jouste governance et remede se facent des pleuseurs compleintz, grevances, et meschiefs moustrez au roy nostre seignur en cest parlement, mesme nostre seignur le roy, a la reverence de Dieux, et a les grantes instances et especiales requestes a luy faitz diverses foitz en cest parlement par les Communes de soun roialme, pur ease et confort de tout soun roialme, ad ordeignez certeins seignurs et autres southescriptz destre de soun grant et continuel conseil '

and twenty-two names follow. The entry is not dated, but as the entries on the roll are in a rough chronological order, the appointment probably took place in March, near the end of the parliament. As in 1401, no great significance attaches to the names. As usual, they are a balanced selection of the estates of the realm, but in practice most of the names were those of men already attending the council, and the records show that attendance changed little as a result of the nomination. The backbone of the council continued to be a small group of administrators who attended frequently while a larger group of councillors attended occasionally. Only two of those nominated are not known to have attended before. Thomas Neville, Lord Furnival, who had served the king in various offices on the Scottish March, was nominated, and until his death in 1407 became an active administrator and one of the most frequent attenders at the council. This *is* a case of a ' new ' man, though he became an assiduous attender at the council only when he became treasurer in December 1404. The other new man was Peter Courtenay, captain of Calais and constable of Windsor, but he is not known to have attended a council meeting either before or after the parliament. In addition a few councillors seem to have been persuaded to attend a little more frequently than in the immediate past—Edward, duke of York, Lord Berkeley, Curson, and Doreward. The impression which the attendances gives is however that the nomination of 1404 had even less effect on membership than the nomination of 1401; on this occasion there was not even a significant rise in attendance.[1]

Again in 1404 as in 1401 there is insufficient evidence to show why the Commons asked for the appointment of the council or where the significance of the concession lay, but it is easier to understand the background to the crisis because the roll records a great deal of criticism by the Commons of the conduct of government. On the second day of the parliament the speaker, once again Sir Arnald Savage and now himself a member of the council,[2] added to his speaker's protest a request for leave to criticise the conduct of government, and the roll gives a clear enough account of the nature of this criticism. Some of the grievances were traditional ones that come up again and again in parliament, for example, that signet and privy-seal letters were interfering with the work of the common-law courts, but the major complaints were that inadequate provision had been made for defence and that the royal finances were badly conducted. Both these complaints are readily understandable. There had been two landings on the south coast in the previous six months and further invasions seemed imminent; and a good indication of the desperate state of the finances is given by a petition presented in this parliament by the king's half-brother, John, earl of Somerset, complaining that as captain of Calais since 1401 he was due over £11,400, almost two years wages.[3] The Commons were particularly critical of the finances, of declining revenues, of the extravagant granting of annuities and royal resources, and of the household which the king admitted had not been properly administered. As a result reform was attempted. The king at the request of the Commons removed some aliens from his household and a variety of revenues amounting to £12,000 were assigned and reserved for it, and war treasurers were appointed to receive the unusual land-tax granted in the parliament.[4] It is undoubtedly against this background of criticism and reform that the appointment of the council must be seen. Its significance does not lie in the names, and again there is not a scrap of evidence that the Commons wished to nominate the council or make it responsible to them. The Commons wanted good government, and they probably thought that a council

---

[1] The table may appear to suggest that there were three victims in 1404, John Scarle, Edmund Stafford, and Guy Mone, but Scarle and Stafford ceased to attend in March 1403, and Mone attended only until he was relieved of the treasurership in September 1403. Nicholas Bubwith, who was not nominated in 1404, began to attend only when he was appointed keeper of the privy seal in March 1405.

[2] *Vide infra*, p. 41.   [3] *Rot. Parl.* iii. 434-5.

[4] The Commons insisted on the appointment of war treasurers and laid down various rules governing their work including one that they should make payments only on the authority of privy-seal warrants ordered by ' le grant conseil '. This can hardly have been intended to refer to the occasional, specially summoned great councils, and in practice it did not do so. More probably it meant the formally-appointed council, and if so it gives an indication of the sort of thing that the Commons expected from this council. Chrimes and Brown, pp. 213-14.

formally appointed and charged to do its duty was the best guarantee that good government would be achieved.

One revealing feature of the parliaments of 1401 and 1404 is the role of the speaker, Sir Arnald Savage.[1] Savage seems typical of quite a few country gentlemen in the later Middle Ages; he was prepared to make a career in the royal service in return for the rewards it brought, undertaking all manner of administrative tasks. He had been a member of Richard II's household for almost twenty years; by 1401 at the latest he was a member of Henry of Monmouth's household, and by the end of that year its steward; and between 1402 or 1403 and December 1406 he was a member of the king's council.[2] But how could the spokesman of the Commons' criticism in 1401 and 1404 be at the same time a favoured royal councillor and servant? One possible explanation is that a distinction was drawn between Savage's own opinions and those of the speaker, but this cannot be the whole story. Savage seems to have been more than an unwilling spokesman. His personality stands out even in the parliament roll, and the St. Albans chronicle singles out his leadership in the parliament of 1401 for praise. Yet three days after the close of this parliament Henry IV confirmed an annuity granted to Savage by Richard II, and his career in the royal service flourished. It is unlikely that he was being bribed, and the weight of evidence suggests that his 'loyal criticism' was considered compatible with royal favour, and he continued to serve the king, on and off the council, until his death in 1410. In Savage's case this means more than that a councillor expected to be able to speak freely to the king. It seems to reflect an accommodating spirit of the first half of Henry IV's reign. Henry received a good deal of blunt though generally loyal criticism and advice in his parliaments, and probably he received very much the same from his council.[3] No king could have liked this, but the criticism never became personal or scandalous as it had become, for example, in the last quarter of the previous century; it was criticism

---

[1] Savage's career is outlined in J. S. Roskell, 'Sir Arnald Savage of Bobbing, Speaker for the Commons in 1401 and 1404', *Archaeologia Cantiana,* lxx (1956), from which many of the facts in this paragraph are taken.

[2] The date of his appointment to the council is problematical. In 1406 when an order was given to pay his arrears of wages he maintained that he was appointed a councillor 'about' Michaelmas 1402, and that it had then been ordained that each knight on the council should receive wages of £100 a year. Exchequer of Receipt, Writs and Warrants for Issues, box 21, no. 270. A parliament met on 30 September and he may well have been appointed in it. On the other hand, when in June 1403 he asked for an annuity to meet his additional expenses as a councillor 'about the king' he said he had been appointed with the assent of the last great council, and a great council had met in May. Ancient Petitions, file 186, no. 9256. The council meeting which considered this request on 4 June was the first he is known to have attended! Perhaps he was appointed in 1402 but could not attend and was again appointed in 1403. One suspects however that there was an element of sharp-practice somewhere in his claims for expenses.

[3] The proof of this statement about the council rests in the events of 1406 and the years following.

of lack of success, primarily in war and in finance. No doubt partly because he had no alternative and partly because he was a sensible man Henry seems to have accepted this without malice. This does not mean that he surrendered his prerogative—on the contrary throughout his reign he was jealous of it. But he was prepared to make concessions, to announce the names of his councillors, and to give promises—though these were perhaps not very material concessions. This is probably why the parliament of 1406 was so lengthy. Henry was then being asked to make material concessions, and then he resisted as long as he could.

All these things can best be judged in the third of these incidents, in the parliament of 1406, which is by far the best-known and the best-documented. On 22 May 1406 the king, after repeated requests from the Commons for good government, announced the names of his council in parliament and made promises which appear to have given it greater authority over the conduct of government. This concession did not satisfy the Commons and they refused to grant sufficient taxation until 22 December when the king accepted thirty-one articles which made further concessions and gave greater authority still to the council. In this parliament if anywhere is the evidence of a Lancastrian constitutional experiment, but surprisingly these events have never been examined and assessed critically; instead a number of extreme and conflicting generalizations have been made about them.[1] To Stubbs ' the parliament of 1406 seems almost to stand for an exponent of the most advanced principles of medieval constitutional life in England '.[2] Wylie thought that the concessions in May ' revolutionized ' government;[3] Professor Otway-Ruthven doubted if they had any constitutional significance at all;[4] while Baldwin wrote of the king ' withdrawing his hand from government entirely '.[5]

The background to the parliament of 1406 is very much the same as that in 1401 and 1404, threats to English security and financial embarassment. The year 1405 is probably the nadir of Henry IV's fortunes; in February there had been an attempt to remove the two young Mortimers to Wales, and in the summer there had been a major rebellion; the Welsh rising still continued and had been reinforced by a French expedition; and every frontier seemed to be threatened. Money was desperately short and there were large unpaid debts. Even the meeting place of this parliament had to be changed twice because of threats from Wales and from an enemy fleet in the Thames. It was perhaps unfair to the king, but it is not surprising that in the circumstances the Commons' repeated demand

---

[1] Some of these conflicting interpretations have been pointed out by C. G. Crump, ' A Note on the Criticism of Records ', *Bull. John Rylands Library*, viii (1924), 146–9.

[2] Stubbs, iii. 59.   [3] Wylie, ii. 429.

[4] J. Otway-Ruthven, *The King's Secretary and the Signet Office in the XV Century* (Cambridge, 1939), p. 32.   [5] Baldwin, p. 158.

throughout the parliament was ' good and abundant governance ' and an end to failure and insolvency.   They did not allege great scandals as they did, for example, in 1376, but they did say that great sums of money had been expended apparently with little effect, and they wanted an end to repeated demands for money and calls to fight for the king.   Parliament lasted from 1 March until 22 December with two adjournments, one from 3 to 26 April for Easter, and a long harvest adjournment from 19 June to 13 October.   The reason for this unprecedentedly long parliament was the unwillingness of the Commons to grant taxation save on conditions, but the selective character of the parliament roll makes it possible to know this prolonged struggle only in outline.   The roll of course does not record any proceedings in the Commons' chamber, and it records only some of the meetings of the full parliament.   For example, when the speaker on 3 April demanded the expulsion of aliens from England he reminded the king that ' as diverses foitz en cest parlement ' he had asked for this on behalf of the Commons.[1]   None of these earlier requests is mentioned on the roll.   More important, in the final session of parliament from 13 October until 22 December, meetings on only the opening and closing days and on 18 November are mentioned on the roll, though during this period the Commons must have been resisting demands that they should grant taxation and preparing their counter-demands in the thirty-one articles.   The point need not be laboured further; the parliament roll records only an outline of events.

The theme of the chancellor's opening sermon was the king's wish for advice from parliament, and it is probable that from the out-set the Commons were critical of how government had been conducted.   The fact that on 3 April the speaker thought it necessary to say that contrary to report the Commons had not spoken improperly about the king's person suggests that there had been plain speaking.[2] On the roll the first full meeting of parliament after the presentation of the speaker was on 23 March when the Commons made the first recorded demand for ' good and abundant governance ' and for immediate provision for the defence of the sea and for Wales and Gascony.   Two of these matters were dealt with at once; an agreement was reached whereby the merchants undertook to defend the sea, and some provision was made for the government of Wales. The only other recorded subject of discussion in this first session was a demand by the Commons that aliens should be expelled from England.   The council is not mentioned at all on the roll, but it is likely that the history of the council nomination of 22 May goes back into this first session of the parliament.   On 22 May the speaker reminded the king that the archbishop of Canterbury had already reported to the Commons that the king wished to be advised

[1] *Rot. Parl.* iii. 569.   [2] *Ibid.* iii. 569.

by the wisest lords of the realm who would have supervision over all that would be done for good government.[1] This promise may well have been given before the Easter recess, an obvious occasion for it would have been after the demand for ' good and abundant governance' on 23 March. A stronger piece of evidence is a memorandum, almost certainly of items considered by the council, and some of them matters for which the speaker asked on 3 April.[2] One of these items is ' Item, touchant les nouns des seignurs qi serront du consail du roy'. The issue is unimportant save to emphasize what is likely in any case, that the nomination of the council on 22 May had a long history behind it, probably going back to the demands of the Commons in the first part of the parliament. Parliament should have re-assembled after the Easter recess on 25 April, but because some lords and members of the Commons had not returned business was not resumed until the 30th. The king himself could not have been present then because on the 28th he had been taken ill at Windsor and could not travel. Items of business are recorded on three successive Saturdays in May; on the 8th the terms of the expulsion of aliens were agreed; on the 15th the king was present to agree to a member of the Commons leaving to serve as an admiral; and on the 22nd the appointment of the council took place. Proceedings on the 22nd began with the speaker coming before the king and the lords and reminding them that ' au commencement de parlement, et puis encea ' he had asked for ' governance habundante ' and asking that this should now be provided.[3] He also reminded the king of his wish reported by Archbishop Arundel to be advised by the wisest lords of the realm who would have supervision over all that would be done for the good government of the realm. The king agreed to provide this good government and personally repeated his good intentions; a ' Bill ' was then read, said to be made by the king himself and of his own free will. The ' tenor ' of this 'Bill' follows on the parliament roll, appparently in the form in which it was read to the parliament. The text deserves very close attention because here is the only surviving account, apparently in the king's own words, of why he appointed the council in parliament. It has often been quoted, particularly item VI in the synopsis below, but it has been interpreted in the most diverse ways, and it is worth-while trying to set out in detail what it seems to say.

I. The king, considering the labour he must expend on the government of his realm and all his possessions, (a) first, for the conservation of the rights of the king and his crown, and so that their revenues will be better collected and increased as far as possible, and so that he can better sustain his estate; and (b) second, for the

---

[1] *Rot. Parl.* iii. 572. [2] *Procs. and Ords.* i. 287–8.
[3] *Rot. Parl.* iii. 572–3 ; Chrimes and Brown, pp. 218–20.

    conservation of the laws and statutes of the realm, so that equal right be done to all;

II. of his own free will, desiring to be supported in ' les suis dites causes ' because he cannot attend to them personally as much as he would wish, and for the great love and trust he has for them, has appointed and charged seventeen named people to be of his council.

III. He asks and commands them to put all their effort into ' les suisdites causes ' for the king's profit and the conservation of the laws and statutes, so that by their labours he personally may be better relieved of the work.

IV. In order that they would serve more willingly on the council he has caused the appointment of these prelates and other lords to be announced in parliament.

V. He will support them all in these things and he fully trusts them.

VI. ' Et qe billes a endorserz par le chamberleyns, et lettres dessoutz le signet de nostre dit seignur le roy a adressers, et autres mandementz a doner, as chanceller, tresorer, et gardeyn du prive seal, et autres officers queconqes, desore en avaunt, *en tielx causes come desuis,* serront endorsez ou faites par advis du consail. Et, qe les ditz chanceller, tresorer, et gardeyn du prive seal, et autres officers, ne facent *en celles causes* sinoun par advis du dit consail;*

VII. toutes voies de chartres de pardoun de cryme, et de collacioun de benefices qe serront voides de fait, et des offices, voet nostre dit seignur le roy faire soun plaisir '.**

VIII. The king wishes that if those of the council are disturbed and cannot bring about the profit of the king nor see that the laws and statutes are protected, then they may depart freely without the ill-will of the the king.

IX. If any of them is found to be acting contrary to the king's profit, his laws, or his realm, let him be corrected or put out of the council.

    The ' Bill ' ends at this point, but the roll goes on to record some further proceedings in parliament which must be regarded either as a pantomine or as giving an unsuspected twist to the incident. The chancellor, Thomas Langley, pointed out that Lord Lovel was included in the council though he had often asked the king to be excused because of pleas pending in the courts, and the king agreed to excuse him. The other councillors then asked to be excused, and had to be asked again by the king; they then agreed to serve, but they asked ' depuis ceste bille fuist la volunte du roy et de sa mocioun propre, et nemye a lour seute ' that it be entered of record on the parliament roll, that it should be carried out, and that if during the parliament they found any way of amending it profitably, that it should be amended and entered of record. The king agreed to all these things. The events of 22 May have been seen as a concession to the Commons and clearly they were designed to please the Commons, but they seem also to have been designed to please the councillors and persuade them to serve. In the ' Bill ' the king says in section IV that he is appointing the council in parliament

to make the councillors more willing to serve and in sections V
and VIII he stresses his trust in them and the genuineness of his concession.   And the proceedings after the 'Bill' had been read suggest
that it was something of a surprise to the councillors and that they
were doubtful and reluctant to serve.   Why else was Lord Lovel
excused after the names had been read out in parliament, and why
else did the councillors demand firm assurances and the security of
the proceedings being entered on the parliament roll?   A feigned
reluctance to serve may have been good manners, but these exchanges
go much beyond this.   Either the proceedings were play-acting
which is difficult to believe, or they were not pre-arranged and the
king had found it necessary to come to parliament and on his own
initiative make a concession to placate the Commons and encourage
his council to continue to serve.

What then was being conceded?   Once again it was not a new
council.   The councillors nominated on 22 May were by and large
those who had been attending the council beforehand; twelve of
the seventeen had been nominated in the parliament of 1404.
There were some changes, but it is convenient to consider these with
the more important changes in membership that took place later in
the parliament.[1]   Certainly, however, the significance of the incident
does not lie in the names.   It must lie in the promises about government contained in the ' Bill '.   It is often said that these amount to
handing over government to the council, but this is certainly untrue.
Most commentators have concentrated on sections VI and VII in the
synopsis, and though these are only glosses on the major part of the
' Bill ' it is convenient to begin by finding out what they mean.
Section VI states that certain matters will require the assent of the
council;   section VII reserves other matters to the king himself.
Section VI states that *all* warrants to the chancellor, treasurer,
keeper of the privy seal, and all other officers ' en tielx causes come
desuis ' must be endorsed or made with the advice of the council,
and that these officers shall not act ' en celles causes ' without the
advice of the council.   Two types of warrant are specifically mentioned, bills endorsed by the chamberlains and letters under the
king's signet, but this has no great significance.   Bills endorsed by
the chamberlains were petitions to the king on which one of the
chamberlains, either the chamberlain of England or the king's
chamberlain, had written that the king had granted it.   The bill
then became the authority on which a letter was issued, most often
a privy-seal letter, very occasionally a letter under the great seal,
and probably not infrequently a letter under the signet.[2]   Letters
under the signet were merely another way of conveying orders from

---

[1] *Infra*, pp. 54-5.
[2] I hope to discuss these warrants more fully in an article on ' The Authorization of
Letters under the Great Seal '.*

the king.   They were most often used as warrants to the keeper of the privy seal; the treasurer would not accept them at all; the chancellor normally accepted them only for very minor matters; and the same is true of other officers.   These two types of warrant can have been cited here only as examples.   They were the most common ways in which orders for grants of the royal grace were conveyed to the privy-seal office, but this is all.   Even orders to the privy-seal office were given in other ways, and, for example, neither type of warrant was used *at all* as a warrant to the treasurer.   Section VI states and means that *all* warrants to *all* officers dealing with *certain subjects* must receive the approval of the council.   This approval must be signified by an endorsement or by a statement to this effect in the text; for example, the clerk of the council might endorse a chamberlain's bill with a record of the council's approval or a privy-seal warrant might state in its text that a grant was made by the king ' par advis de son conseil '.

Much more important than these technicalities is the statement in section VI that the concession refers only to certain matters; the first sentence states that warrants ' en tielx causes come desuis ' must have the approval of the council, and the second states that officers shall not act ' en celles causes ' without the advice of the council. These ' causes ' are not difficult to identify; in sections II and III the king refers to the assistance he hopes to obtain from the council in ' les suisdites causes '.   These ' causes ' must be the two aspects of government which the king has specified in section I—(a) and (b) in the synopsis.   The first is the king's financial profit, and the second is the conservation of the laws and statutes of the realm.   The whole ' Bill ' is a unit which turns upon these opening sentences. There are two parts of government to which the king cannot attend as much as he wishes ; he has therefore appointed his council to help him to deal with them.   Section VI is merely glossing this concession or explaining how it will work; perhaps it is included to emphasize that sections I and II are more than general statements of good-will. These two aspects of government are described in a general way in section I and are paraphrased in sections III and VIII, and probably in section IX also.   The second, ' the conservation of the laws and statutes of the realm ' is expressed generally and it is perhaps significant that it is paraphrased in almost the same words; probably it was never intended to be more than a generalization.   The first aspect can be defined more closely and probably was more important.   In section I it is said to be the conservation of the rights of the king and of his crown, not his rights in general but in particular his financial rights because the remainder of the sentence refers to the better collection and increase of his revenues so that he can better sustain his estate.   In the paraphrases in sections III and VIII this aspect of government is referred to simply as the king's ' profit '.

The idea that seems to lie behind this part of the ' Bill ', indeed
behind the whole ' Bill ', is one that is common in the later Middle
Ages, that if the king was well-advised and did not grant-away his
revenues he would be rich from his own resources and would have
little or no need to ask his subjects for taxation; conversely if he did
have to ask for money this was the result of misgovernment. A
good statement of this view comes from the Commons in 1376 who
said that ' leur semblait pur chose veritable qe si lour dit seignur lige
eust euz toutdys entour luy des loialx conseillers et bon officers,
meisme nostre seignur le roy eust este bien rychez de tresor, et par
tant neust mye grantment bosoigne de charger sa commune par voie
de subside, ou de talliage, nautrement '.[1] Sir John Fortescue's *The
Governance of England* is largely a treatise on the same theme a century
later. In the early years of Henry IV's reign this view was repeatedly put forward by the Commons in parliament who maintained
that if the king would restrain his liberality and refrain from grant-
ing-away his resources, or if at least he would grant them away only
with the advice of his council, he would have little need to tax his
subjects.[2] It would be wrong to interpret the ' Bill ' too narrowly;
a general improvement in government was expected to derive from
the appointment of the council; but there seems to be a direct connection between these earlier demands and the ' Bill ' of 1406.

In 1399 one of the charges made against Richard II was granting-
away his patrimony;[3] and in Henry IV's first parliament the Commons
petitioned that outrageous grants made by the king to undeserving
people, confirmations, and pardons of large sums of money should
be repealed, and that in future these should be granted by the advice
of the council. The king replied vaguely that he would be advised
' par les sages de son conseil es choses touchantz lestat de luy et de
son roialme, sauvant toutesfoitz sa libertee ' and a statute was passed
laying down that petitions seeking certain types of grants must state
their annual value and that of any other grants enjoyed by the
petitioner.[4] A few months later in a great council in February 1400,
no doubt with the rebellion of the previous month in mind, the
lords advised the king to retain forfeited lordships in his own hands
so that he could maintain his estate without charging his people, and
so that parliament could not rebuke him if he had to ask for money.[5]
In the next parliament, in 1401, in which the first of these council
nominations took place, the Commons again petitioned on this
subject. They asked that because some people took advantage of

---

[1] *Rot. Parl.* ii. 32 ; Chrimes and Brown, pp. 106–7.*

[2] B. P. Wolffe, ' Acts of Resumption in the Lancastrian Parliaments 1399–1456 ',
E.H.R., lxxiii (1958), discusses this view in another connection. *Infra,* pp. 61–91

[3] *Rot. Parl.* iii. 417 and 419 ; Chrimes and Brown, pp. 187 and 189.

[4] *Ibid.* iii. 433 ; *Stat. R.* ii. 113 ; and see G. C. Crump, ' Eo quod expressa mentio,
etc. ' in *Essays in History presented to Reginald Lane Poole* (Oxford, 1927), pp. 30–45.

[5] *Procs. and Ords.* i. 108.

the king's generosity and made demands which the community had to pay for, in the future petitions asking for annual profits should say that the grant be made with the advice of the council. The king replied that he would be advised by ' les sages de son conseil ' in making such grants and would moderate the number, saving his liberty. On this occasion the Commons excepted offices and benefices from the grants that should have the assent of the council, two of the three exceptions in section VII of the ' Bill '.[1] In the next parliament, in 1402, the Commons petitioned that grants of the king's revenues should not be made ' forspris offices, corrodies, et baillies ', and the king replied that he did not intend to make any save to those whom he and his council thought deserving, and that others who asked for them should be punished.[2] The next parliament was the Westminster parliament of 1404 in which the second council nomination took place, and again there was strong criticism of the unwise and improper grants of castles, lands, and annuities.[3] In the Coventry parliament later in 1404 the demand was resumed in a slightly different form.[4] The Commons asked for a resumption of all grants from the ancient inheritance of the crown made since 40 Edward III with the object of paying for the expenses of the household. The king's reply was evasive. ' And for als muche that the Comunes desiren that the kyng shulde leve upon his owne, as gode reson asketh, and alle estates thynken the same, the kyng thanketh hem of here gode desire, willyng put it in execution als sone as he wel may.' He promised an examination of the grants, but though a proclamation was issued that all who had such grants should bring copies of the patents before the king and council so that a decision could be made about them, there is no evidence that anything was achieved by this promise. What the king did do was take the issues from annuities and grants for one year from Easter 1404.[5] The concession of 22 May 1406 undoubtedly was made with these earlier demands in mind; the king was then freely making a concession in the spirit of these earlier Commons' demands. The king was certainly conceding something more than that the council should supervise these obnoxious grants, but the exemption from conciliar control in section VII of pardons of crime and grants of benefices and offices, and the events of the remainder of the parliament suggest that it was the old idea that the king should live of his own which governed the incident.[6]

---

[1] *Rot. Parl.* iii. 478–9. [2] *Ibid.* iii. 495. [3] *Ibid.* iii. 523–4.
[4] *Ibid.* iii. 547–9. A council may have been nominated in this parliament also because among the council records there is a list of those assigned of the council in 6 Henry IV. *Procs. and Ords.* i. 243–4. [5] *Rot. Parl.* iii. 549.
[6] No mention has been made of the king's statement that he wished to be relieved of some of the burden of his work. It is true that his health had already begun to fail, and this no doubt made him less unwilling to share some of his responsibilities, but at most this can have been only a contributory factor. He seems to have been forced to

The most surprising thing about the concession of 22 May is that it had so little effect on the Commons. The councillors agreed to serve and the promises began to take effect, but the Commons remained critical. On two further occasions before the summer adjournment the speaker asked for 'good and abundant governance', and they continued to point out examples of past failures. They insisted on the audit of the accounts of the treasurers of war appointed in the Coventry parliament of 1404; and most important of all, in spite of Archbishop Arundel's statement on 24 May that the council would serve only if there were sufficient resources, the Commons on 13 June granted only a small amount of money. Their distrust was clearly not of the councillors appointed on 22 May; they had asked that they should serve and that they should be paid for doing so.[1] It seems to have been rather distrust of the extent or reality of the concession, and what they wished in addition is made clear by some articles which they presented on 19 June.[2] They asked that aliens be expelled; that the household be 'modified' to cut down its outrageous and excessive expenses; and, continuing the theme that the king could live of his own if he cut down his liberality, that the king's resources be conserved by revoking grants made since the beginning of the parliament, by not granting away revenues which came into his hands until household debts had been paid, and by an enquiry by the council before Michaelmas into the value of all lordships, manors, lands, tenements, alien priories, custodies, marriages, or other possessions leased or granted, with authority to increase the farms where possible. The king gave no reply to these articles, and whether as a result or not, parliament was adjourned that same day until 13 October.

The remainder of the parliament is poorly recorded but it was presumably for firm promises of good government on the lines of these articles that the Commons stood out until 22 December; certainly the thirty-one articles which the king accepted on that day in return for a grant of taxation concede most of the demands of 19 June.[3] These thirty-one articles are much more miscellaneous than the earlier articles; for example, six provide merely that various officials should act honestly, and others deal with the appointment of sheriffs and escheators, the holding of county elections, and special assizes; but the more important contain an elaboration of the familiar plan for good government. Its mainstay is the council by whose advice the king is to govern. This council had already been appointed, but a number of articles lay down regulations about its work—for example, members are to be paid and some are always to

make the concessions of 1406 and he was determined that they should not be continued after the parliament of 1407. His conduct throughout the reign suggests a man who clung to authority, not one who surrenders it willingly.

[1] *Rot. Parl.* iii. 577–8.   [2] *Ibid.* iii. 578–9.
[3] *Rot. Parl.* iii. 585–9 ; Chrimes and Brown, pp. 220–5.

be with the king (art. 1), those who are absent are to be consulted where possible (art. 13), members are to leave meetings if matters in which they are involved come before the council (art. 14), and various other well-intentioned general provisions.   The council is to assist the king in all matters, but there are two aspects of government which dominate the articles.   First, there is the household.   The Commons do not propose new regulations for the household but they insist repeatedly that existing regulations must be obeyed and that household officials must do their duty (arts. 11, 21, 22, 26, 27).   And, second, and closely related to the first, is the familiar theme that with economy the king can live of his own.   The councillors are to take notice of all places where revenues are spent (art. 5); all the revenues from ' gardes, mariages, voidances des temporaltees des erceves-chees, eveschees, eschetes, forfaitures, priories aliens, custumes, et toutes autres commoditees, profitz, revenuz, et emolumentz du roiaume, certeins et casuels '* not granted-away before the first day of the parliament and coming into the king's hands before the last day of the next parliament are to be received in the exchequer and not assigned, and paid for household expenses; and no grants or pardons of these or other revenues is to be made until the end of the next parliament, with certain specified exceptions (arts. 6-7).   The Commons had at last succeeded in banning grants and pardons of the king's resources for a period.   Closely connected with the same idea are two articles concerning petitions (arts. 8-9); the king is to receive these only on two days in each week and they are to be examined by those of the council with the king.   The ostensive reason for this is to free the king on the other days, but as he is to be free to grant petitions for offices, corrodies, benefices, and other things which he cannot retain to his own use, the real reason is more likely to have been to restrain his liberality.   This is the familiar Commons' plan and undoubtedly they had won a great victory in forcing the king to accept it.

Unfortunately it is impossible to follow in detail how this Common's victory was achieved.   Parliament had been adjourned on 19 June, apparently with the Commons insisting on their plan for good government; the new session began after several postponements on 18 October, but the only day on which business is recorded on the roll between then and the last day of parliament is 18 November. On that day the Commons through their speaker asked that the lords should be charged to tell the king of the bad government of the realm—presumably the deadlock between king and Commons was unbroken at this date.[1]   The king probably began to make further concessions about the end of that month.   This is indicated by a document in the Cottonian collection which lists those assigned by the king to be of his council on 27 November 1406; nothing more

[1] *Rot. Parl.* iii. 579.

of this incident is known but presumably it represents a conciliatory move by the king.[1] Another similar move must have been the appointment on 8 December of the Commons' speaker, Sir John Tiptoft, as treasurer of the household, and discussion about a new controller, and on the same day the council made some provisions for moderating household expenses.[2] Discussions of the thirty-one articles must have been going on about this time, and a memorandum of advice from the council on an earlier draft of these survives.[3] This tells little about the negotiations save that the council accepted the principle of the articles though they advised some modifications. Some of these were accepted, but it is interesting that though they recommended that grants which had been made with the advice and assent of the council since the beginning of the parliament should stand, article six revokes all such grants, allowing only certain specified exceptions; presumably the Commons held-out for the principle and won.

There is also an account of the last days of the parliament in the St. Albans Chronicle.[4] According to this the Commons held out for a promise from certain lords, presumably the councillors, that they would refund the grant of taxation if it should be misspent. The lords declined to give this promise, the king was furious, and the Commons had to give way three days before Christmas. This could fit well with the chronology given by the record sources. The new council was probably appointed at the beginning of December,[5] and the thirty-one articles may well have been accepted early in the month for the proceedings on 22 December were merely the public acceptance of an agreement reached beforehand. The additional promise for which the Commons are said to have asked is quite in accord with their attitude throughout the parliament, and the king's refusal to concede it accounts much better for the session lasting until three days before Christmas than his acceptance of the thirty-one articles.

Even if the Commons had to accept defeat on this point their victory was still a considerable one. They had rejected the offers the king had made and held out for nine months to win by the thirty-one articles all or almost all they asked. Moreover, unlike many concessions to the Commons, this victory was not merely nominal; the concessions were material ones and they were put into practice. In May the king appointed a council and promised to act in certain matters only with the assent of the council. The council records show that all those and only those appointed to the council attended its meetings. The only business recorded at these meetings is routine administration but, under the influence of the Commons'

[1] *Procs. and Ords.* i. 295.   [2] *Ibid.* i. 295–6.   [3] *Ibid.* i. 297–8.
[4] *The St. Albans Chronicle 1406–1420*, ed. V. H. Galbraith (Oxford, 1937), pp. 2–3.
[5] *Infra,* p. 55.

articles of 19 June, the council began to enquire into financial administration generally and commissions dated 28 June were issued to
enquire in each county into concealment of royal revenues by local
officials, their extortions, and into royal farms and the charges on
them.[1] The greatest visible effect of the concessions was on the
obnoxious grants and pardons of royal revenues enrolled on the
chancery rolls. These continued to be made during the parliament,
but from about the end of June the majority record that they were
granted with the assent of the council, something quite unusual
because these were grants of grace normally made by the king alone.
The thirty-one articles forbade these grants and pardons entirely
until the end of the next parliament, and there is in fact a striking fall
in the number entered on the rolls; they were almost but not completely stopped.[2] They were resumed after the Gloucester parliament of 1407, and some of those who had received grants during the
1406 parliament and had them cancelled by the thirty-one articles,
then received new grants of the same graces.[3] Exchequer evidence
is more complicated, but after May 1406 a high proportion of the
privy-seal warrants to the treasurer and chamberlains ordering payments and assignments were made ' with the assent of the council ',[4]
and Principal Steel has noted that ' there was practically no assignment at all after 13 December' (1406) in the Michaelmas term,
1406-7, and only a small amount during the Easter term of 1407, in
striking contrast with the other years of the reign.[5] The corresponding rise in cash receipts at the exchequer means that the sixth of
the thirty-one articles was being observed to a large extent.[6] There
is also evidence that during 1407 an attempt was made by the council

---

[1] *Cal. Pat. Rolls, 1405–1408*, pp. 153–5, warranted ' per ipsum regem et consilium '.

[2] For example, the number of letters-patent enrolled on the Patent Roll and warranted
'per breve de privato sigillo' in the seventh and eighth years of the reign were—pardons
of crime, 94 and 90 ; grants of benefices, prebends, &c., 42 and 43 ; grants of office, 23
and 23 ; grants of land or custody of land, 36 and 9 ; grants of goods, 16 and 1 ; grants
of money, 46 and 8 ; pardons of money, goods, &c., 11 and 4. Grants which do not
diminish the revenue remain at the same level in both years, whereas those which do
diminish it drop in the eighth year beginning on 30 Sept. 1406. Only seven of the
twenty-two grants in the last four categories in the eighth year were dated after 22 Dec.
1406, and six of these seven are stated to have been given with the assent or advice of
the council.

[3] For example, *Cal. Pat. Rolls, 1405–1408*, pp. 381, 389, 392.

[4] Statistics of this kind are always somewhat misleading but the proportion of privy-
seal warrants ordering payments or assignments made ' with the assent of the council '
was 26 per cent in 5 Henry IV ; 31 per cent in 6 Henry IV ; 20 per cent in 7 Henry
IV up to 22 May 1406 and 60 per cent after 22 May ; and 41 per cent in 8 Henry IV.

[5] A. Steel, *The Receipt of the Exchequer, 1377–1485* (Cambridge, 1954), pp. 94–95.

[6] Another indication that the thirty-one articles were taken seriously is that two
copies were written at the time and survive as Exchequer, K. R., Parliamentary and Council Proceedings, rolls 31 and 32. The king may have had them in mind when he added this
postscript to a privy-seal warrant to the chancellor dated 5 June 1407. ' Et volons auxi
et vous mandons qe encountre nostre venue a nostre dite citee (of London) qe serra
Marsdy prochein ove laide de Dieu, vous facez avoir une copie de touz les estatutz et
ordennances faitz en nostre darrein parlement pur demorer continuelment pardevers
nous '. Chancery, **Warrants** for the Great Seal, file 635, no. 5293.*

to plan how revenue was to be spent rather than rely on the hand-to-mouth methods of the past; some kind of national balance sheet may even have been prepared.[1] But planned spending did not end with the Gloucester parliament of 1407 in which the Commons were put in their place, and it is likely that this was as much the result of pressure put on the king towards the end of 1406 by some of the lords and in particular by the prince of Wales.

This aspect of the events of 1406 is difficult to define, but it has already been pointed-out that the ' Bill ' of 22 May seems to have been designed to conciliate the councillors as well as the Commons, and there is a draft of advice offered by the lords spiritual and temporal to the king in this parliament which shows that they shared some at least of the ideas of the Commons.[2] They advised that grants and pardons of debts should cease for two years so that the king might be more wealthy and would not need to impose on his subjects more than necessary, that certain additional customs should be granted and in part reserved to pay for the grants that had already been made, and that £10,000 should be reserved from other revenues to pay for household expenses. These proposals are not as sweeping as those of the Commons but they are very much in the same spirit, and it is likely that the king was under pressure from all sides and probably for the same reasons. This pressure seems to have come to a head in the last month of the parliament and led to a fundamental change in the composition of the council. The knights and esquires who had been so prominent on the council since the beginning of the reign were completely ousted, and at the same time the prince of Wales began to attend the council regularly and continued to do so until he was dismissed in November 1411. Only a hint of this change is contained in the council appointed on 22 May. Twelve of the seventeen appointed on that day had been appointed to the council in the parliament of 1404, and none was a newcomer. The bishop of Exeter, Edmund Stafford, was again recalled from his diocese to serve; the steward and the chamberlain of the household, Sir John Stanley and Reginald, lord Grey, were formally included; and the only man who was almost a newcomer was Hugh, lord Burnell, who had been serving with the prince of Wales against Glendower. The omissions are possibly more significant, but as no record of the attendance at a council meeting during the first four months of 1406 survives this must be uncertain. But Henry Bowet, bishop of Bath, Richard Clifford, bishop of Worcester, John Doreward, and John Pelham who had all attended quite frequently during

---

[1] The warrants for issues often carefully specify from what revenue a payment was to be made instead of leaving it to the discretion of the treasurer and chamberlains as in the past, and some large block payments were ordered. In March three warrants ordered the payment of £21,000 for war expenses, and in May, after a great council, a group of warrants ordered the payment of over £20,000 for war and household expenses—all from specified sources of revenue.   [2] *Procs. and Ords.* i. 283–7.

1405 were not included and the council became distinctly more aristocratic. All those who were appointed on 22 May, except Lord Lovel who was excused, attended meetings while parliament was in session, and it is noticeable that attendance was limited to these men whereas in the past a wider circle of councillors had attended occasionally. The king seems to have found no fault with these councillors because it is virtually the same men whom he is said to have appointed to the council on 27 November 1406.[1] Lord Lovel and the bishop of Exeter were not included—probably at their own wish; John Prophete who had been appointed keeper of the privy seal on 4 October was added; otherwise it was the council of 22 May re-appointed. A great change however took place between 27 November and 22 December; when the lords of the council were called upon to take an oath to observe the thirty-one articles, only thirteen did so. Lord Willoughby and three knights, John Cheyne, Arnald Savage, and Hugh Waterton, who had been appointed to the council in May and November are omitted. This is a deliberate omission; all save Waterton are recorded at meetings of the council during November; Savage had attended a meeting on 2 December, and yet a warrant of 10 December implies that he is no longer a member[2]; and not one of them is known to have attended again. It must be emphasized, however, that these men were not in disgrace and continued to serve the king in responsible positions. The only newcomer was Sir John Tiptoft, the speaker, who had been appointed treasurer of the household on 8 December, and he is not known to have attended at all until he was appointed treasurer in 1408.[3] More significant, the prince began to attend meetings regularly after 8 December; he was too important to be asked to take the oath to observe the thirty-one articles but article thirteen shows that it was assumed that he would be a member of the council. Evidence of attendance is scant for the next twelve months, indeed for the remainder of the reign, but attendance was limited to those who took the oath and a number received salaries for doing so.[4] Quite clearly a new phase in the history of the council had begun.

This new council is difficult to characterize or explain. It is more aristocratic than the council of the previous years, but it would be wrong to emphasize this element too much because all the lords spiritual and temporal who were members had attended in the

[1] *Procs. and Ords.* i. 295.

[2] Exchequer of Receipt, Writs and Warrants for Issues, box 22, no. 243.

[3] Tiptoft was a king's knight who had received a number of gifts from Henry IV in the past. On 8 December he was appointed treasurer of the household and given goods worth £150 and the custody of some lands in Wales, both of which were exempted from the limitation on grants in the thirty-one articles. *Rot. Parl.* iii. 591. Was he being bribed?

[4] The archbishop of Canterbury, the bishops of London, Winchester, and Durham, the duke of York, and Lords Burnell and Roos were all paid salaries as councillors.

past and almost all had considerable administrative experience; contemporaries would probably have described it as a ' substantial ' council. The omission of the knights and esquires was probably a concession to a prejudice common in the Middle Ages that ' low-born ' councillors thought too much of their own profit.[1] Some explanation like this is necessary to account for the sudden dismissal of men whom the king continued to trust. Another explanation is that these men were in general personal servants of the king, some of whom had been in his service before 1399, and after 1406 Henry IV controlled his government less immediately. It is necessary to be cautious in speaking of this because the king did not cease to control government though he governed in a different way. In the past he had always been at the centre of affairs, at Westminster or dealing with some regional crisis. Now his throne was more secure and his health was not good, and for long periods he was away from the centre of affairs, Westminster, and living in the country. He still ordered many letters and important issues of policy, diplomatic affairs, for example, still required his approval, but he must have relied much more on others, particularly on the council. A good indication of this change is that the privy-seal office which acted as a ' clearing-house ' for government and operated from the place where it could be most useful, now tended to remain at Westminster most of the time though the king was rarely there; in the first part of the reign it had often followed the king when he left Westminster. No doubt the king now used his signet much more than in the past to convey his instructions. The other side of this story is that the council became more active in dealing with major questions than in the first part of the reign. This new phase which lasted from December 1406 until November 1411 requires a separate study,[2] but it is relevant here to ask why it began. Was it the result of the action of the Commons in parliament? No doubt the determination of the Commons in 1406 helped to bring it about, and no doubt the Commons were pleased to see the prince come to the council and the council given greater authority, but it does not appear to have resulted directly from the action of the Commons. The evidence for this is indirect. In the parliament of 1407 the Commons were firmly put in their place. The king was still conciliatory in some ways, but a number of the restrictions of 1406 ceased automatically

---

[1] The poem *Mum and the Sothsegger,* ed. M. Day and R. Steele (Early English Text Society, 1936), which was written about 1403–6 refers (p. 75) to ' Thees knightz of þe conseil þat nygh þe king dwellen ' and plunder his revenue. The value of this remark is however doubtful because the poem attacks *all* the estates of the realm, and there is no concrete evidence that the opinion was aired in the parliament of 1406.

[2] Unfortunately very little of the council records survive for this period and this study will have to be primarily an examination of the attempt to plan the king's finances. These show that many of the changes forced on the king by the prince and his friends in 1410 and 1411 can be traced back to the more friendly arrangements of 1406 and the three following years.

with the end of this parliament, the councillors were excused further obedience to the oaths they had taken in 1406, and it was made clear that there was to be no repetition of the events of 1406.[1] The 'Bill" and the thirty-one articles were dead; and yet the prince and the other councillors continued to serve and exercise their new authority. The initiative was certainly not now coming from the Commons, and it is only possible to speculate on where it did come from. At the close of 1409 the council split into two factions and the prince and his friends forced an unwilling king to retain them alone on the council and to accept their policies. But nothing like this seems to have happened in 1406; bitter enemies in 1410 served together in 1406, and the king was apparently not actively hostile to the new council. The most likely explanation is therefore that the prince, notoriously impatient and confident in his own ability, came forward late in 1406 to try to solve the problem of good government, and to help to rescue the king from his impasse in parliament. As commander in Wales he had suffered considerably from the weakness of government in recent years, and now that the back of the Glendower rebellion had been broken he could more easily serve in Westminster. The king, in bad health, and under fire from all sides in parliament, all sharing the same basic ideas on how good government could be achieved, was obliged to concede. It is impossible to say how much force was used. The probability is that the king conceded with good grace in a situation where he had little alternative; but *at this stage* he was merely conceding greater authority to a council of his son and his friends. By 8 December the new regime had begun, and the king was being given the no-doubt unpleasant advice that after Christmas he should go to some place where with their advice his household expenses could be moderated.[2]

Another incident of the same type took place in 1410; the Commons asked that in aid of ' bone et substanciall gouvernance ' the king should appoint a council and that the members should be sworn in parliament. The king accepted this and some further requests framed in the same spirit as the thirty-one articles of 1406.[3] As far as the Commons were concerned this was no doubt another opportunity to put forward the same ideas as in the other incidents, but on this occasion magnate politics certainly entered in it, and it is better set aside until the whole period 1406-11 is considered.

The evidence of these incidents therefore gives no support to the theory of a Lancastrian constitutional experiment. True, it is easier to point out what the Commons did not ask than to say why they acted as they did, but there is no trace of ' constitutionalism ' in their outlook. At no time did they ask that *they* should appoint the king's council or his great officers; they did not even ask that they should

[1] *Rot. Parl.* iii. 609 ; Chrimes and Brown, pp. 227–8.   [2] *Procs. and Ords.* i. 296.
[3] *Rot. Parl.* iii. 623–34 ; Chrimes and Brown, pp. 229–33.

approve the king's choice.   They appear to have had a prejudice
against men of their own estate being too prominent on the council,
but they seem to have had no strong complaint against the existing
councillors.   Certainly in 1401, 1404, and in May 1406 the membership of the council changed only slightly as the result of the Commons' action; it was re-inforced but not changed.   Only once was
there a distinct change, in December 1406, when the knights dropped
out and the prince began to attend.   No one seems to have gained
admission to the council as a result of the action of the Commons, and
none of those who ceased to be a member was attacked by them or
disgraced by the king.   If then the significance of these incidents
does not lie in the membership of the council, where does it lie?
The answer can only be that the Commons saw some assurance of
better government in the formal, public appointment and swearing
of the council.   The aim of the Commons was 'good and abundant
government' as it was described in 1406.   This should not be conceived narrowly; it meant that the seas would be properly defended,
the war in Wales effectively conducted, the king's household administered economically, that his officers would act honestly, and so on.
The Commons, and everyone else at the time, seem to have believed
optimistically that with good counsel all these things could be
achieved; this theme of good counsel is repeated again and again in
these years.   One aspect of this was particularly prominent in the
minds of the Commons, the economy aspect.   If the king was well-
advised and did not grant-away his resources so liberally, he would
have enough money to live of his own and would not require to ask
his subjects for help so often.   The Commons put forward this idea
in every one of the early parliaments of Henry IV's reign; it lies
behind the ' Bill ' of May 1406 and it is the most substantial part of
the Commons' articles of June 1406 and of the thirty-one articles.
No doubt it is so prominent because it touched their pockets directly
and because it was so simple to grasp and pronounce.   The Commons did not want responsible government or anything as refined
as this; they wanted good, honest, and in particular economical
government by the king; and they thought that the council was
the best means of ensuring this.   They were fighting on the one
hand to ensure that the king took the advice of his council on
certain matters, and on the other to ensure that the councillors
attended regularly and took their responsibilities seriously.   The
public appointment and swearing of the councillors in parliament,
and if possible a specific promise by the king to take their advice,
were the means to achieve this.   It may seem a modest aim now,
but the ' Advice ' of the council in 1401 shows that it was considered
potentially dangerous then, and in 1406 it was forced upon a resisting
king.   This is the only explanation which fits the facts as we know
them.   It confirms that the Commons were capable of sustained

criticism on matters which affected them directly, and that Henry IV by force of circumstances and probably by nature also was conciliatory in dealing with the Commons, but it leaves no room for theories of ' Lancastrian constitutionalism '.

APPENDIX I

Public Record Office, Council and Privy Seal File 28

Tresredoute et nostre soverain seignur nous vous recomandons a vostre hautesse si humblement come nous savons ou plus poons. Et tresredoute seignur vous plese savoir que hier le Venderdy apres que nous departismes hors de vostre noble presence nous estiems assemblez a les Freres Precheours pur pluseurs tres-chargeantes busoignes et matires touchantes (lonur, bien, et seuretee de vostre roiale persone et·le noble)[1] estat de vous et de vostre roiaume; et purposasmes avoir moustrez et declarez nostre entencioun et avys sur ycelles le Samady lendemayn bien matyn entour sept de la clok. Et pur ce que a lors nous estiems certifiez que vous departiscez bien par temps hors de Londres la ou vous plust, nous assemblez depuis a les ditz Freres de nostre comun assent chargeasmes vostre foial lige Johan Dorewarde, un de vostre conseil, de venir a vostre treshonurable presence pur vous moustrer et declarer les ditz busoignes et matires depar nous (en la presence du conte de Somerset, vostre chamberlain, et du conte de Wircestre[2], seneschal de vostre hostel, ou de lun de eux).[1] Sur les queles (busoignes et matires)[1] plese a vostre roiale magestee luy escoutier benignement et lui doner ferme foy et creance en celle partie, et nous ent faire assavoir par les ditz contes (vostre)[1] voloir et entencion a grand confort de nous voz humbles liges et servantz qy prioms a la Benoite Trinitee qil vous ottroie bone vie a longe duree a lonur et plesance de lui et bone gouvernance de vostre roiaume. Escript a Londres le . . . iour de Marz.[3]

Au roy nostre tresredoute
et soverain seignur

Voz humbles liges et
servantz, trestoutz de
vostre grand conseil.*

APPENDIX II

Attendance at the Council

Columns D, G and I indicate those who were appointed to the council in 1404 and in May and December 1406. The remaining columns give the number of times each councillor is known to have attended council-meetings during the periods specified.

[1] The words in brackets have been interlineated in a more cursive hand than the rest of the letter.

[2] The words ' de Wircestre ' are repeated by mistake.

[3] A blank has been left for the day of the month.

	A 1400	B Apr. 1401 / Mar. 1402	C 1403	D parlt. 1404	E Apr. 1404 / Mar. 1405	F Mar. 1405 / Feb. 1406	G May 1406	H Jun.-Dec. 1406	I Dec. 1406	J 1407
Chancellors										
John Scarle, 1399–1401	16	34	10							
Edmund Stafford, 1401–3		40	9		1		x	4		
Henry Beaufort, 1403–5			21	x	39	21	x	16	x	7
Thomas Langley, 1405–7		9	31	x	60	75	x	24	x	6
Thomas Arundel, 1407–9		5	10	x	9	10	x	19	x	8
Treasurers										
John Norbury, 1399–1401	13	4	6	x	12	6				
L. Allerthorpe, 1401–2		24								
Henry Bowet, 1402	2	9	5	x	22	32				
Guy Mone, 1402–3			23							
Lord Roos, 1403–4	1		10	x	15	15	x	7	x	2
Lord Furnival, 1404–7				x	45	63	x	21	x	6
Nicholas Bubwith, 1407–8					20	78	x	21	x	6
Keepers of the Privy Seal										
Richard Clifford, 1399–1401	12	27		x		18				
Thomas Langley, 1401–5	see		under			chancellors				
Nicholas Bubwith, 1405–6	see		under			treasurers				
John Prophete, 1406–15	14	29						14	x	8
Bishop Bottlesham of Rochester		15		x		*died 1404*				
Bishop Trevenant of Hereford		19				*died 1404*				
Bishop Young of Bangor		26	3	x	3					
Prince Henry						1	1			5
Duke of York		1		x	9	2	x	17	x	4
Earl of Northumberland	3	24	4		2					
Earl of Somerset	1	3	5	x	16.	8	x	5	x	6
Earl of Westmorland	1	8	4	x	3					
Earl of Worcester	9	11	5			*died 1403*				
Lord Berkeley		6		x	7	1				
Lord Burnell						1	x	12	x	1
Lord Grey	1	4			4	4	x	6	x	3
Lord Lovel		2	7	x	1	21	x			
Lord Willoughby			4	x		3	x	8		
Sir John Cheyne	8	12	16	x	5	19	x	3		
Sir Peter Courtenay				x						
Sir Thomas Erpingham			6		2	1				
Sir John Pelham					10	16				
Sir Arnold Savage			7	x	17	30	x	10		
Sir John Stanley					1	3	x	6	x	4
Sir John Tiptoft									x	
Sir Hugh Waterton		6	11	x	17	5	x	1		
John Curson	1	18		x	7	1				
John Doreward	9	21		x	8	25				
John Frome	1	25								
Others	35	15			14	21	1			
Number of council-meetings at which the attendance is known	17	45	34		61	80		24		8
Average attendance	7.4	8.7	6		5.7	6		8.1		8.2

2

Acts of Resumption in the Lancastrian Parliaments, 1399-1456 [1]*

by B. P. Wolffe

THE English royal demesne in the later Middle Ages has hardly been studied at all. Though the landed possessions of our later Plantagenet and Lancastrian kings are generally supposed to have been but a shadow of their former size and to have played an insignificant part in our national history, these beliefs are still no more than unproved assumptions. For example, no investigation has been undertaken even to ascertain the extent of royal lands at any time during the fourteenth and fifteenth centuries. There is, of course, one basic fact which no-one would question: by the mid-fourteenth century, if not earlier, our kings had grown quite accustomed to obtaining the major portion of their revenues from other sources, namely from the more profitable source of direct parliamentary taxation and from the even more lucrative and constant source of the customs. But no attempt has yet been made to assess the impact of these financial developments on the attitude of our medieval kings towards their landed patrimony, nor to examine their effects on the royal lands themselves or on the central office which administered them, the exchequer.

These topics are certainly important: there is abundant evidence that by the beginning of the fifteenth century, if not earlier, men of affairs had become very much concerned about them. Twice during the Lancastrian period, between 1399 and 1406, and again from 1449-56, the Crown lands became the central issue of parliamentary controversy. As a result a series of parliamentary acts of resumption were passed designed to recover alienated or deeply pledged royal estates and revenues for the Crown, to overhaul their administration and to redeploy their issues. We are still largely dependent for our knowledge of Lancastrian government and Lancastrian parliaments on Bishop Stubbs and Sir James Ramsay, neither of whom found any reason to attach much importance to these acts of parliament which have never since been studied in any detail. The purpose of this article is to re-examine them. Since Stubbs and Ramsay wrote there has been a steady publication of calendars of the chancery

[1] I wish to thank Mr. K. B. McFarlane for his helpful criticism of this article.

rolls and many detailed guides have been compiled to great
classes of record material in the Public Record Office.[1] This
new evidence, added to the obvious importance attached to these
acts by informed contemporary opinion,[2] justifies a re-assessment
of their political, financial and constitutional significance.

I

Charges of large-scale and wanton alienation of the royal
demesne to the king's favourites were repeatedly voiced during
the fourteenth century, especially in the political manifestos of
baronial opposition. Such charges were sometimes coupled
with the demand that the king should 'live of his own'.[3] During
the early years of Henry IV's reign such questions began to be
raised with unusual vigour and determination in parliament,
and, if we can believe the contemporary chronicle accounts, the
prime movers were the knights of the shire. For a number of
years after 1399, in spite of strong opposition from the king and
his council, these knights of the shire persisted in charges that
substantial royal endowments were being ignorantly or wantonly
squandered and ought to be recovered for the exchequer. A
determined body of critics endeavoured to make further grants
of parliamentary revenue conditional upon a drastic inquiry into
alleged alienations of royal land, upon energetic steps being taken
to recover it, and on new controls being imposed to regulate its
use in the future.

These early years of Henry IV's reign witnessed an unusual
situation which made the amplitude of the king's 'livelihood'
and the uses to which it was being devoted especially obvious
and open to criticism. When Henry Bolingbroke seized the
Crown in 1399 he most probably became the greatest royal landowner that England had seen since the days of the Conqueror and
his sons. As the heir of his father and mother he brought to the
support of the Crown the vast estates of the duchy of Lancaster

---

[1] Vol. iii of Stubbs's *Constitutional History of England* was first published in 1878
and Ramsay's *Lancaster and York* in 1892.

[2] The best known contemporary discussion of the problems here considered is
to be found in *The Governance of England*, ed. Charles Plummer, chapters v–xii and xiv,
attributed to Sir John Fortescue who was appointed chief justice of the king's
bench in 1442.

[3] The earliest instance of the use of this expression quoted by Stubbs, *op. cit.*
(4th edn.), ii. 543 is from the fourth ordinance of 1311. What did it mean ? The
1311 instance shows that the expression on that occasion included the customs as part
of the king's own.* Stubbs's second example of 1332, taken from the parliament
roll, describes an aid as granted to assist the king to live of his own. He quotes
'viver deinz les revenues de votre roialme' as an equivalent. Put in this way it
appears to mean that the king should live on what was lawfully his, *i.e.* within the
limits of his current income from all sources, and not incur debts : economy and
solvency. It does not signify that fourteenth century kings were supposed to live on
the income from their crown lands and feudal dues.

extending over most of the counties of England and Wales.[1] Through his wife he had a life interest by courtesy in half the huge possessions of his father-in-law Humphrey de Bohun, earl of Essex, Hereford and Northampton, which were to vest in his son on his death.[2]   As king he controlled six other great complexes of estates, each with their own treasuries: (1) the duchy of Cornwall with extensive lands in more than a dozen counties besides Cornwall and Devon; (2) the king's lands in North Wales; (3) his lands in South Wales; (4) the county and lordship of Pembroke with the lordships of Tenby, Cilgerran and Ystlwyf; (5) the counties and lordships of Chester and Flint; and (6) the lordship of Richmond in Yorkshire, which included many manors in Lincolnshire, Norfolk, Suffolk and Cambridgeshire besides the Yorkshire lands.[3] In addition there were the numerous other lands scattered throughout all the counties of England which were, in theory, farmed out from the exchequer.   The roll of the proffer for Michaelmas 1400, while professing to exclude certain lands which had been granted out for life or terms of years rent free, lists over 100 separate lordships, manors and towns, the Channel Islands and the Isle of Wight, as charged to farmers or keepers.[4]

---

[1] See *Cal. Close Rolls, 1360–1364*, pp. 201–11 for the lands of Lancaster which John of Gaunt inherited on the deaths of his father-in-law in 1361 and his sister-in-law in 1362.

[2] There is a full list of Humphrey de Bohun's lands as drawn up in two lots by Anne, countess of Stafford, for the final division between her and Henry V in 1421: *Rot. Parl.* iv. 136–8.   The earlier division had differed from this: *ibid.* iv. 138–40.

[3] The chamberlains of North Wales (at Caernarvon), South Wales (at Carmarthen) and Chester each had their treasuries, the duchy of Cornwall had its treasury at Lostwithiel, there was a treasury at Richmond for the lands of the earldom and a treasury at Pembroke, *Cal. Pat. Rolls, 1401–1405*, p. 121.   The royal lands in North Wales in 1399 were the counties and lordships of Caernarvon, Conway with the four commotes, and of Merioneth with the lordships of Criccieth and Harlech.   Thomas Percy, earl of Worcester, was holding the lordship of Nevin and Pwllheli for life, and Henry Percy, earl of Northumberland, the county and lordship of Anglesey for life: *Reports . . . touching the Dignity of a Peer.* v. 126–7.   The royal lands in South Wales in 1399 were the county and lordship of Carmarthen with the lordships of Lampeter and Cantref, and the county and lordship of Cardigan with the lordships of Builth and Montgomery.   Thomas Percy, earl of Worcester, held the lordships of Haverford and Newcastle in Emlyn for life.   The Principality of Chester, created in 1397, was dissolved by act of parliament (Stat. fig. 1 Hen. IV, c. 3).   These palatine counties of Chester and Flint included the castles of Chester, Beeston, Rhyddlan, Hope and Flint, and the manors of Shotwick and Frodsham.

Henry IV ignored Richard II's grant of the Richmond lands to John duke of Brittany's sister.

[4] P.R.O., Exchequer K.R., E. 159/177, mm. 1–4.   This figure does not include liberties, or cities and towns listed as paying feefarms.   At the end of the list of the proffer appears the following: ' Memorandum quod castra civitates burgi ville maneria et hundreda que sunt in manibus diversorum ad terminum vite vel annorum annotantur in memorando de anno septimo Regis Edwardi III^{eti} avi domini Regis nunc in profro de termino sancti michelis et in memorandis annorum precedencium tempore dicti Regis avi in profro.   Set non annotantur in isto profro nec de cetero debent scribi in profro quousque revertantur ad Regem eo quod prius nichil habetur exigi ad opus Regis set finito profro scribatur consimile memorandum in fine cuiuslibet profri.*

Contemporaries saw that Henry IV was a very great landowner indeed: much greater than his predecessor. At the same time they saw that he had few close relatives able to make legitimate demands upon the income from his lands. When he usurped the throne he had no queen and his sons were minors. Queen Joan, the widowed Duchess of Brittany, only arrived in England in 1404. Even by 1404, when Henry met perhaps the most critical of his parliaments at Coventry, only his eldest son Henry (then aged seventeen), heir to the throne and king's lieutenant in Ireland, had received substantial endowments. Little provision had been made for the new queen or for the king's younger sons Thomas, John and Humphrey.[1] Yet the king maintained that he had exhausted his financial resources and the Commons were being repeatedly asked to dig deep into their own pockets to support him.

At the Coventry parliament of 1404 a determined group of ' parliamentary knights ' put forward a reasoned plan to resume into the king's hands all the landed resources which he and his predecessors had ever held in absolute possession since 1366. Their purpose was to strengthen the Crown financially, to place a significant part of the issues from royal lands at the disposal of the exchequer in such a manner that they could be relied upon for a substantial and regular contribution to the royal income. The extent of the king's bounty was obvious to all. Let there be a full inquiry so that men with an honest sense of public duty might be satisfied. In this plan they roused strong opposition which came, according to the St. Albans chronicler, Thomas Walsingham, from the temporal lords in parliament (*i.e.* the most powerful interests close to the king), and from the bishops. The bishops' hostile attitude to these plans for reform, and indeed the chronicler's own, was determined when these same parliamentary knights also directed their attention to the lavish temporal endowments of the church. Would-be despoilers of church property were the enemies of bishops and of monastic chroniclers. Moreover, according to Walsingham, some parliamentary knights were tainted with lollardy.[2] We are indebted to him for his account of the activities of these parliamentary knights but it is not surprising that no defence of their policy can be found in that quarter.

The practice of not listing these Crown lands while granted for life or term of years, rent free, began in 1334 when the dowers of Queens Isabella and Philippa, the lands of John of Eltham and grants to Margaret countess of Kent, absorbed a major part of the whole.

[1] Henry's sons were born in 1387, 1388, 1389, and 1391 respectively.

[2] ' Annales Ricardi et Henrici IV ' in *Johannis de Trokelowe et Henrici de Blaneforde Chronica et Annales* (Rolls Series), ed. H. T. Riley, pp. 392-4; *Historia Anglicana* (Rolls Series), ed H. T. Riley, ii. 266-7; *Ypodigma Neustriae* (Rolls Series), ed. H. T. Riley, pp. 410-11. Professor V. H. Galbraith in his introduction to *The St. Albans Chronicle 1406-1422* proves conclusively that Thomas Walsingham, the most important of contemporary chroniclers, was the author of all these three accounts.

There is, however, an alliterative poem (dated 1403–6) composed by an anonymous author who expounded in popular form the policies which were being advocated with such vigour by the Commons in these parliaments. The author was no great believer in the powers of parliamentary knights, for he saw that the grievances which they took to parliament they most often brought back unredressed. Nevertheless, he regarded their views with respect: what they said was not to be classed with the ill-informed and irresponsible criticism of government he heard all around him, and they had a right and duty to make their views known.[1] His own statements of the need for strengthening the endowed revenues of the Crown merit quotation:

> For nedis moste oure leige lord like his estat
> Haue for his houshold and for his haynous werres
> To maynteyne his manhoode there may no man seye other,
> But of his owen were the beste, who-so couthe hit bringge;
>
> (lines 1664–7)

and again:

> Thenne of fyne fors hit foloweth as me thenketh,
> That a certayne substance shuld be ordeynid
> To susteyne this souurayn that shuld us gouerne.
>
> (lines 1636–8)

He had no doubt about the causes of the king's political weakness and financial straits which at this time, and especially in the Coventry Parliament of 1404, provided an unusually favourable opportunity to air plans for reform:

> There is a librarie of lordes that losen ofte thaym-self
> Thorough lickyng of the lordship that to the coroune longeth,
> And weneth hit be wel y-do but wors dide thay neuer
> Thenne sith thay gunne that game. . . .
>
> (lines 1626–9)

The king's advisers, knights of the council, temporal lords and bishops had 'pulled the pears off the royal tree' and 'were licking even the leaves'. Half the king's livelihood and more was in their hands (lines 1648–53).

Periods of determined personal rule by strong kings were the golden ages of medieval government. Just as in the later troubles of 1450 men would look back to the reign of Henry V, so now in

---

[1] *Mum and the Sothesegger*, ed. M. Day and R. Steele (Early English Text Society, 1936), pp. 27–78. After a round condemnation of irresponsible criticism he continues:

> ' I carpe not of knightz that cometh for the shires,
> That the king clepith (*i.e.* calleth) to cunseil with other;
> But hit longeth to no laborier the lawe is agayne thaym.'
>
> (lines 1460–2)

Professor Helen Cam accepts the date 1403–6 deduced by the editors for the composition of this poem, *Liberties and Communities in Medieval England*, p. 225.

these early years of the century the personal rule of Edward III in his prime had become a legend. Government was weak where once it had been strong. Therefore, contemporaries thought, the evident causes of current weaknesses could not have applied in that earlier period. Edward III must have been better endowed before the policies of the last forty years, 'these fourty wintre', began. So argued the author of the poem, and the sponsors of the petition for resumption did likewise. They proposed a resumption into the king's hands of all castles, manors, lordships, lands, tenements, fees and advowsons, fee farms, annuities, franchises, liberties and customs which had been 'membre et parcelle d'auncien Enheritance de la dite Corone' in the fortieth year of Edward III or since.[1] They believed that if there had been wanton misuse of the king's lands it had occurred since then. This period from 1366 to 1404 was sufficiently long to ensure that the vast majority of Crown manors on lease or grant for term of years or life would have fallen in at least once within that time and so would be brought under the scrutiny of the act. The net was stretched to include all lands leased or granted for a term of years, for life, in fee simple, fee tail or conditional fee. Emphasis was thus not merely on grants in fee, *i.e.* alienations, but also on the leases and grants for life and term of years which were the normal means by which the king bestowed his favour and obtained some income from his lands. The information required to set an inquiry in motion could easily be found by a search of the records, a common enough practice in the exchequer of the later Middle Ages whenever any kind of statistical information was needed.

The basic purpose of the petition was thus to place the landed resources of the crown at the disposal of the exchequer so that they could be let out to farm again at their true value. The revenues so obtained were to have as first charges upon them the expenses of the household, chamber and wardrobe and due provision for the queen's dower. Only after these charges had been met was the residue to be made available to compensate the dispossessed at the king's discretion. In other words the occupation of lands and the enjoyment of its profits were not in future to be given in lieu of fees and wages but were to be at the disposal of the exchequer for the current expenses of Government.[2]

[1] *Rot. Parl.* iii. 54–78: 'L'an du regne le Roy E, aiel nostre Seigneur le Roy q'or est XL et puis en cea', which is repeated as 'Douns ou Grantz que feurent parcelle del dite Corone le dit an XL ou depuis'. The king's answer, in English, took the Commons' request to mean 'al that longed unto the Coroune the fourty yere of Kyng Edward, and sithe hath be departed': *ibid.* p. 549.

[2] Forfeiture of the lands, &c., concerned and three years imprisonment were to be the penalties for retaining anything covered by the operation of the act without authority of parliament. In future any royal officer who executed any gift or grant from these recovered royal possessions was to be liable to loss of office, complete forfeiture and also a sentence of three years imprisonment.

This petition was no isolated incident in one unusual parliament but the culmination of a campaign of criticism in successive parliaments which Henry and his ministers were finding increasingly hard to control.[1] By the autumn of 1404 the king's room for manœuvre was most severely restricted. The expenses of consolidating his usurped authority had made a prompt and substantial parliamentary grant essential. Early in the year he had met a parliament which had granted him little immediate supply and that under the most stringent conditions: a novel land tax of which only £12,000 was at the king's free disposal, the rest to be spent under control of four treasurers of war appointed in parliament and answerable to parliament.[2] This assembly had also launched a most outspoken attack on his lavish grants of lands and annuities and on the cost of his household.[3] He had been driven by its obstinacy to proclaim a priority assignment of £12,000 for his household expenses spread over a wide range of existing revenues,[4] and by the summer of 1404 his financial embarrassment was so acute that he had to suspend payment of annuities.[5] The support of men of substance for his house was at the best lukewarm: he had no alternative but to come to some terms with his persistent parliamentary critics.

In negotiating a bargain under such financial stress Henry IV showed considerable skill. He appeared to yield the main point by giving his assent to an act of resumption, while at the same time claiming that the act could not take effect immediately because the essential information needed to work it was lacking. Consequently he intended to appoint a commission of inquiry composed of certain lords spiritual and temporal, all the royal justices and sergeants-at-law and other persons he might wish to name to prepare a report on what the Crown lands had been in 40 Edward III and what had been granted away since then. Subject to this committee being given time to report he undertook to give effect to the whole petition with all possible haste as far as he might by the law of the land or by his prerogative or liberty.[6]

He followed up this guarded undertaking with the plea that it would be neither honest nor expedient for him to revoke or resume outright any letters patent under the great seal, because of the

---

[1] For attempts in Henry IV's previous parliaments to resume or limit royal grants see *ibid.* iii. 433, 458, 495. In 1400 his council warned him to keep some lordship in hand lest the wasteful nature of grants made should prejudice his chances of generous parliamentary aid: *Proc. and Ord. of the Privy Council*, ed H. Nicolas, i, 108.

[2] *Cal. Fine Rolls*, xii. 251–64. For evidence that the treasurers were effective see *Proc. and Ord.*,i. 220–2: warrants to them for payment dated 23 April 1404.

[3] *Rot. Parl.* iii. 523–4; *Eulogium Historiarum* (Rolls Series), ed. F. S. Haydon, iii. 399–400; ' Annales Ricardi et Henrici IV ', p. 379.

[4] *Rot. Parl.* iii. 528 (1 March 1404); *Cal. Close Rolls, 1402–1405*, p. 343.

[5] *Ibid.* pp. 377, 382 (cancelled under 5 July 1404 but finally issued under 28 August 1404).

[6] *Rot. Parl.* iii. 549.

clamour at home and repercussions abroad which would ensue. By this plea he apparently meant that a wholesale revocation of letters patent at the behest of parliament would further damage the prestige of his house in the eyes of foreign princes. But as an immediate stop-gap measure he agreed that all who held annuities, fees or wages for life or for a term of years of the grant of Richard II or himself should surrender one year's income from Easter 1404 to Easter 1405.[1] At the same time he granted separately that holders of royal castles, manors, lands and tenements, rents and possessions granted for life or term of years by Richard II or himself should likewise surrender a year's income.[2] It should be noted that these two levies of a year's income were not to extend back as far as 1366 but to the accession of Richard II and were only to apply to grants for life or term of years.

In addition, as a further earnest of his intention to carry out a resumption, proclamation was to be made throughout the kingdom requiring all holders of patents of grants for life or term of years made by any king since 40 Edward III to bring them in for scrutiny by the council before Candlemas 1405 to the end that the deserving might be confirmed but the undeserving reduced or quashed.[3]

By these far-reaching promises which, although very carefully hedged about with safeguards, were unprecedented, the Commons were at last induced to be very generous. A further grant of the new land tax was voted, this time in the form of 20s. tax on every £20 of income from land over 500 marks *per annum*, together with a lavish provision of two tenths and two fifteenths in the traditional form plus an extension of the customs for two further years.[4] The royal promises had brought a handsome dividend: how far would they be kept?

Instructions to levy one year's income from Crown grantees were sent out to the shires on 21 January 1405.[5] But the king was in no position to offend any wavering supporters. The returns made by sheriffs and escheators show that he exempted whom he pleased by writs *non obstante*.[6] Many other annuitants had already obtained their payments for the current year before the sheriffs

---

[1] *Ibid.* Only the fees, wages and rewards of the chancellor, treasurer, keeper of the privy seal, justices of both benches, barons of the exchequer, sergeants-at-law and the other royal law officers were exempted.

[2] Exemptions from this second levy were made for all casual revenues (*i.e.* escheats, advowsons, wardships and marriages), for the queen and the king's sons, for confirmations or grants of annuities in parliament, and for castles assigned to meet the defence of the Scottish and Welsh marches and the coasts.

[3] *Rot. Parl.* iii. 549.

[4] *Ibid.* iii. 546–7; the previous parliament had insisted that all record of its land tax be destroyed to avoid creating a precedent. The Coventry parliament now allowed their grant of it to be enrolled.

[5] *Cal. Fine Rolls*, xii. 288 (instructions to sheriffs and escheators throughout England).

[6] See for example P.R.O., Exch. K.R. Sheriffs' Accts., E. 199/8/49 (Devon); E. 199/23/15 (Lincolnshire), E. 199/42/41 (Surrey and Sussex).

and escheators received instruction to make the levy and the enrolled accounts show that the immediate yield, subject to these diminutions, could have been at the most a little over £600 and was probably less than this.[1] The sheriffs were also duly commanded to order the surrender for inspection of copies of all patents of life grants and grants for terms of years received from Edward III, Richard II or Henry IV.[2] This should have provided sufficient material for the committee of inquiry to begin work. But there is no record that it ever met. A committee of inquiry was a traditional medieval device and Henry appears to have fobbed off the Commons nicely with it—until his needs again compelled him to meet another parliament.

This assembly, which met in 1406,* found the king's financial difficulties just as pressing as in 1404. They proved as determined as their predecessors and seized the opportunity presented by the king's financial demands to substitute a full scheme of constitutional reform in place of the act of resumption passed in 1404 but apparently never carried into effect. The Commons now realized that the king could not be trusted. It was also evident by now that he was a sick man. They therefore put their trust in a council which, they hoped, could be called to account in the next parliament. On this council they proposed to base a most comprehensive scheme of reform. In the first session, before the adjournment, Henry made certain concessions which gave extra power to his council. For the moment he surrendered his right to give orders direct to chancery and exchequer by promising to submit his warrants for endorsement by the council. He reserved only the pardoning of criminals and the appointment to offices and benefices actually vacant.[3]

Six days before the adjournment, which took place on 19 June, this strengthened council was charged to discover by all the means it could before the following Michaelmas the true values of all royal manors, lordships, lands and tenements let out for life, for terms of years or for the duration of war (*i.e.* also embracing alien priory lands), either at a fixed annual rent or at nothing at all. These lands were to be relet by the council with the authority of parliament after Michaelmas 1406 at true value. The previous farmers were to have first chance of paying it. If they would not, the lands were to be taken from them after reasonable warning and compensation.[4]

---

[1] P.R.O., Exch. L.T.R., Enrolled Accts., Misc., E. 358/12.

[2] *Cal. Close Rolls, 1402–1405*, p. 478: before Candlemas 1405 on pain of forfeiture.

[3] *Rot. Parl.* iii. 572 (*b*), and see Mr. K. B. McFarlane's account of this document in the *Camb. Med. Hist.* viii. 372. For a different but, I consider, unconvincing interpretation of it, which describes the king acting here as ' the inheritor of the Lancastrian tradition', see C. G. Crump, 'A Note on the Criticism of Records', *Bull. John Rylands Library*, viii (1924), 146 *et seq.*

[4] *Rot. Parl.* iii. 578–9. This measure also stated that annuities already charged on

There are no signs that this heavy task imposed on the council was completed by them in the three and a half months allotted. Parliament reassembled on 15 October and at the final meeting on 22 December thirty-one further articles for execution by the council were ultimately accepted by the king.[1] These included additional measures to strengthen the power of the council as the chief organ of government and to make it an effective instrument in the policy of retrenchment.

For the future the treasurer of England, acting by advice of the council, was to have full freedom to let to farm or to sell all lands, wardships, forfeitures, &c., in the manner appropriate to his office. From 17 December 1406 (presumably the date on which these thirty-one articles had received their final drafting and presentation) until parliament met again, no grant whatsoever, which gave away any source of profit to the crown was to be made, under penalty of its loss and a fine of double the value, to be paid towards the expenses of the Calais garrison. There were to be two days each week, Wednesday and Friday, set aside by the king for receiving petitions and all or at least some of the council were to be present to receive and despatch them. Severe penalties were to be imposed on any member of the household or others who presented petitions to the king at any other time. This was of course to ensure conciliar control of grants.

Further drastic proposals were submitted but not entered on the roll and seem to have been merely discussed in council.[2] As the parliament drew to a close it became obvious that it was no easier to bind the council than the king. Nevertheless the Commons remained adamant in refusing supply. In the end the king's direct intervention secured the taking of oaths by the councillors which were enrolled, but even this concession was not sufficient and the suspicious Commons now made an unprecedented and revolutionary demand: a personal guarantee from certain lords still present in the parliament that they would be individually responsible for refunding any money mis-spent. Only the king's angry threats of violence, the refusal to co-operate of the lords and the compelling desire of members to get home for Christmas at last produced a most reluctant grant after darkness on 22 December.[3]

these lands, and grants of grace and favour already made rent free, would not be disturbed. Some care was thus taken in 1406 not to outrage existing interests but to concentrate on reform for the future.

[1] *Ibid.* iii. 585–9.

[2] *Proc. and Ord.* i. 283–7 .These included the cessation of all grants for two years during which the secret and privy seals should not be valid instruments for making grants. Also an appropriation of £10,000 from the ancient revenues of the Crown to make ready money payments for prises taken for the household, chamber and wardrobe; *cf.* the parliamentary appropriations of 1404 above p. 589, and of 1439–40 and later described below.

[3] *The St. Albans Chronicle 1406–1420*, ed. V. H. Galbraith, pp. 2–3.

This new stand taken by the parliamentary knights had indeed been most remarkable. A most unusual combination of circumstances had made it possible. The king was physically ill, his prestige was low and his financial embarrassment, though temporary, was acute. No medieval king worthy of the name could surrender his power of making grants indefinitely or endure effective conciliar government and parliamentary audits imposed upon him. Henry IV took good care that the royal demesne was not allowed to appear as the main point of contention in politics again for the rest of his reign. Aided by his able sons he succeeded in crushing his rebels and winning over the English aristocracy and gentry to the support of his house. His successors turned their turbulent energies to the heady field of foreign conquests and plunder. But when years of increasingly unsuccessful foreign war and another king's impuissance had reduced the prestige of government to its lowest level since the early years of the century, the political conditions of 1399–1406 began to operate again and, what is more, at a similar point in the history of the royal demesne, when the king had a great number of estates under his nominal control and a dearth of adult members of his family able to absorb a major portion of them. The deaths of Queens Joan of Navarre and Catherine of Valois and of the three royal uncles Clarence (ob. 1421), Bedford (ob. 1435), and Gloucester (ob. 1447), were to leave the sickly Henry VI without near relatives except for two half brothers who were minors and his own young and alien queen. In these circumstances and following a period when the king's landed resources were far more wantonly squandered than ever they had been under Henry IV,[1] the policy of a resumption and reorganization of the royal demesne, advocated with such vigour in the early parliaments of Henry IV's reign, was once more to become the central issue of politics and finance.

II

How well informed were the Lancastrian assemblies about the state of the king's finances? We know that some of Henry VI's parliaments were certainly provided with statistical information in the form of a speech by the treasurer in the opening stages of parliament in which he ' declared the state of the realm '. It must not be supposed that these declarations were budget statements in the modern sense, but equally it would be rash to consider

[1] Between his coming of age in 1437 and 1449 Henry VI was moved to alienate his lands outside the circle of princes of the royal blood to an extent probably unprecedented in English history. In addition, almost the whole income from his remaining lands was placed firmly in the grasp of members of his household. For details see my Oxford D.Phil. thesis, ' The Crown Lands and the Parliamentary Acts of Resumption 1399–1495 ' in the Bodleian Library.

them merely as a few figures hastily concocted with an eye to
obtaining large parliamentary grants, to impress the supposedly
foolish and gullible commons with the king's extreme poverty,
and with the immense, unavoidable financial burden of government.

Kings emphatically did not render account, as Henry IV had at
first angrily replied when the commons asked for an audit of grants
earmarked for his wars.   Nevertheless, the Lancastrians did not
suffer from lack of knowledge of their resources or from any
inability to estimate charges upon them.   There is evidence to
suggest that at least from 1401 exchequer officials were regularly
required to produce a ' state of the realm ', a reasonably accurate
assessment of the year's revenue and expenditure which was laid
before the king and his council.[1]

An apparently new step was taken in 1433 during the minority
of Henry VI, when Ralph lord Cromwell, an able and acquisitive
member of the lesser nobility, was called upon to shoulder the
invidious responsibility of managing the national finances at a
time of maximum expenditure and heavy war debts.   Cromwell
knew the personal dangers which his office might involve, and
that his fellow councillors would use him as a scapegoat without
compunction if the need arose.   There was no adult king to bear
the ultimate responsibility.   He had considerable standing as a
respected protégé of the duke of Bedford and when he took office
he was able to have a full detailed account of the national finances not
only presented to parliament, but also enrolled on the parliament
roll,[2] to demonstrate for all time the serious state of the Treasury
when he assumed responsibility for it.

This practice of declaring the whole matter in parliament,
begun by Cromwell, was continued by his successors even after
the king came of age.   The Issue Rolls of the Exchequer of Receipt
demonstrate how these statements were compiled for the parliaments
of 1435, 1447, 1449 (two in this year), 1453 and 1455.   They also
show that these declarations involved the attendance of exchequer
officials at parliaments, to convey the record to the treasurer there,

---

[1] There survive three reasonably complete statements of revenue and expenditure,
three incomplete statements, and mentions of one other between 1401 and 1429,
Proc. and Ord. i. 154, 342; ii. 7–13, 96–7, 172–80, 312–15; iii. 322.   In addition there is a
statement among the causes for summoning a council in 1437 that the king's progenitors
were accustomed at the beginning of the year to ' purvey by the assent of his great
council for all necessaries and charges . . . likely to fall and ensue all the year after '
(*ibid.* v. 65).   There was a close parallel in France from the mid-fifteenth century
onwards where an annual budget proposal called ' état par estimation ' was presented
to the king and his council; G. Dupont-Ferrier, *Études sur les institutions financières
de la France à la fin du moyen âge*, ii. 192–7.

[2] *Rot. Parl.* iv. 433–8, and the protestation of the Treasurer which follows, 438–9.
For an attempt to assess the financial accuracy of Lord Cromwell's statement see
J. L. Kirby, ' The Issues of the Lancastrian Exchequer and Lord Cromwell's Estimates
of 1433 ', *Bulletin of the Institute of Historical Research*, xxiv (1951), 121–51.

to expound it, and to answer questions which the king's ministers and lords of the council would doubtless wish to raise.[1]

The realization that this expert information and the officials who had produced it were available for reference in parliaments is most important in understanding parliamentary proposals for reducing household expenses, parliamentary appropriations made upon the king's land revenues and parliamentary petitions for resumption. There is an allusion to the frequent practice of presenting such statements, and to the serious financial situation revealed by them, in the Household Ordinance of 1454.[2] The parliamentary petition for a resumption of Crown lands in 1450 begins with a quotation of figures which might very well have come from such a statement.[3] Another set of figures, probably from the same source, was used in the accusations made against Suffolk in 1450.[4] Not only round figures quoted in petitions and in the charges against the king's chief minister, but also the detailed figures which were amassed for parliamentary appropriations most probably originated in the reports drawn up for these declarations of the state of the realm.

Such financial information, when presented to parliament, certainly did not induce the Commons to provide larger grants and probably made them more and more critical of the management of the king's resources. None of Henry VI's parliaments between 1433 and 1450 refused all supply but the growing financial demands of an unsuccessful war made these assemblies increasingly aware of bargaining powers forgotten or waived in the distraction of foreign conquest and the flush of victory. The parliament of 1433 in which Cromwell presented his comprehensive financial review was the first to insist on a special allowance of £4,000 being made from each complete tenth and fifteenth granted, in order to alleviate the burden on certain impoverished towns.[5] Before their adjournment

---

[1] P.R.O., Exchequer, Treasury of Receipt, Issue Rolls, E. 403/721, Mich. 14 Hen. VI; 765, Mich. 25 Hen. VI; 773, Mich. 27 Hen. VI; 775, Easter 27 Hen. VI; 777, Mich. 28 Hen. VI; 779, Easter 28 Hen. VI; 798, Easter 32 Hen. VI; 801, Easter 33 Hen. VI. For example, on 17 February 1447 various exchequer clerks were paid through Thomas Brown, under-treasurer, for attendance at Bury St. Edmunds in 1447 for work in connection with the declaration of the state of the king and kingdom compiled for presentation at the Bury parliament. On 21 July 1449 Brown himself was specially rewarded for his services at the Winchester session of parliament in 1449. Hugh Fenne, an exchequer auditor, was rewarded on 9 March 1450 for his work in compiling a declaration of the state of the realm for presentation in parliament and on 19 May 1450 received his expenses for attending the parliament at Leicester on the treasurer's instructions for the declaration of certain matters for the king's profit to the king, lords spiritual and temporal and the Commons in parliament. I wish to thank Professor J. S. Roskell for help in collecting these references.

[2] *Proc. and Ord.* vi. 221.   [3] *Rot. Parl.* v. 183.

[4] *Archaeologia*, xxix. 325; C. L. Kingsford, *English Historical Literature in the Fifteenth Century*, p. 360.

[5] *Rot. Parl.* iv. 425–6: or on towns which the Commons considered were 'over greatly charged' to the tax.

(13 August) this parliament was told that there would be no more money available for current household expenses until they reassembled on 13 October. They therefore instructed the treasurer to place a ceiling of £2,000 on the total of all payments of assignments allocated up to 20 July 1433. Only payments due to those who had lent the king money were to be exempt and, of course, payments to the household itself.[1] In the parliament of 1439-40 much more significant restraints on the free disposal of revenues were conceded: an appropriation of the issues of the duchies of Cornwall and of that part of the duchy of Lancaster not in the hands of Henry V's feoffees to current household expenses for five years;[2] one quarter of a tenth and fifteenth specifically appropriated for ready money payment of household expenses;[3] and those portions of the duchy of Lancaster revenues still in the hands of the feoffees also appropriated, under certain conditions, to pay the king's debts and to lessen the grievances of household purveyance.[4] In 1442 attempts were made in the Commons to extend this appropriation of the revenues of the two great duchies to current household expenses for a further three years and to add a further annual appropriation of 5,000 marks on the customs but the petition was answered evasively.[5]

Parliamentary action was thus once again concentrated on ensuring that the unavoidable expenses of the royal household should be guaranteed from permanent, reliable sources of income. The method, as in the reign of Henry IV, was to strengthen the exchequer by means of parliamentary directives: by ear-marked grants, by specific appropriations and, in the ultimate resort, by acts of resumption designed to free the Crown's deeply pledged resources.

The reluctance of subsequent parliaments to grant unconditional supply was even more marked. The parliament of 1445-6 at first granted only half a tenth and fifteenth.[6] Later, when a further one and a half tenths and fifteenths were granted, the rate of allowance for impoverished towns was raised to £6,000 for each complete tenth and fifteenth (i.e. £9,000 for that grant).[7] Further measures of appropriation for household expenses, this time on the issues of wardships, marriages and vacant temporalities were made in the parliament which first met on 12 February 1449. Moreover, this assembly not only restricted its grant to a mere

---

[1] Ibid. iv. 420–1.

[2] Ibid. v. 7. As a result of these measures the controller of the household acknowledged receipt of £7,192 18s. 10d. in 1441–2 and £8,481 12s. 8¾d. in 1443–4 from the receivers-general of the two duchies: P.R.O., Exch. K.R. Various Accts., E. 101/409/9, 11.   [3] Rot. Parl. v. 32.

[4] Ibid. v. 8–9. Cf. the parliamentary appropriations of 1404 and the proposals of 1406 above, pp. 67, 70   [5] Rot. Parl. v. 62–3.

[6] Ibid. v. 68–9.   [7] Ibid. v. 69.

half tenth and fifteenth (less £3,000) but was emboldened to demand a large-scale resumption as the price for any further grant. Its persistent agitation for an act of resumption finally led to the dissolution of this parliament at Winchester on 16 July 1449.[1]

Less than four months passed before another parliament had to be called and in temper this assembly was even more determined than its predecessor. At Leicester in the spring of 1450 it impeached the king's chief minister Suffolk, not only for the failure of his foreign policy, but also for his 'insatiable covetise' which, it was claimed, had contributed substantially towards the impoverishment of the king.[2] For the same reason great hostility was shown towards Suffolk's colleagues and all the household men. A new type of household appropriation was drawn up at the instance of the Commons which it was hoped would be much more difficult to set aside in favour of other charges. This measure detailed individual items to be derived from specific farms and feefarms throughout England and Wales, from the ulnage, from the customs and subsidies at the ports and from various other sources totalling £11,002 6s. 1d. *per annum,* all to go entirely to the current expense of the king's household, the arrangement to endure for seven years.[3] A long petition for a resumption followed.[4]

This demand for an act of resumption had aroused great interest and widespread support in the country at large. A resumption promised some relief from direct taxation which had been heavy for a long time [5] with little to show for it in the way of military success, prestige, effective government at home or stable conditions

[1] There is no mention of this petition on the roll of the parliament but the account of this first parliament of 1449, found in Robert Bale's Chronicle (*Six Town Chronicles,* ed. R. Flenley, Oxford 1911, p. 125), stresses the insistence of this parliament on a resumption, and states categorically that this insistence caused its dissolution. This chronicle, according to Flenley and C. L. Kingsford, is a noteworthy contemporary account for the years 1449–51 and most precise in its chronology. Robert Bale was probably a citizen of London, a lawyer, and a judge. (See C. L. Kingsford, *op. cit.* pp. 95–9.)

[2] *Hist. MSS. Comm. 3rd Report,* Appendix, p. 280, a copy of a further list of charges which C. L. Kingsford overlooked in his defence of Suffolk (see his *Prejudice and Promise in Fifteenth Century England,* chapter vi). Cf. *Rot. Parl.* v. 179 (articles 29–31).

[3] P.R.O., Exch. K.R. Mem. Rolls, E. 159/227 (29 Hen. vi), Communia, Mich. m. 17. I owe this reference to Professor E. F. Jacob. The version printed in *Rot. Parl.* v. 174–6 is accurate as far as it goes but is incomplete, details of more than £5,000 of the assignment being omitted. This measure also included a direction to the receiver-general of the duchy of Lancaster to pay his surplus revenues over and above the queen's endowment to the treasurer of the household for seven years.

[4] *Ibid.* v. 183–5.

[5] The average had been a complete tenth and fifteenth every two years since 1429. This aspect of the resumption was seized upon in John Hardyng's rhyming chronicle (ed. H. Ellis, p. 401). As a result of it he says: 'taxe ceased and dymes eke also, In all Englande then raysed were no mo.' He himself lost an annuity of £10 by the resumption. This 1450 parliament refused to make any grant in the traditional form. Instead it granted a graduated property tax on the 1404 model, appropriated to defence, to be paid to four specially appointed treasurers and not to be treated as a precedent (*Rot. Parl.* v. 172–4).

for trade abroad. Coupled with the appropriations for the household it offered some prospect of relief from the abuses of purveyance which had been the subject of vociferous complaints in successive parliaments. It is noteworthy that the Kentish rebels who had risen in arms while this parliament was still sitting at Leicester complained that the king's ministers were preventing the acceptance of the resumption and professed to be acting in support of parliament's demands.[1] Contemporary political lampoons show how bitter was the resentment against holders of Crown lands and the profits from them.[2]

The self-confidence of the king's ministers was profoundly shaken by the impeachment of Suffolk. His colleagues made no attempt to stand by him [3] and when Suffolk was removed from the political scene Cromwell, Say, Beauchamp, Sudeley and the rest decided to try a limited policy of concession to their critics. Consequently they advised acceptance of the resumption petition to quieten the persistent importunity in parliament,[4] confident that they could best defend the interest of those most threatened by allowing and supervising a resumption ' in summe, but nat in alle '. These were the words of John Crane sending the news of its acceptance from the parliament at Leicester on 6 May 1450. He also mentioned the spate of private bills being submitted, many of them, no doubt, for exemption from the act, and told his master to hurry if he had any of his own to put forward.[5]

The petition for a resumption of all grants made since the first day of the reign (1 September 1422), together with fifteen modifying and largely uncontroversial clauses, was finally turned into an act of parliament simply by appending a brief royal assent to it.[6] The king qualified this assent by reserving the right to

---

[1] *Three Fifteenth Century Chronicles*, ed. Gairdner (Camden Soc., N.S.) xxviii. 95; *Six Town Chronicles*, p. 130.

[2] *Political Songs* (Rolls Series), ed. T. Wright, ii. 229.

[3] According to 'William Worcester' the Commons were actually instigated to attack Suffolk by the secret work of Lord Cromwell among them : *Wars of the English in France, Henry VI* (Rolls Series) ed. J. Stevenson, II. ii. 766.

[4] ' And the commons of the parliament (i.e. which first met on 6 November 1449) laboured evermore that the king should admit and receive to have his resumption ', *Six Town Chronicles*, p. 126.

[5] *Paston Letters* (1904 library edn.), ii. 148 (no. 121).

[6] Petition and royal assent: *Rot. Parl.* v. 183–6 with modifying clauses printed as follows: (i) The queen. (ii) Eton and King's Colleges. (iii) The provisions of the king's will. (iv) Alien priory lands granted to churches, monasteries, colleges, hospitals, chantries. (v) Grants given specifically to maintain a dignity (*e.g.* viscount) on an accepted scale. (vi) Purchases made by Cardinal Beaufort for St. Cross, Winchester. Interest in any possessions owned by any person before 1 September 1422 though that person only obtained possession of it after that date. Letters patent for restitution of lawful inheritance. Discharge of towns, &c., for over-payment of farm. (vii) Grants made by Henry VI to replace grants made by his predecessors and lost through no fault of the grantee. (viii) Exchanges of land made with the king if a fair exchange. (ix) All lands which yielded their full value to the king as at the

add any provisos of exemptions he considered necessary, on the understanding that they were put in writing during the remaining life of the parliament. We know that the act had only recently been passed on 6 May 1450 and parliament was dissolved about 8 June.[1] Added to the roll were 186 provisos of exemption.[2] From dates upon the original petitions for exemption it appears that the time limit set for admitting exemptions was no mere formality. Almost all those enrolled were reviewed by the lords spiritual and temporal during the remaining life of the parliament at Leicester. The petitioners knew that even if the king accepted late petitions after the dissolution of parliament their legal validity might be doubtful. Hence perhaps the somewhat elaborate subscriptions put on two petitions for household men not presented in time, designed to prevent their validity being questioned.[3] No other petitions bear subscriptions of this kind and the latest date found on others is 6 June.

When one considers that the act would render doubtful the legal validity of most of the royal grants entered on the Patent, Charter, and Fine Rolls between 1422 and 1450 a total number of 186 exemptions is not surprisingly large in itself.[4] Many of the exemptions had little if any connection with the alienation of Crown lands and revenues. There were matters like the restitution of bishops' temporalities, letters patent of naturalization, and debts and obligations of state.[5] A number of provisos are accounted for by the royal approval given by patent under the great seal to family arrangements from which the king could only have profited

time of the grant. (x) Lands for which the king was a trustee. (xi) Wages at the scale operating under Henry V for the chancellor, treasurer, keeper of privy seal, barons of exchequer and other officers. (xii) Letters patent to children born overseas to English fathers of foreign mothers granting rights of inheritance. (xiii) All grants to All Souls College, Oxford. (xiv) Grants to towns of freedom from the jurisdiction of the admiral of England or the wardens of the Scottish Marches. (xv) Grants of murage to towns. The act was to take effect from 6 November 1449, the day on which the parliament had been assembled.

[1] *History of Parliament, 1439–1509, Register*, p. 115.

[2] *Rot. Parl.* v. 186–99.

[3] Thomas Parker's, dated 8 August, was subscribed: ' per dominum cardinalem de mandato Regis infra parliamentum signeto facto ' and bears the sign manual. The petition from Thomas Pope, whose proviso follows Parker's on the roll (*Rot. Parl.* v. 198 (*b*)), and so was probably of the same date or later, was marked ' per signetum factum in parliamento per testimonium J. Stanley et B. Hawley et aliorum'*: P.R.O., Chancery, Parliament and Council, C. 49/62/51 and 52.

[4] Students of the Lancastrian period, in the absence of contrary evidence, have assumed that the high number of 186 exemption clauses was sufficient to make the act ineffective. This should be contrasted with the claim of Professor J. D. Mackie that Henry VII in 1485 ' found means to enrich the Crown by an enormous act of resumption ', *The Earlier Tudors* (Oxford, 1952), p. 63. The act of 1485 contains 461 clauses of exemption.

[5] *E.g.* Debts to Leonard lord Welles as Lieutenant of Ireland, to John earl of Shrewsbury as Steward of Ireland and to Humphrey duke of Buckingham as Captain of Calais.

by outraging accepted conventions.[1] Confirmations of bene-
factions touching the king's interest, made to the church by the
king's family or others of his subjects, accounted for a number of
exemptions. In many cases these exemptions concerned reversions
of alien priory manors which contemporary opinion felt should
not remain permanently in lay hands. Some exemptions were for
charters granted to towns which involved civic authority and
dignity or arose out of mere economic necessity due to flood,
inundations of the sea, tempests, &c.[2] A number of legitimate
rewards for valuable public services were exempted as these services
had been costly to the doers.

Read consecutively on the parliament roll all these exemptions
may give an impression of excessive largesse and benevolence on
the part of a medieval king to those who were set in authority
under him, but in fact they represented no more than his normal
duty. The crucial exemptions were personal ones for members
of the government and their supporters, that is, for the household
men. These exemptions actually appear at first sight to have been
less likely to make the act ineffective than the other exemptions
because they specifically state that the grantees were to surrender
certain of their grants. Nevertheless, what they gave up was only
a fraction of what they retained. Further consideration of their
exemptions reveals how they hoped to placate the interests
clamouring for resumption while actually consolidating their own
position about the king.

The original Commons' petition for a resumption had probably
been under discussion for about six months before it was accepted.
At some time before individual petitions for exemption began to be
submitted a conference or committee of household men appears
to have determined what each of their members should give up
and what he should retain. This is shown by a contemporary
document containing a list of 101 members of the household headed
by Beaumont, Say, Sudeley, Cromwell, Beauchamp, St. Amand,
Stourton, Hungerford, and Stanley, stating the amounts which
the king had granted them to keep and also those which he had been
moved to resume.[3] The form of the original petitions for exemptions submitted by some of the household men who appear in this
list show that before they submitted these petitions they had been

---

[1] *E.g.* To John viscount Beaumont, in possession of the lands of his wife's family
the Bardolfs; to John Holt of Aston, Warws., as the heir of his cousin Margery;
the settlement of the lands of the Beauchamp earls of Warwick; the jointure
of Jacquette, widow of the duke of Bedford and the interests of her husband
Lord Rivers; to William FitsAlan, earl of Arundel, in the recovery of his family
lands.

[2] There were twelve grants to towns among the exemptions.

[3] P.R.O., Exch. K.R., Miscellanea, E. 163, bundle 8, no. 14: 'Paper roll of
resumptions by the crown.'

told what they would be allowed to keep and what they must be resigned to losing.[1]

The household men thus gave up only what they had agreed among themselves and with the king to surrender. Some of their surrenders, totalling *c.* £700 *per annum* in value, can be seen enrolled in their provisos on the parliament-roll. But Cromwell, Say, Sudeley and the other chief ministers were given exemption in the widest possible terms on the roll and it is only from the paper list of 101 members of the household that we know that they had agreed to give up anything. A combination of amounts from these two sources shows that these household men who held most of the Crown lands and endowed revenues firmly in their grasp were prepared to make surrenders worth about £1,800 *per annum*. The amounts to be retained, as listed in the paper list, total rather less than £3,750, excluding reversions. These figures take no account of profits made from lands held at the rate of the extent, of wardships, *ad hoc* gifts of forfeitures, or innumerable special allowances and privileges which came the way of these men. Nevertheless, as a valuation of lands held rent free and of fees from offices at the ancient rate it may well be a reasonably accurate figure.

Apart from the surrenders, totalling about £1,800 for the whole household, this act of resumption could have had little immediate or ultimate effect on the state of the king's finances. Administrative action was dilatory and ineffective, though no doubt this was partly due to the disturbed state of the capital and countryside. No copy of the act was sent to the exchequer until 15 October 1450 though exemptions were reaching them by 13 August 1450.[2] The exchequer did not begin to send out writs to the sheriffs ordering local inquiries about holders of Crown lands until the spring of 1451.[3]

Nevertheless, in spite of its shortcomings the acceptance of this first act of resumption at Leicester in May 1450 had actually brought about a state of great uncertainty among holders of royal lands and offices. There were members of the household ready to profit from the expected misfortunes of their colleagues. Many of the land-hungry gentry and nobility were prepared to take a chance on the market. ' As for the Duche on this side Trent ', wrote Thomas Denyes to John Paston, on 13 May 1450, ' Sir Thomas Tudenham

---

[1] These are in the main to be found in P.R.O., Chancery, Parliament and Council (C. 49), but some are in Ancient Petitions (S.C. 8).

[2] P.R.O., Exch. K.R. Mem. Rolls, E. 159/227 (29 Hen. VI) Communia, Mich., m. 23; *ibid*. Brevia directa baronibus, Mich., m. 2.

[3] The enrolled accounts called Sheriffs Seizures give the date of the writs: *e.g.* 16 March 1451 (Beds. and Bucks.), 17 March 1451 (Cambs. and Hunts.), 27 March 1451 (Lincoln city), 21 June 1451 (Somerset), 3 December 1451 (Devon and Dover and Cinque Ports), 7 November 1451 (Norwich), 13 February 1452 (Cumb.): P.R.O. Exch. L.T.R., E. 379/175.

had a joynte patent with the Duke of Suffolk, which, if it be resumed, Sir Thomas Stanley hath a bille redy endossed therof '.[1] At an earlier date (16 April 1450) John Hampton, an esquire of the body, had already prudently surrendered a life grant of Kempton manor in Middlesex and paid an increment to have it converted to a twenty-five years lease. His colleague Thomas Daniel lost a rent-free life grant of Geddington (Northants) and Lord Rivers took out a ten years lease of it at £28 *per annum* as early as 2 June. Stephen Cote, a valet of the chamber who held the manor of Westley (Suffolk) for life at a rent of 13s. 4d., found himself superseded on 3 June by two ushers of the chamber who were willing to pay £5 per annum for a twelve years lease. By 20 February 1451 he had recovered it by offering £5 13s. 4d. for a twelve years lease himself.

Suffolk's family were not allowed to retain any of the royal lands which he had been given whether granted for term of years, for life, or in fee. An esquire of the body, Philip Wentworth, was appointed receiver of the lordship of Cilgerran (18 May 1450), and Lord Beauchamp took out a twelve years lease of the county and lordship of Pembroke (31 May 1450). There was some competition for Suffolk's manor of Swaffham in Norfolk. His Oxfordshire lands [2] were taken over by Lord Sudeley from Michaelmas 1450.

The dukes of York and Somerset who were abroad were both affected by this act of resumption. York had an exemption for his lieutenancy of Ireland only, and Somerset only for the lands he held as heir of his uncle, Cardinal Beaufort.[3] It appears that the king's ministers acted without partiality for either in their own scramble for self-preservation and, no doubt, for the preservation of what they considered to be the king's vital prerogative right.

A new parliament was summoned to meet on 6 November 1450. Taking stock of the position at this date we find that the sheriffs

---

[1] *Paston Letters*, ii. 150 (no. 123). Denyes was referring to the stewardship of the duchy south of Trent.

[2] Woodstock, Handborough, Wootton, and Stonesfield.

[3] The manors of Bassingbourne and Babraham which Somerset held in tail male were leased to Thomas Cotton, a citizen and draper of London, for twenty years (7 June 1450). Three months later the duke of Exeter and three others took out a lease of them for ten years. On 20 June 1450 the manors known as Gurney lands in Somerset and Dorset, which Somerset also held in tail male, were leased to Exeter and four others for ten years. John Everdon took a lease of York's manor of Hadley (Essex) on 18 May, but on 7 September surrendered it and this too passed to Exeter. Lands and rents in Great Wratting (Suffolk), another of York's manors, were leased to Hugh Fenne, clerk of the exchequer (25 May 1450). The king ordered Lord Beauchamp to see to the rule of the Isle of Wight which York held, and Beauchamp was made steward there for life on 7 June 1450. The foreign accounts show that a receiver, Thomas Chamberlain, a valet of the chamber, was appointed with effect for 6 November 1449 on 27 June 1450, but that he only acknowledged responsibility for the issues from the Nativity of St. John the Baptist (24 June) 1450. Until that date York's officers continued to collect the rents. Full details of these resumptions and new leases, taken mainly from the Fine Rolls, are given in Appendix C (pp. 324–34) of my D.Phil. thesis cited above.

had as yet received no writs from the exchequer to order inquisitions pursuant to the act of resumption. The exchequer itself had only received a copy of the act some three weeks before. Nevertheless, there had been considerable activity in the transaction of new leases. A number of the king's subjects who had not been on the spot when the act was passed had good reason to feel aggrieved because the lands they held from the king had been given to others. Even York and Somerset appear to have been treated in this cavalier fashion. The men about the king had not only handled the rebellions of the summer with firmness and skill, but had also managed to preserve their hold over the king's patrimony in spite of almost nation-wide support for the efforts of the Commons in parliament to secure a drastic resumption. Although the king's chief minister, Suffolk, had been destroyed and the treasurer, Lord Say, murdered by the mob, the rest had closed their ranks and, at the price of comparatively small concessions, were actually turning the resumption to their own advantage.

III

Such a half-hearted resumption was sure to come under fire as soon as a new parliament met and political circumstances favoured the Government's parliamentary critics when this new assembly was summoned to Westminster for 6 November 1450. Late in August Richard, duke of York, the king's most powerful subject, had returned unbidden from Ireland, had forced his way into the king's presence with an armed escort, had openly censured the policies of the last few years and had demanded changes. When the first session of the new parliament was only a fortnight old he and his kinsmen Norfolk and Warwick brought strong forces to the capital. York was reported to desire ' meche thynge qwych is meche after the Comouns desyre ':[1] his chamberlain Sir William Oldhall was chosen speaker. Edmund Beaufort, duke of Somerset, the next male heir of John of Gaunt and Suffolk's close associate, had in the meantime become the king's foremost counsellor. But on 1 December York's influence prevailed at court and the duke of Somerset was placed in ' protective custody '. York had taken no part in the policies of the Suffolk régime at home or abroad. Now his successful intervention and his open stand against these policies emboldened the advocates of resumption to put forward another petition because, as they justly claimed, the act of the previous parliament had ' not been effectually had '.[2]

Though the attitude of York no doubt increased its chances of success, this new petition was essentially a continuation of the policy

---

[1] *Paston Letters*, ii. 174 (no. 142), dated 6 October 1450.
[2] *Rot. Parl.* v. 219 (*b*).

consistently advocated in so many previous meetings of the Commons. It was in fact the petition which had already been accepted at Leicester in the spring of 1450, now submitted all over again but subjected to a very careful revision in the meantime. While much of the wording was repeated exactly there were significant alterations. Whereas, for example, the original petition had made a generous exception for the king's new scholastic foundations at Eton and Cambridge this revised petition, while making some exemption for them, described their endowments as ' over chargefull and noyus '. A new request was made that all exchanges of land to which the king had been a party should be reversed. Most important of all, there was a clause in the new petition requesting the appointment of a committee to supervise all the king's future grants, consisting of the chancellor, the treasurer, the keeper of the privy seal and six lords of the council, who were to write their names on all letters patent authorized by them. Any person accepting letters patent not so subscribed would render himself liable to loss of title to all his freehold lands. All grants, &c., made by Henry since the first day of his reign (1 September 1422), were to be again annulled with effect from 6 November 1449, the operative date specified in the earlier act of 1450.

Judging from the bold temper of this petition it was presented during the first session of the parliament, when the king was temporarily overawed by York's presence and prestige and in fact appears to have submitted to some form of conciliar control.[1] The Commons' petition was framed in the spirit of that moment when the king's prestige was low.

The answer to this resumption petition most probably came some time later and was framed in different circumstances. Shortly after Christmas Henry felt strong enough to have Somerset released from the Tower. His intention was to establish a balance between his two most powerful subjects. Both York and Somerset were employed on commissions of oyer and terminer in the troubled area of the south east. Somerset was made Captain of Calais. Parliament, prorogued on 18 December, was summoned to reassemble on 20 January 1451. But the king left London on 28 January and made a royal progress in the south east. On 23 February he returned to London and ' rode right royally through the city '.[2] The petition for resumption now received a favourable but firm and considered answer. It was not accepted wholesale

---

[1] Thereby fulfilling a promise to York to appoint a ' sad and substantial Council, giving them more ample authority and power than ever we did before this ': the king's answer to York's bill of complaint, *Paston Letters*, i. 84. Evidence that for a time the king did submit to a measure of conciliar control is supplied by a royal writ to the exchequer dated 25 January 1451 cancelling an earlier restriction upon the validity of warrants not passed by advice of the council, *Proc. and Ord.* vi. 104.

[2] *Chronicles of London*, ed. C. L. Kingsford, p. 162.

like its predecessor with a brief royal assent.   This act of resumption consists of a detailed reply to the petition : those portions of the petition not specifically accepted were declared to be rejected, among them most notably the proposed supervising committee of the council to licence the king's grants.   Exchanges of land made by the king were to stand.   His scholastic foundations at Eton and Cambridge were to have full immunity.   The new act was to take effect not from 6 November 1449 but from Lady Day 1451.   The exemptions which the Commons had themselves made to their petition were accepted and the king reserved the right to add what further exemptions he pleased during the remaining life of the parliament.   Parliament was again prorogued on 29 March, re-assembled on 5 May and was dissolved some time between 24 and 31 May by which date the king had added forty-three provisos of exemption in all.[1]

Sir James Ramsay was quite mistaken in assuming that all the 186 provisos of exemption made to the previous act of resumption at Leicester in the spring of 1450 also automatically applied to this new act.[2]   In fact none of those 186 exemptions, least of all the personal ones which had largely rendered the earlier act ineffective, applied to the second act.   The forty-three provisos of exemption to the new act, with very few exceptions, were framed on general not personal lines.   The chancery and receipt rolls show beyond any possible doubt that the resumption, which had been begun half-heartedly at Leicester in the previous summer, was now made effective.

On 2 August 1451 writs were sent out under the great seal to sheriffs and escheators throughout England ordering inquisitions to be held under their joint supervision pursuant to this new act. All lands, tenements, annuities, privileges, franchises, and offices, granted by the king since the first day of his reign (1 September 1422), were to be taken into their hands with effect from 25 March 1451 and extents made.   Details of these extents were to be sent to the exchequer before the morrow of All Souls Day under penalty of £100.[3]   When these writs of great seal were sent out some of the sheriffs had still not received the writs under the exchequer seal ordering similar inquisitions to be held pursuant to the previous act.   The two acts were now operated concurrently.

Action at Westminster did not wait upon sheriffs' and escheators' returns.   The act of parliament destroyed the validity of grants and

---

[1] Petition, answer and provisos of exemption are printed in *Rot. Parl.* v. 217–25. The petition had provided for exemption for the queen, limited exemption for Eton and King's Colleges and Pembroke Hall, Cambridge, grants of alien priory lands in 'spiritual men's hands', leases made by treasurer's bill at truly competitive rates, salaries of officers of state, law officers, and civil servants, money due to the duke of Buckingham as Captain of Calais, and grants to corporate bodies of various kinds.

[2] *Op. cit.* ii. 139–40.   [3] *Cal. Fine Rolls*, xviii. 229–30.

leases the moment it was passed. Exemption from it could only be obtained while parliament was sitting. By 1 June 1451 the parliament had dispersed and only forty-three exemptions had been made. Consequently there was a spate of new leases of Crown lands taken out in June and July 1451. In the last three months of the year, when the sheriffs' and escheators' returns were being received at the exchequer, the number of these new leases suddenly rose again. At least eighty-five new leases were made in 1451. Then the rate fell sharply until stimulated again by a further resumption in 1455 which to some extent supplemented the earlier acts.

As a result of the acts of 1450 and 1451 there were at least seventeen cases of alienated estates and properties recovered and let out to farm for terms of years at the rate of the extent, several cases of alienated estates kept in hand after recovery, and at least forty cases where life grants were changed to leases for terms of years only. In addition, a number of life grants resumed were not granted or farmed out again, and in at least thirty-five cases leases for terms of years were shortened and/or the farms raised. All new leases were made subject to a condition imposed by the act of resumption of 1451, namely that the rate of the extent should be the basis, but that any man who would offer to pay more without fraud should have the lease in preference, unless the holder would himself match or surpass the competitive offer.[1]

Some resumed lands were for the time being retained in the hands of local officers. In the case of the duchy of Cornwall lands this could easily be done. There had long been competent local officers there and 'foreign' auditors to audit their accounts at least since the reign of Richard II. In other cases where farmers or grantees were displaced and the lands kept in hand, special officers and auditors had to be appointed.[2]

There appears to have been no political discrimination against would-be lessees of the resumed lands. In many cases the existing holders, including the household men, took them back on the new terms. A marked increase in the number of jointly-held leases and even syndicate leases, many to men who made no appearance on the political scene, suggests that financial considerations were allowed to be of primary importance.

The act of 1451 also annulled various liberties and privileges and also many annuities, not merely on land but on other sources of revenue including the customs at the ports. The very greatest

---

[1] New leases counted between the years 1450 and 1458 total: 1450, 16; 1451 and 2, 102; 1453 and 1454, 24; 1455 and 1456, 40; 1457 and 1458, 22. They range from whole lordships like Pembroke and substantial groups of a dozen manors or more like the Gurney lands to single tenements in London. For full details see Appendix C of my D.Phil. thesis, pp. 269–323.

[2] E.g. the king's lands in the counties of Cardigan and Carmarthen and the honour of Richmond lands in Lincolnshire, Norfolk, Suffolk, and Cambridgeshire.

suffered in this way, including both York and Somerset, as well as most of the household men. The patent rolls show that many of these annuities were quickly regranted and back-dated to 25 March 1451, but a more significant point is that many were not.[1]

Without the resumption the parliamentary appropriation made in May 1450 for current expenses of the household from the revenues of royal lands, sheriffs' issues, feefarms, customs, ulnage, &c., to the total of £11,002 6s. 1d. *per annum* would most probably have been quite ineffective. It is very difficult to find evidence from the chancery calendars or exchequer records that any of the amounts charged on the king's lands in this appropriation were available when it was made. For example, in the case of seventeen items examined there seems to have been only about £150 available in May 1450 to meet a charge of almost £2,700. However, the same records show that from Easter 1451 there was certainly £1,700 available in the case of these seventeen items, due to the resumption of rent-free grants, grants at nominal rents and annuities and to the making of new leases.[2] Sheriffs' issues, feefarms, customs and ulnage appropriated to the household in 1450 were similarly freed by the resumption of annuities.

The immediate effect of the resumption on the national finances can best be gauged from the Receipt Rolls. Prior to the resumption not only were cash payments by farmers or keepers of crown manors at the exchequer negligible but assignments made on them were almost equally so. As a result of the resumption farms and rents from the resumed lands reappear on the rolls as sound assignments for the payment of debts, for the defence of the borders and generally for the current expenses of Government.[3] The parliamentary acts of resumption had restored a considerable measure of control over the endowed revenues of the Crown to the exchequer

---

[1] See Appendix C of my thesis cited above.

[2] *I.e.* details of grants, leases and annuities for Bradwell, Hadley, Havering (Essex), Kingsthorp, Fawsley, Geddington, Brigstock (Northants.), Swaffham (Norfolk), Bassingbourne and Babraham (Cambs.), the Gurney manors (Soms. and Dors.), Woodstock, Cookham and Bray (Oxon and Berks.), Marston Maisey (Wilts.), Rockingham Forest (Northants.), the county of Carmarthen (S. Wales), Pembroke and Cilgerran lordships, Isle of Wight manors.

[3] This statement is based on an examination of the Receipt Rolls from Michaelmas 1446 to Easter 1452 (P.R.O., Exch. of Receipt, E. 401/796, 800, 804, 807, 808, 811, 814, 816, 820, 821, 824, 827). Note especially assignments made on the king's lands in the two periods May–August 1451 and June and July 1452 for John Stourton, treasurer of the household, John Merston, treasurer of the king's chamber, William Cliffe, clerk of the works, Henry Percy, warden of the East Marches, William Cotton, clerk of the great wardrobe, for money owed to Richard duke of York and for fees and wages of the officers of the exchequer, &c. Very few were cancelled. Principal Steel in his book *The Receipt of the Exchequer, 1377–1485* makes no reference to this significant change on the Receipt Rolls except for as brief note on p. 237 under Easter 1451 that 'all the larger drafts were unexpectedly on the hereditary revenues'. Following Ramsay he summarily dismisses the resumption, describing the act of 1451 as 'even more useless' than its predecessor of 1450: *op. cit.* p. 236.

D

and the inescapable expenses of the king's household, the nerve centre of the Government of the realm, had been made a primary charge on this newly-freed income.

The prayer of the Commons that the resumption might 'take good and effectuell conclusion' had thus at last been answered. There could now be little cause for complaint. While declining to accept those portions of the petition which infringed his prerogative the king had been moved to further a genuine resumption. The extraordinarily lavish grants and alienations of 1437–49 were almost entirely undone. York, Somerset, and other great nobles, lords, knights, and esquires of the household had surrendered grants in fee and grants for life in a manner quite unprecedented in English history. The rates of farm for Crown manors had been significantly increased by competitive leasing. In addition there was a marked reduction in the value of annuities and pensions on the king's lands, on feefarms and on the issues of the counties, on the ulnage and on the customs and subsidies at the ports. If the king's resources were still gravely inadequate for the legitimate expenses of government he now had a very strong claim on the generosity of parliament.[1]

The next parliament which met at Reading on 23 March 1453 was indeed the most co-operative assembly Henry VI ever summoned. His stock had undoubtedly risen throughout the country. King's men were more acceptable in the constituencies;[2] the knights of the shire were more co-operative than ever they had been before. One is reminded of an *ex post facto* belief that the king who made a thorough resumption by act of parliament would be amply rewarded : 'And yff it (the king's livelihood after a resumtion) wolde not than be so gret, I holde it for undouted that the people off his lande woll be well wyllunge to graunte hym a subsidie, uppon suche comodites off his reaume as bith be ffore specified, as shall accomplishe that wich shall lakke hym off such livelod.'[3] Henry had made the gesture. This assembly responded with a remarkable act of generosity for which there were only two

---

[1] This 1450-1 parliament made no grant of supply. In addition to the resumption it enacted that a strict priority payment of £20,000 for two years from Christmas 1450 should be enforced for the defence of the realm on the customs of London and Southampton with exemptions only for the wages of the Calais garrison and for those who had lent the king money, with special mention of the Merchants of the Staple: *Rot. Parl.* v. 214. This measure prevented payment of £1,000 *per annum* of Qùeen Margaret's dower in 1451 and 1452 (*ibid.* v. 258–60).

[2] There certainly was a higher number of members of the household elected to this parliament. Professor J. S. Roskell gives the following figures: 47 members of the household (20 knights and 27 burgesses) being 17 per cent. of the total house of commons elected in 1453 compared with 17 members of the household (3 knights and 14 burgesses) being 6 per cent. of the total house of commons elected in the 1450–1 parliament: *The Commons in the Parliament of 1422*, p. 136.

[3] *The Governance of England*, pp. 136–7, and *cf.* p. 143.

precedents in English history:[1] a life grant of the subsidy on wool, the tax on aliens and of tunnage and poundage. In addition, by the end of its second session, the king had been granted one and a half tenths and fifteenths and a force of 13,000 archers, apparently for service at home. No wonder that on 2 July 1453 he thanked the Commons in person.[2]

The long history of the demand for a resumption,[3] associated with continual complaints against wasteful grants, with resentment at the abuses of purveyance and with numerous measures of parliamentary appropriation demonstrates that these acts of resumption were essentially measures to induce financial retrenchment and solvency. Nevertheless, there was an obvious need to balance any success in these financial aims against the danger to the king's prerogative inherent in acts of parliament calculated to restrict his power freely to dispose of his landed patrimony. It is no surprise therefore to find this Reading parliament endowing the royal family with the best of the resumed lands.[4] In March 1453, following a petition of the Commons, the king's two half-brothers Edmund of Hadham and Jasper of Hatfield were solemnly declared legitimate, created earls and endowed with the lands of Richmond and Kendal and of Pembroke respectively.[5] They also received a number of other resumed manors in 1453 and 1454. When provision had had to be made for Queen Margaret's dower in 1446 there had been no land available with which she could be endowed and she had received only a general reversionary claim on the king's lands. Since the resumption the assertion of her reversionary claim had temporarily secured her the lordship of Pembroke lands but in 1453 she surrendered her claim to these and by authority of parliament received a permanent endowment of other resumed lands

---

[1] To Henry V immediately after Agincourt and to Richard II at Shrewsbury during the so-called tyranny (1398). This new sense of identity of interest and purpose between king and Commons also resulted in a display of hostility towards the over ardent supporters of York and of loyal enthusiasm towards the king hitherto unknown during his reign. An 'act of resumption' was passed known only from its recital on the roll of the 1455–6 parliament which repealed it as casting doubts on the allegiance of some of the king's subjects: *Rot. Parl.* v. 329–30. It was directed only against those who had taken the field at Dartford with York, and those who had contrived to be specially exempted 'by name of baptism' for fee simple grants from the resumption of 1451. This latter provision can have affected very few men: Ralph lord Cromwell and possibly one or two others. It is not a true act of resumption but rather a forerunner of the later acts of forfeiture and attainder.

[2] *Rot. Parl.* v. 236.   [3] *I.e.* dating from the Ordinances of 1311.

[4] Compare the situation in the early years of Henry IV's reign when the same parliament which petitioned for a resumption also petitioned for a better endowment of the queen, the king's younger sons, the Beauforts and Edward duke of York: *Rot. Parl.* iii. 547, 612; and when Queen Joan received an increase in income from Crown lands it was specifically stated to be pursuant to the request of the Coventry parliament: *Cal. Pat. Rolls, 1405–1408,* p. 438. For a similar request in 1377, also coupled with a demand for a resumption, see J. G. Edwards, 'Some Common Petitions in Richard II's First Parliament', *Bull. Inst. Hist. Res.* xxvi (1953), 203, 207.

[5] *Rot. Parl.* v. 250–4.

in part satisfaction of her dower.[1] As a result of these arrangements for the royal family the parliamentary appropriations on the hereditary revenues for the expenses of the household would clearly be affected. The appropriation of 1450 was in fact annulled from 17 April 1454 and a new detailed appropriation for the household substituted with a reduced ceiling of 10,000 marks per annum.[2]

To end the story of the Lancastrian resumption at this point on a note of success and co-operation between king and parliament would of course be unrealistic. While it is certainly true that in some ways the summer of 1453 was indeed the most auspicious point of Henry VI's long reign, in others it was the most disastrous. Even the final loss of Gascony was a blessing in disguise, but the king's first attack of helpless insanity which followed within a brief time of his speech of thanks to parliament [3] was an overwhelming catastrophe. It hopelessly bedevilled the problem of creating a strong and solvent kingship at the very moment when the attainment seemed within grasp. Politics degenerated into an open struggle for power between York and the queen.

In these radically changed circumstances less than two years passed before a petition for a further resumption was submitted.[4] This petition was presented in the first session of the 1455-6 parliament which ended on 31 July 1455.[5] Less than two months previously the Yorkist lords had taken the field against the king's household at St. Albans. As a result they were in forcible control of the Government, were apprehensive lest parliament would not approve their actions and had made strenuous efforts to influence

[1] *Ibid.* v. 260–3. For Queen Margaret's lands see also *Foedera* (1727 edn.), xi. 155; *Cal. Pat. Rolls, 1446–1452*, p. 559; *ibid. 1452–1461*, p. 340. The accounts of the keeper of the wardrobe of the household show that Queen Margaret's receiver, under her obligation to pay £7 a day to the expenses of the king's household, contributed nearly £12,000 in the eight years Mich. 1446–Easter 1454 (E. 101/409/20).

[2] *Rot. Parl.* v. 246–7. The details of the assignment given appear to be incomplete. They do not amount to 10,000 marks. The exchequer copy (K.R. Mem. Rolls, E. 159/231 (33 Hen. VI), Communia, Mich. m. 39) is identical but a copy in Ancient Petitions (S.C. 8/24/1187 B) has an additional item at the end of the list which is crossed out.

[3] Possibly in July and certainly by early August 1453.

[4] The accounts of the keeper of the wardrobe of the household show a spectacular and unique drop in receipts from the exchequer from Easter Term 1453. £6,105 7s. 1½d. for Michaelmas Term 1452 was well above average. For Easter Term 1453 receipts were only £552 0s. 4d. (E. 101/409/20). They substantially recovered by 1455: Easter 1455 £5390 12s. 8½d., Michaelmas 1455 £5205 1s. 10¼d. (E. 101/410/15). The accounts for most of 1454 do not survive.

[5] *Rot. Parl.* v. 300–20 (petition, answer and 143 provisos of exemption). The petition undoubtedly belonged to the first session (9 July–31 July 1455). *The History of Parliament 1439–1509, Register*, p. 217 erroneously places it in the third session. The act took effect from Michaelmas 1455 and the petition requested this operative date in the form '. . . from the Fest of Seint Michell th' Archangell next comyng . . .'. It could not have been presented in the second session which did not begin until 12 November 1455.

the elections.[1] Undoubtedly their endeavours were sufficiently successful to enable them to give an anti-Lancastrian bias to this petition.[2] Yet it is important to realize that all sections calculated to infringe the king's prerogative were carefully removed before this petition was accepted. The act itself in its final form cannot therefore be considered partisan.[3] However, in the autumn of 1455 the king again became completely insane and York held the office of Protector from 17 November 1455 until 25 February 1456 when the king appeared in person in parliament and relieved him of it. Consequently for much of the period during which petitions for exemption were being submitted to the lords spiritual and temporal the Yorkist lords were in complete control.[4] How they used this act of resumption to carry out a thorough reduction of annuities and pensions still held by members of the king's household is shown by the survival of the original petitions for exemption as submitted by grantees, with the comments of the ' lords spiritual and temporal ' upon them, scaling down their grants before any exemption was allowed.[5]

When it was known that the king was recovering it was thought in some quarters that the resumption would not go forward, a view which adds support to the belief that it was being applied in a partisan manner.[6] However, it was carried out, its effects on annuitants and pensioners being mitigated to some extent by means of letters patent under the great seal regranting what had been resumed and back-dating the regrants to Michaelmas 1455. A certain number of new leases operative from Michaelmas 1455

[1] See Stubbs, op. cit. iii. 178 and references to Paston Letters, Proc. and Ord. and Rot. Parl. there cited.

[2] For example, the resumption of all duchy of Lancaster lands placed in the hands of feoffees either by the king or his father to perform their wills was specifically requested; the petition also requested that Queen Margaret's dower should not exceed 10,000 marks; no exemptions were requested for the king's two half-brothers Jasper and Edmund Tudor; the petitioners sought to have any exemptions the king might wish to make sent to them first for their approval.

[3] It was accepted, saving the king's prerogative in all things; a request in the petition that the penalty of the Statute of Provisors and a forfeiture of 1,000 marks should apply to all who contravened the act was specifically rejected; the king reserved the right to make such exemptions as he pleased by advice of the lords spiritual and temporal, to be put in writing during the lifetime of the parliament; and there was to be no question of submitting these provisos of exemption for the Commons' approval. Complete exemption was made by proviso for the queen and for the king's two half-brothers.

[4] Parliament was dissolved on 12 March 1456.

[5] P.R.O., Special Collections, Ancient Petitions (S.C. 8) and Chancery, Parliament and Council Proceedings (C. 49) passim. Examples of these are given in my D.Phil. thesis, Appendix C, pp. 345–8. None of the original personal petitions for exemption from this act bear the king's sign manual. Almost all those for exemption from the 1450 act do so.

[6] Paston Letters, iii. 75 (no. 322); 9 February 1456, John Bocking to Sir John Fastolf, ' The resumpsion, men truste, shall forthe, and my Lordes of Yorkes first power of protectorship stande, and elles not, etc.'.

began to be taken out in November 1455. Once more the new act of resumption was closely associated with detailed appropriations for the expenses of the household, again stressing the primary financial purpose of these resumption proposals.[1] The king again exercised his undoubted prerogative right by setting aside the best of the estates resumed under this last Lancastrian act of resumption for the endowment of the infant prince of Wales.[2]

The impact of this act on the Crown lands was not very great, not primarily because of partisan action and its subsequent annulment but because of the effective resumption of 1451 : as a result of it those Crown lands which were not now held by the royal family had already been almost entirely leased out for terms of years at the rate of the extent plus the best increment obtainable.

The chief characteristics of the Lancastrian parliaments can be listed as follows: a growing reluctance to make money grants without some evidence of retrenchment; a persistent endeavour to obtain a more stable and purposeful direction of public affairs; close contact with public opinion ; an eager response to any gesture of co-operation from the throne. In this setting their acts of resumption both under Henry IV and Henry VI must be treated as the seriously intended measures which they undoubtedly were. By 1451 a stage had been reached in the history of the Commons in parliament when they were able to insist that the lavish and conspicuous waste of late medieval government would not be tolerated indefinitely. The final disasters of the great foreign adventure produced a political and financial crisis even more acute than in the years 1404–6 and this provided the opportunity to achieve drastic retrenchment and reform. Had the Commons been demanding that all normal expenses of government should be met out of the revenues of Crown lands and feudal dues and that national expenditure should be commensurate with those revenues then they might legitimately be considered foolish and impractical critics. But they were not demanding this. They believed that the permanent revenues of the Crown, efficiently administered through an exchequer backed by parliament, could be made to provide a substantial and regular contribution to the national income as had been done in much earlier times. They may not always have been sure

---

[1] *Rot. Parl.* v. 320–1; *Cal. Pat. Rolls, 1452–1461*, pp. 295–8. These combined appropriations totalled £6520 9s. 5d. for the year 1455–6, *i.e.* almost 10,000 marks as in the previous parliament.

[2] Notably the Gurney lands in Somerset and Dorset. This resumption also freed the duchy of Cornwall and Welsh lands from certain grants. When the infant prince of Wales was endowed with the duchy and principality and with the earldom of Chester in this parliament (*Rot. Parl.* v. 293–5) assignments made on these lands for the king's household were specifically reserved and all surplus revenues above a sum for the prince's own household were also to be employed for the expenses of the king's household and for no other purpose.

of their facts, but there is evidence that on the whole they were well informed. Before granting supply they required and ultimately obtained an earnest of good faith from the king and his advisers.

A more detailed examination of the Lancastrian acts of resumption than was possible to Stubbs and Ramsay suggests that although they were forced upon an unwilling government in the first instance, they were in the end made effective to a significant degree. The amount of alienation of Crown lands and revenues between *c.* 1437 and 1449 had been unique and had undoubtedly mirrored the weakness and low prestige of Henry VI's government. Nevertheless, the resumption of these lands and revenues in the interests of retrenchment and solvency might have done more harm than good by depriving the king of the means of exercising his legitimate and vital political influence not only at the centre but also locally in the shires. The detailed history of the acts passed, however, shows that even under a weak ruler these crucial interests were in fact safeguarded at every stage against undue restriction and against partisan exploitation until at the very end of our period the recurrent insanity of the king* introduced new problems which were beyond the constitutional resources of the age. Only in 1461 was this impasse surmounted by the accession of a strong young king who was in full possession of his faculties and victorious in battle, a king who surrounded himself by commoners and house of commons men able and not afraid to take the initiative in government under his leadership. The policies of parliamentary opposition in the Lancastrian parliaments then became governmental policies under the Yorkists. Here lies the answer to the obvious query as to what became of the Commons' dogged determination after 1461. Yorkist kings and Commons, unlike their Lancastrian predecessors, found themselves able to unite in a policy of resumptions and forfeitures accompanied by a reorganization of royal lands and revenues designed to strengthen the monarchy.[1] The king himself took an initiative in this legislation which his Commons in parliament gladly welcomed. Fifteenth-century England had no concern with the problems which might arise if her kings were made too strong and the activities of the Lancastrian Commons had in no sense been a sign of an incipient struggle for supremacy between king and parliament. Such ideas were even more remote from the political thought of that age than the spectre of an over-mighty king. England had still to be taught the hard lessons of Tudor rule.

---

[1] I have discussed the effect of these policies on the royal demesne and on the royal finances between 1461 and 1485 in *E.H.R.*, January 1956, pp. 1–27, ' The Management of English Royal Estates under the Yorkist Kings '.

3

ATTAINDER AND FORFEITURE, 1453-1509[1]*

By J. R. LANDER

ATTAINDER was the most solemn penalty known to the common law. Attainder for treason was followed not only by the most savage and brutal corporal penalties and the forfeiture of all possessions, but in addition the corruption of blood passing to all direct descendants, in other words, by the legal death of the family.[2] Before proceeding to an examination of the effects of parliamentary acts of attainder[3] in the late fifteenth and early sixteenth centuries it is necessary first of all to define the scope of forfeiture for treason as it affected landed property. Bracton's classic definition of forfeiture had involved for the traitor 'the loss of all his goods and the perpetual disinheritance of his heirs, so that they may be admitted neither to the paternal nor to the maternal inheritance'. Feudal opinion had always been very much opposed to the stringency of this conception and the Edwardian statute *De Donis Conditionalibus*, confirmed implicitly by the treason statute of 1352, had protected entailed estates from the scope of forfeiture, thus leaving only the fee simple and the widow's dower within the scope of the law. The wife's own inheritance or any jointure which had been made for her, because they ante-dated her husband's treason, as distinct from her right to dower which did not, were not liable to ultimate forfeiture—though a married woman could claim them only when 'her time came according to the common law', that is after the death of her husband when she ceased to be 'femme couvert'. This equitable principle was confirmed by a statute of the Merciless Parliament of 1388 which, however, included for the first time the rule that lands held to the use of a traitor were also included in the scope of forfeiture. Thus, by 1388, of the lands held by a traitor (as distinct from the wife's inheritance and jointure), only those held in fee tail fell outside the scope of the treason laws. This loophole was closed by Richard II in 1398 when Parliament declared forfeit entailed estates as well as lands held in fee simple and to the use of a traitor, thus reverting with one exception to Bracton's view of forfeiture.[4] This

---

[1] I wish to thank Dr E. B. Fryde for criticism and advice on this paper.

[2] Bracton, *De Legibus et Consuetudinibus Anglie*, ed. G. E. Woodbine (4 vols., 1915-42), II. 335, on the heinousness of treason.

This article is limited to a study of attainders for treason passed by the English Parliament. Parliamentary attainders for felony and attainders for treason passed by the Irish Parliament, the common law courts and special commissions are not dealt with.

[4] I.e. the wife's inheritance and estates settled on her jointly with her husband or otherwise. In the late fifteenth century the wife was entitled to them after the death of her husband and such estates could descend to her heirs not attainted, e.g. *Rot. Parl.* v, 481-2.

comprehensive and implacable definition was taken over completely in fifteenth-century acts of attainder,[5] although, as we shall see, public feeling against so extreme a position probably affected quite considerably the actual execution of penalties.

During the fifteenth century the penalty of attainder was for the first time imposed by act of Parliament.[6] It was a procedure that had the virtues of speed and simplicity. All that was necessary to condemn opponents was the reading of a bill in the parliament chamber, the mere acquiescence of the commons and its acceptance by the king.[7] Such action became common during the Wars of the Roses when the alternations of conflict placed in power one government after another which, it has been said, from motives of both security and revenge wished to destroy its opponents 'as speedily, as utterly, and with as much appearance of legality as possible'.[8] These motives were undoubtedly the immediate objective of the acts[9] and the fullest statement by a contemporary on the point is Friar Brackley's remark that the attainder of the Yorkists in the Coventry Parliament of 1459 had been contrived by the 'most vengeable labour' of Dr Aleyn, Chief Justice Fortescue, Dr Moreton, John Heydon and Thomas Thorpe.[10] Successive generations of historians have since put forward various conjectures about the results of attainders which have been strongly influenced by such meagre contemporary statements about their aims—issues, in fact, which it is wiser to keep distinct. These conjectural results may briefly be described as financial and political. C. H. Plummer in the notes to his edition of *The Governance of England* states that forfeitures must greatly have increased the

[5] For the general contents of this paragraph see C. D. Ross, 'Forfeiture for Treason in the Reign of Richard II', *E.H.R.* LXXI (1956), 560–75.

[6] Procedure in the treason cases of 1388 and 1397–8 had taken a different form. Acts of Attainder in the fifteenth century sometimes followed judgements in the common law courts or by special commissions (increasingly so under Henry VII).

[7] Henry VII at first did not even consult the Commons but the judges held that their consent was necessary. K. Pickthorn, *Early Tudor Government: Henry VII* (1934), 119; A. F. Pollard, *The Reign of Henry VII From Contemporary Sources* (3 vols., 1913–14), II, 19.

[8] K. Pickthorn, op. cit.

[9] Contemporary writers, where they mention the acts, usually state merely that revenge was taken on opponents and that they greatly enriched the exchequer, e.g. *The Great Chronicle of London*, ed. A. H. Thomas and I. D. Thornley (1938), 191, 198; under 1459 merely mentions the attainders and under 1461 states that many lords and barons were convicted and their possessions escheated. It mentions no other acts under Edward IV or Richard III. Polydore Vergil, however, implies (an implication which Bacon made explicit) that avarice was one of Henry VII's motives in pressing through the attainders of his reign. *The Anglica Historia of Polydore Vergil*, ed. D. Hay (Camden Soc. 1950), 126–9. The Somnium Vigilantis, dated *c.* 1459–60 and sometimes attributed, rather dubiously, to Fortescue, printed by J. Gilson, *E.H.R.* XXVI (1911), 512–25, stresses the intransigence of the Yorkists and the need for repression if orderly government was to be achieved.

[10] *The Paston Letters*, ed. J. Gairdner (4 vols., 1910), I, 535 (see also p. 522). Thomas Thorpe was a baron of the Exchequer and had been Speaker in 1453–4. For his notorious quarrel with the duke of York at that time, see Wedgwood, *Biographies*, 850. The group expected that they 'schuld be made for evir' if their plans succeeded but 'yf it turnyd to contrary wyse, it schuld growe to her fynal confusyon and uttyr destruccyon'.

landed possessions of the Crown under Edward IV, especially after the battle
of Tewkesbury, and that the increase became even greater under Henry VII.[11]
On the political side an extreme theory, dying but not yet completely dead,
has been advanced that the battles, executions and attainders of the Wars of
the Roses resulted in the destruction of a great part of the nobility—a destruction alleged on very flimsy evidence to have been definite government policy
under both Edward IV and Henry VII. While admitting that some of the
greatest names (York, Beaufort, de la Pole, Holland) disappear, recent
scholarship has spoken more cautiously of the extent of the decline of the
nobility under Henry VII and of its corollary, his reliance on middle-class
support, and tends to emphasize the greater tractability of the aristocracy
rather than its decline.[12*] It is one of the aims of this paper to attempt,
if possible, to assess the effect of acts of attainder in bringing about this
change.

In view of the extent of the evidence which has been in print for a long
time[13] and the fairly general realization that the full penalties of the law were
not always exacted, it is somewhat surprising that the number of people who
have from time to time found it necessary to comment on the financial and
political consequences of attainder have not attempted to work out the effects
of the acts with any degree of precision. A glance at the figures provided in
the tables at the end of this article should be enough to show that caution is
necessary in discussing the problem. Between 1453 and 1504, 397 people
(excluding members of the houses of Lancaster and York) were condemned
by process in Parliament, and of these no less than 256 (possibly 265),[14]
or about 64 per cent ultimately had their attainders reversed. It tells very
much against any theory of a calculated destruction of the nobility that the
highest percentage of reversals was amongst the peerage as a whole (just over
84 per cent followed by the next highest ranks the knights and squires (79 and
67** per cent, respectively) followed at a considerable distance by other
ranks. Obscurity, it thus appears, contrary to received opinion, was no

[11] C. H. Plummer, *The Governance of England* (1885), 277. In fact during the 1470's
attainders were notably fewer than during the 1460's and the sessions of the parliament of
1472–5 are more conspicuous for the reversal of old than for the passing of new attainders
(see below, pp. 100–3).†

[12] For these opinions expressed with varying degrees of emphasis, e.g. H. Hallam, *The
Constitutional History of England, Henry VII to George III*, (3rd ed. 1832, reprinted Everyman), 15; A. D. Innes, *England Under the Tudors* (1905), 7; C. Oman, *The Political History
of England, 1377–1485* (1910), 450, 472; K. Vickers, *England in the Later Middle Ages* (1913),
495; W. P. M. Kennedy, *Studies in Tudor History* (1916), 4; K. Pickthorn, *Henry VII*,
op. cit. 93–6; S. T. Bindoff, *Tudor England* (1950), 29–30; A. R. Myers, *England in the Late
Middle Ages* (1952), 115, 188, 193, 197–8, 209; J. D. Mackie, *The Early Tudors, 1485–1558*
(1952), 13, 15, 18. For a change of emphasis compare G. R. Elton, *The Tudor Revolution in
Government* (1953), 33–34, and *England Under the Tudors* (1955), 7–8, 43–6.

[13] Mainly in the *Rotuli Parliamentorum* and the *Calendars of Patent Rolls, 1452–85*.

[14] See Table 1, nn. 5 and 6. Figures quoted in various notes to this article do not always
tally exactly owing to the fact that a number of people were attainted twice and therefore
figures vary slightly at different times.

protection and the lower a man's rank the more difficult it was to obtain restoration in blood and lands; or, at any rate, restoration for some reason was less usual.

It is now proposed to examine attainders and restorations in some detail to see if differences of policy can be detected at different times. No record of the attainders passed in the Re-adeption Parliament of 1470 has survived.[15] The Lancastrian attainders of 1459 and those of Richard III can be quickly disposed of as they were reversed after the political revolutions which almost immediately followed. In spite of Friar Brackley's gossip about the 'vengeable labour' of the Lancastrians in the Parliament of Devils there are signs that Henry VI did not altogether approve of the proceedings of his friends and was personally inclined to a more merciful attitude.[16] Richard III's record is more debateable. After Buckingham's rebellion he attainted a hundred people. His actions seem to show that he was in the grip of something like panic. A wholesale proscription of known opponents was accompanied by bribery of possibly wavering supporters on a very considerable scale.[17] Once again, however, the quick turn of political fortune undid the effects of his own proscriptions and his ultimate intentions are doubtful.

It remains, therefore, to consider the actions of Edward IV and Henry VII whose comparatively long reigns gave them time, had they been so inclined, to work out a consistent policy. It is first of all necessary to say something about the process of reversal. An attainder could be reversed either by letters patent under the great seal or by act of Parliament. With one proviso reversals by act of Parliament present no difficulty—the proviso being that under Edward IV they do not always indicate the real date of restitution. There were long intervals between the meetings of parliament, and some acts of Parliament, although they do not always state the fact, were in effect confirmation of

[15] It is probable that the Parliament Roll was destroyed by the victorious Yorkists and any acts which it may have passed were treated as null and void.

[16] Henry gave his consent only on condition that he should be free to show mercy to any person he might wish to pardon. Three men had their lands confiscated, five were fined, but were spared the full consequence of attainder. Henry also rejected a bill for the attainder of Lord Stanley whose conduct during the Blore Heath campaign had been most suspicious. Abbot Whethamstede also testifies to the king's personal intention of showing mercy *Rot. Parl.* v, 346–50, 368–70; J. Whethamstede, *Registrum Abbatiae Johannis Whethamstede* (Rolls Ser. 1872–3), i, 355–6.

[17] E.g. see his generous treatment of Sir John Fogge, ex-treasurer of the Household to Edward IV, of Lord Hastings' widow, and his brother, Sir Ralph. The Second Anonymous Croyland Continuator lays great stress on the large number of attainders under Richard though this may be due to prejudice, and Gairdner states that the King's Bench Controlment Rolls show that there were numerous prosecutions for treason in that court. (J. Gairdner, *Richard III* (new ed. 1898), 98, 111, 199; *Cal. Pat. Rolls*, 1476–85, 460, 462, 496, B.M. MS. Harl. 433, fols. 108d–109, 159–160; J. Gairdner, *Letters and Papers Illustrative of the Reigns of Richard III and Henry VII* (Rolls Ser. 1861–3), i, 15, 46–8). Sir Thomas More stated that Richard with great gifts won for himself unsteadfast friendships. (*The English Works of Sir Thomas More*, ed. W. E. Campbell and others (1931), i, 37.) B.M. MS. Harl. 433, fols. 282 ff., show the exceptionally lavish way in which Richard rewarded his adherents.

pardons issued under the great seal or completed what may be described as partial restorations[18] made by force of letters patent. As to pardons granted by letters patent under the great seal it is necessary to distinguish between various types.

Those described in the calendars of chancery rolls as 'general pardons' need to be used with caution. What is usually described as a 'general pardon' normally had no particular political significance at this period[19] (except at certain times when a general pardon was proclaimed covering a particular series of events). The stock phrasing of the pardons enrolled on the Pardon Rolls (nowadays called Supplementary Patent Rolls) was changed from time to time to meet new circumstances and in 1461 the form was changed so as to exclude the pardon of attainders.[20] The pardons enrolled on the Patent Rolls themselves between 1461 and 1485 present greater difficulties. Unfortunately the printed calendars leave much to be desired for although the formulae of these pardons are most divergent the summaries seem to have been made without taking this sufficiently into account (the same terms in the summaries covering a variety of offences) and it is unsafe to use them for this purpose without comparing them with the original rolls.[21] In the examples which follow, therefore, no general pardon has been accepted as evidence of the reversal of an attainder unless the full entry on the roll itself specifically states that it covers an attainder passed in some previous Parliament. Nor, even more unfortunately, is this the only difficulty. Pardons like people are not always what they seem. Even in this category of pardons the formulae vary and promises given in them were not always kept to the letter. Some state that the man concerned was pardoned his offences only; others that the penalties and forfeitures involved were remitted. In fact, as far as landed property was concerned most of them, irrespective of the wording, seem to have been subsequently interpreted in one way only. To use the contemporary phrase the men concerned were 'enabled to the laws',[22] that is to say

18 For pardons by letters patent in the 1460's (see below, pp. 96-7). Those granted in 1471-2, e.g. Dr John Morton, Sir John Fortescue, may have been complete in effect as they were reversed in the next parliament and none of their lands were granted away after pardons under the great seal had been issued.

19 The state of the law, both civil and criminal, at this time was so complicated that it was almost impossible to avoid technical offences. The Supplementary Patent Rolls contain many pardons, e.g. to executors and accountants, with no variations of phrasing, which can only have this significance. Like the privilege of freedom from arrest for knights of the shire and parliamentary burgesses the issue of general pardons was usually intended as a protection from the vexatious processes of the common law.

20 Supplementary Patent Roll, C. 67/45, ms. 47, 49. Similar clauses are found on the entries of all rolls up to 11 Edward IV, C. 67/46, 47 and 48. No formula is given on the roll of 12–17 Edward IV which is merely a list of names, C. 67/49. There are no rolls extant for 18–21 Edward IV. The formula appears again for 22–23 Edward IV, C. 67/50.

21 Some entries in the calendars, like the full text on the roll, mention attainder by parliament, others do not.

22 This phrase is used in the final parliamentary reversals of Sir Nicholas Latymer, Sir Thomas Tresham and Robert Bollyng (see below, pp. 112-4).

they were resurrected from the legal death which was the penalty of attainder and became capable in law of making contracts including the purchase of land, but the restoration of their estates (even in some cases in which the forfeitures are declared by the pardon to have been remitted) required a separate grant. Only the subsequent reversal of the attainder by act of Parliament made the restoration complete.[23] It is probable that in some cases where a pardon remitted forfeitures Edward soon found inexpedient the revocation of grants made to supporters from the forfeited estates which it involved.[24] It is also probable that he used this piecemeal process of restoration as a form of political control; ex-Lancastrians had to 'work their way back' into favour and prove their loyalty before they were allowed complete restitution. Nor can the possibility be ruled out that the process conceals bargains between Edward and the attainted under which they were made to surrender part of their estates to obtain the restoration of the remainder, though there is no proof of this.[25] Probably it was because experience had made plain ambiguities of this kind in the operation of extra-parliamentary pardons that Henry VII and Henry VIII both consented to acts of Parliament authorising them to reverse attainders by patent.[26] After 1485, therefore, reversals by patent had full legal effect and no such difficulties in their interpretation arise.[27]

In the first session of the Parliament of 1461–3 no less than one hundred and thirteen people were attainted.[28]* At first sight this would indicate as vindictive and vengeful a spirit as that which Friar Brackley had attributed to the victorious Lancastrians two years earlier. So it was interpreted by J. R. Green who wrote of all these families as reduced to 'beggary and exile'.[29] Such an impression of the wholesale elimination of opponents is, however,

---

[23] See the cases of Sir Nicholas Latymer, Sir Thomas Tresham and Sir Thomas Fulford (see below, pp. 100, 112-4).   Robert Bollyng received a pardon in 1463 but some of his estates were granted out between 1465 and 1468. Although no grant in his favour is enrolled his petition for reversal in 1472 states that although his pardon did not restore his livelihood 'by the King's grace he enjoys the same to the great relief of himself and his wife and their ten children' (*Rot. Parl.* VI, 20; *Cal. Pat. Rolls, 1461-7*, 271, 476; *1467-77*, 31, 46, 50, 479. Also Thomas Cornwaille, *Rot. Parl.* VI, 21-2. *Cal. Pat. Rolls, 1467-77*, 18, 45). Even in the case of Henry Percy IV whose restoration was so politically expedient, 1469–70, his estates were restored by a separate grant not by his pardon. J. M. W. Bean, *The Estates of the Percy Family, 1416–1537* (1958), 109–10.   [25] See below, pp. 107 ff.

[24] See below, pp. 112-3   [26] *Rot. Parl.* VI, 526; VII, cxxi-cxxxi.

[27] Still allowing, however, for the possibility of concealed bargains. Henry VII's act was not passed until 1504 but there were only two cases of complete reversal by patent before this date. The other pardons all contain specific limitations or other definite special features.

[28] The figure usually given is about 133, see below, J. R. Green, n. 29; Sir J. H. Ramsay, *Lancaster and York* (2 vols. 1892), II, 282-3. This is arrived at by adding the defenders of Harlech and a number of people 'provisionally' attainted whom I have excluded. For reasons see the notes to Table 1. The Annales until recently attributed to William Worcester (see K. B. McFarlane, 'William Worcester, A Preliminary Survey', in *Studies Presented to Sir Hilary Jenkinson* (1957), 206-7), give 108 names 'et xlij plures' making a total of 150 (the author incorrectly gives a total of 154). J. Stevenson, *Letters and Papers Illustrative of the Wars of the English in France* (Rolls Ser. 1861-4), II, Pt. ii, 770-1. Names found in these Annales but not in the *Rotuli Parliamentorum* have been ignored.

[29] J. R. Green, *History of the English People* (4 vols. 1877–80), II, 27.

quite incorrect. Far from being in a strong enough position to maintain its security by destroying the leaders of the vanquished the Yorkist government was so insecure that it could not neglect any opportunity of winning over opponents, especially prominent opponents. Ample opportunities were allowed to such men to make their peace: a process all the easier as contemporary opinion saw such changes of allegiance as a normal and far from reprehensible matter, once God had shown a cause to be righteous through victory on the battlefield.[30] Even if in the first flush of success prominent Yorkists (some of whom had every reason for harbouring bitter feelings) were set on revenge, a milder attitude prevailed at court from the beginning; mild enough to provoke resentment amongst some of the government's own supporters.[31] The Yorkists did not look back beyond the immediate events of 1460–1 and adherents of the house of Lancaster, such as the earls of Westmorland and Oxford, who had not been personally involved in the recent conflicts, were not attainted, and even some who had taken part, like Lord Ryvers and Lord Scales, were allowed to take their seats in Parliament.[32] Consideration of the cases of some of those who were attainted is likewise revealing. Sir Henry Bellingham, for example, had fought on the Lancastrian side at Towton, had fled after the battle and had taken part in the Lancastrian raid on Carlisle in June 1461. For all this he was attainted later in the year. Then, captured at the seige of Naworth, after a period of imprisonment in the Tower of London he was pardoned his attainder under letters patent (though his property was not restored) and released to take part in the earl of Worcester's naval expedition along the east coast in 1463. His adherence to the house of York turned out to be shortlived and he fled to the Lancastrians at Bamborough. For this he was again attainted in 1465. Captured at the surrender of Harlech in 1468, he was again imprisoned for a short time in the Tower. In spite of all he received a pardon the following October. He apparently joined the Lancastrians under the Re-adeption and on Edward's return in 1471 a commission was issued for his arrest. There was to be no forgiveness after this and the second attainder was not reversed until after the Tudor victory in 1485.[33]

[30] See J. R. Lander, 'Council, Administration and Councillors, 1461 to 1485', B.I.H.R. XXX (1959), 155–6.

[31] '... for they grudge and sey, how that the Kyng resayvith sych of this cuntre, &c as haff be his gret eanemyes, and opresseors of the Comynes; and sych as haff assystyd his Hynes, be not rewardyt; and it is to be consederyd, or ellys it wyll hurt' (Paston Letters, II, 30, 16 July 1461).

[32] The Fane Fragment of the 1461 Lords' Journal, ed. W. H. Dunham Jr. (1935), 5–24.

[33] Rot. Parl. v, 476–83, 511–12; VI, 320–1; Cal. Pat. Rolls, 1467–77, 98, 288; Cal. Close Rolls, 1461–8, 167; Paston Letters, II, 111; William Worcester, op. cit. 791; C. L. Scofield, The Life and Reign of King Edward IV (2 vols. 1923), I, 180, 292, 313, n. 3. There is no means of determining the exact date of Bellingham's flight but he was with the Lancastrians in the Spring of 1464. The Paston Letters wrongly report that he was beheaded after the capture of Naworth. The attainder of 1461 had never been formally reversed but the act of 1465 states that he had received a pardon under the great seal. I have been unable to trace this pardon. He was dead by 1485 and the reversal was for his son, Roger.

This is by no means an isolated case. The histories of Sir Ralph Percy,[34] Sir Humphrey Neville of Brancepeth[35] and Henry Beaufort, duke of Somerset, are equally outstanding in modern eyes as examples of political amnesty and political treachery. Somerset's case is the most significant of all. The enmity of the families of York and Somerset had been deep and bitter since the mid-1440's and when Somerset was captured on the surrender of Bamborough Castle in December 1462, he had been Margaret of Anjou's most prominent and active supporter since 1458. Sent to Edward at Durham he swore allegiance. Edward never neglected the art of propaganda. He so exulted in this very prominent conversion that he flaunted it to a degree so unwise as to produce an angry reaction. Somerset's attainder was reversed, first under letters patent and afterwards by Parliament. His property was restored. The king made him gifts of money and bestowed annuities on him and on his mother.[36] The duke was sent to take part in the siege of Alnwick, jousts were specially arranged for him, he shared the king's bed and they went hunting together with no more than six horsemen of whom three were the duke's followers. Moving north in the summer of 1463 Edward even made Somerset captain of his guard and rode to Northampton surrounded by two hundred of the duke's men. 'The garde of hym was as men shulde put a lombe a monge wolvysse of malyscyus bestys' wrote the outraged chronicler and the men of Northampton, remembering the sack of the town in 1461, stormed the royal lodgings and would have torn the duke limb from limb. Edward got him safely away to North Wales, where he turned traitor again, fled to Henry in December and was executed after the skirmish at Hexham the following May and again attainted after death (1465).[37]

---

[34] Sir Ralph Percy submitted by Michaelmas 1461, early enough to avoid attainder in the parliament of November. He was put in charge of the key fortress of Dunstanborough for Edward. By the end of October 1462 he had gone over to Margaret of Anjou but in December Bamborough and Dunstanborough surrendered on condition that he was given the command of both fortresses. By mid-March he had the government's confidence to the extent that he was given authority to receive repentant rebels but at about the same time he went over to the Lancastrians again. He was killed at Hedgley Moor and attainted in 1465 (Scofield, I, 204, 261, 264–5, 274, 287, 329–30, 365. Rot. Parl. v, 511–12).

[35] Neville, with the Lancastrians in the North in 1461, was captured and imprisoned during the summer and attainted in November. In February 1462 he was pardoned all executions against him on account of his attainder and granted his life on condition that he would remain in prison during the king's pleasure. Escaping from the Tower he stirred up insurrection in the North in 1463 and in April a commission for his arrest was issued. In June he was received into the king's grace and pardoned all offences and most of his lands were restored. At the end of the year he fled again and joined Henry at Bamborough. In 1464 he surrendered Bamborough to Lord Montagu on condition that the garrison should be received into the king's grace. His life was spared but in 1465 he was again attainted. In 1468 he was stirring up rebellion in Northumberland and again in the North in 1469. He was then (1469) executed by Warwick and his second attainder was never reversed (Rot. Parl. v, 478–83, 511–12; Cal. Pat. Rolls, 1461–7, 122, 267, 269; Scofield, I, 186, 220, 313–14, 329–30, 337, 365, 423, 501, 503). [36] But prudently kept his brother Edmund as a hostage in the Tower.

[37] Rot. Parl. v, 476–8, 511, 512; VI, 288; Cal. Pat. Rolls, 1461–7, 261, C. 66/505, m. 18 (the calendar does not refer to the attainder; the roll does); Gregory's Chronicle in Collections of a London Citizen, ed. J. Gairdner (Camden Soc. 1876), 219, 221, 223–5; Scofield, I, 117, 120–1, 129, 132, 134–5, 145, 154, 165, 169, 188–90, 208, 209–10, 220, 231–2, 241, 253, n. 2, 261–5, 273–4, 292, 312–13, 315, 320, 329–34.

The story of Sir Thomas Fulford shows that ex-Lancastrians felt secure enough at times to take violent action against Yorkist supporters. In the autumn of 1461 the prominent Lancastrian captain, Sir Baldwin Fulford, had been captured by one, John Staplehill, and executed at Bristol. He was attainted in the parliament of November following, and between November 1461 and August 1464 Staplehill was granted the greater part of the Fulford estates. Baldwin's son, Sir Thomas, in spite of the attainder, was evidently living unmolested in the countryside for in March 1463, he petitioned the king for permission to take down his father's head from Exeter Market Place and bury it. In November 1464 he was granted most of the family estates, although his attainder was not reversed and there is no record of a pardon on the Patent Rolls.[38] This grant to Fulford covered the estates which had been granted to Staplehill only three months before in August. Staplehill apparently refused to give up his gains and in April 1465 Fulford, according to an *ex parte* complaint made by his opponent, went to Fulford with 2000 people, broke into the house, carried off goods to the value of £300, bound and beat his servants and so menaced and disturbed his wife that her life was still in danger. Staplehill, the following month, brought a case against Sir Thomas in Chancery alleging that he had been wrongfully dispossessed 'by colour of' the letters patent granted to Fulford in November. Although a commission was issued for Fulford's arrest Staplehill was apparently unsuccessful.[39] The attainder was reversed in 1467. Sir Thomas was on the Lancastrian side during the Re-adeption, fled to the Westminster sanctuary on Edward's return but escaped and, making his way into Devonshire, began to stir up insurrection and was condemned by name in a proclamation. Nevertheless, he had obtained a general pardon by December.[40] Even after this, far from living quietly, which one assumes it would have been wise to do, his aggressive instincts asserted themselves. He continued to harass the unlucky Staplehill and in 1477 his servants even dared to attack those of Sir Thomas St Ledger, the king's brother-in-law.[41]

Edward's first decade was the period during which nine-tenths of the

[38] The only pardon I have been able to trace is one dated 28 January 1465, Supplementary Patent Roll, C. 67/45, m. 7, which has no political significance as it specifically excludes the reversal of attainder and therefore merely shows that Fulford, in spite of it, was living unmolested.

[39] *Rot. Parl.* v, 476–82; *Cal. Pat. Rolls, 1461–7*, 54, 227, 359, 372, 490–1; *Cal. Close Rolls, 1461–8*, 314–15. For details of Sir Thomas' exploits and the reasons for the successive grants made to Staplehill see *Scofield*, I, 53–4, 55–7, 61, 64, 145–6, 179, 200–1. *Scofield*, I, 201, and C. L. Kingsford, *Prejudice and Promise in the Fifteenth Century* (1925), 60, seem to have overlooked the grant of November 1464 to Fulford and therefore assumed that the attack on the house at Fulford was simply a case of violent dispossession.

[40] *Rot. Parl.* vi, 231; *Scofield*, II, 20; *Cal. Close Rolls, 1468–76*, 188–9; *Cal. Pat. Rolls, 1467–77*, 303.

[41] In 1475 he had to enter into a bond of £500 not to enter Devon nor maintain rioters nor prevent their arrest, in 1476 a bond of £200 to keep the peace and protect Staplehill from attacks by his servants and in 1477 a bond of 100 marks to pay Stephan Spycotte, St. Ledger's servant, £20 in recompense for wounding and beating (*Cal. Close Rolls, 1468–76*, 428, 440; *1476–85*, 68–9).

attainders of his reign were passed but, during the same period, as an urgent necessity of policy, he gave his opponents every opportunity to make their peace though it is true that in some cases attainders were not reversed immediately and the terms on which individuals were taken back varied according to the king's whims or his need for their services.[42] In the 1470's when both the Lancastrians and the Nevilles had been finally defeated and the need to win over opponents was no longer so urgent as it had previously been Edward might well have indulged an urge for revenge. New attainders, however, were few and reversals for those old opponents who had been condemned to forfeiture in the earlier part of his reign are far more conspicuous. No less than thirty attainders were reversed (or in some cases reversals under letters patent completed) in the Parliament of 1473–5, followed by six more in the last two Parliaments of the reign as against only thirteen new attainders during the same period. Prominent ex-Lancastrians who had previously been pardoned under letters patent finally secured reversal by act of Parliament[43] and others put forward excuses plausible enough for the government to accept.[44] Chief Justice Fortescue returned and made his peace at the price of refuting his defence of the Lancastrian title and soon became a councillor.[45] Another prominent exile, John Morton, was soon appointed Master of the Rolls and during the king's later years was one of his most trusted councillors.[46] It was Edward's policy towards the offenders of his earlier years to temper justice with mercy; an attitude vouched for later by Sir Thomas More and Polydore Vergil who were in a position to know as they had first hand information from survivors and had no reason for giving Edward more than his due.[47]

Only thirteen attainders followed the political upheavals of 1469 to 1471. So strikingly small a figure calls for explanation. It is possible, even probable, that in 1471 Edward had in mind another mass series of attainders, but was diverted partly because by the time his first Parliament of the 1470's met (it was not until nearly eighteen months after his return to England) severe punishment in the

[42] Twenty people had their attainders reversed or were pardoned under letters patent by 1470, although in some cases they were subsequently condemned again.

[43] E.g. Richard Tunstall and Henry Percy, earl of Northumberland. Tunstall had been attainted in 1461 and had carried on the defence of Harlech Castle until 1468. On the surrender of the castle he was pardoned his attainder under letters patent and a few months later served on an embassy. The attainder was reversed in Parliament in 1473 (*Cal. Pat. Rolls, 1467–77*, 97, C. 66/521, m. 6). The calendar does not mention the attainder but the roll does (Rymer, *Foedera*, XI, 591; *Rot. Parl.* VI, 47–8). For Northumberland, see below, pp. 105, 116.

[44] E.g. Sir John Scudamore, the defender of Pembroke Castle in 1461, Edward Ellesmere, Margaret of Anjou's Treasurer of the Chamber (*Rot. Parl.* V, 483; VI, 29–30, 130–1, 327. Chancery Diplomatic Documents (Domestic), no. 945. *Scofield*, I, 197). Ellesmere came under suspicion again later and because of this failed to get all his lands back; a situation which he later attributed to the malice and false accusations of the king's physician, Jacques Frus.

[45] *Cal. Pat. Rolls, 1467–77*, 296; *Rot. Parl.* VI, 69; Plummer, op. cit. 72, 78–9; S. B. Chrimes, *Sir John Fortescue* (1942), lxvii.

[46] *Cal. Pat. Rolls, 1467–77*, 261, 334; *Rot. Parl.* VI, 26–7. For his later influence see J. R. Lander, 'Council Administration, and Councillors, 1461 to 1485', *B.I.H.R.* 157, 161.

[47] For More and Vergil, see J. R. Lander, 'Edward IV; The Modern Legend and a Revision', *History*, XLI (1956), 38–9, and the references there given.

way of heavy, even crushing, fines had already been meted out to those who had survived the hazards of the battlefield and partly by the persuasions of his brothers, the dukes of Clarence and Gloucester, who had very cogent reasons of their own against attainders at this time. There is a tradition, supported by fragments of record evidence, of heavy fines imposed in the period following the battle of Tewkesbury. Fines amounting in total to over £2000 were imposed by special commissioners on numerous men of Kent, the Cinque Ports, Surrey, Sussex and Essex. It may well be that such punitive measures extended elsewhere for it is only from his son's Inquisition Post Mortem taken fifteen years later that we learn that Sir John Arundel of Uton, Devonshire, was fined 6000 marks for being with the Lancastrians at Tewkesbury.[48]

Even allowing that such heavy fines had been imposed on numbers of men greater than we now know it seems suspicious that the list of those attainted was so small and even more suspicious that none of these attainders was passed until the seventh and final session of the Parliament of 1473–5.[49] Then, apart from the earl of Oxford and his two brothers who had continued in armed rebellion until 1474 and were therefore probably attainted as a warning to others (and even then it must be remembered that Edward spared their lives), the list consists only of the three leaders of the Lincolnshire Rebellion of 1470, three esquires and a yeoman who had fought at Barnet and two knights and an esquire who had fought at Tewkesbury; ten men of whom certainly six and possibly nine were already dead by the time the act was passed in 1475.[50] The bigger fish escaped the net completely. The list is so plainly vestigial that some explanation must be sought for it. My own conjecture is that the explanation

[48] The tradition starts with Warkworth who wrote c. 1474–98 and is therefore a reliable witness. J. Warkworth, *A Chronicle of the First Thirteen Years of King Edward the Fourth*, ed. J. O. Halliwell (Camden Soc. 1839), 21–2; R. Fabyan, *The New Chronicles of England and France*, ed. H. Ellis (1811), 662; 'The Great Chronicle of London', op. cit. (1938), 220–1, 'Such as were Rych were hangid by the purs, and the othir that were nedy were hangid by the nekkis'; Polydore Vergil, 'Three Books of Polydore Vergil's English History . . .', op. cit. 155; *Three Fifteenth Century Chronicles*, ed. J. Gairdner (Camden Soc. 1880, 185). Commissions for Essex and the Cinque Ports, *Cal. Pat. Rolls, 1467–77*, 287–8. No commission has been found for Kent, Sussex and Surrey, but commissions certainly acted there, see the original reports sent into Chancery. Ancient Correspondence, LXVII, nos. 107–110 and 112. For the fines, see J. H. Ramsay, *Lancaster and York*, II, 387–8 and 388, n. 1; the list of names of those who received pardons after making fine and ransom covers three and a half pages in *Cal. Pat. Rolls, 1467–77*, 299–303. For Arundel, *Inquisitions Post Mortem Henry VII*, I, no. 30. Sums totalling £12,904 appear in the Tellers' Roll, E. 403/844, as gifts during the autumn of 1471. These 'dona' include £3333 in money or securities from Arundel and the sums from Kent. It may be that more of the total really consisted of fines. (Ramsay, op. cit. II, 390–1). A. Steel, *The Receipt of the Exchequer 1377–1485* (1954), 298–9, suspected that not all these sums were paid at the time. This suspicion is confirmed by the Arundel Inquisition Post Mortem referred to above.

[49] *Rot. Parl.* VI, 144–9.

[50] Richard Welles was executed in 1470, Robert Welles and probably Sir Thomas de la Launde were killed at 'Lose-cote' Field, Robert Harlyston and William Godmanston were slain at Barnet, John Delves at Tewkesbury and Sir Thomas Tresham executed after the battle. Robert Baynton's attainder was reversed for his son. John Durraunt was still alive when his attainder was reversed. Robert Gybbon's case is doubtful (*Rot. Parl.* VI, 218–19, 259–60, 281–3, 286–7, 307–8, 317–18, 526–7).

lies in a prolonged dispute about the Neville inheritance within the royal family itself. Edward's brothers, the dukes of Clarence and Gloucester, had married the earl of Warwick's two daughters and co-heiresses. Although the two royal dukes quarrelled bitterly about the division of the Neville estates they had at least one common aim—to gain possession of them and continue in possession, as far as possible, by inheritance at common law in right of their wives rather than by royal grant. The quarrel began in 1471. In May 1474 Edward consented to an act which treated the widowed countess of Warwick as if she were legally dead and thus, before its due time, transferred their maternal inheritance to her two daughters and co-heiresses, the duchesses of Clarence and Gloucester. There still remained the question of their paternal inheritance. Now two other acts passed in 1475 debarred the heirs male of Marquis Montagu from the Warwick inheritance—a significant proceeding for Montagu's son was (after Warwick's daughters) the heir at law to Warwick's own estates, the paternal inheritance of the two duchesses. If the two ladies died without leaving heirs of their bodies, which seemed very likely at the time, their husbands would lose these immensely valuable estates to Montagu's son. The two acts which were meant to prevent this possible loss reveal in passing that Edward had originally intended to attaint Marquis Montagu but had desisted at the request of Clarence, Gloucester and other lords. Now if Montagu had been attainted the same result would have been achieved; his son could not have inherited the Warwick estates. However, it would not have been consistent with justice to have attainted Montagu and other offenders without at the same time attainting Warwick, the greatest offender of all. If Warwick had been attainted, his daughters and their husbands could have obtained possession of the estates only by royal grant and such possession (particularly in view of the recent and numerous acts of resumption) would have been much less secure than if the estates had been obtained by direct inheritance. The clauses referring to the intended attainder in these acts, together with the fact that an act of attainder, so peculiar in its contents and so long postponed, was in the end passed only in the same session of Parliament as that in which the question of the Neville inheritance was finally settled, makes it reasonably plausible to suggest that the immunity of the Nevilles provided an umbrella for others. It was probably the resistance of Clarence and Gloucester which prevented the introduction of another whole-sale act of attainder.[51]

---

[51] *Rot. Parl.* VI, 101, 124-7; *Cal. Pat. Rolls, 1467-77*, 455-6, 486-7, 487-8. The marriages of Clarence and Gloucester had taken place in 1469 and 1472 respectively; Clarence, wishing to obtain all the lands himself, being vehement in opposition to his brother's marriage. Gloucester's only legitimate child, Edward, was born in 1473, and Clarence's son Edward, earl of Warwick, c. 21/25 February 1475 at the same time as the acts against Montagu's heir were passed. Any children which had been born previously no longer survived. In the conditions of the day the danger of the two duchesses dying without children surviving them was a real one. The oblique statement about attainder is for our purpose as important as the act itself, for it shows that the king's plans had changed under pressure. A statement of 18 March

In view of the often repeated asseverations of his cruelty and vindictiveness towards them Edward's attitude towards the nobility deserves special consideration. These accusations are based mainly on Commynes' *Mémoires*[52] and are picturesquely but dubiously illustrated by stories of the duke of Exeter, barefoot and ragged in the Low Countries begging his bread from door to door, of the disconsolate countess of Oxford deprived of her jointure and forced to live on the charity of her friends 'or what she myght get with her nedyll or other suche conynge as she excercysed', and of Henry Clifford concealed by his mother for a quarter of a century and brought up as a shepherd for fear of Edward's vengeance. These accusations and anecdotes seem at first sight to be supported by the fact that twelve out of sixteen attainders against noble families were still unreversed in 1483. The matter is, however, too complicated to be dealt with merely by reference to a few figures and a few colourful stories. Investigations of particular circumstances are called for.

Each of these cases has its special features. The Oxford family had shown very clearly that it would not co-operate with the Yorkists. Even after the twelfth earl and his eldest son had been executed for treason in 1462 his second son, John, in accordance with Edward's general policy of reconciliation, was soon restored to his inheritance, was made a knight of the Bath and acted as Great Chamberlain at the queen's coronation in 1465. Edward was so anxious to secure the friendship of the Oxfords that he even reversed Robert de Vere's attainder of 1399 and thus restored the original earldom of Oxford. In spite of all this Earl John was suspected of treason in the obscure plots of 1468, supported Warwick, fled to France and returned to fight with him at the battle of Barnet and later seized and held St Michael's Mount. Although after his capture when the Mount was taken he was imprisoned at Hammes, even then the act of attainder passed against him expressly spared

1472 on the Patent Roll shows that Edward had at some previous time granted both the paternal and the maternal lands to Clarence (I have not been able to trace the grant itself) who had then been forced to disgorge a 'parcel' of them for Gloucester but had received the promise that he should not be deprived of the remainder by act of parliament or otherwise (*Cal. Pat. Rolls, 1467–77*, 330). Clarence was created earl of Salisbury and earl of Warwick on 25 March 1472 (*Cal. Charter Rolls, 1427–1516*, 239–40). Clarence was clearly feeling insecure and all parties were well aware that any property settlements or grants made under any of the royal seals were automatically invalidated by an act of resumption unless exemption was obtained. The Resumption Acts of 1467 and 1473 expressly covered lands granted from the estates of the attainted. Clarence had obtained exemption from the act of 1467 but seems to have lost heavily in 1473. The Croyland Continuator comments on his resentment under the act of 1473 of the loss of the honour of Tutbury 'ac alias terras quam plurimas, quas ex Regia concessione prius obtinuerat'. *Rerum Anglicarum Scriptorum Veterum*, ed. W. Fulman (1684), i, 561. Gloucester was exempted from the 1473 act (*Rot. Parl.* v, 572, 578–9; vi 71, 75). Possession of the Warwick lands by royal grant, following attainder, would therefore have spelt insecurity.

    52 P. de Commynes, *Mémoires*, ed. J. Calmette and G. Durville (3 vols. 1924–5), I, 202; II, 333. Statements about the deaths of nearly all the nobles in the realm in *Cal. State Papers Milan*, ed. A. B. Hinds (1912), I, 77, the 'First Anonymous Croyland Continuator', Fulman, op. cit. 529–30, and the *Italian Relation of the Island of England*, ed. C. A. Sneyd (Camden Soc. 1847), 69, are clearly absurd.

his life.[53] His countess may have been living in poverty immediately after his attainder as during her husband's lifetime she was not legally entitled to either her own estates or her jointure, but in 1481 the king granted her an annuity of £100 during the life of her husband.[54] The story of the Shepherd Lord is very dubious indeed. It only makes its appearance for the first time eighty or ninety years later and in fact Henry Clifford was living unmolested in England as early as 1472,[55] though Edward never reversed his father's attainder nor restored his estates. Just as the countess of Warwick suffered from the cupidity of Clarence and Gloucester, it is probable that their sister Anne opposed the restoration of her husband, the duke of Exeter. In 1471 Anne of Exeter was already contemplating divorce in order to marry her paramour, Thomas St Ledger (one of Edward's squires of the Body), and she was equally determined to keep possession of the portions of the Exeter estates which had been granted to her in addition to her jointure.[56]

If we turn to others who were not so closely connected with the royal family a different story emerges. Somerset (whose case has already been described), the only other duke attainted under Edward, had after all been ostentatiously pardoned and in the end the family died out in the male line with the death of his brothers at Tewkesbury. Of the five earls and viscounts, one, Northumberland, was restored in 1469–70. Although the earl of Devon was executed in April 1461 his brother and heir, Henry Courteney, was given part of the family estates in Devon as early as June 1461 and but for subsequent treasons[57] might well have been allowed 'to work his way back' as others were. The earl of Wiltshire's brother, John, was recognized in 1474 as earl of Ormond and allowed the family's Irish lands.[58] Possibly the influence of Lord Hastings stood in the way of complete restoration as it also probably stood in the way

[53] *Scofield*, I, 231–3, 366, 376, 480–1, 494–6, 521, 529–30, 536–7, 542, 544, 547, 560, 568, 571, 573–4, 579–80; II, 29, 58–60, 85–9, 190–1, 213–14; G. Smith, *The Coronation of Elizabeth Wydeville* (1935), 18, 22, 23, 56, 61, *Rot. Parl.* v, 349 38; VI, 144 9. He, his two brothers and others of the garrison were promised their lives when the Mount surrendered.

[54] This was confirmed by Richard III. There seems to have been no intention of depriving her permanently of her property; it would only be hers in law after her husband's death. She received general pardons in 1475 and 1479 (*Cal. Pat. Rolls, 1467–77*, 507; *1467–85*, 157, 254, 450). The needlework story is found in Fabyan, op. cit. 663. It is not mentioned in either the Paston Letters or the Howard Memoranda, the sources most closely connected with the Oxford family.

[55] W. Dugdale, *The Baronage of England* (1675), I, 343; *Cal. Pat. Rolls, 1467–77*, 327, C. 66/529, m. 22. Hall tells the story that his father John, Lord Clifford slew the young earl of Rutland in cold blood after the battle of Wakefield. According to Holinshed the same Lord Clifford cut off the duke of York's head (he was killed in the battle) and sent it crowned with paper to Margaret of Anjou. The stories appear too late to be worthy of much credence. (*C.P.*)

[56] She married St Ledger in 1472. For estates see *Rot. Parl.* v, 548–9; VI, 215–17; *Cal. Pat. Rolls, 1461–7*, 9–10, 486; *1467–77*, 32–3, 137–8.

[57] He was implicated in the treasons of 1468 and executed in 1469. John, the youngest and only surviving brother, was slain at Tewkesbury, 1471. The title was re-created for the heir male, Edward Courtenay of Boconnock, Cornwall, a descendant of Edward, earl of Devon (1377–1419), in 1485. (*C.P.*)

[58] James, earl of Ormond, created earl of Wiltshire in tail male, 1449, was beheaded at Newcastle after the battle of Towton. He and his two brothers, John and Thomas, were

of the restoration of Viscount Beaumont, for Hastings had been granted a great part of their Midland estates. For political reasons it was essential to maintain Hastings' influence in an area as predominantly Lancastrian as Leicestershire had been before 1461.[59] Jasper Tudor, earl of Bedford, was far too closely connected with the house of Lancaster and with Richmond to be trusted. Of the barons, one had been executed in 1461 leaving no heirs.[60] Apart from this only two were shown no mercy before 1483; they both continued in rebellion, one until his capture and execution in 1469,[61] the other, like Oxford, was imprisoned after he was taken with the earl in St Michael's Mount in 1474.[62] A fourth, after receiving very generous treatment, again became implicated in seditious activities.[63] In two other cases attainders were reversed for heirs in 1472–3.[64] When the particular circumstances of each case are examined the impression emerges that it was not difficult before 1470 for attainted nobles to make their peace if they so wished and that the same is true of the 1470's, except where powerful interests greedy for property (particularly the king's siblings) intervened or Edward felt unable (or was unwilling) in one or two instances to take a risk.

Henry VII is generally credited by modern writers with pursuing a policy of mercy and comprehension—a 'mercy of the head not heart'—which has been compared very favourably with Edward's alleged cruelty.* This is certainly true (with reservations)[65] of his attitude towards those Yorkists who were attainted in 1485. Twenty attainders out of twenty-eight were reversed by 1495 and two more by the end of his reign. Although Henry encouraged Yorkists to make their peace and though he kept his head in a crisis and consistently refused to take panic measures, early writers were much harsher in

attainted by the English parliament in 1461 and in Ireland in 1462. The attainders were reversed in Ireland in 1475, but not in England until 1485. The earldom of Wiltshire lapsed as it had been granted to John in tail male and he died without direct descendants. (*C.P.*)

[59] For Edward's attitude towards Lord Hastings and the Central Midlands see Lander, *B.I.H.R.* op. cit. 154 and n. 5.

[60] Lord Rougemont-Gray. Nor was this attainder reversed under the Tudors.

[61] Lord Hungerford. Robert, Lord Hungerford and Moleyns, attainted (1461), was taken prisoner at Hexham and beheaded in 1464. His son, Sir Thomas, was convicted of treason in 1469 and beheaded. For the ultimate reversal of the attainder and the division of property between the heir general and the heir male see *C.P.*

[62] Edmund, Lord Roos. Thomas, Lord Roos was executed after his capture at Hedgley Moor, 1464. His son, Edmund, was a child and therefore could not be considered in any way a political asset. He escaped overseas sometime before 1485 for his father's attainder of 1461 was reversed before he returned to England, but even then the lands were reserved during the king's pleasure. In 1492 he was found to be weak-witted and this may already have been suspected earlier.

[63] Richard, Lord Welles and Willoughby. Leo, Lord Welles was attainted in 1461. His son Richard, in spite of the attainder, sat in parliament in his wife's right as Lord Willoughby in 1461, 1463–5, and 1468. This is all the more significant as she was dead by 1460. In 1464 he was given his father's chattels, in 1465 some of his father's lands were restored to him and the attainder was reversed in 1467. In the course of the Lincolnshire rebellion he was beheaded in 1470 and a formal act of attainder passed against him in 1475 (*Cal. Pat. Rolls, 1461–7*, 357, 468; *Rot. Parl.* v, 617–18; vi, 144–9).

[64] John, Lord Neville and Randolph, Lord Dacre (*Rot. Parl.* vi, 24–5, 43–5).

[65] With regard to his attitude to their property, see below, pp. 107 ff.

their judgements of the king's attitude towards those who took part in the various plots and risings of his reign. A careful reading of the Great Chronicle of London and of Polydore Vergil shows that he could be quite ruthless in dealing with the aftermath of conspiracy.[66] Polydore Virgil indeed emphasized his notable severity and Bacon quite failed in his attempts to explain away his fluctuating attitude, now merciful, now harsh, remarking 'it was a strange thing to observe the variety and inequality of the king's executions and pardons: and a man would think it at the first a kind of lottery or chance'.[67] Although at the beginning of his reign opposition to wholesale attainders made itself heard, so far as we know, for the first time in Parliament,[68] Henry's subsequent record does not compare favourably with Edward's. Henry attainted 138 people in the course of his reign as against Edward's 140 and they reversed forty-six and forty-two attainders respectively which had passed at their own instigation, but whereas under Edward after the mass attainders of 1461–3 only twenty-seven new names were added to the list each crisis of Henry's reign was followed by new attainders right up to 1504 when more were passed than in any other Parliament of his day.[69] Once again, however, it is unfair to pass judgement on numbers alone as Edward never had to face a major conspiracy after 1471.[70] Even allowing, however, that political circumstances justified the upward curve of Henry's attainders as compared with the downward curve of Edward's an examination of the terms on which the proscribed obtained their reversals throws an unfavourable light on Henry's attitude and to some extent, perhaps, upholds the traditional but now challenged view of his avarice.

Petitions for the reversal of attainders presented under the early Tudors show that some of those suing for reversal had to compound with the king beforehand—a practice which, if it existed under Edward IV, has left no traces on the Parliament Rolls of his reign or elsewhere. Such petitions also seem to show that Henry VII and Henry VIII were much readier to allow

[66] 'The King wished (as he said) to keep all Englishmen obedient through fear . . . .' He emphasizes Henry's fear of riches in his greater subjects and Henry's own rapacity. Polydore Vergil, *Anglica Historia*, ed. D. Hay (Camden Soc. 1950), 126 9.

[67] *The Works of Francis Bacon*, ed. J. Spedding and others (6 vols., 1858), VI, 183. Bacon speculates on the reason for this saying that Henry must have had cause for such variation and states that he probably distinguished between 'people that did rebel on wantonness, and them that did rebel upon want' but admitted that this was mere supposition.

[68] In 1485 'Howbeit, ther was many gentlemen agaynst it, but it wold not be, for yt was the Kings pleasure', *The Plumpton Correspondence*, ed. T. Stapleton (Camden Soc. 1839), 49. The Third Anonymous Croyland Continuator, Fulman, op. cit. 581, states that although the attainders were much more moderate than under Edward IV they aroused considerable censure in parliament. This seems to have been a spontaneous protest whereas that of 1473 had been inspired by Clarence and Gloucester. See also *The Red Paper Book of Colchester*, ed. W. G. Benham (1902), 64.

[69] The figures are 1485–6, 28; 1487, 28; 1489–90, 8; 1491–2, 1; 1495, 24; 1504, 51. Viscount Lovell was attainted twice—in 1485–6 and 1495. The only parliament without attainders was that of 1497.

[70] There was, however, a fair amount of disturbance and disorder in various parts of the country judging from commissions issued to various people to admit to grace those who had stirred up insurrections, e.g. *Cal. Pat. Rolls, 1467–77*, 515.

courtiers and officials to hang on to their gains at the expense of those pardoned. Though some of the attainted under Edward IV bought back their
lands from grantees, there are only two cases (and those quite minor) where
the actual enrolled petition specifies a reservation for a particular person.
Although after 1485 the legal formulae of reversals were much more carefully
and precisely drafted it is hard to believe that the far richer detail given about
particular reservations is entirely due to such a change of practice.[71] Now as
far as the nobility are concerned there were only nine attainders during Henry's
reign and of these he himself reversed five and Henry VIII one more. This
appears to be not ungenerous, but particulars of individual transactions show
a rigid aspect quite unlike Edward's ostentatious mercy in the 1460's. There
is only one reversal of a nobleman's attainder under Henry VII which shows
no special features.[72] All the rest exhibit reservations in some degree or other.
With John, Lord Zouche, for example, Henry's attitude fluctuated at first,
then hardened into meanness. In July 1486, Zouche had to produce sureties
in 2000 marks to be of good behaviour and a few days later was granted a
pardon under the great seal for his offences. Ostensibly the pardon also
restored his lands but unless Henry changed his mind after the pardon had
been issued this must be interpreted as permission merely to *acquire* his lands
again for when the attainder was reversed in Parliament in 1489 the reversal
was not to extend to the estates forfeited under the act of 1485. Zouche was
permitted to inherit only the lands of his grandmother, Elizabeth, the wife of
Lord Scrope of Bolton. The attainder was completely reversed in 1495 by
another act—at a price. In November, Zouche sold five manors to Sir Reynold
Bray for £1000 'since Sir Reynold helped to obtain grace for Sir John from
his liege lord to repeal the attainder and recover his lande'. These five manors

[71] The greater number of reservations in petitions for reversal may possibly be due to
petitioners including clauses safeguarding the interests of grantees with whom they had
previously reached some agreement. On the other hand evidence from sources other than the
Rolls of Parliament is also much less for the period before 1485. Under Edward IV I have
found only three cases of reservation or bargaining (apart from the sales referred to in the
reversals of Sir Nicholas Latymer and Sir Thomas Tresham, see below, pp. 139–41), two on
the Rolls of Parliament (Thomas Danyell and John Delves) and one (Sir Robert Whittingham)
elsewhere (*Rot. Parl.* vi, 104–5, 218–19; *Cal. Pat. Rolls, 1467–77*, 329; J. S. Roskell, 'William
Allington of Bottisham', *Proc. Camb. Ant. Soc.* LII (1959), 51–2). In none of these cases did
the king himself benefit. It should also be added that we have no evidence from before 1485
in any way comparable to the Act of Authority of 1523 (*Rot. Parl.* VII, cxxi–cxxxi), which gave
Henry VIII power to reverse by letters patent attainders passed under Richard III and
Henry VII. Henry appears to have made very little use of the act (only one attainder was
reversed under its powers) but appended to it are thirty-nine clauses exempting grantees from
the consequences of reversal. Many of these clauses refer to attainders which had already
been reversed and also reveal that several persons whose petitions for reversal contain no
reservations had not succeeded in recovering all their property. The question could only be
decided one way or the other by evidence of negotiations between parties carried on before
the reversal of attainders but on balance greater difficulties after 1485 seem to be indicated.
   Although there were a few royal sales of land in both periods these seem to have been
exceptional.
   [72] Walter Devereux, Lord Ferrers, reversed for his son John (*Cal. Pat. Rolls, 1485–94*, 61;
Rot. Parl. VI, 414–15; *C.P.*).

had previously been granted to Bray by the king. The act also protected the interests of Giles, Lord Daubeney and his heirs in certain properties which had been granted to them. The act stated that Zouche might take over any of these reserved properties only if he could persuade the grantees to sell them. Nor is this the end of the tale of losses. Other Zouche estates which had been granted to three prominent courtiers, Sir John Savage, Sir Richard Edgecombe and Robert Willoughby, were still in the hands of their descendants in 1523.[73] Lord Zouche had to pay a high price to obtain the reversal of his attainder.

The story of the Howards shows rather different features—the way in which an attainder was used as a form of control over a potentially dangerous, but also potentially useful man. Even a much less avaricious and grasping character than John, Lord Howard would have had reason to feel aggrieved against Edward IV for the king had denied him the moiety of the lands of the Mowbray dukes of Norfolk to which he was the heir at law.[74] Richard III, who resorted to political bribery on a large scale, not only allowed him the inheritance[75] but also gave him additional rewards on a very considerable scale. By the time of his death at Bosworth Field, Howard was duke of Norfolk and a great magnate with estates extending into nearly a dozen counties. After the disasters of 1485 rumour went round that Henry intended to execute Norfolk's heir, Thomas, earl of Surrey. Although both father and son were attainted and all the Howard properties seized, Surrey escaped execution; he was imprisoned in the Tower of London under the terms of a pardon which left him completely at the king's mercy.[76] A curious incident then followed. During the earl of Lincoln's invasion of England in 1487 the Lieutenant of the Tower is said to have offered him the opportunity to escape. This attempt to lure Surrey to final ruin (as the episode is usually interpreted) failed for he refused the offer saying 'he wolde not departe thens unto suche tyme as he that commaunded hym thether shuld commaunde hym out agcyn'.[77] He remained in the Tower until January 1489 when he was released after taking an oath of allegiance. Release did not mean return to the eminence and riches to which the Howards had so quickly risen under Richard III. During the session of Parliament which began in the same month as his release from the Tower the

[73] Cal. Close Rolls, 1485–1500, 34–5, 270; Cal. Pat. Rolls, 1485–94, 93, 96, 101–2, 129, 231, 315, 380; Rot. Parl. VI, 424, 484–5; VII, cxxiv–cxxv, cxxviii, cxxx. The five manors sold to Bray had been granted to him successively for life, in fee tail and in fee simple. Grants of Zouche's lands were made after the act of 1489, e.g. Cal. Pat. Rolls, 1485–94, 315, 340–1.

[74] The king married Anne, the Mowbray heiress, to his son, Richard, then aged six, and although she died almost immediately arranged for his son to keep the lands (Rot. Parl. VI, 168–71, C.P.).

[75] That John Howard actually received possession of the lands is shown by the statement in Rot. Parl. VI, 478–9.

[76] '... provided that he stand his trial if anyone implead him of the premises, and that it shall be lawful for the King to imprison him during pleasure....' (Cal. Pat. Rolls, 1485–94, 86, 27 March 1486).

[77] See the epitaph in J. Weever, Ancient Funerall Monuments (1631), 834–40.

act of attainder was reversed but with wide reservations. He was restored to the title of earl of Surrey only and the restoration of property was limited to the lands of his wife's inheritance, any lands which he might inherit from ancestors other than his father and lands which the king had granted to the earl of Oxford and Lord Daubeney. Within three months of his release,[78] after the assassination of the earl of Northumberland at Topcliffe Park, he was sent north with a force to quell the insurgents. In the second session of the same Parliament later in the year Surrey was rewarded with an extension of the terms of his reversal. He was now given back the lands of the Howards except those which the king had already granted away but with the agreement of the king he might buy back such lands. This second act did not restore to him his moiety of the lands of the Mowbray dukes of Norfolk nor the grants which he had received under Richard III.[79] Further service followed when Surrey became under-warden to the young Prince Arthur in the wardenships of the Eastern and Western Marches. In the spring of 1491 he put down a second rising at Ackworth near Pontefract and by his merciful attitude won considerable popularity in the North.[80] He received his reward the following year when another act of Parliament was passed in his favour. At last Surrey was allowed to inherit all his property except for the reservation that all grants previously made by the king were to stand, though any reserved rents paid to the king were in future to go to Howard. This means that Surrey had now recovered those estates of the Howards and of that part of the Mowbray inheritance to which he was entitled which the king had not already granted away. The king, however, by certain legal concessions in the act made it easier for him to negotiate with grantees to buy them back.[81] Henry recognized loyal service and according to his own cautious lights he rewarded it. Surrey had shown both loyalty and efficiency. He had been tested and he was restored by stages. He never recovered the immense grants from the Crown Lands which had enriched his family under Richard III; that was not to be expected; grants which had been gained and lost under such circumstances were generally lost for ever. He received his lawful inheritance—the Howards' hereditary lands and the moiety of the Mowbray estates to which he was entitled as one of the heirs of the Mowbray family.[82] Henry was not, however, prepared to alienate supporters by revoking grants which he had made from these estates. Surrey apparently had to rely on negotiations with the individual

[78] Weever, op. cit., says ten weeks, but he was not apparently sent north until after Percy's death which took place on 28 April.

[79] It also provides for exemptions in favour of particular persons.

[80] *Cal. Pat. Rolls, 1485–94*, 314; Weever, op. cit. The Plumpton Correspondence, op. cit. 95–7. He severely punished the ringleaders but sued to the king for pardon for the rest.

[81] For the restoration of title and lands, see *Rot. Parl.* VI, 410–11, 426–8, 448–50.

[82] In 1507 Surrey was granted licence to enter 'on lands of the inheritance of the said John (duke of Norfolk) or the said earl which Elizabeth late duchess of Norfolk held for life with remainder to the said earl' (*Cal. Pat. Rolls, 1494–1509*, 543). Elizabeth Talbot was the widow of the last Mowbray duke.

grantees.[83] Nor did Henry ever restore the title of duke of Norfolk—that only came after nineteen more long years of service as soldier, ambassador, councillor and administrator and after his victory over the Scots at Flodden Field.[84]

The treatment of all other nobles whose attainders were reversed shows similarities to the treatment meted out to Zouche or Howard.[85] The reversals of men of less than noble rank tell the same tale. The way in which the system of control operated can be seen from the career of a 'gentleman' of London, Thomas Kyllyngworth. He was attainted in 1504 for his support of Perkin Warbeck and granted a pardon in 1506 which contained the proviso that whenever the king wished to examine him alone or cause him to be examined by someone of the royal council upon any matter touching the king's majesty or the security of the realm, on any treasons and misprisions done with his knowledge and consent he should clearly declare them and the circumstances surrounding them.[86] Other cases show Henry imposing much harsher conditions on those who sought the reversal of their attainders[87] and even obscure yeomen were made to pay for it.[88]

[83] For cases of Surrey buying back estates or rents see *Cal. Close Rolls, 1485–1500*, 117, 276, 362–3. In March 1490 the earl of Derby, to whom considerable estates had been granted, was sufficiently concerned at what was happening to take out an exemplification of the second act of 1489 in Surrey's favour (*Cal. Pat. Rolls, 1485–94*, 318).

[84] Together with very considerable additional grants of land (*Rot. Parl.* VII, xlv–xlvi, xlvii–xlix).

[85] (1) Lord FitzWalter, att. 1495, and later executed after attempted escape from imprisonment in Calais. Under indentures dated 24 July 20 Henry VII his son Robert bound himself to pay the King £5000. It seems reasonable to connect this payment with the reversal of his attainder under letters patent the following November. He was allowed to pay in instalments of £1000 p.a. This did not mean complete restitution for grants were made from his property in 1506 and in 1509 he was granted the lease at a rent of £100 p.a. of the manors of Hampnell and Disse, Co. Norfolk, which had been forfeited under the act of attainder. He took the precaution of getting the attainder repealed in Henry VIII's first Parliament. At least two payments of £1000 each were made under the indentures (*Cal. Pat. Rolls, 1494–1509*, 444–5, 454, 467, 483, 522; *Letters and Papers Foreign and Domestic of the Reign of Henry VIII*, I, nos. 341, 811, 4347; P.R.O. E. 36/214, 511; B.M. Lansdowne MS. 127, fol. 18 d).

(2) Lord Audley, att. 1497. The act of reversal of 1514 for his son John exempts grants made to Lord Dudley and others. In 1523 John had still not recovered an advowson granted away in 1508 (Parliament Roll, C. 65/132, m. 4; *Rot. Parl.* VII, liiii–lv, cxxvi–cxxvii; *Cal. Pat. Rolls, 1494–1505*, 592).

(3) The de la Poles were, because of their royal blood and extreme unreliability, atypical. Nevertheless their treatment shows similarities to that of other families, e.g. the allotment in 1493 for £5000 to Edmund de la Pole of certain lands and manors as though his brother had never been attainted and his reduction from duke to earl. See *Rot. Parl.* VI, 397–400, 474–8; VII, cxxii; *Cal. Pat. Rolls, 1494–1509*, 259–61.

[86] *Rot. Parl.* VI, 544–8; *Cal. Pat. Rolls, 1494–1509*, 468. The pardon of 1506 was limited in its application. It only 'abled to the laws'. The attainder in this case was never apparently reversed.

[87] Thomas Tyrell had to pay £1738 for the reversal of his own and his father's attainders (E. 36/214, 519; B.M. Lansdowne MS. 127, fol. 41 d). Roger Wake, att. 1485, in order to obtain reversal in 1487, agreed to leave the king free to grant away certain of his lands and grants already made to Viscount Welles, Sir Humphrey Stanley and others were reserved (*Rot. Parl.* VI, 275–8, 393–4). Elizabeth Brews paid the king £500 for the lands of Sir Gilbert Debenham and a promise to get his attainder reversed at the next parliament (*Cal. Pat. Rolls, 1494–1509*, pp. 238–9). For the hard conditions imposed on George, son of William Catesby (att. 1485), see *Rot. Parl.* VI, 275–8, 490–2. A priest, James Harrington, had to pay 80 marks (E. 36/214, 445).   [88] For footnote see following page.

Under both the Yorkists and the early Tudors the way to reversal for men of less than noble rank was not always the simple process of petitioning the king in Parliament for a pardon under the great seal. It was often a case of 'working one's way back' to the king's satisfaction from legal oblivion to full legal rights. Some achieved their restoration step by step, either being pardoned their offences but having their lands restored to them only some time later, or, conversely, received a grant of a fraction of their forfeited estates followed some time later by the reversal of the attainder and fuller restitution. Others were less fortunate in that they found it necessary to buy back their lands between the date of their pardon under the great seal and the formal reversal of their attainder in Parliament. Edward IV, though he does not seem to have made offenders compound to his own advantage, was not always prepared to risk alienating useful friends by depriving them of their gains when exercising his prerogative of mercy. One of the most interesting cases is that of Sir Nicholas Latymer. After fighting on the Lancastrian side at the battles of Wakefield and Towton, Latymer was attainted in 1461 and some of his lands were granted to Sir John Howard and to Edmund Grey. Latymer was still with Queen Margaret in the North and was at Dunstanborough when the garrison surrendered in December 1462. He swore allegiance to Edward at the same time as Somerset and received his pardon at the end of June 1463—the period in which Edward, for urgent political reasons, was trying to win over all the ex-Lancastrians he could. In his final petition for reversal Latymer stated that the earls of Warwick and Worcester had promised him all his former possessions and this is allowed in the full text of his pardon, but in fact it was interpreted only as 'habled unto youre Lawes, but not restored unto his lyflode'. Frustrated though he must have been by this interpretation Latymer lost no time in setting about the recovery of his property. During the next few months some of his actions can be traced in the financial memoranda kept by Sir John Howard and his household officials. At the end of October Howard paid William Farnevelle for riding to Sir Nicholas; a matter which Howard must have regarded as of some importance, for the payment was made in the middle of his journey to take part in the northern campaigns. This is the first of a number of entries scattered amongst the Howard memoranda recording negotiations between Howard and Latymer for Sir Nicholas to buy back the manors of 'Develeche' and 'Donteche'—the properties which the king had granted to Howard. On 26 March, Howard and Latymer discussed certain matters at the Mermaid Inn in Bread Street following which an indenture was drawn up. Under this indenture various payments were made to Howard. Some time, still early in 1464, they met again at Sonning where various payments were made and others agreed upon. Then, on 12 March 1465, a new agreement was made (possibly as a result of

---

[88] E.g. the Cornish yeoman Thomas Polgreven paid £40 and six others paid £30 between them, see B.M. Lansdowne MS. 127, fol. 34 d (entry on Thomas Gosworthdogga).

difficulties which Latymer was experiencing in raising money punctually) stating that Howard should receive 1000 marks of which £40 were to be paid cash down the same day and arrangements were made to pay the balance in instalments. Judging from the terms of his reversal Latymer had also been buying back land from other people besides Howard. This case raises the problem of how a man like Latymer who was supposed to have forfeited every acre and every penny in 1461 contrived to raise very considerable sums of money both in cash and loans until at least the middle of 1466 (when the king made him a special grant of some of his former estates)—a period of rather over two years from the time he received his pardon. The Howard jottings, though tantalizingly obscure, make it clear that the sale of the two manors was not the only financial transaction between Howard and Latymer. Howard was powerful at court. Latymer needed help in high places.[89] Howard presumably knew the terms of Latymer's pardon and, fully aware of Edward's very conciliatory attitude towards ex-Lancastrians at this time, was shrewd enough to realize that it might become more difficult for him to retain the two manors if Latymer petitioned for reversal at the next parliament and therefore drove a hard bargain while he could.[90]

At least one man recovered all his property by purchase. This was Sir Thomas Tresham, one of the most notorious of all Lancastrians, who had been speaker of the parliament of 1459 which had proscribed the Yorkists.[91] His petition for reversal is of great interest for it shows the insecurity in which a man under attaint was forced to live even though he had received a pardon and had recovered his lands:

the seid Sir Thomas, by the Licence of your Highnes, hath bargayned and agreed with all suche persones as it hath liked your Highnes to graunte his Lyvelode unto, and the same Lyvelode he hath aswell by your Graunte to hym and to his heires, as by the releases, astates and confirmations of the seid persones, the whiche sommes by hym content for the same, amounte to the somme of MM Marc and more, for which of grete parte he resteth yette endetted to dyvers of his frendes, for the contentment whereof he can make noo chevysaunce of his Lyvelode, in asmuche as noo persone wolle take it for any suerte of their payment, nor bargeyn, nor marye with

[89] Latymer had manors of Howard's at farm, though they were not his own former manors. It is tempting to think (although there is no proof) that Howard, having obtained his pound of flesh, used his influence in the grant of 1466 and the reversal of 1468.

[90] Wedgwood, *Biographies*, 527; Scofield, I, 265; *Cal. Pat. Rolls, 1461–7*, 269, 525; *Manners and Household Expenses of England in the Thirteenth and Fifteenth Centuries*, ed. T. H. Turner (Roxburghe Club, 1841), 176, 177, 231, 251–2, 466, 468–9. It has to be remembered that these notebooks consist of jottings only and are by no means a complete record of Howard's financial transactions. William Worcester, op. cit. 780, incorrectly states that his lands were restored in 1462. The full text of his pardon shows that it was originally intended to restore his lands '. . .relaxavimus eidem Nicholo universa et singula forisfacta. . .' (Patent Roll, C. 66/505, m. 10). His petition for reversal in 1468, *Rot. Parl.* vi, 230–1, states, 'he hath bargayned and agreed *with dyvers such persones* as it hath lyked your seid Highnes to graunte his said lyvelode unto . . .; the which somes he hath content unto the seid persones by payment and suerte, to his importable charge.'

[91] *Rot. Parl.* v, 616–17. By his pardon he had merely been 'abled unto youre Lawes'.

his sonne and heire, because of the seid Acte, withoute that he, by the merciable favour and socour of your good grace, may be restored by auctorite of youre Parlement.

The effects of attainders on different families varied enormously. We have just discussed the cases of two men who were pardoned their treasons within three years of their proscription and had been restored in blood and lands within seven but were presumably left saddled with a heavy load of debt because powerful interests ranged against them had seen to it that they paid heavily for their restoration. Others like the squire Robert Bollyng and his wife and children were reduced to 'povert and miserye'[92] and Sir James Harrington who was attainted in 1485 and admitted to allegiance in 1486 died in 1488 too poor, it is said, even to pay the chancery clerks for his pardon.[93] Yet by no means all families were reduced to debt or destitution. Some had settlements outside the scope of the acts which left various of their members with considerable incomes. Dowagers, whose length of days could be such a curse to their heirs under normal conditions, became a blessing when the head of the family was attainted for their jointures rescued a considerable proportion of the family income from forfeiture. In the 1460's, for example, during the attainder of Henry Percy IV, the two dowager countesses of Northumberland may have enjoyed between them as much as £1850–£1900 a year gross from their own estates and jointures.[94] The private estates and jointures of Margaret, Lady Hungerford, Katherine, Viscountess Beaumont and Eleanor, duchess of Somerset were by no means insignificant. Other types of settlements were also useful in such circumstances. Even where there were no settlements outside the scope of the law of forfeiture wives and families were not always left destitute. Small allowances were made sufficient for their support but insufficient to allow their diversion to treasonable political activities.[95]

---

[92] There is less reason to doubt this statement than some of a similar kind for it was made after at least some of his property had been restored. Although his attainder was not reversed in Parliament until 1473 he had received a pardon which covered the attainder and the king had separately granted him some of his lands (*Cal. Pat. Rolls, 1461–7*, 271, C. 66/505, m. 7).

[93] *Rot. Parl.* VI, 275–8; *Inquisitions Post Mortem, Henry VII*, ii, no. 44; W. Campbell, *Materials for a History of the Reign of Henry VII etc.* (Rolls Ser. 1873–7), I, 542.

[94] The widow of the second earl had a dower interest of £500 p.a. from her first husband Richard, Lord Despenser and settled estates worth £650–£700 p.a. She also had an annuity of £200 on the Yorkshire estates. The widow of the third earl held the Poynings' inheritance worth £500 p.a. in her own right (J. M. W. Bean, *The Estates of the Percy Family, 1416–1537* (1957), 83, 85, 91). For proof that the second earl's widow was still living in 1465 see *Cal. Pat. Rolls, 1461–7*, 455. For a general account of the incomes enjoyed by dowagers in the fifteenth century see T. B. Pugh and C. D. Ross, 'The English Baronage and the Income Tax of 1436', *B.I.H.R.* XXVI (1953), 4–13, 26–8.

[95] Isabel Horne, 40 marks p.a., Catherine Arundel £100 p.a. (*Cal. Pat. Rolls, 1461–7*, 7; *1476–85*, 417). It was more usual, however, to place a small income or lands in the hands of reliable officers to be administered for their use, e.g. Elizabeth Fulford, Philippa, Lady Roos Elizabeth Tailboys, Eleanor, Lady Hungerford, Anne Hampden, Joan, Lady Zouche (*Cal. Pat. Rolls, 1461–7*, 64, 87, 89, 181; *1485–94*, 222, 223).

Although attainder did not necessarily mean beggary, on the other hand reversal did not necessarily imply complete restitution. Even if all his estates were ultimately returned to their owner they may have been much impoverished. It was generally realized that the tenure of forfeited estates was insecure[96] and some of the new owners undoubtedly took the opportunity to squeeze as much as possible out of such estates while the going was good.[97] Worse still, the reversal of an attainder was one thing; persuading the grantees to whom the estates concerned had passed to give them up was another and often much more difficult thing. It was easiest to recover possession if, in the meantime, the grantee had died without heirs or had turned against the government.[98] Others, particularly under the early Tudors, found it impossible to compel restitution from powerful grantees who were determined to hang on to their gains. Some people, as has been said, recognized such harsh facts when they petitioned for reversal and the wording of their petitions, which include exemption clauses in favour of particular people, shows that they had previously come to an agreement with some of the grantees. Sir Humphrey Stafford of Grafton, whose father had been attainted in 1485, never managed to recover his paternal lands. They had been granted to far too powerful a man, Sir Gilbert Talbot. He managed to recover only his maternal inheritance and even that was denied him until 1514, ten years after the reversal of his father's attainder (an interval of time which probably shows that he had considerable difficulty in doing so), and henceforward the Staffords of Grafton became the Staffords of Blatherwick.[99]

The Berkeleys of Welley never managed to recover the manor of Northfield and Welley which Lord Dudley had bought from the king in 1486 for 1000 marks after the attainder of Sir William Berkeley, even though they were prepared to buy it back and Sir Richard Berkeley even obtained parliamentary authority to bargain with the Dudleys for the purchase of his family's former property. The struggle went on for years but in vain.[100]

[96] See remarks on public opinion and forfeiture (see below, pp. 118-9 and nn. 104 and 105).

[97] When Thomas, Lord Roos' estates were restored to him in 1485 after a quarter of a century in other hands he alleged that they had suffered great waste and destruction—a plausible enough complaint, for it is known that Lord Hastings (to whom most of his Midland properties had been granted) had stripped the lead from the roofs of Belvoir Castle *c.* 1475 and had left the building to tumble into ruin. Stoke Albany, another Roos property, is said to have suffered the same treatment (*Rot. Parl.* VI, 310–11; N. H. Bell, *The Huntingdon Peerage* (1820), 20).

[98] E.g. the greater part of Sir John Fortescue's lands had been granted to Lord Wenlock who was killed in the battle of Tewkesbury in 1471, leaving no heirs, and they were therefore in the king's hands again when his attainder was reversed in 1473.

[99] Wedgwood, *Biographies*, 792–3; *Rot. Parl.* VI, 275–8; *V.C.H. Worc.* III, 125–6. Stafford's name is included in the act of 1504 (*Rot. Parl.* VI, 526) giving the king power to reverse attainders by letters patent but no reversal is enrolled on the Patent Roll.

[100] The story, though very interesting, is too long and complicated to give in detail here. It was also somewhat confused by grants made to Jasper Tudor. The matter came before Parliament in 1495, 1504 and 1523 as well as being the subject of numerous discussions elsewhere. In 1531 Lord Dudley sold the manor to Richard Jervaise, a London mercer (*Rot. Parl.*

Nor did the acts affect only those specifically condemned. The prospect of forfeiture could adversely affect the prosperity of near relations and excessive zeal or mistakes in administration could cause inconvenience and loss of property to quite innocent parties from the dower duchess of Somerset to a simple squire, thus adding to the already very considerable risks and troubles of fifteenth- and early sixteenth-century landowners.[101] On the other hand, one exceptionally fortunate family emerged from the confusion of an attainder with its estates increased. When the third earl of Northumberland was attainted in 1461 his family had not completely recovered the lands which they had lost as a result of their rebellion under Henry IV. Under the terms of their restoration of 1414, confirmed in 1439, the family had recovered only the lands which they had held in fee tail; those held in fee simple were excluded. When, however, in 1469–70 Edward restored the fourth earl because at that moment he so badly needed his influence to counteract that of the Nevilles in the North, some of the manors held in fee simple were also restored.[102]

It is now possible to draw at least some tentative conclusion from these investigations. It seems, in the light of the evidence available, that a re-appraisal of the actual effects as distinct from the consequences possible if the law of attainder had been fully enforced is appropriate. If Friar Brackley's statement is correct the first comprehensive act passed in the Parliament of Devils was intended by its authors to compass the utter ruin of their political opponents and we may well believe that in 1461 the triumphant Yorkists were

vi, 483–5, 487–8, 552–4; vii, cxxix; *Cal. Pat. Rolls, 1485–94*, 64, 83–4, 260, 266; *1494–1509*, 59, 224; *Cal. Close Rolls, 1485–1500*, 115–16; *V.C.H. Worc.* iii, 194–5). Northfield and Welley were one manor though records often refer to 'manors'.

For other cases of reservation see Edward, duke of Buckingham and John, Lord Audley (*Rot. Parl.* vi, 43–4, 213, 285–6; vii, liv–lv).

[101] In 1464 when the dowager duchess of Somerset was imprisoned for a time after her son's flight she complained that certain of her tenants were refusing to pay their rents (*Scofield*, I, 313; Scofield, 'Henry, Duke of Somerset, and Edward IV', *E.H.R.* xxi (1906), 300–2). In February 1461 Sir John Fortescue attempted to settle his wife's jointure. Because he was then 'in trouble and jeopardy' the conveyances were hastily and carelessly drafted and there was trouble and uncertainty about the settlement as late as 1480 (*Cal. Close Rolls, 1476–85*, 199). See also the cases of Hugh Moyne and John Fauntleroy (*Rot. Parl.* vi, 495–6; *Cal. Pat. Rolls, 1494–1509*, 88–9). For other allegations of wrongful seizure, *Cal. Pat. Rolls, 1461–7*, 231, 549–50; *1467–77*, 127–8, 193–4, 200, 445–6, 453–4, 522–3, 584–5; *1476–85*, 364–5, 508, 523, 523–4, 530, 539–40; *1485–94*, 208, 307–8, 397–8, 399–400, 439–41, 473–4; *1494–1509*, 208. In some cases those who had been attainted are alleged to have wrongfully occupied the lands. For the normal hazards of the fifteenth-century landowner see K. B. McFarlane, 'The Investment of Sir John Fastolf's Profits of War', *T.R. Hist.S.* 5th ser. vii (1957), 111–14, and P. S. Lewis, 'Sir John Fastolf's Lawsuit over Tichwell 1448–1455', *Hist. Journal*, I (1958), 1–20.

[102] For the very complicated history of the Percy estates in the fourteenth century, see Bean, op. cit. 69–111. The manors formerly held in fee simple which were restored in 1470 were Shilbotle, Pennington, Guyzance and Beauley. Mr Bean suggests that the crown then lost sight of the distinction between the entailed estates and those held in fee simple; confusion partly due to the fact that in 1461 the third earl had been holding them on lease from the crown. Moreover, Henry Percy IV seems to have been able to bilk some of his father's creditors as the attainder of 1461 had extinguished certain of the financial dispositions made by the third earl (ibid. 134 and n. 4). Henry Percy IV made very considerable acquisitions under Richard III (ibid. 112).

no less revengeful in their attitude towards those who had proscribed them. If the letter of the law had been carried out and the proscriptions had remained permanently enforced a number of noble (and other) families would have disappeared from English life, vast estates would have escheated permanently to the Crown and attainders would have been one of the major factors in renewing the landed endowment of the Crown—the system which, in its most advanced form, has come to be known as 'Tudor feudalism'. For various reasons, however, attainders in the majority of cases were not permanent. The acts of attainder passed under Henry VI and Richard III were quickly and completely reversed. Of the attainders of Edward's reign which were never reversed, only nine affected men above the rank of esquire, while the corresponding figure for Henry VII is thirteen. Within this total of twenty-two, five attainders (affecting four families) were those against nobles and in three of these cases there were no direct male heirs to carry on the line.[103] Acts of attainder, as such, can therefore hardly be said to have produced any significant diminution in the numbers of the greater English families.

Though Edward IV and his advisers may for a short time have intended that attainders should stand for ever there is no evidence that they ever intended to exact the extreme penalty. In 1461, itself, the process of attainder seems to have been somewhat haphazard. A considerable number of quite obscure men were condemned while prominent Lancastrians were allowed (possibly intentionally) to escape. During the 1460's the desperate need for support from almost any quarter led the king to pardon and make use of prominent Lancastrians like Sir Henry Bellingham, Sir Humphrey Neville of Brancepeth, the duke of Somerset, and, rather later, Sir Richard Tunstall and the earl of Northumberland. The 1470's saw few attainders, possibly due almost accidentally to disputes within the royal family, but perhaps we should offset against this a policy of severe fines and heavy financial penalties. At the same time Edward adopted a policy of comprehension and mercy towards those who had suffered attainder in his earlier years and even the notorious exiles of Bar-sur-Mighel made their peace and recovered most of their property, and some like Morton even became trusted councillors at the court of the monarch whom they had so long opposed.

Henry VII's reign, if the evidence is strictly comparable, shows a marked contrast to Edward's. Although Henry was merciful to the Yorkists who were attainted in 1485, his reign as a whole, much more than Edward IV's, shows a continued resort to the process of attainder. Each new conspiracy against the king was followed by punitive action in Parliament. Only one Parliament of Henry's reign—that of 1497—was without its act of attainder. Moreover, towards the attainted noble especially, but also towards others (unless again

---

[103] Henry, duke of Exeter, Francis, Viscount Lovell (left only daughters), Thomas, Lord Rougemont-Grey. The other two were John de la Pole, earl of Lincoln, and Edmund de la Pole, earl of Suffolk. The last male representative of the family died c. 1539 or later.

the evidence is uneven), Henry's attitude seems to have been more severe than Edward's had been, and his attitude towards the bargains which he allowed his courtiers and servants to make with the attainted was distinctly cynical. When attainders against nobles were reversed he rarely allowed complete restitution of their property. Men like Lord Zouche and Thomas, earl of Surrey, were pardoned their lives but their estates were in a greater or lesser degree withheld from them and the hope of recovery held out, often over long years, as an incentive to loyalty and good service. With lesser men, when the attainted sued for pardon, Henry, in some cases, unlike Edward, reserved to himself a proportion of their property and he was much more inclined to countenance (and even to assist) his courtiers and officials in their determination to retain grants of forfeited lands when their former owners were in law restored to their rights. This is not to say that Henry on the whole showed less inclination than Edward to allow his opponents to make their peace but they certainly had to submit to stiffer conditions. The contrast traditionally drawn between Edward IV's cruelty and Henry VII's inclination to mercy can hardly be sustained. Though this particular contrast must not be pushed too far, in Edward's later years proscriptions died away; under Henry they reached a ferocious climax in his last Parliament. Although under both kings men had to 'work their way back' to restitution Henry imposed by far the harder conditions.

Apart from the very sensible desire of these insecure régimes to encourage support from whomever was prepared to give it, contemporary opinion amongst the landed classes had a strong effect on the attitude of rulers. Stubbs summed up this point in his usual concise, clear way:

The landowner had a stake in the country, a material security for his good behaviour; if he offended against the law or the government, he might forfeit his land; but the land was not lost sight of, and the moral and social claims of the family which had possessed it were not barred by forfeiture. The restoration of the heirs of the dispossessed was an invariable result or condition of every political pacification; and very few estates were alienated from the direct line of inheritance by one forfeiture only.[104]

Throughout the fifteenth century opinions of this kind were forcibly expressed, in action as well as in theory. The tenant in fee simple had the sole interest in his estate. It could, therefore, be confiscated without necessarily injuring others. By contrast the tenant in fee tail had only a life interest. Consequently, in spite of the confiscatory legislation of the 1390's and later, men felt very strongly that lands held in fee tail should go to the heir, sentence

---

[104] Stubbs, III, 610. It may also be added that Stubbs' opinion is given added force by the fact that the number of reversals passed in favour of collaterals is by no means insignificant. E.g. the following attainders were reversed for other than sons; Sir Robert Whittingham, John Floryl, Sir Anthony Notehill, Sir Walter Notehill, Sir Alexander Hody. The act of 1489 for the reversal of Sir Robert Brakenbury's attainder in favour of his sisters and co-heiresses even contained a proviso that if the co-heiresses died without leaving direct descendants his bastard son should inherit (Rot. Parl. VI, 27–8, 108–9, 175–6, 219, 433–4).

of forfeiture notwithstanding, when his time came at common law after the death of the convicted traitor.[105] To fly in the face of this opinion would have been to outrage one of the strongest of contemporary sentiments.

It may be that this insistent public opinion, so strongly in favour of ultimate restoration, contributed to one aspect of attainders which a close examination of the acts quite clearly brings out. As time went on, however unpremeditated such a thing may have been in 1459 and 1461, attainders came to work, at least in part, as a kind of probation system;[106] a system of political control, the extreme form of the current system of recognizances for good behaviour (the Close Rolls both under the Yorkists and under Henry VII are crowded with recognizances exacted from men as highly placed as they were unreliable) and the heavy suspended fines imposed on prominent men (and others) by Henry VII. Its workings must certainly have appeared thus to men who were first pardoned and then allowed to recover their lands by purchase or partial grant before the final act of oblivion and mercy.

It remains to assess the effect of attainders on the holding of property. In the present state of research on the subject it is impossible to assess accurately

[105] In 1423 it was declared in parliament that Henry V on his deathbed had been greatly troubled in conscience because he had granted away certain forfeited lands of Henry, Lord le Scrope of Masham which were asserted to be entailed. It was stated that the grantees were willing to surrender the lands if this were so. It was therefore decided that the question of fact should be tried at common law. In 1425 the case was settled in favour of John le Scrope, brother and heir of Henry (*Rot. Parl.* IV, 212–13, 287–8). There had been some vacillation as to what type of lands attainder covered. In the de Vere case, 1392–3, entailed lands were not to be forfeited by attainder (*Rot. Parl.* III, 302–3). The rebels of 1 Henry IV, the earls of Kent, Huntingdon and Salisbury, Thomas, Lord Despenser and Sir Ralph Lumley, were to forfeit all lands and tenements which they held in fee simple (*Rot. Parl.* IV, 18). On the other hand the forfeitures of those condemned in 1406 extended to entailed lands (*Rot. Parl.* IV, 604–7), but a declaration in parliament in 1439 confirmed restorations of lands held in fee tail but not in fee simple (*Rot. Parl.* V, 12). For the Percies see above, p. 143 and n. 102. There was a similar proviso in St. 9 Henry VI, c. 3, which confirmed the proceedings against Owen Glendower (Plummer, op. cit. 278). The petition against William de la Pole in 1451 seems to represent the opinion of the landowner. It asks that his heirs should be corrupt of blood and unable to inherit any lands, tenements, rents, services or any other manner inheritance or possessions of fee simple as heirs to him. His goods and chattels were also to be seized (*Rot. Parl.* V, 226). The petition does not mention entailed estates or estates held to his use. As late as 1453 a proviso exempting entailed estates was expressly introduced into the act of attainder against Sir William Oldhall (*Rot. Parl.* V, 265–6). The provisions of the acts of attainder from 1459 onwards for the confiscation of estates in fee tail were therefore flying strongly in the face of public opinion. When Edward IV returned in 1471, according to Polydore Vergil, none dared, for fear of Warwick, join him in his attempt to recover the crown. He therefore gave out that he sought only for his dukedom of York 'to thintent that by this reasonable and rightewouse request he might get more favor at all handes. And yt ys incredible to be spoken how great effect that feygnyd matter was of, suche ys the force of righteuousnes generally among all men; for whan they herd that King Edward mynded nothing lesse than to require the Kingdom, and sowght simply for his inherytance, they began to be movyd ether for pyty to favor him, or at the leest not to hinder him at all from thattayning of that dukedome' (*Three Books of Polydore Vergil's English History* . . ., ed. Sir H. Ellis (Camden Soc. 1844), 137).

[106] The method was not new. Very similar measures had been taken under Edward II. See the case of Bogo de Knovill in 1326. *Cal. Pat. Rolls, 1324–7*, 333. I owe this reference to Dr E. B. Fryde. It may also be compared as a method of governmental discipline with the taking of hostages from feudal tenants under the Angevins and the enormous fines imposed (but generally uncollected) under King John.

either the extent or the value of the property which passed into the royal hands at one period or another of the civil strife. Nevertheless, it is clear enough that vast estates and goods and chattels of enormous value passed to the crown as a result of the acts. After the attainder of Sir William Stanley, Henry VII netted the prodigious sum of £9062 in cash and jewels[107] and similar though smaller windfalls must have been very useful to Edward IV in the 1460's when he so desperately needed money.[108] As to estates, sums obtained from the sale of custodies, a few outright sales of estates and sums taken from the attainted before the restoration of their lands were by no means negligible.[109] The income received from the estates themselves in comparison with the Crown's annual budget must at certain times have been very considerable.[110] The permanent effect on the landed endowment of the Crown is, however, a different matter. It is true that after each successive revolution and conspiracy the lands of the dispossessed were available for distribution to the victors, thus reducing the insistent pressure for grants of Crown Lands. The relief of pressure is, however, a very different thing from the permanent building up of the landed endowment of the monarchy. After all only five (or at the most seven) noble estates were never returned,[111] either in whole or in part, to their original owners,[112] and only seventeen estates of men of knightly rank. The remaining one hundred and nineteen estates which were permanently forfeited were those of squires, yeomen, merchants and minor ecclesiastics, the greater number of them most probably of small value.

Perhaps more important was the effect of attainders on the fortunes of individual landowners. The probability that the possession of forfeited estates

[107] W. C. Richardson, *Tudor Chamber Administration 1485–1547* (1952), 12.

[108] E.g. from Edward Ellesmere £2000, see above, p. 128, n. 44, Henry, duke of Exeter, £1100 (jewels and silver plate), Henry, duke of Somerset, £1000 (jewels and plate) (*Cal. Pat. Rolls, 1467–77*, 121), William Tailboys (cash and debts), £108 (*Cal. Pat. Rolls, 1461–7*, 295).

[109] E.g. for part of the estates of the following, Henry, duke of Exeter, £4666. 13s. 4d., (Ramsay, *Lancaster and York*, II, 459); Clarence, £2000 (*Cal. Pat. Rolls, 1476–85*, 212); Berkeley of Welley, £666. 13s. 4d. (*Cal. Pat. Rolls, 1485–94*, 83–4). Sir Henry Bodrugan, £320 (*Cal. Pat. Rolls, 1494–1509*, 503). Including 600 marks which Lord Audley paid to Edward IV to save his brother Humphrey's lands from forfeiture (*Rot. Parl.* VI, 127–8), £5000 paid by Edmund, earl of Suffolk, £5000 by Lord FitzWalter, £1728 by Thomas Tyrell and other smaller sums the total amounts to over £20,000 and it is by no means complete.

[110] A list of sixteen estates (and the values of some of these are far from complete) gives a total value of nearly £18,000 p.a. Not all these estates, however, were in the crown's hands simultaneously. The figure includes the estates of Clarence and Gloucester, £3500 and c. £3666 net respectively. It seems legitimate to include these as the figures include the old Salisbury, Spenser and Warwick lands as well as royal grants. As the figures are only an approximation detailed references have been omitted to save space.

[111] Those of the dukes of Exeter, Somerset, Suffolk, Viscount Lovell and Lord Rougemont-Grey. The figure is brought up to six if the Salisbury and Warwick estates are counted. These fell to the crown after the attainders of Clarence (1478) and Richard III (1485).

[112] It is also improbable that attainders to any great extent permanently reduced the acreage of land in the hands of the aristocracy, though the distribution of lands between its various members may have been altered or diverted. E.g. the Howards, although they had to wait for many years, finally emerged with their lands greatly increased, including their moiety of the Mowbray estates and the grants made to Surrey from the Crown Lands after Flodden.

was likely to be temporary may well have led to excessive exploitation by those to whom they had been granted and to their return wasted and impoverished to their original owners. Others of the proscribed ran deeply into debt to get back their estates and may have done so in order to live. The process may also have increased the already considerable hazards of the fifteenth-century land market by adding further complications to titles already insecure and uncertain. It must have embittered some to the extent of making them the more ready to plot treason again. Even so, the system as it actually operated, as distinct from the way it could have operated (and has so often been assumed to have operated) if the full penalties allowed by the law had been exacted, cannot have brought about any significant numerical reduction of the aristocracy nor even the decimation of an unruly element in English society. The co-operation of the nobility was essential to firm government as the history of both Edward IV and Henry VII shows.[1] What the attainder system ultimately achieved in combination with other things, like fines, bonds and recognizances, was to hold the sharpest of legal swords over recalcitrant heads and helped to bring about that greater tractability which some historians have noted as one of the more prominent characteristics of the upper ranks of English society in the early sixteenth century.

[113] See my article, 'Council, Administration and Councillors, 1461 to 1485', *B.I.H.R.* op. cit. 153–6. I hope to deal more fully with this question elsewhere.

TABLE I

A. Total figures of attainders and reversals (excluding royal families)

(*a*, number attainted; *b*, number reversed or ultimately reversed for heirs; *c*, number unreversed.)

Attainder under ...	Henry VI			Edward IV			Richard III			Henry VII			Total	Reversals	Unreversed	Percent reversed
	a	*b*	*c*	*a*	*b*	*c*	*a*	*b*	*c*	*a*	*b*	*c*				
Dukes	—	—	—	2	1	1	1	1	0	1	1	0	4	3	1	75
Marquises	—	—	—	—	—	—	1	1	0	—	—	—	1	1	0	100
Earls	3	3	0	5	5	0	1	1	0	3	1	2	12	10	2	83
Viscounts	—	—	—	1	1	1	—	—	—	1	0	0	2	1	1	50
Barons	2	2	0	8	7	7	17	17	0	4	4	0	15	14	1	93
Knights	7	7	0	38	31	7	53	53	0	23	13	10	(84)*85	(67)*68	17	79
Squires	9	9	0	55	31	24	20	19	1	53	22	31	170	115	55	67
Yeomen	—	—	—	15	5	10	3	3	0	30	8	22	65	32	33	47
Ecclesiastics	—	—	—	11	3	8	2	2	0	5	1	4	(18)*19	(6)*7	12	36
Merchants	—	—	—	—	—	—	1	1	0	10	1	9	17	5	12	29
Miscellaneous	—	—	—	5	2	3	1	1	0	8	1	7	9	2	7	22
Grand totals	21	21	0	140	86	54	100	99	1	138	52	86	(397)*400	(256)*258	141	64

Combined peerage figures (Dukes, Marquises, Earls, Viscounts, Barons): Total 34, Reversals 29, Unreversed 5, Percent reversed 84.

Figures in brackets marked * give the actual number of persons involved as distinct from the number of attainders and reversals—allowing for the fact that Sir Nicholas Latymer and Dr John Morton were each attainted in two periods.

B. Member of royal families

Yorkist	Attainted	Lancastrian	Attainted
(1) Richard, Duke of York	1459	(1) Henry, Earl of Richmond (Henry VII)	1484
(2) Edward, Earl of March (Edward IV)	1459	(2) Margaret, Countess of Richmond	1484
(3) Edmund, Earl of Rutland	1459	(3) Henry VI	1461
(4) George, Duke of Clarence	1478	(4) Margaret of Anjou	1461
(5) Richard, Duke of Gloucester (Richard III)	1485	(5) Prince Edward	1461
(6) Edward, Earl of Warwick (Clarence's son)	1504		

Notes to Table 1

General

(a) If a man has been attainted *twice* in *one* period, e.g. Edward IV and the attainders twice reversed once 'in' and once 'out' of the period only the reversal in the period 'out' has been counted for this table, e.g. Sir Thomas Tresham, att. 1461, pardoned by patent 1464, reversed by Parliament 1468, attainted 1475, reversed for heir 1485, therefore included in Tudor reversals only. If a man was attainted in *two* different periods he is included as attainted in *both*, e.g. John Morton, att. 1461, rev. 1473, att. 1484, rev. 1485.

(b) '*Provisional*' *attainders*. In the Parliaments of 1461–3 and 1463–5 a number of men were to be regarded as attainted unless they surrendered for judgement by certain dates. Where it is known that these 'provisional' attainders became effective they have been included in the figures in the table. The residue for which no further information has been found is as follows: esquires and gentlemen 12, yeomen 3. Of the three yeomen one later received a general pardon but as this is enrolled on the pardon roll (C. 67/48, m. 2) it has no political significance.

(c) *Defenders of Harlech.* In 1461 eighteen of the defenders of Harlech were declared attainted unless they surrendered by the feast of the Purification of our Lady. I have found no evidence that any of them gave themselves up to the royal officers. These have not been included in the table. One was definitely attainted and two more 'provisionally' attainted in 1463–5.

Special cases

(1) Somerset. Although the family was extinct in the male line Henry VII reversed his attainder in 1485.

(2) Wiltshire. James Butler (see above, p. 132 and n. 58).

(3) Sir Robert Chamberlain's attainder (1491–2) was reversed in 1531 but no property was to be restored.

(4) Dan Miles Salley, att. 1489–90, after the Abingdon conspiracy. A monk of Abingdon, of the same name, received a pardon in 1492 (which does not cover attainder) (*Cal. Pat. Rolls, 1485–94,* 381). The name is unusual and (in spite of the fact that there is no evidence of the reversal of attainder) he may be the man who afterwards became abbot of Eynsham and bishop of Llandaff and whose splendid tomb is in John of Gaunt's Hospital, Bristol.

(5) In addition the following seven men received general pardons (which do not, however, specifically mention reversal of attainder) and should possibly be counted as restored: esquires and gentlemen, James Dalton, Thomas Tunstall, Thomas Blandrehassett, William Antron, Richard Cockerell; ecclesiastics, John Whelpdale; yeomen, Thomas Carr.

(6) John Hooe of London was the only man attainted by Richard III who was not included in the mass reversal of 1485. This was probably merely due to inadvertence.

TABLE 2. *Details of attainders and reversals*

Attainted under	Category											Attainder reversed under
	Dukes	Marquises	Earls	Viscounts	Barons	Knights	Squires	Yeomen	Ecclesiastics	Merchants	Miscellaneous	
Henry VI	—	—	3	—	2	7	9	—	—	—	—	Henry VI*
	—	—	3	—	2	7	9	—	—	—	—	Richard III
	—	—	—	—	—	—	—	—	—	—	—	Henry VII
	—	—	—	—	—	—	—	—	—	—	—	Henry VIII
Edward IV	2	—	5	1	8	38	55	15	11	5	—	Edward IV
	—	—	1	—	3	16	15	3	3	1	—	Richard III
	1	—	4	1	4	15	16	1	—	1	—	Henry VII
	—	—	—	—	—	—	—	—	—	—	—	Henry VIII
Richard III	1	1	1	—	1	17	53	20	3	2	1	Henry VII
	1	1	1	—	1	17	53	19	3	2	1	Henry VIII
Henry VII	1	—	3	1	4	23	53	30	5	10	8	Henry VII
	1	—	1	—	3	12	19	7	1	1	1	Henry VIII
	—	—	—	—	1	1	3	—	—	—	—	

* In the Parliament of 1460, which was Yorkist controlled.

4

London and Parliament in the Reign of Henry VIII*
by H. Miller

IN THE sixteenth century London was represented in parliament by four members, two chosen by the aldermen and two by the commonalty.[1] London's members and the two citizens from York were customarily accorded seats of honour beside the privy councillors on the front bench.[2] This tribute to the wealth and prestige of England's two largest cities was no doubt gratifying to their self-esteem; did it imply more than a formal deference? One disgruntled commentator early in Elizabeth's reign thought that there had been a recent and disastrous increase in mercantile power.

Marchants are growne to be so conninge in the trade of corruptinge, and have founde it so swete, that sens the first yere of the kinge your fathers raigne of famous memorye untill nowe there cold never be wonne any good lawe or order which towched the lybertie and state of the marchaunte, but that they stayed it, ether in the common howse, or higher howse of parliament, or ells by the prince himself.[3]

Such negative triumphs are difficult to assess but the parliamentary record of London during the reign of Henry VIII can be partially reconstructed and may prove illuminating.

London was unique in the early sixteenth century in the hopeful attention which it paid to parliament. Other cities and boroughs preferred bills from time to time: London alone regularly devised a parliamentary programme. The court of aldermen decided on the bill or bills which the city was to promote, often after having called for suggestions from the court of common council or the wardens of the livery companies, and exercised control over the city's members. In the early years of Henry VIII's reign the court of aldermen tried to dominate the election of the commonalty's two members by presenting to the common council the names of those from whom the members were to be chosen. In 1509 the common council elected outside the suggested list; in 1512 it conformed and chose two members from the twelve named by the court of

[1] List of M.P.s in A. B. Beaven, *The Aldermen of the City of London* (1908–13), i. In the reign of Henry VIII the aldermen regularly elected one alderman and the recorder, the commonalty two citizens below the rank of alderman. If one of the members elected by the commonalty subsequently became an alderman, he forfeited his seat and a by-election was held.

[2] John Hooker, quoted by E. Porritt, *The Unreformed House of Commons* (1903), i. 426.

[3] Hatfield House, Cecil Papers 152, fos. 96–99.

aldermen.[1] But by 1523 the right of nomination was exercised by the commonalty and from 1529 the two members were elected not by the common council but directly by the commons of the city.[2] Yet the power of the court of aldermen was unbroken: no member of parliament for London, however elected, disputed the authority of the mayor and aldermen.

Their authority was, however, challenged on occasion by the livery companies. The court of aldermen insisted that it should direct all London's legislative efforts, that no individual company should present its own bills to parliament without the sanction of the court. Before the parliament of 1515 assembled, the court of aldermen appointed four aldermen and seven commoners

to have communicacion for a reformacion of suche thinges as they shall seme convenient to be redressyd at this next parliament . . . and to have the examinacion of all suche billes as shall be exhibit to this parliament before that they be presentyd to the same.[3]

The greater companies probably secured a verbal authorization: the mercers and the grocers, both well represented in the court of aldermen, were never reproved for their parliamentary activities, although never expressly licensed to put forward bills. The wardens of other companies were called to account for infringements of the rule. The clothworkers in 1542, questioned about a bill introduced into parliament in their name, were able to plead ignorance and had to resort to the clerk of the parliaments to discover that the bill had been put in by the company of weavers, whose wardens later confessed to this manoeuvre. The clothworkers then devised a bill of their own, but the court of aldermen would 'in no wyse' consent to its introduction into parliament, although leaving the company 'att theyr lybertye to do as they shall thinke good therin'.[4] The following year a butcher was ordered to deliver to the mayor 'a true copye of the byll that he and hys companye have caused to be preferryd and putt furth into the parlyament house'; and in 1544 the cordwainers were commanded by the aldermen to 'cease theyr . . . sute in the parlyament house untyll they shalbe dysmyssyd from thys court, upon payn of dysfraunchesment', while the wardens of the ironmongers, interviewed about a bill 'put in to the parlyament house concernyng the regratyng of stele and other merchaundyse', were only licensed to depart 'upon a newe warnyng'.[5] It was clearly becoming increasingly difficult to maintain

[1] City of London Corporation Record Office, Repertory 2, fos. 77, 125v, Journal 11, fos. 93, 147v. The repertories and journals of (respectively) the court of aldermen and court of common council of the city of London are hereafter cited as Rep. and Jo.

[2] Jo. 12, fo. 213v; *Narratives of the Reformation*, ed. J. G. Nichols (Camden Soc., 1860), pp. 295–6.

[3] Rep. 2, fo. 205v.

[4] Rep. 10, fos. 241v–242v, 243v, 245.

[5] *Ibid.*, fo. 325; Rep. 11, fos. 23, 26.

aldermanic control and under Elizabeth the number of London bills was to be an embarrassment to the house of commons,[1] but in the reign of Henry VIII the city of London spoke in parliament with one voice, the voice of the court of aldermen.

I

The closing years of the reign of Henry VII were marked by a series of incidents which to Londoners at any rate bore the impress of tyranny. The death of the king reversed the fortunes of the handful of people involved in these episodes, which have recently engaged the attention of historians.[2] But rivalries within the city were as important in their way as disputes between individual citizens and the central government, and could on occasion bring the city authorities to more lasting grief. In the parliament of 1504 they suffered a defeat which only parliament could reverse: for years afterwards London concentrated its legislative efforts on trying to recover the ground lost then by the passage of an act for the regulation of gild ordinances.[3] This statute, so much detested by the mayor and aldermen, they did much to bring upon themselves by their opposition to the incorporation of the merchant tailors under letters patent of 6 January 1503, a seemingly innocuous act of the royal prerogative which bred a chain-reaction involving king, council and parliament, the government of the city and all the London companies.

The immediate effect of the letters patent[4] was to incorporate the fraternity of tailors and linen armourers of London under a new name, the gild of merchant taylors of London. At the same time the master and wardens of the new company were authorized to admit any number of Englishmen into the fellowship, without regard to any other craft or mystery in London, and to ordain and execute ordinances for the government of their company, provided only that these were not 'contrary to the laws and customs of our realm of England or in prejudice of the mayor of the city of London'.

To the tailors, who did not hide their jubilation that the name of their fraternity had been, as they expressed it, 'brought to light, . . . which has long lain hid in concealment and shade',[5] the grant was seen primarily as a victory over the drapers, a recognition of their own development from a craft to a trading gild. The drapers had long resented the incursion of the tailors—who specialized, as they did, in the buying and selling of

---

[1] Brit. Mus., Harley MS. 253, fos. 33v, 34v.

[2] G. R. Elton, 'Henry VII: rapacity and remorse', *The Historical Journal*, i (1958), 21–39; J. P. Cooper, 'Henry VII's last years reconsidered', *ibid.*, ii (1959), 103–29; Elton, 'Henry VII: a restatement', *ibid.*, iv (1961), 1–29.

[3] 19 Hen. VII, cap. 7.

[4] Printed in full by F. M. Fry and R. T. D. Sayle, *The Charters of the Merchant Taylors' Company* (1937), pp. 34–9.

[5] *Ibid.*, p. 41.

woollen cloths—and retaliated (or so the tailors believed) by using their superior weight in the court of aldermen against their rivals. In particular the tailors ascribed the repeated failure in the mayoral election of one of their company, Sir John Perceval, to the malice of the drapers: not until his fifth attempt, in 1498, when the king wrote to the city on his behalf, did Perceval become mayor, the first tailor to do so. But the court of aldermen as a whole mistrusted Perceval's 'hot appetite' for the mayoralty, thinking (according to the *Great Chronicle of London*) that he intended to make more of its powers than previous mayors had done.[1] Although this fear proved false the general suspicion of the tailors seemed justified when the terms of their letters patent, secretly negotiated, were made known. Every company in London stood to lose by the merchant taylors' right of free recruitment and the authority granted to make ordinances at will left the mayor and aldermen powerless to intervene in matters which could affect the whole city.

The court of aldermen quickly prepared to counter-attack. On 9 February 1503 they arranged to hear the opinion of learned counsel for both the drapers and the tailors.[2] Some weeks later, having marshalled their arguments, four aldermen and the recorder were sent to inform Henry VII of 'the grugge that is tayn by the hole body of thys cite by reason of his letters patentes late grauntid to the ffealoship of taillors. And to perswade his grace to reforme the same'.[3] In May the court of aldermen decided to boycott the tailors' annual feast, although in the end they went because foreign ambassadors were to be present.[4] In November the lord chief justice reported to the king that the clause in the merchant taylors' patent safeguarding the rights of the mayor applied only to the immediately preceding article and the council ordered the mayor and city of London to appear and show cause why the tailors should not enjoy the effect of their letters patent and why the king should not by his prerogative grant to the company the name of merchant taylors.[5]

This marked the end of the first round for the mayor and aldermen. Their legal arguments had evidently been rejected; a new approach had to be devised. Their first reaction may have been to allow popular demonstrations in London against the merchant taylors: on 24 November the council warned them that they would be held responsible for any disturbances in the city 'under pretext of the letters patent granted to the tailors'.[6] On 10 December the court of aldermen, convinced that the name of merchant taylors 'myght not stond neither by convenyencie of reason nor with good ordor of this cite', determined to sue to the king for redress 'asmoche as by possibilite and duetie of their alegeaunce myght be don'[7];

[1] *The Great Chronicle of London*, ed. A. H. Thomas and I. D. Thornley (1938), pp. 245–6, 288, 323; Jo. 9, fos. 239, 280, 280v; Jo. 10, fos. 79, 108v, 141v.
   [2] Rep. 1, fo. 122.   [3] *Ibid.*, fo. 129.   [4] *Ibid.*, fo. 135.
   [5] *Select Cases in the Council of Henry VII*, ed. C. G. Bayne and W. H. Dunham (Selden Soc., lxxv), p. 35.
   [6] *Ibid.*, p. 36.   [7] Rep. 1, fo. 148.

and on 23 December they agreed to offer £5,000 for the confirmation of the city's charter 'and for adnullyng and revocacion of the newe charter late graunted . . . to the taillors of this citee . . . and to put the same taillors in case that they were in byfore.'[1] Early in January 1504 this decision was approved by the city's legal counsel.[2]

For the moment, however, attention was turned to parliament, which opened on 25 January. The dispute between the merchant taylors and the mayor and aldermen of London had focused attention on the relationship between city authorities and livery companies in general and in this parliament the first attempt was made to bring all companies into a nation-wide system of regulation by the central government. The local battle which London had been fighting was suddenly removed to the national arena.

The act of 1504[3] began by referring to a statute of 15 Henry VI[4] imposing on all corporate bodies the duty of having their ordinances confirmed either by justices of the peace or by the municipal authorities: which act, to endure 'as long as it shall please our . . . lord the king', the act of 1504 declared, 'is nowe expired'. Since its expiry, the preamble continued, many ordinances had been made 'contrarie to the kinges prerogatyfe, his lawes and of the comon weyll of his subgiectes'. Therefore it was enacted that henceforward no ordinances should be made or executed without the approval of the chancellor, treasurer and two chief justices, or any three of them, or of the justices of assize on their circuit, on pain of £40 fine for every infringement; and that no company should make any order preventing its members from suing in the king's courts.

The genesis of the act is obscure. The clerk of the merchant taylors, preparing to submit the company ordinances to the chancellor and other royal officials for approval, blamed the 'great labour, subtle wit and crafty means' of the recorder of London, Sir Robert Sheffield, one of the city's members of parliament. The motive the clerk ascribed to him was the recovery of that legal business lost to London lawyers by the peaceful settlement of disputes by arbitration, to which potential litigants were forced by ordinances of the companies forbidding their members to implead each other without the permission of the master and wardens.[5] Yet this is to attempt to explain the passage of the act by reference solely to its second, and less important clause, allowing members of companies free access to the king's courts; and to suppose that the recorder of London, for his own private profit, could promote a bill which in its main intention was directly opposed to the interests of the city.

There is no doubt that the statute was regarded by the authorities in London as an infringement of their rights over the companies. The act of 1437 which it replaced is thought to have been the result of pressure

[1] Rep. 1, fo. 149.   [2] *Ibid.*, fo. 150.
[3] 19 Hen. VII, cap. 7.
[4] 15 Hen. VI, cap. 6.
[5] C. M. Clode, *The Early History of the Guild of Merchant Taylors* (1888), i. 39–41.

from the city,[1] and its expiry at some unspecified date in the past, announced in the parliament of 1504, seems to have come as news to London.
The court of aldermen had never abandoned its claim to supervise gild
ordinances. If the act had expired with the deposition of Henry VI—
perhaps the likeliest date—the practical effects were negligible. In 1462
the fishmongers were called before the court of aldermen and forbidden
to use any ordinance until it had been confirmed by the court: any hope
they may have had of a new freedom from control was clearly dashed, and
for the rest of the century the lesser London companies regularly submitted their ordinances to the court of aldermen for approval.[2] Nor was
this situation peculiar to London. In York, for example, the ordinances
of the smiths were confirmed in 1503,[3] less than a year before parliament
announced the expiry of the legislative basis of any such system of
municipal control.

The greater London companies were not normally accustomed to bring
their ordinances to the mayor for approval, but even they, on occasion,
consented to do so. In the parliament of 1487 'grete grudge and displeasure' were expressed against London companies 'for sellyng of dere
stuffe, excedyng price resonable', during which their ordinances came
under fire: 'everyche withyn them self by reason of theire corporacions do
make ordenances and statutes in comen hurt of the kynges liege people'.
(The specific complaint of high prices, not mentioned in the act of 1437,
was to be interpolated into it in the preamble to the act of 1504.) The
mayor, to appease these complaints, undertook to reform abuses 'by mean
and auctoritie of his courte' and ordered the wardens of every company
to bring in their books of ordinances. The mercers agreed to send in their
ordinances 'and all suche of them as the mayre and aldremen fynde
convenyent and good ben by them well allowed, and alle other refourmed
or anulled'.[4]

London and other cities may have retained control over their companies
without the sanction of statute. But if the act of 1437 had expired, it had
done so with remarkably little ceremony: an act of parliament affecting
all the gilds and fraternities of the country should surely be annulled with
at least the publicity which had attended its enactment. Moreover, if it
had indeed been annulled—as it could have been at any time at the king's
pleasure—what purpose would have been served by removing the existing
system of control and replacing it by nothing at all? It seems more likely
that the act of 1437 had been forgotten and was only brought formally to

[1] G. Unwin, *The Gilds and Companies of London* (3rd edn., 1938), pp. 162, 170.
[2] *Calendar of Letter Books of the City of London, Letter Book L*, ed. R. R. Sharpe
(1912), p. 16 and *passim*.
[3] *York Civic Records* (Yorks. Archaeol. Soc. Record Ser.), ii. 180.
[4] *Acts of Court of the Mercers' Company, 1453–1527*, ed. L. Lyell and F. D.
Watney (1936), p. 183. In Dec. 1487, as parliament was ending, the mayor and
aldermen forbade the making of ordinances without their approval and the wardens
of 'divers misteries' brought in unauthorized ordinances for cancellation: *Letter
Book L*, p. 246.

an end in 1504 in order that the new act might be passed. In this case the disorders alleged to have followed its expiry would take their place simply as arguments in favour of the proposed act: the writers of preambles not infrequently allowed themselves a politician's licence.

Probably, therefore, this was a government bill suggested by the council's inquiry of the previous autumn into the London dispute. It was, however, in the form of a Commons' petition: 'Prayen the comens in this present parliament assembled that. . . .' Although there was no necessity for such petitions to be read first in the house of commons, they normally did appear there before going to the Lords. Of the seven acts couched in this form which passed in 1504, only two were begun in the Lords, this act and another almost equally disliked in London, an act for scavage.[1] The payment of scavage, a duty levied by towns on all merchandise sold by 'foreigners', had recently been extended by London to all merchants who were not free of the city. The people of Exeter had contested London's right to do this[2] and a month before parliament met the court of aldermen in London set about collecting evidence 'for the prove of the dutie of scavayge'.[3] The act of 1504 ordered that in future, as in times past, scavage was to be paid by aliens only, but a separate proviso annexed to the bill permitted London to levy scavage on denisens' goods if the consent of the king and council were first obtained. This proviso—our proviso, as the town clerk entitled it—and the enacting clauses of the act for the supervision of gild ordinances were both entered in the repertory kept by the city.[4]

In these two matters London was forced on to the defensive. The one attempt known to have been made by the city, or at least agreed upon, to extract some positive advantage from this parliament met with no success. On 17 February 1504, in the fourth week of the session, the court of aldermen

determyned that a bill be conceyved by the counsell etc. to be put to the parlement for the probate of testamentes, and for letters *ad coligendum*, and also for reformacion that th' ordenaries kepe all the goodes and paye not dettes for that, that all creditors come not at a certen day lymitted.[5]

Complaints about the testamentary jurisdiction of the church were to receive a ready hearing in the Reformation parliament: if London's bill was indeed presented in 1504, it was some twenty-five years too early to be acceptable.

The parliament over, the city returned to the fight against the merchant taylors. On 22 May the common council repeated the offer of £5,000 to

---

[1] 19 Hen. VII, cap. 8. The original acts, in the House of Lords Record Office, reveal the provenance in their superscriptions.

[2] *Select Cases before the King's Council in the Star Chamber, 1477–1509*, ed. I. S. Leadam (Selden Soc., xvi), pp. 71–95; Jo. 10, fo. 281.

[3] Rep. 1, fo. 147v.

[4] *Ibid.*, fos. 157, 158v, 160v.   [5] *Ibid.*, fo. 153.

the king for the confirmation of London's charter—'with convenient
explanacion of suche articles as be doubteos and ambiguous'—and the
repeal of the letters patent to the merchant taylors. If Henry would not
'absolutely and clerely take away the name of merchaunt taillors, but
altere it unto any other name than taillors oonely', the sum was to be
adjusted accordingly.[1] The king stood firm and in March 1505 the common
council agreed to pay 5,000 marks (in five yearly instalments) for the
confirmation of the charter, with no reference to the tailors' patent.[2] The
dispute seemed to be settled.

Eighteen months later, however, the old scars were reopened when
Henry VII forced the election as sheriff of William Fitzwilliam,[3] the merchant taylor who was held responsible for negotiating the letters patent
of 1503.[4] Even his enemies did not suppose that Fitzwilliam—who paid
£100 'for the kingis gracious favour for being sherif'[5]—wanted the office
for financial gain, but believed that his motive was 'to put in question the
ffranchyse of the cyte, or at the lest that men shuld knowe how he stood in
the kyngis ffavour and that he mygth opteyne of his grace, that many
othir mygth nott'.[6] In October 1508 the king again intervened in a city
election, requesting the choice of another merchant taylor, Stephen
Jenyns, as mayor[7]: there was no attempt at refusal.

The accession of Henry VIII the following April was hailed in London
as elsewhere as the dawn of better things. The usual confirmation of the
city's charter by the new king could be made the opportunity not only of
the recognition of old liberties which the citizens had been 'enterruptid of'
but also of new privileges which might be added.[8] There was also the
possibility—although this was not mooted in the court of aldermen until
a new mayor had succeeded Jenyns—of being released from the payment
of the last instalment of the 5,000 marks due to Henry VII for his confirmation and even (a wilder flight of fancy) of recovering the money already
paid.[9] Yet little was in fact achieved beyond a private vengeance. In 1510
the city elected Fitzwilliam as sheriff, affecting to believe that his earlier
election was invalid.[10] Fitzwilliam refused to serve again and sued the

---

[1] Jo. 10, fo. 312v.

[2] Ibid., fo. 333v; Great Chronicle, p. 328.

[3] Great Chronicle, pp. 332–3.

[4] G. Cavendish, Life and Death of Cardinal Wolsey, ed. R. S. Sylvester (E.E.T.S.,
243), p. 34.

[5] Brit. Mus., Lansdowne MS. 127, fo. 31.

[6] Great Chronicle, p. 333.   [7] Rep. 2, fo. 50.

[8] Ibid., fos. 66, 67v. The accession of Edward VI was greeted in the city in
strikingly similar terms. The recorder in 1547 sued (unsuccessfully) to the council
for 'the more full explanying and declaracion' of those liberties 'wherin they be
now, by reason of certeyne darke and ambiguous termes comprysed within the
same, impeached and interrupted': Jo. 15, fo. 313v.

[9] Rep. 2, fo. 75v. The collection of the last instalment of the 5,000 marks was
not ordered by the mayor until Nov. 1512: Jo. 11, fo. 166v.

[10] Jo. 11, fo. 120v; The Customs of London, otherwise called Arnold's Chronicle
(1811), p. xliv.

mayor (a draper elected against the opposition of the merchant taylors)[1] for acting out of malice; the mayor, Sir William Capel, sued Fitzwilliam and the merchant taylors and the city started a case against Fitzwilliam.[2] A decree of the star chamber then stayed all proceedings and on 10 July 1511 the council advised the mayor and aldermen to restore Fitzwilliam to the freedom from which he had been expelled—adding sanctimoniously that 'good and circumspect governors ought rather to train a member to good than to cut off the same member'—and forbade them, until further notice, to collect the fine of 1,000 marks which they had imposed on him.[3] In the event Fitzwilliam left the city, was befriended by Wolsey, entered his service, was preferred by him to the king's council, bought the manor of Milton in Northamptonshire—where the family (raised to the peerage in the seventeenth century) still lives—and generally prospered in despite of London's attempts to teach him the error of his ways.

The much more important matter of the act of parliament remained. In the first parliament of Henry VIII's reign a bill which may represent an attempt by London to recover its lost authority appeared briefly in the Lords: after its first reading it was heard no more.[4] At the same time a persistent campaign conducted by the mercers' company in and out of parliament to prevent the grant of tonnage and poundage to the new king —a campaign supported by the city's members of parliament—ended in failure. Sir Thomas Seymour, one of the wardens of the mercers, reported to his company that

he perceyved well that it was the kynges mynde to have the subsidye graunted at this parlement, notwithstondyng that it is not the myndes of the marchauntes; and that the most parte of the parlement hous stondith by gentilmen which bayre no charge of the said subsydie and be willyng to graunt the same.

Seymour then consulted the mayor 'and certen burges of the parlement' and with the assistance of the city's legal advisers they drew up three provisos to be added to the bill before it left the Commons, limiting its effect. The provisos were approved by the merchant adventurers, who appointed members of their company to ask the lord privy seal (the bishop of Winchester), Sir Thomas Lovell, treasurer of the household, and Sir Robert Sheffield, the late recorder of London, to support a request to the king for payment after the rates set down in 4 Henry VII, the old book of rates to be annexed to the grant. But all to no effect: the provisos failed in the house of commons, the lord privy seal refused to speak in the merchants' favour and the company was told that it was 'but foly' to try to prevent the passage of the act: the stubborn resistance of London's M.P.s had done no more than earn them the 'displeasour' of the council.[5] Before the next parliament met, early in 1512, the court of aldermen appointed five of their number, with twelve commoners, 'to here maters

[1] Rep. 2, fos. 80, 86v–87.   [2] Clode, ii. 46.
[3] Ibid., pp. 46–9.   [4] L[ords'] J[ournals], i. 8.
[5] Acts of Court of the Mercers' Company, pp. 346–50, 357.

for the next parliament'.[1] On 3 February, the eve of the opening day, the
aldermen decided to give a tun of wine to the lord chancellor, the duke of
Buckingham, the lord treasurer, the lord steward and the lord chamberlain,
and two hogsheads of wine to the king's secretary, the treasurer of the
household and the vice-chamberlain.[2] The speaker chosen for this
parliament was Sir Robert Sheffield, and half-way through the session the
city increased his annuity, originally granted when he resigned the
recordership, from forty shillings to five marks.[3] Yet again results were
disappointing. If the city tried to repeal the act for gild ordinances the
bill must have failed in the Commons for it made no appearance in the
Lords. That the merchant taylors feared legislation against their company
appears evident: they prepared a proviso to protect their interests (probably
in the general terms customarily used by the merchants of the Hanse)
and got it signed by the king before sending it in to the house of lords.
The lord chancellor and the bishop of Winchester decreed that the proviso
for the Hanse, received on the same day as the merchant taylors', being
signed by the king, needed the assent of neither Lords nor Commons.[4]
Presumably this ruling applied also to the merchant taylors' proviso. For
the rest a bill concerning juries in London was brought in to the Lords
either by Thomas More (the under-sheriff of London) or his father, by
order of the lord chancellor, but got no further than a first reading, while
a bill for tonnage and poundage, passed by the Lords after four readings,
failed in the Commons.[5] The *Great Chronicle of London*, alongside a
brief description of this parliament, records in the margin that it 'was
callid the parliament off powndage',[6] reflecting the importance which
London attached to the bill, which perhaps contained some concession
to the merchants.

Parliament was adjourned on 30 March and re-assembled on 4 November 1512. On 5 November the court of aldermen decided to speak to the
recorder 'for the bill put in to the parliament howse concernyng bieng
and sellyng in groos, and also for the bill concernyng the apparaunce of
juries at Seint Martyn's.'[7] The first of these came to nothing, but an act
for juries within London was passed.[8] This, originating as a Lords' bill,
extended the duty of jury service to citizens worth a hundred marks in
goods, where before only those were liable whose lands were worth
forty shillings a year; the act passed with a separate schedule limiting its
endurance till the next parliament only. Although no mention of St.
Martin's was made in the statute, a clarifying act of the next session[9]
declared that it had been made 'for the good expedicion of justice, for to
have quyke apparence of jurours, citizens of London, at Saynt Marteyn's

---

[1] Rep. 2, fo. 127.   [2] *Ibid.*, fo. 128v.
[3] *Ibid.*, fo. 130v. The recorder in office was never at this time elected speaker,
but, besides Sheffield, Sir Thomas Nevill (speaker in 1515), Sir Thomas More
(1523) and Sir John Baker (1545) had previously been in the city's employment.
[4] *L. J.*, i. 17.   [5] *Ibid.*, pp. 14, 17.   [6] *Great Chronicle*, p. 378.
[7] Rep. 2, fo. 145.   [8] 4 Hen. VIII, cap. 3.   [9] 5 Hen. VIII, cap. 5.

the Graunt within the said citie', and it was evidently the bill in which the court of aldermen was interested: whatever the reception it got from the citizens, the act made the sheriffs' job of impanelling juries easier and no doubt the recorder was told to support it in the house of commons. It is even possible that the bill (without the limiting clause) was drawn up by London in the first place. The common council had several times discussed measures to overcome the difficulties experienced in collecting juries in the city, the last time only a week before the opening of this session of parliament, when two aldermen and seven commoners were appointed 'to examyn the boke for apparaunce of enquestes'.[1]

But the city's greatest efforts were again directed to a repeal of the act for gild ordinances. On 17 November 1512 the court of aldermen called before them the wardens of ten companies. All of them, except the wardens of the merchant taylors, 'consented to the peticion late moved in the parleament house that all craftes shall hereafter be under the rule of the maire and aldermen' and agreed to go to parliament the next day 'and appere before the lordes', taking with them Thomas More and the common serjeant of London to speak for them.[2] On 7 December aldermen and law officers of the city were appointed in groups of two, three or four to lobby the duke of Buckingham, the bishops of London and Norwich, the prior of St. John's, the lord privy seal, Lord Bergavenny and Lord Berners, all 'for the acte concernyng corporacions'.[3] No such act passed. But there was again a proviso for the merchant taylors, signed by the king, evidently designed to protect them against the act if it did get through:

Providyd alwey that this acte nor noon other acte . . . may extende or be pre-judiciall to any graunte . . . by the kyng . . . by his lettres patentes or by the lettres patentes of his moste noble fadre . . . to the felasshyp of merchauntes taillours within the citie of London.

The proviso was not in fact attached to any act and was entered by itself at the end of the parliament roll.[4]

The last session of this parliament opened on 23 January 1514. On 12 January the court of aldermen agreed that 'sich order as my lord maier and the recorder thyncke best to be taken for the exspedicion of a bill passid the neder howse in the parliament shall be taken and pursued'.[5] On 7 February two aldermen were appointed 'to speke with the busshopp of Norwich for the exspedition of the bill of corporacions and for the puttyng back of the bill of wynes to be solde in groos and also of cloth by strangers to foreyners in London'. Half a dozen other aldermen, the mayor and recorder and Thomas Nevill, the under-sheriff, were assigned in groups of two or three to lobby the lord chancellor, the bishop of London, the prior of St. John's, Lord Bergavenny and Lord Berners.[6] Two days later the court of aldermen decided to give the speaker £5 'for

[1] Jo. 11, fos. 118v, 137, 163.
[2] Rep. 2, fo. 146.
[3] Ibid., fo. 148.
[4] Statutes of the Realm, iii. 91.
[5] Rep. 2, fo. 169v.
[6] Ibid., fo. 171.

the expedition of certain causes of the city in parliament'.[1] Sufficient progress was made for the mayor to send round to the wardens of a number of companies to seek their support, informing them that he and the aldermen

entended to sue in the parlement hous for to have alle the corporacions in the citie of London to be yolden into the mayres hondes, and that lykewise other dyvers cities, towenes and borowes in this realme of Englonde be mynded to make labour for theym self to stonde in the same case, and thynk that it shall be more beneficiall to the comunaltie, aswell of this citie as of all other, to be ruled, ordred and governed by the mayre and other hedd officers than for to sue alway for their remedie to the chaunceler of Englond or elles to the kynges counseyll.

The mercers, asked by their wardens 'yf they thought it necessary thus to do', answered 'that lyke as all other compenyes shuld do in this behalfe, so will they be content to doo and non otherwise'. The impression of some lack of enthusiasm in this case is reinforced by the marginal heading: 'A pretens to have the corporacions in the citie to be yolden into the maires hondes etc.'[2] The day after the mercers had made their answer to the mayor's proposition, thirteen aldermen and both the sheriffs were assigned to go to parliament on 25 February, with representatives of other companies, 'for the bylle of corporacions'.[3] For all this activity the bill failed to pass.

Nor was London any more successful in the other two bills it had shown interest in, for the sale of wines and cloth. Moreover there was one act, for the export of cloth,[4] little to the liking of the merchant adventurers, which London had apparently been unable to prevent. One of the city's members of parliament was shortly afterwards elected governor of the merchant adventurers in England. He then advised his company to obey this act 'and eschew the daunger that may fall by doyng the contrarie'; the merchant adventurers thanked him for his 'advise and counseyll' and announced that they would carry on as before and risk the danger.[5]

The city's one success was an act confirming Edward IV's letters patent to London for the packership of cloth; in the form of a petition to the king from the mayor and commonalty of London, it was read first in the Lords and at some stage suffered a long erasure of its original text, before receiving the royal assent.[6] After this parliament had been dissolved the court of aldermen gave Dr. Taylor, the clerk of the parliaments, what was probably the customary reward of forty shillings 'for his labour hadde in the seid parliament in causes of this citie', with six and eightpence for his clerk.[7]

In November 1514, less than nine months after the dissolution of parliament, writs went out for new elections. There was some attempt by

[1] *Ibid.*, fo. 171v (in Latin).
[2] *Acts of Court of the Mercers' Company*, p. 417.
[3] Rep. 2, fo. 172v.
[4] 5 Hen. VIII, cap. 3.
[5] *Acts of Court of the Mercers' Company*, p. 436.
[6] 5 Hen. VIII, cap. 16.
[7] Rep. 2, fo. 174.

the government to secure the return to parliament of the same members who had been elected in 1512, and London (whether in response to such a request or not) in December re-elected the same four members.[1] Five bills were put forward by the city in the first session.[2] One of them concerned the payment of scavage and was presumably decided upon after the failure of a petition to the king, ordered by the court of aldermen in July 1514, 'for a restreynt from hensforth of makyng of eny straungers denyzens in preiudice and losse of such scavage as the cite shuld have, fforsomoche as such denyzens shall pay no scavage by th' acte of parlyament Anno xix⁰ H. vij'.[3] The bill proposed that denisens should still be subject to taxation as aliens.[4] The other four bills were to prevent the repacking of merchandise after it had been shipped and received its docket, to regulate the making of bills of assurance, to allow ducats, crowns and other foreign coin to be current, and to prevent foreign merchants standing surety for each other. Not one of the five bills became an act. In the second session of parliament, later in 1515, a bill of corporations—no doubt promoted by London—did at last pass the house of commons. It was brought up to the Lords on 14 December, was given a first reading there on 17 December, and a second three days later.[5] Then on 22 December parliament was dissolved and the bill for corporations was lost once more, and for the last time.

Perhaps the city would have tried again if the opportunity had come sooner, but eight years were to go by before another parliament was summoned, and by 1523 new problems had arisen. Relations between the city and the central government deteriorated sharply with the rise to power of Wolsey, and London, far from being able to plan for an extension of its authority, was hard put to it to retain what it already had. The soft words traditionally used by English kings towards the city of London found no echo in Wolsey's conversation. In March 1516 the court of aldermen determined to make every effort to secure the cardinal's 'favour and speciall good lordship',[6] but almost at once had to face instead charges of maladministration[7] and illegality,[8] followed in the autumn by the threat of exact assessment to the subsidy.[9] In some, perhaps all of these particular issues, Wolsey had justice on his side: this did not ensure greater appreciation of his actions in the city.

Henry, too, through Wolsey, on occasion resorted to strong language, threatening in 1521 'to punyshe the citie with such sharp and grevous punyshement which they be not nor shalbe able to beere' for its demonstrations against the execution of his 'great enemy', the duke of Buckingham. People were going daily to Tower Hill and visiting Buckingham's grave, 'reputyng hym as a saynte and a holy man' and saying he died guiltless;

---

[1] Jo. 11, fo. 204.   [2] Rep. 3, fo. 8.   [3] Rep. 2, fo. 182v.
[4] Text of bill, without preamble or opening clause, entered some years later in Rep. 5, fo. 58, and misdated 7 Hen. VIII.
[5] L.J., i. 53–4, 56.   [6] Rep. 3, fos. 70v–71.   [7] Ibid., fo. 80.
[8] Ibid., fo. 93.   [9] Ibid., fo. 116.

and the king was 'in a grete suspicion' of London's loyalty.[1] This alarming news was relayed by Wolsey to the recorder of London at the same time as a report of the king's displeasure at the city's refusal to appoint his nominee to an office within London: the crisis over Buckingham's supporters may even have been magnified on purpose in retaliation, and certainly served to keep the mayor and aldermen in high trepidation for some weeks. The right to appoint to offices within the city gave rise in these years to a series of conflicts as bitter as the more celebrated disputes over subsidies, loans and benevolences. London fought tenaciously to retain control over appointments to such offices as garbeler of spices, keeper of Blackwell hall, and common weigher of London, sought by courtiers and others with royal support: from time to time the city had to concede the substance, while striving to keep the forms of a free choice. And when parliament at last re-assembled, this was the issue on which the city decided to make its sole attempt at legislation, fourteen commoners having previously been appointed 'to devyse what thynges be most necessary and behovefull for the common weale of this citie to be moved at this next parliament'.[2]

The act that London hoped to get would have ratified a grant by the king to the city of the right to appoint to certain specified offices: old, disputed claims would then be settled beyond a doubt, at the cost of allowing a royal grant of liberties which Londoners believed already theirs by charter. The court of aldermen approved the draft bill, which contained a special proviso for the office of common weigher, at that moment a subject of controversy, and ordered London's M.P.s to present it to parliament.[3] How it fared there is not known, beyond the fact that it failed to pass. The livery company most interested in this bill, or at least in its proviso, was the grocers'. The appointment of the common weigher lay with them, for they had the right to present their nominee to the mayor and aldermen, and earlier in 1523, before parliament met, they had announced to the court of aldermen that they intended to sue to Wolsey 'for their mater of corporacion' and for the recognition of their right to this office. The aldermen had given their approval and promised, if the grocers were unsuccessful, to join with them in a second petition.[4] After the failure to reach a settlement sanctioned by parliament, the city decided to take action on its own for the 'matter of corporation', if it could do nothing directly for the company over the office, and the grocers agreed to bring their ordinances to the common council for approval.

All concerned were fully conscious that, if this action became known to the Crown, it might be judged—as it surely was—an infringement of the act of 1504 against which the city had struggled so persistently in earlier years. The grocers presented their ordinances with an acknowledgement that they had all been 'weale and ripely examynd and perused and

[1]Rep. 5, fos. 199v, 204.   [2]Rep. 4, fo. 145v.
[3]Rep. 6, fos. 32, 36v.   [4]Ibid., fo. 15.

diligently correctid' by the chancellor, treasurer, and two chief justices in 1508, 'and by them allowed, ratified, confermyd and subscrybed'. Nevertheless,

forasmoche as it shall not be thought to eny persone that the . . . company entende to attempte eny thyng in the said book that shuld be inconsonant to reason, hurtefull or preiudiciall to the liberties or ffree customes of the . . . citie or in enywise soundyng in to the derogacion or breche of them,

the company asked that their book of ordinances might be examined by persons to be named by the common council. Four aldermen and nine commoners then considered the grocers' ordinances, approved most of them, amended four and added one, 'which they have not doon', they declared, 'ne mynded nor entended to doo of any presumpcion to correcte and countroll nor in enywise to abrogate that that is doon to the said book by the said iiij lordes'. Yet the fact remained that the grocers' ordinances were altered without reference to the royal officers who should have given their approval, and the revised book was entered of record in the city journal.[1]

Tentative moves towards such a solution had been made before. Immediately after the act of 1504 the presentation of ordinances to the mayor and aldermen had ceased. The only mayor at this time prepared to ratify gild ordinances was Sir William Capel, the opponent of Fitzwilliam and the merchant taylors. But gradually the old ways were resumed. In 1517, 'uppon the contynuall sute of the ffelishep of tylers', the court of aldermen agreed to authorize certain new ordinances, but only at the company's own 'perylles and charges concernyng the statutes made . . . concernyng ffelissheppes makyng eny actes or ordinaunce amonges theym selfes',[2] while by 1520 the cutlers had reached the point where they 'dare not presume to make any newe ordynaunces or rules without favour and lycence' of the mayor and aldermen.[3]

A few years later municipal supervision, transferred to the common council, became general once more. In 1528 six commoners were appointed to examine 'suche bokes of actes and ordynaunces as heretofor were geven and grauntid by the mayre and aldermen to diverse ffelyssshippes' to see 'whether that they be goode and resonable and ought to be confermyd by auctorite of commen counsell or not'.[4] Acts of common council were hopefully said to be 'of noo lesse strength then actes of the high court of parliament',[5] but not even the most sanguine Londoner could suppose that an act of common council could override statute, and the parliamentary act of 1504 remained, an ever-ready refuge for any company which was unwilling to submit its ordinances to the city for

---

[1] Jo. 12, fos. 263–72, printed by J. Aubrey Rees, *The Worshipful Company of Grocers* (1923), pp. 70–84.

[2] City of London Corporation Record Office, Letter Book N, fo. 37v.

[3] Jo. 12, fo. 38v.

[4] Jo. 13, fo. 96v.   [5] *Ibid.*, fo. 23v.

approval. London had done something to retrieve its lost authority but it had totally failed to impose its will on parliament.

II

Twenty-five years after the passage of the act of corporations, the city of London finally abandoned its attempt to secure the act's repeal and turned its attention to wider issues. In 1529, for the first time in the century, there seemed to be the opportunity for an extensive legislative programme. The fall of Wolsey, already current knowledge before parliament assembled, aroused hope and expectation in the city. On 14 October 1529 the court of aldermen ordered thirteen of the greater London companies 'to assemble all their companyes at their halles and there to counsell togeder what thinges they shall thynk to be goode and beneficiall for the commen weale' and to present to the aldermen a written statement of their suggestions 'to th' entent that the knyghtes and burgessys of this citie may preferre the same at this next parliament'.[1] The wardens of the mercers' company seized their chance and on the following day read to a general court of the company the text of the answer which they had prepared. In five articles, devised by the wardens in consultation with half a dozen other members of the company, the mercers gave free rein to their hatred of Wolsey and produced a wholesale indictment of his rule as it had affected London.[2]

The first of their five points consisted of a general statement that

they fynde that the citezeins of London been empeched and restrayned of their liberties and custumes graunted to them by the kynges noble progenytors and ratified and confermed by his grace, as in scavage, gevyng of their offices, and otherwise.

Secondly they complained that 'of late daies' many protections had been granted under the great seal, 'by reason wherof the persones enjoying the same deteyneth and kepeth in their handes greate sommes of money of the goodes of the kynges propre subgiectes', amounting to £20,000 or more in a year. The suggested remedy lay with the king:

for reformacion wherof, it may please the kynges highnes to have respecte from hensforth in graunting of such proteccions, so that noon may enjoye them oonles the persone suyng for suche proteccion bryng certificat under a seale autentique of suche citie, towne or borowe within this the kynges realme where he is inhabitant and dwellyng, wherby may evydently appere the maner and cause of his mysfortune and decay.

Thirdly

it is to be considered the greate charge of subsedie paid by the merchauntes, graunted to the kynges grace by acte of parliament, to th' entent the said

---

[1] Rep. 8, fo. 66.
[2] Mercers' Company, Acts of Court, 1527–60, fos. 24v–25v. For permission to consult this MS. I am grateful to the wardens of the Mercers' Company.

marchantes his subgiectes shuld be waffeted, salvegarded, conducted and surely defended on the see from pirates and other their notorious enemys the Frenche-men;

this service had nevertheless not been provided and as a result English merchants in the past twelve years had lost to the French goods worth at least £200,000. Although French goods captured by Englishmen had been restored, Englishmen had not yet been able to recover their goods in France, being 'delaied from courte to courte, from towne to towne, from admyrall to vice-admyrall, and from the Frenche kyng to his council'.

The mercers' fourth point was directed at the clergy.

Item, to have in remembrans howe the kynges poore subgiectes, pryncipally of London, been polled and robbed without reason or conscience by th'ordenarys in probatyng of testamentes and takyng of mortuarys and also vexed and trobled by citacions with cursyng oon day and absoilyng the next day, *et hec omnia pro pecuniis.*

Finally, the foreign merchants in London came under review. 'It is to be noted that the greate nombre of licences graunted by the kyng owr soveraigne lord to marchantes estrangiers, the long respite for the payment of their custume, and the greate sommes of money lent to them by his grace' have encouraged them to raise prices and engross goods, 'by reason wherof the marchantes his subgiectes, havyng not suche recourse or traffique of marchandise as they have had in tymes passed, been greately decayed and enpoverished'.

Although their sufferings were clearer to the mercers than the means of relieving them, two of their complaints were discussed in parliament in 1529. A bill against the recognition of protections was committed to Thomas Cromwell, Paul Wythipole, one of London's members, Edward Hall, the chronicler, and two others, but was never passed.[1] The attack on clerical exactions, on the other hand, brought London into line with national sentiment. Hall's account of the six grievances which especially moved the house of commons began with the two cited by the mercers, probate of testaments and mortuaries. Bills on these subjects were drawn up by a committee of the Commons and referred to a conference of both Houses. While they were still under discussion a bill came down from the Lords remitting to the king all the loan money advanced to him, which, according to Hall, was 'sore argued' in the house of commons.[2] Nevertheless Sir Thomas Seymour, the senior member of parliament for London and former Master of the mercers, reported to a general court of his company on 20 November that the act for the release of the loan had been passed by both Lords and Commons, 'for certein high consideracions them movyng'.[3] The words are common form but may conceal the manoeuvre outlined by Hall, who ascribed the grant of a general pardon

[1] P.R.O., S.P. 1/236, fo. 133 (cal. *L. & P. Hen. VIII*, Add. I. i, No. 663).
[2] *Hall's Chronicle* (edn. 1809), pp. 765-7.
[3] Mercers' Company, Acts of Court, fo. 25v.

and the passage of two new bills for probate of testaments and mortuaries to the intervention of the king, 'entendyng somewhat to requite' the Commons for their release of the loan money.[1]

Seymour finished his account of proceedings in parliament by relating Henry VIII's promise

that oonles right urgent causes move hym (which shalbe evident to all his said subgiectes) his grace woll never demaunde peny of them duryng his lyff naturall, and further, in case they coulde study any thyng that myght be for the publique welth of this his roialme and citie of London, his grace wold right gladly condescende therunto.[2]

Seymour's report was surprisingly well received; the mercers 'all admytted the same to be very well doon, and praied God to save his grace, and sende hym prosperous fortune and long lyff'.[3] If they really looked forward to a happy tax-free future they were bound for disillusion. By 1536 the mercers were lamenting the 'greate summes of money . . . lately takeyn from this house by severall actes of parlyament'.[4] Indeed, the years after 1529 brought few of the city's expectations to fruition. The number and scope of its bills increased, but not its ability to transform them into acts.

During the fifteen-thirties and fifteen-forties (up to 1547) the city tried, and failed, to carry acts of parliament to confirm the court of requests set up in London by the common council,[5] to transfer to the court of aldermen the right to administer the goods of city orphans,[6] to limit the bounds of the sanctuary of St. Martin's the Grand,[7] to clean the Fleet ditch,[8] to define the city's rights in Southwark,[9] to extend the mayor's jurisdiction over the Thames,[10] to prevent the deceitful packing of woad,[11] to stop the

[1] *Hall's Chronicle*, p. 767.
[2] Mercers' Company, Acts of Court, fo. 25v.
[3] *Ibid.*, fo. 26.
[4] *Ibid.*, fo. 93v.
[5] In 1533: Rep. 8, fo. 274.
[6] In 1536: Rep. 9, fo. 181v; previously discussed in common council, Jo. 13, fos. 461v–462. Bill passed the Commons and was rejected on its third reading in the Lords, *L.J.*, i. 98–9.
[7] In 1539: Rep. 10, fo. 97. Royal commissioners had previously heard the arguments of the city and the owner of the liberty, the abbot of Westminster, Jo. 13, fos. 453, 467–8; P.R.O., St. Ch. 2/20/57, 323–4, St. Ch. 2/23/266.
[8] In 1542: four lawyer M.P.s (Townshend, Caryll, Pollard and Catlyn) to be lobbied, Rep. 10, fo. 242v. A bill for this purpose was read once in the Lords on the opening day of the next session, but got no further, *L.J.*, i. 199.
[9] In 1542: Sir John Gage, the royal steward of Southwark, to be lobbied, Rep. 10, fo. 242v.
[10] In 1543 and 1544: Rep. 10, fo. 303, Rep. 11, fo. 44; text of bill, Jo. 15, fos. 201–2. The bill passed the Commons in 1543 and received a promise of support from the council in 1544, but was not enacted: Rep. 10, fo. 330v, Rep. 11, fo. 44.
[11] In 1543 and 1544 (if the city's legal counsel considered 'that yt may nott well be establysshyd for a lawe by acte of commen counsayll here'): Rep. 10, fo. 308, Rep. 11, fo. 30.

conversion of mansions into lodging houses,[1] to make all the inhabitants of the city liable with the citizens to local taxation,[2] and to bring under the rule of municipal authorities all hitherto exempt places in cities, towns and boroughs.[3] The court of aldermen also promised (vain) support for bills prepared by the London pikemongers[4] and the young men of the merchant adventurers, led by Henry Brinklow[5]; and opposition which proved effective to an unauthorized bill promoted by the ironmongers[6] and to another, much disliked by the mercers, against the alleged smuggling of gold and silver in merchants' bales of cloth.[7]

Positive success came rarely. An act of 1531 making denisens pay customs and other dues as aliens[8]—for which London had hoped in 1515 —was presumably still welcome, although there is no evidence that the London members were in any way responsible for it, and clear indication that the proviso to the Commons' bill, added by the Lords, imposing government control over London's rates of scavage, was resented in the city.[9] Two acts removed technical obstacles which impeded the mayor and aldermen, one assuring to the city a vacant plot in Cheapside[10] and the other giving compulsory powers for the improvement of London's water supply.[11] A bill drawn up by the city's legal counsel to lower the property qualification of jurors in London was also passed, but only at the second attempt and after some alteration.[12] Finally, the citizens of London may be accounted the victors in a long drawn out dispute with their curates over tithes. This, however, was not essentially a parliamentary victory. It was achieved outside parliament, in negotiation with a government commission, after the city had repeatedly failed to obtain a comprehensive statute settling the whole controversy.

The court of aldermen first tried for such an act in March 1534, presenting to parliament for ratification a book detailing the tithes due by

[1] In 1544: text in Jo. 15, fo. 203. The bill was read once in the Lords, L.J., i. 252.

[2] In 1545: Rep. 11, fo. 220v.

[3] In 1545: *ibid.*, fo. 227v. The bill as originally envisaged in the city was more restricted: 'that all the foreyn lybertyes' within London 'may be resumed into the kynges highnes handes and incorporate to the seyd citie, yf it may be obtayned': *ibid.*, fo. 220v.

[4] In 1543: Rep. 10, fo. 313v.

[5] In 1544: Rep. 11, fo. 44. This bill, against merchant strangers, had passed the Commons and been sent to the Lords before Brinklow appealed to the court of aldermen for assistance, and was then in the hands of the lord chancellor; it was read three times in the Lords but did not pass: L.J., i. 253, 256–7.

[6] In 1544: Rep. 11, fos. 26, 34.

[7] In 1544: *ibid.*, fo. 38.

[8] 22 Hen. VIII, cap. 8.

[9] The 'table' of rates was still under negotiation in 1534: Rep. 9, fo. 57v.

[10] In 1536: 27 Hen. VIII, cap. 49.

[11] In 1544: 35 Hen. VIII, cap. 10.

[12] In 1544 and 1545: Rep. 11, fo. 27; 37 Hen. VIII, cap. 5 (qualification 400 marks in goods). Text of original bill (qualification £200 in goods) in Jo. 15, fos. 202v–203; read once in Lords in 1544, L.J., i. 254.

Londoners to their curates.[1] This followed an interim award of arbitrators, headed by the archbishop of Canterbury, fixing the rate of tithe within the city at 2s. 9d. in the £ on house rents, where formerly 3s. 6d. in the £ had been due.[2] There was no quarrel in the city with the new rate, but many other causes of dispute remained, in particular over the definition of titheable property, and the city's bill, besides giving parliamentary sanction to the award, would have imposed its own solution to these problems.[3] When the session ended without the bill having passed, a royal proclamation was issued ordering payment of tithes at 2s. 9d. in the £ until a final award was made,[4] thus reinforcing a decision agreed by the court of aldermen nine days before.[5] A year later a further proclamation reissued the order[6] and early in 1536, when London was exempted from an act of parliament regulating the payment of tithes throughout the country,[7] a separate act continued the terms of the award in the city until the whole question should be settled by the king and the thirty-two commissioners to be appointed to review the ecclesiastical law.[8] London, still awaiting this final settlement, was again exempted from a further general tithe act passed in 1540.[9]

In the early fifteen-forties tithes in London were discussed in every session of parliament. A bill was read three times in the Lords during March 1542, described as 'for tenths and offerings' and 'for offerings to be made according to usage'.[10] It is not clear whether this represented a counter-attack by the clergy or an attempt at unauthorized intervention by a London grocer, Thomas Nott, who had busied himself in the tithe dispute for the past six years.[11] Nott was reproved by the mayor and aldermen on 9 March 1542 for acting without their knowledge or consent in preparing a bill for this parliament.[12] In either case, the court of aldermen was forced into action when a parliamentary committee was appointed to discuss the tithe question. On 14 March the court nominated four commoners to go to the Temple the following day 'to assyste theym of the parlyament howse that have the hering of the matter of tythes to be payed by the cytezens of thys cytye to theyr curates'.[13] Two days later these four men and the recorder were ordered to be at Sir John Baker's

---

[1] Rep. 9, fo. 50v. Bills for tithes in London were read in the Commons in 1532, but there is no evidence to show who put them in; *L. & P. Hen. VIII*, vi, No. 120.

[2] Jo. 13, fo. 395; C. Hill, *Economic Problems of the Church from Archbishop Whitgift to the Long Parliament* (1956), p. 275.

[3] Jo. 13, fo. 404.

[4] R. Steele, *Tudor and Stuart Proclamations* (1910), i, No. 140; text in Jo. 13, fos. 417v–418.

[5] Rep. 9, fo. 51.   [6] Steele, i, No. 148.

[7] 27 Hen. VIII, cap. 20.

[8] *Ibid.*, cap. 21; text entered in Jo. 13, fos. 471v–472.

[9] 32 Hen. VIII, cap. 7.   [10] *L.J.*, i. 181–2, 186.

[11] Rep. 9, fo. 76; Rep. 10, fo. 197v; Jo. 14, fo. 122v.

[12] Rep. 10, fo. 249v.   [13] *Ibid.*, fo. 250.

chamber in the Temple at 1 o'clock of the afternoon of 18 March, where the town clerk would attend them with the book of the earlier composition made for payment of tithes within the city.[1] On 21 March the court of aldermen 'longely debatyd' the whole question and finally decided 'that Mr. Recorder shall aunswere the matter in the parlyament howse as he shall thinke good, not confessyng eny auctorytye to be gyven unto hym therin by thys howse'.[2] The session ended on 1 April without producing any new tithe act.

When parliament reassembled, in 1543, the court of aldermen took the initiative and sponsored Nott's bill; the curates also produced a bill of their own.[3] Both were read several times in the Lords[4]; neither was passed. In the last session two bills for tithes again made their appearance. One, 'concerning the true payment of personal and privy tithes', was read first in the Lords on 12 February 1544 and a second time a week later; the other, for tithes in London, passed the Commons and was read in the Lords on 1 March.[5] Neither was heard again.

Finally, in the last parliament of Henry VIII's reign, the curates once more put in a bill; the recorder read the gist of it to the common council on 10 December 1545. It aimed at preventing the evasion of tithe in London by such means as subdividing houses, reducing rents and raising entry fines, and maintained the jurisdiction of the ecclesiastical courts in cases of dispute.[6] The city mobilized all its forces against it: the evasions listed were to become part of the traditional way of life in seventeenth-century London, sanctioned by no less an authority than Sir Edward Coke.[7] The common council after a long debate agreed that two of the city's legal counsel, advised by six commoners, should draw up an answer to the bill.[8] This was then submitted, as the curates' bill had been, to 'the lordes of the kynges most honorable counseyll in the parlyament howse', but was roundly rejected by them as unreasonable. They recommended instead an 'indyfferent examinacion' of all outstanding points at issue—in effect a return to the earlier method of arbitration—which the common council agreed to accept.[9] The first bill, which had been committed to the lord chancellor and other peers on 11 December, was then replaced by another ordering a new award to be made by arbitrators headed by the archbishop of Canterbury. This was read three times in the Lords on 17 December and sent down to the Commons; they returned it six days later and it received the royal assent at the end of the session.[10]

The award was made on 24 February 1546 and by the act had the force of statute.[11] It left unaltered the 2s. 9d. rate and went far to meet the

[1] Rep. 10, fo. 251.   [2] Ibid., fo. 252.   [3] Jo. 15, fo. 20.
[4] L.J., i. 208, 216.
[5] Ibid., pp. 246, 249, 251–2.
[6] Jo. 15, fos. 214–15.   [7] Hill, p. 276.   [8] Jo. 15, fo. 214.
[9] Ibid., fo. 310v (misplaced in 1547).
[10] L.J., i. 274, 276–7, 281–2; 37 Hen. VIII, cap. 12.
[11] Appended to 37 Hen. VIII, cap. 12.

demands of the curates in matters of detail; but it transferred to the mayor
all jurisdiction over tithe disputes. This was soon to arouse bitter resentment in convocation and was seen in the seventeenth century as one of the
prime causes of the decline of tithe payments in London.[1] As in the
earlier struggle over company ordinances the city, with a persistence
which some might deem worthy of a better cause, had found a way
round the obstacle created by parliamentary stalemate. If London merchants had indeed grown 'cunning in the trade of corrupting', it was not
in parliament that they exercised their art.

[1]Hill, pp. 278–9. The curates had earlier complained of being 'thretened by
the officers of the citie that in case they do conventt their paryssheners afore any
spirituall iudge', they would be 'sued upon the statute of the premonire': P.R.O.,
S.P. 1/105, fos. 213–215.

5

THE COMMONS' PRIVILEGE OF FREE SPEECH IN PARLIAMENT*

by J. E. Neale

THE antiquarian movement of the Elizabethan and Stuart ages, which was graced by such scholars as Cotton, Coke, D'Ewes, and Prynne, conjured into mediæval history a golden age of parliamentary liberties. Liberty may have been fully justified of her apostles, but history was set in bondage to a myth, the influence of which has not easily spent itself. Even Stubbs, massive as his scholarship was, gave new life to an old creed when he wrote that never before and never again for more than two hundred years were the commons in parliament so strong as they were under Henry IV.[1]** And though to-day the Lancastrian experiment of our text-books be suspect, still the evidence that led Stubbs to believe in it has not been re-interpreted, so that one who sets out to trace the history of freedom of speech in parliament under the Tudors, finds himself—with a traditional background to his subject which is unconvincing—compelled first to attempt a re-fashioning of its earlier history.

Whether for the earlier or the later period, the task is not easy. In the first place the evidence is so sparse. The commons' journal does not appear before 1547 : indeed, for a satisfactory narrative of parliamentary proceedings, we must wait until 1571. Then the vast mass of documents in the *Letters and Papers* of Henry VIII's reign is for the parliamentary historian little better than a wilderness ; and as for the domestic discussions of the commons in the Middle Ages, they are wrapt in a gloom pierced but by a ray of light from a narrative of the Good Parliament, only recently discovered.[2] A negative argument is thus the most dangerous of expedients, and

[1] *Const. Hist.*, iii. p. 73.

[2] An Anominal Chronicle of St. Mary's Abbey, York, which is being edited for the Manchester University Historical Series, by Mr. V. H. Galbraith.† I am greatly indebted to Mr. Galbraith for placing his transcript of the chronicle at my service.

positive evidence is so partial as to be misleading.   Nor is this
the only difficulty.   The word ' freedom ' itself is a term whose
content is unfixed, depending not so much upon the nature of
any restraint, as upon the nature of the reaction to restraint.
Its meaning varies for different ages and individuals, and
consequently any study that takes account simply of precedents,
becomes a study of the letter which kills the spirit.   Inevitably
we must sweep into our review broader questions of parliamentary development.

However, despite the inaccuracy involved in delimiting
freedom, we may for convenience' sake assume that freedom of
speech in the house of commons was achieved when the house
became the sole arbiter upon the conduct of members in parliament, save only where treason or felony had been committed.
It is true, such freedom was not fully achieved until after the
days of the Tudors, but the important point for us is that, to
control members, the house needed the power to imprison and
fine, that is, to act as a court.   This fact enables us at the outset
of our essay to stress the fundamental distinction between the
power of the commons in modern times and in mediæval ; for
whatever may have been the corporate spirit of the commons in
the Middle Ages, they certainly possessed no jurisdiction of
their own as a court.   They could defend their privilege of
freedom from arrest, only by petitioning the king, or the king
and lords.   Their speaker had no power to procure a writ
of privilege by his warrant, and they themselves could not
summon an imprisoned member and his gaoler before them,
as they did later.   They had no control over elections, nor
could they license any member to depart early from the parliament ; and even on such a purely domestic matter as the time
of their meeting, the speaker had at least once to petition the
king to issue an order.[3]   It was only in Tudor times that the
commons began to assume these powers and to fashion a new
creed which taught that they were themselves a court as were
the lords, and that though the high court of parliament was
but one, yet its nature was dual ; so that it was a sounder
remark than either he or his irate colleagues imagined, when
Arthur Hall, a factious Elizabethan, once scornfully said that
the commons were a new person in the Trinity.[4]   But if the

[3] *Rot. Parl.*, iii. pp. 523*a*, 530*a*, 542*b*, 572*a* ; iv. pp. 357–8, 453*a* ; v. pp. 7*b*, 239–
40, 374–5 ; vi. pp. 160–1, 191*b*.
[4] Townshend, *Hist. Collections* (1680), p. 260.

commons possessed no right of discipline over members in the Middle Ages, the right must have reposed somewhere, and it reposed in the king.

With this fundamental distinction made, we may proceed to inquire whether a privilege of free speech really existed before the sixteenth century. But first it is as well to lay the ghost of Haxey's case, which has troubled us too long. Haxey was condemned by the lords in parliament in 1397, because he had delivered a bill to the commons complaining of extravagance in the king's household. The judgment was reversed in Henry IV's first parliament, and into the commons' petition then made on his behalf, with its mention of the ' Libertes de lez ditz Communes,' historians have read a declaration that his condemnation was a breach of parliamentary privilege. It was a hasty interpretation. In the first place privilege of free speech covers members alone, and there is neither any evidence that Haxey sat in parliament, nor any need to suppose that he did, in order to explain his putting a bill into the commons. Moreover, privilege was never a plea against a charge of treason ; and in reality the petition in favour of Haxey was either grounded upon the irregularity of the trial, since, though not a peer, he was tried by the lords as a court of first instance ; or it was grounded upon the contention that the offence was not treason. In fact it should be coupled with the other petitions in the parliament of 1399, for reversing the newly-made treasons of Richard II's reign. As for the phrase ' Libertes de lez ditz Communes,' which has been so great with meaning in modern eyes, it was a commonplace of the time : ' Libertes ' did not include freedom of speech, and ' Communes ' was not restricted to the representatives in parliament.[5]

Haxey's case, then, does not prove the existence of a privilege of free speech, and our inquiry remains open. In pursuing it we must take care to distinguish between any formal privilege, and the practice of the time. So far as the former is concerned, our conclusions must be based upon the entries in the rolls of parliament of the protestations made to the king by the speaker ; and these fortunately are full enough, during the critical reigns of Richard II and Henry IV, to be of service. Mediæval protestations divide themselves into two classes, the first usually made down to the year 1413, the second thereafter. For the moment our concern is with the

[5] *Rot. Parl.*, iii. pp. 339, 341, 407, 430, 434.

former. They contained two sections, either taking precedence in the entry, of which one was the speaker's request to be allowed to amend his report of the commons' proceedings should he by chance misrepresent them. In all probability the formal character of legal procedure gave rise to the request, and an analogy may be found in the right that a mediæval litigant enjoyed of amending his counsel's plea.[6] But it was not legal formality alone that troubled the speaker. Occasionally he showed that his real anxiety was to transfer all responsibility for his speeches to the commons. For example, John Doreward in 1399 prayed ' qe ceo q'il deust ensi parler en cest Parlement pur les dites Communes ne serroit pris q'il le face de son propre motif ou voluntee singulere.'[7]*

The other section of these early protestations was a prayer that if the commons—or often if the speaker—should say anything displeasing to the king, or infringe his prerogative, it should be forgiven, since the offence would not be intentional. I quote an example from 1378 : 'Et primerement pur la dite Commune, qe si par cas il y deist chose qe purroit soner en prejudice, damage, esclaundre, ou vilanie de nostre Seigneur le Roi ou de sa Coroune, ou en amenusement de l'honour & l'estat des grantz Seigneurs du Roialme, qe ce ne feust accepter par le Roi & les Seigneurs, einz tenuz pur nul, & come rienz n'ent eust este dit ; desicome la Commune n'est en autre volentee, mais souvrainement desirent l'oneur & l'estat de nostre Seigneur le Roi & les dreitures de sa Coroune estre maintenuz & gardez en touz pointz, & la reverence d'autres Seigneurs estre duement gardez toutz partz.'[8]** The petition appears in nearly every protestation down to the year 1413, with variations only in detail. If we ignore the phrases about the lords, the implicit theory is clear : the commons or the speaker could not prejudice the king's estate or slander him— or often it is displease him[9]—without being liable to punishment. If the protestation was more than a mere formality, then the speaker's concern was not to safeguard a right to free speech, of which in fact there is no hint, but to turn away the king's wrath in anticipation by an apology.

In the light of these protestations, I think we may safely

---

[6] Cf. Pollock and Maitland, Hist. of Eng. Law, i. pp. 190–1. Also Michael de la Pole's similar protestation when impeached in 1386 (Rot. Parl., iii. p. 216b).

[7] Rot. Parl., iii. p. 424b. Also cf. ibid. p. 5b.

[8] Ibid. iii. pp. 34–5.

[9] Cf. ibid. pp. 73a, 357a, &c.

say that there was no formal privilege, at least before 1413. But, with Stubbs' assertion in mind, we are driven on to ask whether in practice the commons did not enjoy a large measure of free speech. It must be a very tentative reply from one whose reading has been chiefly in another period.

Few people reading through the rolls of parliament would escape thinking of the constitutional struggle under Henry IV as Stubbs thought of it, for the attacks upon the crown in that, and to some extent in Richard II's, reign were seemingly launched by the commons ; and through their petitions were conducted the assaults upon the royal household and the agitation that captured the council for the barons, handing the government patronage over to them. But we are beginning now-a-days, with the growing study of conciliar and administrative history, to realize that scholars of Stubbs' age thought too much in terms of parliamentary government, and it seems likely that to the new historical school Henry IV's reign will appear, not as a premature rehearsal of the seventeenth century, but as an episode in the mediæval struggle between the baronage and the king for control of the government. Indeed, let us but ask of these attacks upon the crown, *cui bono?* and we shall find it incredible that the magnates were so quiescent as they appear in parliament, leaving to the knights of the shire the whole initiative in what actually was their own cause.

And so we are faced by a puzzle. Perhaps a solution of it may be suggested by examining the parliamentary procedure of the time. In the early days of parliament the lords had been a group or groups, very much as the commons, outside the operative part or core of parliament, which was the king and council. Then they had been able to move the king by petition, like the commons[10]; but as they fused with the council, sharing an increasing proportion of parliament's decisions, they shed this function of corporate petitioning. It is true, individual lords may on occasions still be found petitioning without an intermediary, but the commons were now the petitioners *par excellence*,[11] and for general business it was they who were the initiating organ of parliament—at least, while procedure by petition lasted. This was their function, certainly

[10] *Rot. Parl.*, i. and ii. *passim*, e.g. i. pp. 292, 295 ; ii. pp. 56, 64*b*, 67, 69*b*, 127, 136*a*, 137*b*.
[11] Cf. *ibid*. iii. p. 427*b*.

from the Good Parliament to the death of Henry IV, when, if ever, there was a ' Lancastrian ' experiment. They were used by the lords as a body, to initiate their requests : for example, the petition against the Lollards in 1406 begins, 'supplie . . . votre humble fitz Henry Prince de Gales & les Seigneurs Espirituelx & Temporelx'*; yet it was presented to the king by the speaker in the name of the commons.[12] Individual lords also used the commons,[13] and so did the king. It was on their initiative that Richard II in 1391 made a demonstration in defence of his prerogative ; and when Henry IV wished to make a similar *démarche* in 1411, he sent the chancellor to them to suggest a verbal petition, and this served to raise the question of the prerogative for him.[14]

Now if the commons were, as I suggest, the initiating organ of parliament, we need see no more than formal significance in that activity of theirs under Henry IV which so impressed Stubbs. But if this be so, how, one must ask, did the lords communicate their requests to the commons ? Is there any evidence of a *liaison* between them which would suggest that the real initiative in parliament, in part or whole, came from the lords ?[15] Fortunately there is. From 1373—probably from an earlier date—down to 1407, it was the practice for a number of lords to be assigned as advisers to the commons.[16] Usually the commons named those they wanted.** True, we do not find the entry in every parliament, but clerks were not equally diligent, nor was their choice of entries for the rolls constant, and the practice may have continued after 1407. The reason the commons gave for the conference in 1382 is striking.

[12] *Rot. Parl.*, iii. p. 583. The petition was probably handed to the commons already drafted. A petition of 1371 begins, ' Et pur ce qe . . . fu monstre a . . . le Roi par touz les Contes, Barons & Communes . . . ;' but the formal petition is a commons' petition (*ibid.* ii. p. 304). Another commons' petition begins, 'se pleinont Countes, Barouns, Chivalers, & autres de la Commune' (*ibid.* ii. p. 305*b*) ; *cf.* also *ibid.* ii. p. 368*a* (No. 39).

[13] *Ibid.* iii. *passim.* Surely such important petitions as those on pp. 525-6, 547*b*, 574-5, were prompted by the interested parties.

[14] *Ibid.* iii. pp. 286*a*, 658. In 1406 the Archbishop of Canterbury reported to the commons, 'qe le Roi vorroit estre conseillez par les pluis sages Seigneurs.' Thereupon the speaker formally raised the subject in a brief verbal petition, and the King had a bill read, already drawn up by himself, appointing councillors (*ibid.* iii. p. 572*b* ; cf. *Trans. Roy. Hist. Soc.*, 4th ser., i. p. 179) ; *cf.* also the proceedings in September, 1397, *ibid.* iii. pp. 348, sq.

[15] The articles for reforming the government presented by the speaker in 1406 do not seem to have been drawn up by the commons, at least not by them alone : *cf.* the speaker's words, *ibid.* iii. p. 585*b*. Also *cf. ibid.* p. 100*b*.

[16] *Ibid.* ii. pp. 316, 363*b*, &c. ; iii. p. 610*a*.

It was ' Qe purtant qe lour dit Charge a eux donez touchast si hautement & si pres l'estat de lour Seigneur lige, leur pleust a eulx granter certeins Prelatz, Contes, & Barons de Roialme . . . pur entre-communer avec eux.'[17]*

It would be a hasty conclusion, and one palpably untrue, to imagine in the light of this practice that the commons were no more than instruments of the lords.   They were clearly more in the Good Parliament.[18]   They were aggrieved—or some were—and they had a general idea why.   But there is a great gulf between their vague talk amongst themselves as the chronicler gives it, and the astonishing detail of their impeachment articles ; and one fancies that it was bridged by the lords sent to confer with them.   What actually were the relative parts played by the lords and commons in attacks upon the crown, it is beyond my competence even to suggest : no doubt we shall have an authoritative opinion from the administrative historian.   But if the line of my argument be sound, then the commons, by the normal procedure of parliament, were necessarily saddled with the task of petitioning.   And if the speaker's protestation was something more than a formality—and there are indications that it was[19]—then the commons realised the danger of their task.   Perhaps it is straining the fancy to suggest that when in the parliament of 1406, which in Stubbs' theory was an important parliament, the speaker made his protestation no less than seven times, it was because he was unusually anxious lest he should give offence.   At any rate, we need no longer conclude that the real test of strength in parliament was between the king and commons.   In all likelihood it was between the king and lords.[20]   And some support

---

[17] *Rot. Parl.*, iii. p. 145a.   The author of the Anominal Chronicle makes one speaker in the Commons in 1376 say, ' et de treter de si graundes poyntes et grevouses maters . . . saunz conseil et aide de plus graundes et sages qe nous ne sumez et ne serra poynt profitable ne honurable a nous tiel processe comencer saunz assent des seignours.** Therefore they should ask for certain lords, ' pur nous aider et conseiler et oier et tesmoigner ceo qe nous dirroums.'†

[18] An Anominal Chronicle . . . (*ut supra*).

[19] *Cf. Rot. Parl.*, iii. pp. 339b, 466a, 569b, 658b.

[20] The parliaments of 1386, 1388, and 1397–8 offer striking illustrations of my thesis.   In them all, the formal initiative, as the rolls and statutes record the procedure, was overwhelmingly the commons' ; yet Stubbs does not attach to that initiative the significance he attaches to it under Henry IV, for the realities are known to have been different.   In 1386 and 1388 Gloucester's party was in the ascendant.   Even from the rolls and statutes of those years one might draw the following conclusions : (i) The lords and commons worked closely together, knights of Gloucester's party no doubt supplying the leadership of the commons.   (ii) The commons' petitions, demanding the com-

for such a thesis comes from the newly-discovered account of the Good Parliament, where the commons appear as an un-organised body, and their speaker, not as a chairman, but as a member elected to report their wishes when they were on the eve of proceeding before the king.   To the Tudor historian, reading history backwards, this seems natural, and what slight evidence of the speakership the rolls contain appears to confirm the chronicler's picture of procedure.

A prologue, however, has no right to usurp the place of the play, and so we must leave this argument, stated no doubt too simply to fit all the intricacies of a developing procedure, and must conclude our introduction.   After 1413,—though not necessarily immediately after—the speaker's protestation sheds the prayer for the king's forgiveness, a change which may indi-cate the tendency of phrases to become formal and curt when often repeated,[21] or may reflect the passing of baronial politics from the parliamentary stage under Henry V, or again may represent the gain in independence accruing to the commons from time and an unpleasant apprenticeship under Richard II and Henry IV.   In the middle of the century we have Yonge's case.   In 1451 he proposed in parliament that the Duke of York should be declared heir to the crown, and for his temerity was imprisoned in the Tower.   A swing of fortune's wheel placed the government in the duke's control, whereupon Yonge petitioned for compensation for his sufferings, urging ' that by the olde liberte and fredom of the Comyns of this Lande had, enjoyed and prescribed, fro the tyme that no mynd is,' all

mission of reform, &c., were prompted, directly or indirectly, by the lords. (iii) The lords compelled the king to agree to their conversion into statutes, and perhaps coerced the judges to agree to the obnoxious statute of 1386, which later was declared treason-able.   The point I would make is that Gloucester's policy was embodied in commons' petitions, not because he wished to shirk responsibility—that would have been a futile and childish deception—nor merely to give the semblance of national support to a party programme, but because it was the normal procedure of parliament.   The commons were the strategic point of parliament.   The fight was between the crown and Gloucester's party in the lords.   And perhaps Richard tried to obtain knights, ' in debatis modernis magis indifferentes,' in 1387, because he hoped that without definite leadership the commons might boggle over shouldering a dangerous burden.   In 1397–8 the balance of power was changed where it really mattered—in the lords.   The king was dominant, and determined parliament's policy.   But the formal initiative was again with the commons.   Here is a simple explanation of a *volte-face* in the commons.   It is needed several times in this period. (*Rot. Parl.* and *Statutes of the Realm* for 1386, 1388, 1397–8.)

[21] Chaucer lapsed into extreme brevity in 1411 ; but the king suspected some scheme of innovation, and made him repeat his protestation at full length.   *Rot. Parl.*, iii. p. 648.

members ' ought to have theire fredom to speke and sey in the Hous of their assemble, as to theym is thought convenyent or resonable, withoute eny maner chalange, charge or punycion therefore. . . .'[22]   It is a claim unique in the Middle Ages. Yet how much more than a personal opinion his definition of free speech was, it is hard to say.   Certainly it cannot be taken at its face value ; and it would be absurd, considering Yonge's connection with party politics, to urge that the favourable answer of the government was an implicit recognition of his definition.   However, a certain, or more probably a very uncertain, freedom of speech had evidently come to be regarded as a customary right ; and at that it remained until the Tudor period.

The fundamental change which led to the transformation of parliament into two more or less co-ordinate houses, no doubt was the change from procedure by petitioning, as in the French Estates General, to procedure by a bill, containing in itself the form of an act, and read and assented to both by lords and commons.*   It was a slow change, too subtle to yield its secret to any but the most careful research.   It was accomplished before 1509 : indeed it is very doubtful whether any bill in Henry VII's reign passed without the consent of both lords and commons.   Nevertheless one may still be approximately right in assigning Henry VII's reign to the mediæval evolution of parliament, and in setting forth anew with the reign of Henry VIII.   For then the commons began to assume those new powers which led them to function as a court ; and since they assumed them with the acquiescence and probably with the encouragement of the crown, there is much truth in the paradoxical description of Henry VIII as the architect of parliamentary liberties.

The first of the new powers was granted to the commons by an act of 1515, which forbade members to leave parliament before its close without the license of the speaker and the commons.[23]   How members secured leave of absence in Henry VII's reign we do not know, but probably this act for the first time transferred the granting of permission from the king to the commons.   Its contemporary significance was slight—no doubt but a step of administrative convenience ; and it did not deprive the crown of its ancient disciplinary rights.   Time, however, was to show that the penalty for the

<hr />

[22] *Rot. Parl.*, v. p. 337a.   [23] *S.R.*, iii. p. 134.

disuse of power is the loss of it. In 1555 there took place a great secession of members from parliament in contempt of the queen's commands, and Mary then asserted her control over attendance by prosecuting the offenders in the Queen's Bench.[24]   Whether they regarded her action as *ultra vires*, one cannot say ; but Elizabeth's reign must have educated the commons to such a view, and it is significant that Coke, in commenting upon this incident, assumes it unhesitatingly.

Our real concern with the act of 1515 is, however, as the first recorded assumption by the commons of control over their members.   It leads logically and in all likelihood led historically to the house reviewing other questions affecting its membership.   Thus the crown began to leave it to the speaker to move the chancellor for a new writ when a member, chosen for two constituencies, had decided for which he would sit—and again, no doubt, the innovation was a matter of convenience ; it did not forbid the house to examine the charters of new borough constituencies, probably because they would not be disputed if they were in order ; and then at last it dared not fight out the constitutional quarrel when the commons went on to settle a disputed election in 1586, for in that session there was the great business of Mary Queen of Scots, and minor issues might have distracted them from it.[25]

Hence the act of 1515 launched the commons on a new career ; and in 1543 they broke with mediæval practice still more strikingly when they assumed jurisdiction over their old privilege of freedom from arrest and molestation.   This was in Ferrers' case, the first precedent of its kind that we know, and seemingly the first that Elizabethans could quote.   That it was novel the very ill-success of its initial stage suggests; for when the serjeant of the lower house was sent to release Ferrers, his mace was broken in an undignified scuffle, and he failed to fulfil his mission.   But setting aside the proffered help of the chancellor, as though conscious of the great constitutional issue that was involved, the commons renewed their attempt. They were successful, and, to mark the affront to their honour, imprisoned those who were concerned in Ferrers' detention.[26] The precedent once set, they clung tenaciously to it, and won new dignity in their own and in others' eyes by the readiness

[24] Coke, *4th Institute* (1669), pp. 15, *sq.*
[25] *C.J.* Edw. VI and Mary, *passim* ; D'Ewes, *Journals*, pp. 393*a*, 396–7, 398–9.
[26] Holinshed, *Chronicles* (1587), iii. pp. 955–6.

with which they took to punishing contempt of their court by imprisonment.

Whilst the commons were acquiring these new powers, the petition for free speech appeared. It first occurs in the entry of the speaker's protestation in 1542.[27] The question is, can we assume that that really was the first time that it was made ? The lords' journal for the previous parliament, 1539, contains no protestation ; for 1536 there is a protestation, but no petition for freedom of speech ; and the petition appears in no earlier protestation.[28] It looks, then, as though we might say that until 1539, at least, the petition was not made. But we dare not, and for this reason. After 1542 the speaker's protestation reappears in the lords' journals only in Mary's last parliament ; but it is then mediæval in form and free speech is not mentioned.[29] Yet that the petition was made, we can be practically certain, for it was made previously in November 1554, and subsequently in Elizabeth's first parliament, and in every parliament thereafter.[30] Clearly, the clerk's entries cannot be trusted. Common form walks like a ghost after death ; and probably we owe the entry in 1542 to nothing more than the virgin energy of mind of a new clerk, Thomas Soulement. The lords' journals are therefore untrustworthy, the parliament rolls are for this purpose useless, and we escape from speculation only by the unexpected help of Roper's *Life of Sir Thomas More*. Roper seems to have had by him a draft of the speech which More made as speaker in 1523, and this he quotes *verbatim*. It contains two petitions, the one personal, such as had been made since mediæval days, and of no great length ; the other for freedom of speech, prefaced by a long preamble, and containing with the preamble from six to seven hundred words.

It is clear that More did not consider his petition a petition of right : free speech is not yet a formal privilege, we gather. Parliament is the king's court ; he may be displeased with what members say ; and as discipline is his to maintain, he may punish the too bold or too rash for their speeches. But, More urges, to instil fear will prejudice the king's business : ' as much folly is uttered with painted polished speeches, so many boysterous and rude in language see deepe in deed,' and ' the mynd is often so occupied in the matter, that a man rather

---

[27] *L.J.*, i. p. 167.
[29] *Ibid.* i. pp. 514-15.
[28] *Ibid.* i. pp. 4, 11, 19, 86.
[30] *C.J.*, i. 37 ; D'Ewes, *op. cit. passim.*

studieth what to say, then how.' The petition itself is as follows: 'It may therefore like your most abundant Grace . . . to give to all your Commons here assembled your most gratious license and pardon freely, without doubt of your dreadfull displeasure, every man to discharge his conscience, and bouldly in every thinge incident among, declare his advise, and whatsoever happneth any man to say, it may like your noble Majestie of your inestimable goodnesse to take all in good part, interpretinge every man's words, how uncunningly soever they may be couched, to proceed yeat of a good zeale towardes the profitt of your Realme and honour of your Royall person. . . .' [31]

It seems hardly to differ from the protestations made down to 1413, except in this fundamental fact, that More wants liberty of speech, whereas his predecessors wished to avoid punishment, thereby tacitly renouncing the liberty which More claims. Let us notice, however, that it is speech and speech only with which he is concerned. He is not asking, not dreaming of asking, that members shall be allowed 'to frame a form of Relligion, or a state of gouernment as to their idle braynes shall seeme meetest.' [32] Henry VIII would have retorted like his daughter, 'no King fitt for his state will suffer such absurdities.'

Now if we turn to Elizabeth's reign; in 1563 we have a full account of speaker Williams' speech, occupying more than four folio columns in D'Ewes' *Journals*. Despite its length the petitions are very briefly put, especially the one for free speech, which reads as follows: 'That the Assembly of the Lower House, may have frank and free Liberties to speak their Minds, without any Controulment, Blame, Grudge, Menaces or Displeasure, according to the old antient Order.' [33] There is no preamble, as with More, to justify the claim. Time and a rising spirit of independence had formalised it and had converted free speech into an ancient and undoubted privilege. The contrast with More's petition is so remarkable that I am inclined to argue that the claim could not have been an old one when More spoke his long apology ; and his own experience of the need for freedom of speech, his independence of mind and courage, make it probable that he himself

[31] More's *Utopia*, ed. J. R. Lumby, pp. xi–xii.
[32] The Lord Keeper's speech in 1593.   *E.H.R.*, xxxi. p. 137.
[33] D'Ewes, *op. cit.* p. 66a.

originated the claim. His successors may all thereafter have repeated it.

With the theories of More's petition, expressed and implied, the practice of Henry VIII's reign seems to have been very much in keeping : although so lamentably deficient is our information that we hazard a guess, rather than state a fact. Whatever the earlier official attitude to the house of commons—and Wolsey was rather truculent—with the opening of the reformation Henry VIII took it into partnership ; and it is significant that while at the beginning of the reign government legislation seems to have been introduced into the lords, many of the reformation measures were initiated in the commons. The crown threw the weight of its favour into their scale and hastened that descent of the beam which social changes were also aiding. The long Reformation Parliament proved an invaluable school of experience, a nursery for the corporate spirit of the commons. And it was a necessary corollary of the king's policy that instead of controlling by a naked display of power, he managed the house by a group of ministers. When, for example, Lord Lisle's agent in England spoke to Bishop Gardiner about a motion which a Calais member, Broke, had made against the sacrament, he was answered that Broke ' beying a burgesse . . . might well declare his mynde and opynyon. Neuertheles hee was there [in the house of commons] imedyatlye fullye answeryd by sir William Kyngston comtroller of the Kinges . . . howshold.' [34]

It is a remarkable fact that a masterful man like Henry VIII chose to persuade rather than coerce members. When two of them suggested that he should take back Katherine, his wife, and treat her well, he was displeased ; but we do not know that he did anything more than defend his policy before the commons. [35] When Sir George Throckmorton opposed the act of appeals, the king merely sent for him, justified himself, and forgave his conduct. [36] But we must not be too charmed with this method of Henry's of ' confounding them all with his learning.' [37] Argument might be a little one-sided in an age familiar with the saying that the wrath of the

[34] P.R.O., Lisle Papers, vi. f. 27 (L. & P., Hen. VIII, xiv. pt. i. 1152).
[35] L. & P., Hen. VIII, v. 989, 1059.
[36] S.P., Hen. VIII, cxxv. ff. 246, sq. (L. & P. Hen. VIII, xii. pt. ii. 952).
[37] L. & P., Hen. VIII, xiv. pt. i. 1040.

prince is death, and familiar too with its truth. Too bold
speech was an offence, though it might be forgiven ; and even
supposing we could argue that because we do not know of
anyone in the house of commons who was imprisoned for
licentious speech, therefore nobody was imprisoned, still our
scanty information contains some sinister hints. Throckmorton said that ' the common house was much advertised
by my lord privy seal ' and ' few men there would displease
him.' [38]   Bishop Gardiner, after the remark about Broke
already quoted, went on to say, ' And concernyng further
examynacyon whether the forsaid Artycles and motyon soo in
the parlement made cam and proceedyd of other, to that . . .
yow shall not nede to dowbt but that hee shall bee otherwyse
after a more dewe and strayt facyon examyned then hee haue
ben yet.' [39]   Broke became so obnoxious that the king took
advantage of his connection with the Calais sacramentarians
to suggest that he be put to death.[40]   Again, Marillac, the
French ambassador, thought that a wealthy merchant who had
been imprisoned and his goods forfeited for succouring a
priest in prison, had really been punished because ' the year
past at the parliament he spoke too boldly in prejudice of this
King's rights and prerogatives.' [41]   So, too, we find Throckmorton needing Henry's forgiveness a second time for his
behaviour in parliament [42] ; and Gostwick, another member,
threatened for maligning Cranmer.[43]

   While it would be absurd to believe Chapuys when he
asserts that no man in parliament ' dare open his mouth
against the will of the King and Council ' [44]; and while Marillac's comment about the wealthy merchant is at least as notable
because it implies that he was not immediately and not directly
punished for prejudicing the royal prerogative, still one
imagines that if there was formal tolerance, there was also
informal coercion, and nuisances were not suffered gladly.[45]

   The period from 1547 to 1558 is hardly more than a
bridge between two reigns of outstanding importance, and

[38] S.P., Hen. VIII, cxxv. f. 246.   [39] Lisle Papers, vi. f. 27.
[40] L. & P., Hen. VIII., xv. 473.   [41] Ibid. xv. 697.
[42] S.P., Hen. VIII, cxxv. ff. 246, sq.
[43] Strype, Memorials of Abp. Cranmer (1812), p. 177.
[44] L. & P., Hen. VIII, xxi. pt. ii. 756.   Also cf. ibid. xiii. pt. ii. 771 (2).
[45] I need hardly point out that Strode's case has no concern with the relations of
the crown and the commons. The act concerning him asserts the obvious principle
that an inferior court cannot punish members of a superior court for their actions in
that court.

I propose to treat it somewhat cavalierly by merging its incidents into a survey of the constitutional position affecting freedom of speech at the close of the period. For very soon after 1558 the veil lifts from parliamentary history, revealing a ceaseless conflict between the crown and the commons, constant interference with the proceedings of parliament, and the imprisonment and coercion of members for what seems to be their courageous championship of parliamentary liberties. Traditional history has given its verdict upon Elizabeth's policy with no uncertain voice, and her acts have been condemned as unconstitutional. If we are to review this verdict, then it behoves us to discover what constitutional practice and theory were on the eve of Elizabeth's accession to the throne.

In the first place the speaker by 1558 regularly petitions for freedom of speech at the opening of a parliament. It is true that since More's speech we have had only two notices of his doing so, the one in 1542, the other in 1554 : that is an accident with no special significance. Constant repetition and Henry VIII's fatherly policy have shortened and formalised the request, so that it has shed its apologetic character, and free speech has come to be regarded as a privilege similar to the ancient privilege of freedom from arrest and molestation. In consequence, the claim is by 1558 as vague and elastic as the term ' freedom '; and members of a house of commons which is growing rapidly in corporate capacity, whose independence is increasing with ripening experience and ability, whose traditions, too, are beginning to defy time as membership becomes the lifelong hobby of the gentry, and whose victories over the crown can now be consolidated by registering them in the new journal—members of such a body may and will read into ' freedom ' the most radical ideas, and claim for them the sanctity of privilege. Hence the change from the fifteenth century, when free speech was a customary right, if a right at all, to the Elizabethan age, when it is a formal privilege, formally petitioned for, and formally granted, is a profound change. Its public assertion in each parliament revives it in members' minds. Its lack of precise definition encourages its expansion. As yet the crown has hardly awakened to the danger. The reply it makes to the petition in 1542 is vague, at least in the clerk's short entry : ' honestam dicendi Libertatem,' says the chancellor, ' non negare

Regiam Majestatem.'[46]* And in 1559, when we have the actual text of the lord keeper's speech, it is still vague : the petition is granted, Sir Nicholas Bacon says, but so the commons ' be neither unmindful, or uncareful of their Duties, Reverence and Obedience to their Sovereign.'[47]

As yet the commons do not seem to have claimed that they are the sole interpreters of their privilege. The claim, however, lies in the logic of events. As we have seen, they have already established a fairly extensive jurisdiction. They control their own membership in certain election questions ; they exercise discipline over attendance. More important still, they are now the defenders of their privilege of freedom from arrest and molestation. They can imprison and fine. Why then should they not extend their control to another privilege, determine the limits of free speech, and punish licence ? Here, as so often happens, practice preceded theory. In 1548 when Story attacked the act of uniformity in a vehement speech, crying, ' Woe unto the land whose king is a child,' the commons did not wait for the privy council to act, but committed him at once to the serjeant's ward, judged his case on the two following days, and on the third sent him to the Tower. But they did not carry their assumption of jurisdiction through to the end, for when they desired his release, they forwarded their resolution to the king with the request that he should forgive him.[48]   As yet, then, there is no theory that the commons alone should punish licentious speech : there is the beginning of a practice, however, that may well result in the theory. The same comment may be made upon an incident in Mary's last parliament. A member named Copley used ' unreverent words about the Queen's Majesty,' saying that a certain bill might enable the Queen to give away the crown from the right inheritors. The house again took immediate cognizance of the offence. It wished to excuse Copley on the ground of his youth, and perhaps because of sympathy with his zeal ; but conscious that it had not full jurisdiction, it committed him to the serjeant's custody and announced his fault to the Queen, at the same time pleading for mercy. Mary's reply seems to indicate that she intended the council to investigate the matter.[49]

[46] *L.J.*, i. p. 167.   [47] D'Ewes, p. 17*a*.
[48] *C.J.*, i. pp. 6, 9 ; *D.N.B.* ; *Harl. Misc.* (1745), iii. p. 100.
[49] *C.J.*, i. pp. 50-1.

So far we have noticed the following facts. First, a formal privilege exists in 1558, which is not precisely defined, except so far as practice has defined it. Second, the right of the crown to enforce discipline in the house of commons has been kept alive by use, although the tendency of the commons to anticipate the crown's action by action of their own threatens encroachment. We must now discover more accurately what the content and the limitations of free speech were.

Our starting-point is the vague, earlier mediaeval protestation. Under Richard II and Henry IV, as we have seen, it seems to have been supposed that members might find themselves in trouble, either by saying or doing anything displeasing to the king, or by infringing his prerogative. The second offence is really a more heinous form of the first ; and since the prerogative became an acute question in the reign of Elizabeth, we may postpone discussion of it for the moment, merely remarking that as parliamentary sovereignty was born only in the seventeenth century—though in the womb, no doubt, in the sixteenth—parliament had no right to threaten damage to the prerogative without the crown's consent. We are left to draw what precise conclusions we can from the offence of displeasing the king.

In the late fifteenth and early sixteenth century this offence must have undergone a sinister extension. Whilst the old procedure by petitioning lasted, the crown had had no need of a legislative policy in parliament.[50] The formal initiative had come to be with the commons ; and their petitions suggested administrative reforms and provided the basis of statutes. If the King had a policy, he enforced it through the council. But the evolution of procedure by bill, the decay of the council, and the growing authority of parliamentary measures, made a crown policy in parliament not only possible but necessary ; and it is notable that Fortescue advocated it in his scheme for an ideal government.[51] One's impression is that Henry VIII developed the practice to the full. Inevitably the relations of the crown and the commons took on a new complexion, and the question was bound to arise, whether the commons could with impunity attack and reject govern-

[50] Of course the crown did sometimes have a policy, as Richard II in 1397. (Cf. supra, p. 153.) Also cf. Trans. Roy. Hist. Soc., 4th Ser., i. p. 172.
[51] Governance of England (ed. Plummer), p. 148.

ment measures. Even supposing that the danger to individuals was decreased when there was practical unanimity in the assembly, leaders of opinion might still feel the crown's displeasure ; and as the team spirit was in fact a slow development, it was imperative that there should be some security when criticising government bills. A story from Roper will illustrate the point. He tells us that Sir Thomas More incurred the bitter wrath of Henry VII by his opposition to a money grant, and that ' had not the King soone after died, he was determined to have gone over the sea, thinking that beinge in the King's indignation he could not live in England without great daunger.' [52]

If the petition for freedom of speech was first made by More, as seems likely, then it requires no great act of faith to believe that it was out of this need for unrestrained criticism of government measures that the petition really arose ; and if the conjecture be accepted, it follows that the object of the petition furnishes us with a practical and positive description of the privilege ; one, moreover, which agrees with the construction put upon it by Henry VIII and his Tudor successors, who all honoured it as such—formally, at least. It was a valuable right, by no means to be disparaged because Elizabethans had grown out of its swaddling clothes. Whether this description of the privilege would have been accepted by a parliamentarian in 1558 I find it impossible to guess, although I doubt if he would have opposed it so vehemently as the history of the two next decades might suggest.

We may assume, then, that the commons after 1523 were privileged to oppose and amend government proposals. That involved liberty of speech : but liberty was not licence, which still remained punishable ; and the danger was that while the crown retained the right to enforce discipline in parliament, it necessarily defined licence. Slander of the crown, as Story's or Copley's, and Gostwick's attack upon Cranmer, would come under the head of licence. So too would riotous conduct in the house of commons, of which an interesting example reaches us from the parliament of 1555. That year there was a formidable opposition to the crown, enlivened by a radical section in the commons, at whose head was Sir Anthony Kingston. The bill for releasing firstfruits and tenths was carried on a close division of 193 to 126, and then only by a

[52] More's *Utopia*, p. viii.

manœuvre; for its third reading was delayed a week, and probably rushed through unexpectedly at the close of a long sitting. This annoyed the opposition, and they determined that a bill for recalling absentees should not be passed by similar tactics. Accordingly, Kingston and his group seized the keys of the house, locked the doors, and forced a division in which the bill was rejected. They were summoned before the council for their outrage and committed : Kingston was sent to the Tower, and a fortnight later was released on his humble submission.[53]

A further limitation must be noticed before we turn to Elizabeth's reign—namely, that the privilege of free speech covered speech inside parliament, but not outside. It was the Tudors' consistent policy to forbid the discussion of public affairs in private assemblies, and therefore the development of parties and of concerted action in the house of commons met from the first with legal obstacles, not removable by any existing privilege. Already under Henry VIII a letter of Sir George Throckmorton to the King shows a group of members dining frequently at the same inn and discussing the proceedings of the house. But they were careful to dismiss their servants before talking, and Throckmorton insists upon the casual nature of the meetings, for their legality was in question.[54] Also Kingston and his friends in 1555 had invited themselves to dine with Cecil, and it was only the fact that the cautious Cecil had forbidden them to discuss parliamentary business—an injunction they ignored—that saved him from sharing their imprisonment.[55]

If in Elizabeth's reign the aspect of our subject changes, if parliaments are full of strife, if liberty begets martyrs, and martyrdom a new mentality, and if privilege in consequence becomes an obsession, the explanation lies in that alteration of the crown's powers in parliament which had been steadily proceeding since the fifteenth century, and which, no less than the rapid growth of independence in the house of commons, placed Elizabeth in a worse predicament than any of her predecessors. As early as 1376 the speaker had claimed that ' ceo qest fait en parlement par estatute ne serra poynt defait saunz parlement.'[56]* But not all petitions, especially not

---

[53] *C.J.*, i. p. 46 ; *Acts of P.C.*, v. pp. 202–3, 208 ; Peck, *Desiderata Curiosa*, p. 9 ; *Venetian Cal.*, vi. pt. i. p. 283 ; Noailles, *Mémoires*, v. p. 246.

[54] S.P., Henry VIII, cxxv. f. 248.   [55] Peck, *Desiderata Curiosa*, p. 9.

[56] An Anominal Chronicle of St. Mary's Abbey, York.

those more intimately affecting the royal administration, had become statutes and been more or less given the legal character of Elizabethan acts of parliament. Moreover, until the sixteenth century, even with procedure by bill, a king had been able to amend acts at the moment of assenting to them—at any rate by way of lessening their scope.[57] Edward IV added provisos to an act of resumption in 1472–3 which fill pages of the printed rolls : and not only that, but by letters patent six years later he amended the form of his assent and added further provisos.[58] The power of amendment lapsed under Henry VIII, probably owing to the encroachment of legal and parliamentary opinion, and also because the crown now had ministers in parliament to steer legislation through the houses.[59] By Elizabeth's reign not a word of an act could be altered without the assent of the lords and commons, and the crown's power had thus been limited to a veto. The queen kept her veto alive by vigorous use of it, quashing twelve bills in a single session.[60] Yet this remnant of power was not unqualified. One of the remarkable features of her reign was the focussing of public attention upon parliament. Men strove for membership for experience' sake and ' to learn and sea fashiones.'[61] Puritan synods were held and pamphlets published in London during its sessions [62] ; and parliamentary business became the talk of taverns, the city following the great monopoly campaign of 1601 with passionate interest. As Elizabeth sought to establish her throne upon the affections of her people, she was conscious that she might shake its foundations by quashing a bill in which the public was interested. In 1566, when the lords co-operated with the commons in the succession question, she complained bitterly of her isolation and of the sole responsibility being thrown upon her for refusing to nominate a successor ; and at the close of the

[57] Amendments of this character to one another's bills could be made either by the lords or commons without the other's special assent. Cf. *Y.B.* (1601), 33 *Hen. VI, Term Pasch., plea* 8, ff. 17*b*–18.*

[58] *Rot. Parl.*, vi. p. 74 *sq.*, 92 *sq.* An act in Henry VII's reign fills three and a half pages of the *Rolls*, whereas royal provisos fill forty-five pages (*ibid.* pp. 339 *sq.*) ; and this sixth volume abounds with other examples.

[59] In 1511 the lord chancellor and the bishop of Winchester ruled that the king could add a proviso for the Hanse merchants without the assent of the lords and commons (*L.J.*, i. p. 17*b*). The implication is that the king's right was exceptional in this case. It is the last instance of the right of amendment that I know.**

[60] *E.H.R.*, xxxiv. p. 586 ; xxxvi. p. 480. [61] Harleian MS. 253, f. 32.

[62] Usher, *Presbyterian Movement* (Camden Soc.), p. 98 ; Fuller, *Church Hist.* (1845), v. p. 83.

session she spurned at those who had thought to work her that mischief which never foreign enemy could bring to pass, the hatred of her commons.[63]   Again, in 1572 she made a pathetic but futile attempt to convince parliament that her veto upon the bill against Mary was only a suspension of judgment.[64]   And on another occasion she told the Spanish ambassador that if certain bills on church matters were passed, she feared that ' such pressure would be brought to bear upon her that she could not refuse her consent.'[65]

Nor was the restraint upon her veto the only handicap she suffered.   The reformation had engendered passion and had raised an issue where the divinity of kings could not prevail against a higher loyalty to God.   Once more the difficulties of her predecessors were negligible alongside hers, for whereas the crown had hitherto carried through the religious changes and had preserved its initiative without much trouble, after the opening years of her reign Elizabeth's policy ceased to be progressive, and she had to fight to withhold the initiative from a vigorous, legally-trained puritan opposition, in whose hands the opinion of parliament was moulded.   Inhibitions and threats were of little avail.   Said Pistor, one of the puritan members in 1571, ' This Cause is God's, the rest are all but Terrene, yea trifles in comparison ; call you them never so great, or pretend you, that they import never so much; Subsidies, Crowns, Kingdoms, I know not what they are in comparison of this.'[66]   Similarly in the problem of the succession, the crown had but a negative policy which seemed no policy; and yet upon the future of the throne depended the future of religion.   'It importeth more,' wrote Wentworth, 'than all the members' heads and ten thousand more be worth.'[67]   The same conflict of loyalties arose here ; and the initiative was again taken by the puritans, but with more general and influential support than in their religious campaign.

Elizabeth dared not let bills upon the succession or religion be framed.   She might not count upon the lords as a certain obstacle, and the bills might gather such momentum that to stop them with her veto would cause a shock to the constitution.   The sphere of the crown and of parliament in

---

[63] Cf. *E.H.R.*, xxxvi. p. 505.   [64] *Ibid.* xxxix. p. 42.
[65] *Spanish Cal., Eliz.*, i. p. 604.
[66] D'Ewes, p. 166.   I have turned the quotation into direct speech.
[67] Harleian MS. 1877, f. 38*b*.

initiating legislation thus became an acute problem—as I believe, for the first time ; and the queen was compelled to attempt control of the commons through her ministers, and this failing, was compelled to interfere with their proceedings. A great contest over freedom of speech opened, and continued until the final victory of parliament in the next century.   It was well that in 1558 the privilege of free speech was so indefinite.   It was also well that history was then in its infancy, so that liberty's upholders might pervert it with a good conscience.

In 1559 the lord keeper's reply to the petition for free speech was, as we have seen, in general terms only, like the petition itself.   In 1563 it was no more.[68]   But in the two sessions of that parliament the succession agitation began. Members refused to be satisfied with royal promises which they knew were evasions ; and when the Queen peremptorily forbade further discussion, they talked of their privilege. It was only the masterly tact of the queen that saved a serious crisis.[69]   One thing was clear : the crown must reply by a definition of its own to the definition of free speech advanced in 1566 by Paul Wentworth ; and therefore when in the next parliament the speaker made his usual claim, he was answered that the petition ' was such that her Majesty having Experience of late of some disorder, and certain Offences, which though they were not punished yet were they Offences still, and so must be accompted, therefore said, they should do well to meddle with no matters of State, but such as should be propounded unto them, and to occupy themselves in other matters, concerning the Common-wealth.' [70]   As the trouble continued, the definition was reiterated.

Elizabeth construed the privilege of free speech in a perfectly clear manner.   On the positive side her construction cannot be better put than in the lord keeper's speech of 1593. ' For libertie of speech,' he said, ' her majestie commaundeth me to tell yow, that to saye yea or no to Bills, god forbid that any man should be restrained, or afraide to answar accordinge to his best likinge, with some shorte declaracion of his reason therin, and therin to haue a fre voyce, which is the verye trew libertie of the house.' [71]   In essence it is the positive description of the privilege that I suggested earlier in this essay.

[68] D'Ewes, pp. 66b.   [69] Cf. E.H.R., xxxvi. p. 497 sq.
[70] D'Ewes, p. 141b.   [71] E.H.R., xxxi. p. 136.

Negatively the queen imposed certain limitations, the first of which, namely, that excluding licentious speech, I have already discussed : ' fitt obseruacion of persones, matters, tymes, places, and other needfull Circumstances,' was required, she said.[72] But there were two other limitations which we must now examine. The one concerned her prerogative, the other banned all talk of the succession.

The queen's prerogative included her ecclesiastical powers as supreme governor of the church—powers, as she professed, that existed ' by law of the crowne ' and ' by law posityue by statute.'[73] It included also her right to issue letters patent, for example creating monopolies ; and her right to control the administration. The commons attempted to frame bills entrenching upon all these and upon other branches of her prerogative ; and she was compelled to keep vigilant watch and to engage in numerous struggles. But it was impossible for the queen entirely to exclude matters of prerogative from the business of parliament ; nor did she desire to. Her rights might inflict hardship upon the commonwealth, as the abuse of purveying or the granting of monopolies did ; or the church might be corrupt and need reform. All the queen asked was that a constitutional procedure might be observed ; for as a subject could not sue the crown without first petitioning it, so the commons ought not to discuss her prerogative without first asking her consent. By way of remedy she might allow them to frame an act of parliament, or she might use her own power to redress their grievances ; or, of course, she might forbid any action. The best legal opinion in the house of commons was with her, for legally her position was unassailable. The queen, Fleetwood said, was sworn to preserve her prerogative ; and to talk of it, *rege non consulto*, was perilous.[74]

It can hardly be argued that the prerogative included the right to nominate an heir. The constitutional position was rather that where the best right was, there was the heir ; and it was a matter for adjudication between claimants, though which was the proper adjudicating authority was a disputable point. Parliament had passed acts regulating the succession under Henry VIII, but the crown no doubt had introduced them, even when framed as petitions. And though Norton, backed by a fervent majority, had inserted a clause into the

[72] *E.H.R.*, xxxi. p. 136.   [73] Harleian MS. 6853, f. 285b.
[74] D'Ewes, p. 160b.

government's treason bill of 1571, whereby it became a treasonable offence to deny parliament's right to determine the succession, yet that could not gain members the right of initiating a discussion.   The question after all was one of high policy, neither pertaining to them, as Elizabeth would have said, nor within the capacity of a subject to understand ; and she forbade talk of it, since it was liberty and not licence that the commons enjoyed.   If my earlier description of free speech be sound, then no more need be said upon the correctness of the queen's ban.   And though Yonge's case might seem to offer a precedent on the commons' behalf, it is really valueless in a historical enquiry, unless one can show that practice or theory afterwards sustained it.

The prominence of the prerogative in Elizabeth's reign might suggest a reversion to the days of Richard II and Henry IV.   There was an important difference, however, which, though it has been suggested before in this essay, may well be stated again more explicitly.   In the earlier period parliament's initiative was by petition, the more important of the petitions entrenching upon the crown's powers being made verbally by the speaker.   The king's assent no doubt was often exacted under duress, but even so there was no formal threat to the prerogative in a mere request for remedy of a grievance, unless on the one hand the petition was converted into a statute, or, on the other, the pressure of parliament could be—as it was not—sustained long enough for custom to turn a temporary into a permanent victory.[75] In reality the petitions more closely affecting the royal administration were not embodied in statutes,[76] and unless their fulfilment was possible in parliament, the king's assent was but a promise recorded on the roll of parliament.   Even those petitions incorporated in a statute were merely the moving instruments upon which the king framed the statute, and his replies to them might qualify their sense and the sense of the statute.   Elizabethan petitions or bills were very different. The hand of the past might pen their form, but they were more than petitions.   They were the actual texts of laws, enforcible in the law courts, once the royal assent had been

[75] Theoretically no time ran against the king ; but obviously time has run against him.

[76] In 1386 and 1388 the lords forced Richard II to convert such petitions of the commons into statutes : hence his indignation and the appeal to the judges in 1387. But this was exceptional.

given ; and that assent had been reduced to an unqualified yes, and the veto to an unreliable weapon. Though the crown by a *non obstante* had wide powers of dispensing with laws, still, when bills encroached upon the prerogative there was a threat of limiting it by law, and Elizabeth once was warned by one of her ministers against restricting her rights by act of parliament, since another act would be needed to restore them. The queen's whole endeavour, in fact, where her prerogative was concerned, was to re-establish the old procedure by a genuine petition ; but she found that all grievances tended to precipitate themselves in the form of a bill, and as circumstances brought ' matters of state ' frequently forward, she was bound to defend herself by solving in the crown's favour the essentially new problem of initiating legislation.

' Matters of state,' as Elizabeth used the phrase, were matters reserved as part of the royal estate or prerogative ; and this royal estate was transcendent under the Tudors. It had been busy absorbing the other estates, its last great victim being the church. But outside the royal estate there lay the commonwealth, and one of the problems of the sixteenth century was how political power was ultimately to be organised. There were three possible solutions. On the one hand, the royal estate might absorb the commonwealth, and the state of Louis XIV—mediæval ' status ' and modern ' state ' wedded —might result. That possibility vanished when Henry VIII went into partnership with the commons in parliament. Or ' state ' might retain the mediæval tinge that Elizabeth gave it, be kept distinct from ' commonwealth,' and a system of divided powers be maintained, the crown alone controlling one sphere of action and the crown in parliament another. To attempt this, as Elizabeth did, without the aid of a written constitution and in face of a quickening public opinion, for which parliament served as a safe and effective organ, was to attempt the most delicate of political feats. Men like Peter Wentworth, whose legal training had been long enough to equip him with a sense of constitutional principles, yet brief enough not to qualify his passion by a lawyer's conservatism, turned a blind eye to the queen's distinction between matters of state and commonwealth matters ; and what they aimed at, not less effectively because not deliberately, was the third solution of the political problem, namely, the absorption of the

royal estate into a new and wider conception of the commonwealth.   They were pragmatists, but parliamentary sovereignty lay at the end of the road they were travelling.   Let us
see what these men thought of the most important of parliamentary privileges.

The first attempt to define free speech of which we know,
other than Yonge's, was made in 1566, when Paul Wentworth
propounded three questions to the house of commons as a
retort to the queen's veto on their discussion of the succession.
First, he asked, was the veto a breach of their liberty ?   Second,
should the crown's ministers command silence, and were their
orders to be regarded as royal commands ?   And third, supposing this was so, was a member not free to dispute such an
interpretation ? [77]   The move was a fundamental one, assuming,
as it did, that the commons were arbitrators upon their own
privileges.   But the man who carried the task of definition
furthest was Paul Wentworth's brother, Peter.   Starting from
his experience of royal opposition in the two causes which he
had most at heart, the puritan reformation of the church and
the succession, he grasped, perhaps more clearly than any of
his contemporaries, that the fundamental cause upon which
all others depended was freedom of speech.   His theories he
deduced from consideration of parliament's powers ; and he
argued that as free speech was due to every council, so *a maiore*
was it due to parliament, the highest court and greatest council
of the realm.   Without it the prince and state could not be
preserved or maintained, and hence it constituted a special
law to which the queen was subject ; for though she had no
peer or equal in her kingdom, yet was she subject to God and
the law.   A plenitude of freedom, he maintained, was
parliament's right, both on theoretical and practical grounds.
Once he employed the historical argument.   Henry VIII in
his wisdom, he wrote, saw the injury which would result to
the realm if any member of the house were either blamed or
punished for any speech or bill preferred in parliament, other
than by the authority of the house itself.   As for introducing
bills, why, he asked, should the commons not ' innovate ' ?
Nay, were they not bound in honour to ' innovate ' good
orders as well as good laws ?   And had not former parliaments, to their enduring honour, left many precedents

---

[77] S.P., Dom., Eliz., xli. No. 16 ; *cf.* the similar tactics of Richard II in 1387. *Rot.
Parl.*, iii. p. 233.

thereof, as examples of their power to be imitated ? He attacked particular invasions of free speech, and followed his brother's tactics, in 1587, seeking by means of leading questions to obtain rulings from the house on its privilege. He would have had the crown's right of punishment limited to traitorous words, all commands and prohibitions to the house denounced and bearers of them punished for contempt, and the widest competence asserted for parliament.[78] Wentworth, however, was an extremist, with the defects and qualities of the martyr. Few members were prepared to go so far, though most were affected by his spirit and tributes to free speech were abundant. Even the ministers of the crown posed as its advocates.[79]

We have examined the rival theories of the crown and of Wentworth. Let us now see what the practice of the reign was. The queen showed herself in her parliamentary policy a person of infinite tact. Whether it was her instinct or Burghley's common sense, or a happy combination of both, she knew when she must bend before a storm. Yet she could be as imperious as any sovereign and trounce the commons in the most vigorous language. But her bluster should not deceive us. No one blended wrath with clemency more successfully, or plucked up ' dismayed spirits ' more graciously. She played the prince with consummate art. When, for example, puritan propaganda so far stirred the commons in 1585, that they broke through all previous restrictions and launched bills that encroached upon her ecclesiastical supremacy, she asserted her rights in a very characteristic message : 'her majestie,' said the speaker, 'is greatlye greued that she hathe occasyon to cause this thus to be delyuered vnto you whom she dothe know and affyrmethe to be as louing subiectes as any prynce in the world hathe. And therfore of her great and tender fauor she could not choose but as a mother ouer her children eftsones to warne you to forbeare any further procedinges in this course.'[80]

Then in 1589, when the commons managed to pass two bills through their house, the one concerning purveyors, the other the exchequer, and when, after the queen had stopped the bills in the upper house, they retaliated by searching for precedents and by asking for access to explain and justify

---

[78] Cf. *E.H.R.*, xxxix. pp. 36 *sq.*, 175 *sq.*   [79] *Cf.* D'Ewes, pp. 175*b*, 259.
[80] Harleian MS. 6853, f. 285*a*.

their action, this being thought best to stand with their liberties and honour, it certainly seemed that there might be
trouble. Elizabeth handled the situation masterfully. She
assured them of her 'great and inestimable loving Care towards her loving Subjects'; and explained that she had
herself taken steps to redress their grievances. Nor was this
all ; for a week later she invited the commons to appoint a
committee to confer with the ministers to whom she had
entrusted the drafting of needful reforms.[81]

Did space permit, we might analyse the great monopoly
campaign of 1601, and show that old age had not soured her
or robbed her of her art. But we must refrain. By a
certain amount of coercion, by practical concessions, and by
astonishing tact, Elizabeth generally got her way. On the
succession question she issued an imperative 'No'; and
though the problem of Mary Queen of Scots made it impossible
always to repress the subject, she ultimately succeeded either
in converting people to her policy or in coercing them into
silence—except, of course, the irrepressible Wentworth.

It remains only to review the queen's acts of coercion. It
must be done summarily. In 1566 Dalton was summoned
before the council because he was said to have impugned the
Scottish title to the succession ; but the charge was dropped,
as one of several concessions to win over a stubborn house.[82]
Then in 1571 Robert Bell was sent for and reprimanded by
the council for a speech which touched upon the prerogative :[83]
and other members, as Hobby in 1585,[84] were unofficially
rebuked for what they had said. In the hearts of the
timorous, if we are to believe Wentworth, fear strove for
mastery with conscience and too often overcame it. Yet
so wide were the legitimate powers of the queen, that she
had no need to strain them : indeed, though there was no
lack of speeches which on a strict interpretation of free speech
might have been regarded as licentious, she punished no one,
so far as I know, for any speech used in parliament. Cope,
Lewknor, Hurlston, Bainbrigg and Wentworth, it is true,
were imprisoned in 1587, and Wentworth, Bromley and
Stephens in 1593, but they were imprisoned for holding what
we may call party meetings out of parliament, and arranging
campaigns for church reform and the settlement of the suc-

[81] D'Ewes, pp. 440–6.   [82] Cf. E.H.R., xxxvi. pp. 507–8.
[83] D'Ewes, pp. 158–9, 167–8, 242.   [84] Ibid. pp. 432, 433–4.

cession—not for their speeches in parliament [85] : privilege
therefore could not cover them.   There was no jesting with
parliament over this question of free speech.   It was clear
that the commons might become as stubborn as a mule, should
members be imprisoned for speeches only.   If a speech went
beyond the bounds of decency, then they thought that they
should punish the speaker themselves, as they did Wentworth
in 1576 [86] ; and the ministers of the crown were practically
brought to recognise the doctrine.

The introduction of a bill, such as a church bill, contrary
to the queen's commands, was another matter ; and Strickland
was confined to his house for this offence during the parliament
of 1571.   But so threatening was the storm which this step raised
that in prudence the queen gave way and he was freed.[87]   It was
a false move and was recognised as such ; and the same offence
was committed with impunity,[88] until in 1593 the queen took
alarm at Wentworth's conspiracy to effect a settlement of the
succession, and not knowing, but fearing its ramifications,
placed James Morice under restraint for the same offence
as Strickland.[89]   Immediate and drastic action had seemed
necessary.   The danger past, she reverted to her policy of
tolerance, and though her two last parliaments caused her
great anxiety, she punished no one.

Elizabeth's reign, as it has been interpreted here, was one
of the most critical in parliamentary history.   Her church
and succession policies, from one point of view so successful,
were from another disastrous : they hurried on the growth of
the house of commons, as a hot-house hastens the growth of
a plant.   Not a parliament met after 1559 but the commons
came into conflict with the crown : restrictions hardly noticed
before were bitterly resented ; and the illusion of freedom
gradually vanished from men's minds.   Parliament was
schooled as the hostile critic of the prince, and moderation,
of all qualities the most difficult to retain, was preserved
only by the consummate tact and ability of a woman, and the
chivalrous loyalty of her people.   In her reign, if ever, the
monarchy should have stood upon its rights and contested
every inch of ground with the parliament.   But Elizabeth's

[85] Cf. *E.H.R.*, xxxix. pp. 51–2, 195.
[86] D'Ewes, pp. 241–4.   *Cf.* the instance of Parry in 1585, *ibid.* pp. 340–2.
[87] *E.H.R.*, xxxix. pp. 39–40.   [88] For example, in 1585.
[89] D'Ewes, pp. 474–6, 478 ; Baker MSS. (Cambridge), xl. pp. 105–34.

genius was opportunist. She was well content to win a practical victory without inflicting a constitutional defeat. She left unused powers which her unique personality rendered unnecessary. She overlooked offences the commission of which immediately served as a precedent for committing them anew. 'By these degrees,' as Harrington said, 'came the house of commons to raise that head, which since has been so formidable to their princes that they have looked pale upon those assemblies.'[90] The very measure of her success was the measure of the crown's ultimate failure. For, 'converting her reign through the perpetual love tricks that passed between her and her people into a kind of romance,'[90] she made of the crown in parliament a rôle which no man could have played, unless perhaps it had been her father, and trained an audience, which, if sometimes barely tolerant of herself, would be charmed by no other. She passed away, the splendid though involuntary betrayer of the cause of monarchy.

[90] *Oceana* (Morley's Univ. Library), p. 60.

6

PARLIAMENTARY DRAFTS, 1529-1540*
by G. R. Elton

THE period which opened with the meeting of the Reformation parliament on 3 November 1529 and closed with the fall of Thomas Cromwell on 10 June 1540 was one of revolution. A great many things were done that overthrew accepted notions, and a great many more were planned. A new 'polity' was being shaped, though the revolutionaries were conservative to a degree in the manner of their work. The characteristic note of those years is one of calm assurance that things ought by rights always to have been even as they are now being fashioned; there is really no innovation—only a clearing away of the false and usurped encrustations of the ages. The preamble of the Statute of Appeals with its invocation of 'histories and chronicles' sets the tone. In keeping with their backward-looking words, the revolutionaries also employed the strictest legality in putting through their measures. There was no attempt to do away with the supremacy of the law; on the contrary, nothing was done without giving the courts a hand in applying it. The place of parliament in the establishment of the royal supremacy and in dealing with the vast social and political consequences of that establishment has been consistently misunderstood. Henry VIII and Cromwell did not appeal to parliament for moral authority, nor did they use it (having perhaps packed it) to pretend a unity in the nation for propaganda purposes. They had no choice in the matter if they were to make their measures enforceable at law—if they hoped, as everything shows they hoped, to carry their revolution through on conservative and legal lines. The reformation statutes do not make the king supreme head—they accept that fact as their starting point; what they do is to work out the administrative details and impose the penalties which alone could secure the revolution against opposition. Only parliament—only the lawmaking body—could do this; there was nothing new in this use of parliament, though a great deal that was new in the scope and magnitude of the work.[1]

The importance of legislation in parliament has not been overlooked, and ever since the existence of drafts for acts of parliament was revealed by the publication of the *Letters and Papers . . . of Henry VIII* historians have remarked

---

[1] It is, of course, true that one result of the 1530's—part of their revolution—was parliament's greatly enhanced standing as a maker of law.

on their significance. Stubbs and Maitland, great guides indeed, were the first
to point it out.[1]   Some have since investigated the genesis of enacted legislation from the sequence of extant drafts, false starts and dead ends; the treason
law, the Statute of Uses, the Act of Appeals and the Supplication against the
Ordinaries have all received this treatment.[2] Others have discovered some of the
very interesting plans cast in the form of parliamentary bills which never came to
fruition, and have sought to divine the government's intentions from them.[3]
But here the difficulty begins. It has been too easily assumed that every draft
act of parliament preserved among the state papers necessarily represents government planning. This was an age of turmoil, not only among the makers of
policy but also among men of ideas unconnected with the government. The
'commonwealth's men' of the 1540's[4] had their predecessors in the 1530's.
Though more obscure, the Clement Armstrongs and Rastells were no less active
in thought than the Haleses and the Levers, and Latimer, so prominent in the later
group, provides a link with the earlier. Such treatises as those on the staple and
the provision of labour for industry and agriculture which are ascribed to Armstrong[5] display a lively interest in reform and incidentally an equal predilection
for the term 'commonwealth' or 'common weal'. It is at least not inconceivable
that some of the more extravagant ideas may have sprung from brains less committed to responsibility than those of Thomas Cromwell and his staff. Rastell's
plans for the reform of church and state included suggestions for five statutes
('bills to be drawn against the next Parliament')—to permit priests to marry, to
prohibit offerings to images, for reforms in the common law and the court of
chancery, to prevent the taking of excessive fees in the various courts.[6] There
was but a small step from suggesting reforms and asking that bills be prepared
for them, to the drawing up of such ideas in usable form and sending them to the
man who could use them.[7] They would then survive as parliamentary drafts
among Cromwell's papers. It should be possible to discover some means of

---

[1] W. Stubbs, *Seventeen Lectures*, p. 321; F. W. Maitland, *English Law and the Renaissance*, n. 11.

[2] I. D. Thornley, 'The Treason Legislation of Henry VIII', *Trans. R. Hist. Soc.* (1917), pp. 87 ff.;
W. S. Holdsworth (on the Statute of Uses), *Hist. of Eng. Law*, iv. 449 ff.; G. R. Elton, 'Evolution of
a Reformation Statute', *Eng. Hist. Rev.*, lxiv (1949), 174 ff. and 'The Commons' Supplication against
the Ordinaries', *ibid.*, lxvi. 507 ff.*

[3] T. F. T. Plucknett, 'Some Proposed Legislation of Henry VIII', *Trans. R. Hist. Soc.* (1936),
pp. 119 ff.; L. Stone, 'The Political Programme of Thomas Cromwell', *B.I.H.R.*, xxiv. 1 ff.

[4] Cf. S. T. Bindoff, *Tudor England* (1950), pp. 129 f. I owe much in this paragraph to points made
by Professor Bindoff in conversation, but he is not, of course, in any way responsible for the conclusions
at which I have arrived.

[5] Tawney and Power, *Tudor Economic Documents*, iii. 90 ff., 115 ff.

[6] *L.P.*, vii. 1043. That this paper was composed by Rastell was proved by A. W. Reed, *Early
Tudor Drama*, p. 24.

[7] Armstrong sent his treatises to Cromwell (S. T. Bindoff, 'Clement Armstrong and his Treatises
of the Commonweal', *Econ. Hist. Rev.*, xiv. 68). Cf. also his scarcely veiled appeal to Cromwell: Tawney
and Power, *op. cit.*, iii. 112.

determining whether a draft emanated from the government or not, and all that will be attempted here is to provide such a classification and discuss the 'private' drafts. The sixty-odd extant drafts of those eleven years have therefore been studied and compared. It was supposed from the start that a government machine as highly developed as that of the early Tudors, working moreover through most of this time under the direction of one chief minister, would show a marked uniformity in its products, and this supposition has been borne out.[1]

Taking those drafts that resulted in legislation—drafts, that is, whose government provenance can nearly always be taken for granted—the following characteristics emerge. They are written on one side only of large sheets of paper (about 18 in. by 12 in.); spaces one to one and a half inches wide are left between the lines for corrections; they are almost invariably in a typical clerical script otherwise found in the offices of the privy seal and especially the signet;[2] corrections on them, when not by the drafting clerk, are nearly always in an identifiable government hand, either Cromwell's or Lord Chancellor Audeley's. In other words, they are obvious drafts, written out so as to make correction easy, and in fact are as a rule corrected. The form does not appear to have been original, for there are among Cromwell's papers drafts of indentures and patents which would seem to be its prototype. They are, then, lawyers' drafts. Some evidence, mostly of the negative kind, suggests that the application of this form (and indeed the practice of prolonged drafting and redrafting) to parliamentary business may have been due to Cromwell, but this point does not matter in the present context and cannot be pursued any further. The point to note is that the typical genuine government draft of an act of parliament cannot be mistaken.

It would be too much to expect no exception to this simple rule, and a number of drafts which do not obey it while yet being part of enacted legislation must be mentioned. It will be seen that they do not really affect the rule because there is something out of the ordinary about all of them. They will be taken in order as they are listed in the calendar.

(a) A draft of the Supplication against the Ordinaries:[3] on smaller sheets and written on both sides; but in the clerkly script and corrected by Cromwell. This is a draft of the year 1529 and part of Cromwell's work before he became a

---

[1] All the drafts have been studied in the original MS., but for simplicity's sake they will, wherever possible, be cited by reference to the calendar (L.P.).

[2] Handwriting in the offices of the lesser seals was not so definitely departmental as were exchequer and chancery hands. At this period, however, it can be identified within limits: it is a large, round and well-formed mixture of late Bastard and early Secretary which is met with occasionally in other clerical scripts but predominantly among government clerks; it can never be mistaken for anything but a professional hand and is easily distinguished from more individual writing.

[3] L.P., iv. 6043 (7).

member of the government; though connected with Cromwell, it had nothing to do with the government.[1]

(*b*) Two drafts for the Act of Appeals (24 Henry VIII c. 12) are a little out of the ordinary.[2] They are the first in the series, a draft which is 'proper' in every respect except that it was written on sheets smaller than the usual size, and the draft made when it became apparent that a fresh start on the problem was required. This second draft was again 'proper' but for the handwriting; not a clerk but men a little higher in the official world wrote it (Sir Richard Riche? and others) because it required renewed thought and fresh phrasing. There is nothing in these drafts to make nonsense of the definition given. They were different in minor details and for special reasons.

(*c*) A draft for the attainder of the Fitzgeralds (26 Henry VIII c. 25).[3] Closely written on both sides of smaller sheets, in an uncharacteristic clerical hand; uncorrected and cast in the form of a Commons' prayer. It is likely to be the first draft and the work of the Irish opponents of the defeated Fitzgeralds who may have been asked to submit a suitable bill as they were the party most interested and most knowledgeable.

(*d*) A draft for the bill to exonerate the universities from the payment of first fruits and tenths (27 Henry VIII c. 42).[4] Correct in every way, except for narrow spaces between lines. This together with a decorated first line suggests a final draft ready for submission to parliament.

(*e*) A draft of the act extinguishing the authority of the bishop of Rome (28 Henry VIII c. 10).[5] Like (*d*); endorsed by Cromwell's clerk 'An Acte towch . . .' and by Cromwell (?) 'the busshop of Rome'. Also likely to have been the final draft.

(*f*) Two papers concerning theological matters.[6] Though endorsed 'An Acte of parliament concerninge the true vnderstandinge of holy scripture', these papers are not draft bills; the endorsement may have been a note as to steps to be taken. The form of the papers—smaller sheets written on both sides in a clerical script with narrow spacings—is quite typical of the many treatises, opinions and memoranda on such matters.

(*g*) Three drafts identical in form; one for the Act of Six Articles (31 Henry VIII c. 14),[7] and two for the Statute of Marriages (32 Henry VIII c. 38).[8]

[1] Cf. my 'Commons' Supplication', *Eng. Hist. Rev.*, lxvi. 508 ff. The other drafts of the supplication may be included here; only a brief notice is required as they are discussed in full in that paper. The first of them (*L.P.*, v. 1611, 3) is a Commons' draft; of the remaining three, one (*ibid.*, 4) is also Cromwellian and non-government, while the others (*ibid.*, 1, 2) come from Cromwell and the government. Only no. 2 is an altogether 'proper' draft.*

[2] The drafts are E and F in my numbering (cf. *Eng. Hist. Rev.*, lxiv. 174, n. 5). For F cf. also *ibid.*, p. 181.

[3] *L.P.*, vii. 1382 (1).   [4] *L.P.*, x. 246 (11).
[5] *Ibid.*, 1090.   [6] *L.P.*, xii. 1313 (1, 2).
[7] *L.P.*, xiv. I. 868 (9).   [8] *L.P.*, xv. 499 (1, 2).

They are on both sides of smaller sheets (15 in. by 11 in., to 12 in. by 9 in.), in one of the known clerical scripts, with well-spaced lines, and corrected by the king. It seems certain that this special form was adopted only for drafts which Henry VIII himself wished to see and revise. Only these matters of theological interest attracted him, and his hand does not appear on any other draft except on one of the many for the Act of Appeals which is also a little unusual in form, having originally been a roll.[1] Specially handy drafts were apparently made for the king.

(h) A draft preamble to an act for a subsidy.[2] Though written on both sides of smaller sheets, this is otherwise a 'proper' draft; it is endorsed by Cromwell ('ffor a subsidie'). Whether it was ever used is not certain, and in any case it was a draft of only part of a bill and therefore does not have to conform to the pattern.

(i) A draft for an act concerning maltsters.[3] A 'proper' draft except that the spacing is very narrow, and that it is in the hand of John Uvedale, clerk of the council in the north. Endorsed by Cromwell's clerk: 'Againste Maltes— merchauntes of yorke.' It adopts the form of a petition. In fact, it was drafted not by the government in London but by the government in the north, in deference to local interests, and was never enacted.

These are all the drafts which we can be sure had some connexion with the government and which do not fit the normal pattern. It will be seen that they do not affect the argument; there are reasons why they should be a little different, and in any case it would be surprising if the form had been always followed without fail. The great number of 'proper' drafts still makes it possible to say that government draft bills were written on large paper, one side only was used, the lines were widely spaced, and the writer was as a rule a government clerk (usually a signet clerk?) with a distinctive clerical hand. Corrections and endorsements in the hand of ministers or their known servants confirm the identification. From this it follows that a considerable number of drafts which never resulted in legislation, but which answer to the description of 'proper' government drafts, may be taken to have emanated from the government. With them we are on safe ground; plans outlined there may be used to illustrate the lines on which the government was thinking and working.

However, there is nothing very striking among these abortive government drafts. Sometimes the ideas are interesting enough, but as a rule they are dull— simply details of administration. The vast plans embodied in the drafts printed, for instance, by Professor Plucknett and Mr. Stone are not among them. But ought we really to be surprised at this? It is, on the face of it, much easier to believe that the government was worried about the rebuilding of Dover harbour

---

[1] This is draft H in my numbering (*Eng. Hist. Rev.*, lxiv. 174, n. 5), now cut up and bound in separate sheets in Brit. Mus., MS. Cotton, Cleop. E. vi, fos. 179–202.

[2] *L.P.*, xv. 502 (1).   [3] *L.P. Add.*, 1453.

G

or the fate of the weaving trade, than that it wished to set up revolutionary courts to supersede the common law or build a standing army. That is merely on the face of it: intrinsic improbability does not disprove a case otherwise sound. We must see how sound the case is for ascribing a number of interesting drafts to the government, and it must in the first place be remembered that none of the documents now to be discussed answers to the description of true government drafts which has already been given. 'Diplomatically' they are not government drafts. Indeed, it is really incumbent upon those who would have them be such to prove their case, for they can only have been government drafts if they broke all the ordinary rules. Once again we shall do best by taking the drafts in turn as they are listed in the calendar and discuss them individually. There are only nine of them. The points to consider, apart from their diplomatic appearance, are such details as corrections and endorsements, and their contents; the language employed can be a useful guide to the source whence the idea came.

(1) Draft bill to restrain the bishops from citing or arresting any of the king's subjects for heresy.[1] The draft is written on one side of large sheets of paper, but there are no spaces left for correction, and it is in an individual hand, so far unidentified. Its contents suggest the amateur at work. Citations for heresy were not to be allowed unless the bishop or his commissary was free from any private grudge against the accused, and there were to be at least two credible witnesses. The accused was to know the charge and the names of his accusers. The draft embodied, in effect, standing grievances against ecclesiastical courts, especially in their attitude to heresy trials, grievances which also found expression in the Supplication against the Ordinaries. Since these grievances were entertained by the Commons themselves (the Supplication originated in that house),[2] it seems likely that this draft represents work on the part of the Commons, or of some one individual interested in these matters and connected with the Commons. It should probably be ascribed to the first (1529) session of the Reformation parliament. Nothing seems ever to have followed from it.[3]

(2) Draft bill to prohibit the sale of goods except at fairs and markets.[4] Almost a 'proper' draft, but in an individual and unknown hand. Endorsed: 'Mr. Gybson—A bill concernyng Cyttes borowhs towns and portes.' The suggestion in the calendar that this referred to Richard Gibson, member for Romney,[5] is quite unsupported; we suggest instead that the endorsement referred not to the man entrusted with the bill or responsible for sponsoring it in the house, but to the author who had sent the document to Cromwell (the endorsement is

---

[1] *L.P.*, vi. 120 (2).
[2] Cf. *Eng. Hist. Rev.* lxvi (1951), 507 ff.
[3] There is only the vaguest echo in the act restraining bishops from citing suspects out of their dioceses, passed in 1532 (23 Henry VIII c. 9), but this too arose out of a clause in the Supplication.
[4] *L.P.*, vii. 67.   [5] *Ibid.*, footnote.

by a Cromwellian clerk). The significance of this will appear below.[1] The contents of the bill bear strong marks of a special kind of source: they speak of the engrossing of merchandise by rich men and their unethical dealings in the privacy of their own houses, of the decline of market towns and the impoverishment of artisans compelled to seek a living in the countryside or go begging. The bill provides for public and controlled trading and compels all artificers, except blacksmiths and farriers, to reside within some town or borough. Not even pedlars are to sell any goods except at markets and fairs. The draft evinces a concern for decaying towns of which there is much in the programme of the economic reformers of the 1540's, but nothing in government action until 1554;[2] it attacks merchants much as Armstrong did;[3] and the absurdity of its desire to restrain craftsmen within the limits of towns sufficiently indicates that we have here no responsible government plan. It reads like the suggestions of an ardent reformer with ideas of his own on the troubles of the realm. Needless to say, there is no trace of such a plan in any other document of the period.

(3) Draft bill for the setting up of a court of six Justices or Conservators of the Common Weal.[4] This is the draft printed and brilliantly commented upon by Professor Plucknett.[5] To him it was a sign both of high juristic reasoning and administrative skill. It planned the erection of a court, assisted by a police force (serjeants of the common weal), to enforce 'statutes penal or popular', statutes creating offences breach of which was brought to trial by private persons (informers) bringing a civil action and taking part of the statutory fine. The scheme outlined would have given England an early system of public enforcement of the law in criminal cases by means of a true criminal procedure, and would have saved such matters both from the malice of individuals and the confusion introduced by the principle of civil action. Whether it could have been established in a society whose local government was so markedly unbureaucratic is another matter. There is no other trace of so far-reaching a revolution in the administration of the law; the common practice then and for many years before and after was to commit the enforcement of penal statutes to conciliar committees, especially the 'king's council learned'.[6] The draft would therefore show the government considering the adoption of entirely new methods. But whether one can, in fact, see the hand of the government in this draft, is the question. It is written on both sides of small sheets with a little space between lines for corrections; the scribe, though a clerk of some sort, did not write any known government draft. All the few corrections are by him. There is thus no trace of government provenance in the appearance of the draft.

[1] P. 186.
[2] 1 & 2 Philip and Mary c. 4.
[3] Tawney and Power, *op. cit.*, iii. 122 f.
[4] *L.P.*, vii. 1611 (4).
[5] *Trans. R. Hist. Soc.* (1936), pp. 125 ff.
[6] Cf. R. Somerville, 'Henry VII's "Counsel Learned in the Law" ', *Eng. Hist. Rev.*, (1939), liv. 427 ff., and such statutes as the 'Star Chamber Act', 3 Henry VII c. 1.

Many points about the document suggest an origin outside government circles. The reiteration of 'common weal'—the catchword of the later economic pamphleteers—not only in the title of the officers to be appointed but also in the sweeping adjurations of the last clause, is in itself significant. There is the fact, remarked by Mr. Plucknett, that the one citation of a previous statute is a serious misquotation.[1] The extreme provisions of clause 20, extending the competence of the court to offences not yet created and left to its discretion, are very different from the almost painful legalism commonly observed in the statutes of the 1530's. There are some very odd and oddly phrased sentences which it would be difficult to parallel in known government work: acts are not observed 'and bettir it were they neuer had bene made onlesse they shuld bee put in due and perfite execucion',[2] 'there is neuer at any tyme any sutis . . . entreated of but oonly such as concerne meum and tuum',[3] 'the prisone of the flete shalbe the place to commytte all such offendours vnto'—a curious inversion suggesting the sermon rather than the statute.[4] There are others. The enacting clause is highly peculiar, especially in that it refers in general to the ordinances following instead of to the first section, an invariable practice in genuine acts. Equally unusual is the use of 'Item' instead of 'Also' to introduce each section. Finally, there is the business of the seal of the court. Several new courts with seals of their own were erected in this period, but this is the only one to be described. And in so strangely romantic a way—a ship and the king's arms on one side, a plough with two handcarts, a hammer, and a spade on the other—to signify the place occupied by husbandry, crafts, and fishing in sustaining 'the greate bourdene of the Common weale of the Realme'.[5] One might be reading a political pamphlet; indeed, the seal suggested to Mr. Plucknett the hand of Thomas More and echoes of *Utopia*,[6] though—as he himself says—the draft cannot be earlier than 1534 by which time More, two years out of politics, was awaiting his fate in the Tower. The last folio seems to clinch the matter: it suggests the words to be engraved on the seal 'if it bee the kingis pleasure', surely no way to express things in a statute prepared by the king's ministers.[7]

To sum up: this is almost certainly not the work of the government, but was produced by one of those men interested in economic and social reforms of whom there is growing evidence in the 1530's. If we could point to a man closely associated with Latimer, Armstrong and Hales, whose chief interest lay in the law, we might be able to identify the author. The plan was in any case too vast and difficult to find favour with the government to whom it was sent.

---

[1] Plucknett, *op. cit.*, pp. 128, 137.

[2] *Ibid.*, p. 135.

[3] *Ibid.*, p. 136. These two sentences provoked Mr. Plucknett's special admiration, and rightly so: but are they in any way comparable to the usual tone of statutes at the time?

[4] *Ibid.*, p. 140.   [5] *Ibid.*, p. 138.

[6] *Ibid.*, p. 132 f.   [7] *Ibid.*, p. 144. The words underline the ideas represented on the seal.

(4) A bill described as 'The copye of an Acte of Parlyament agaynste Pilgrimages and supersticious worshippinge of Reliques &c.'[1] It is drawn up in a very 'improper' manner: on both sides of smaller sheets, with hardly any spaces between lines but very wide margins, and in an unfamiliar clerical hand. Its phrasing gives it away. The preamble is full of moral reflections, which is not unusual, but also adopts some very fanciful words; thus it inveighs against the man who 'addict hym self to any priuate or common place where yn ease and ydlenes he may lede his lyfe and like a drone bee eate and suke vpp suyche allmys and sustentation as shulde be geven to poore impotent and miserable persons'. The bill uses sermonizing terms like 'spices of ypocrisy' and is vague when it comes to legal points. Throughout the enactment phrases of moral censure and justification recur, whereas they ought to have been concentrated in the preamble. Altogether, taking into account appearance, purpose and phrasing, this paper was most likely drafted by an advanced religious reformer, perhaps at the instigation of interests either in parliament or government, and must not be taken as evidence of the government's considered intentions. The fact that it was described as a 'copye' does not mean it was taken from a real draft of an enacted statute; 'copye' here signifies much the same as draft.

(5) Draft bill (the preamble only is now extant) concerning the payment of tithes in London.[2]* Nearly a 'proper' draft, but the clerk's hand is unfamiliar and the spacing is unusually narrow. The paper seems originally to have formed a roll. The point at issue, affecting only the interests of the citizens and parsons of London, and the fact that the bill was intended to clarify doubts arising out of an arbitration made between them, make it plain enough that this bill was drawn up by the city authorities; that it was submitted by them to Cromwell is suggested by the endorsement, in the hand of one of his clerks, of the description 'Bytwene the Cytizens and Curattes of London'.

(6) Draft bill for 'A Reformacion for the pow[re] benefices thorough the Realme'.[3] 'Proper' except for spacings and handwriting which is very individual, though so far unidentified. The bill grants powers to abolish poor benefices and transfer their emoluments to others; it envisages a necessary and not very difficult reform. The fact that the vicegerent in spirituals is specifically given authority by it also suggests that it may have come from Cromwell and the government. Against this is its form, not a very weighty objection since it is nearly enough correct and may be a first and rough draft to be worked up later; more important, a correction (not by the draftsman) has changed the perfectly accurate reference to the authority of 'the kinges highnes . . . and of his lordes spirituall and temporall and comens in this present parlament assemblyd' to 'the three estattes assemblyd in this present parlament', a meaningless and unparalleled form of the enacting clause. For the rest, the phrasing is not inconsistent with

[1] *L.P.*, x. 246 (16).   [2] *L.P.*, xi. 204.   [3] *L.P.*, xiv. I. 868 (15).

official origin. Possibly this draft was in some way commissioned by the government but never got near enough acceptance to be put in the hands of official draftsmen. As it is, its provenance must remain suspect.

(7) Draft bill concerning the use of confiscated monastic lands, the creation of a standing army and the erection of a court of centeners to administer it.[1] This draft recently acquired special importance when it was used to clinch a general argument alleging vast plans to build a 'Renaissance despotism' in England.[2] Mr. Stone used his view of this document to support his general thesis, and his general thesis to prove that this document was drafted by the government; his circular argument makes it necessary to tackle both these points.

The document is quite 'improper': written on both sides of small sheets with hardly any spacing between lines, it does not look like a government draft. The handwriting is individual and not clerkly; I have kept an eye open for its recurrence in four years' reading in the records of this time without ever coming across it again, in itself not a bad argument for suspecting that it did not belong to any one connected with the government. Most significant is an endorsement on it of the name 'Thomas gybson'. This is not only contemporary (and not, as Mr. Stone supposes, possibly Elizabethan),[3] but moreover in the familiar hand of a Cromwellian clerk much employed in endorsing the names of senders on Cromwell's incoming correspondence. It is at least likely that a Thomas Gibson sent the paper to Cromwell, and—despite Mr. Stone's failure to make anything of the name—there is a Thomas Gibson, obscure enough but interesting, in this context. He was a protégé of Latimer's, an executor of Clement Armstrong's will, a grocer turned printer and a man who communicated some rather absurd ideas to Cromwell.[4] In other words, he admirably fits the part for which the endorsement seems to cast him, and it is quite probable that the endorsement on document (2)[5] refers to the same man. 'Diplomatically', the paper suggests private provenance.

Its phrasing and contents support this conclusion. Mr. Stone's view that

---

[1] *L.P.*, xiv. I. 871.

[2] L. Stone, 'The Political Programme of Thomas Cromwell', *B.I.H.R.*, xxiv. 1 ff.

[3] *Ibid.*, p. 11.

[4] His figure emerges from the following few notices: Thomas Gibson, grocer of London, signed Clement Armstrong's will (Bindoff, *op. cit.*, in *Econ. Hist. Rev.*, xiv. 72; Armstrong himself was a grocer before he turned pamphleteer—*ibid.*, p. 69); he may still have been a grocer in 1538 (*L.P.*, xiii. II. 1192); before that, however, he had taken up printing in the reforming interest, and Latimer recommended him to Cromwell for the 'Bishops' Book' of 1537 (*L.P.*, xii. II. 295). The Thomas Gibson who some time in 1537–8 wrote to Cromwell, offering to prove the king's coming victory over the pope from many curious prophecies which he had collected (*L.P.*, xii. II. 1242), may well have been the same man; such mild forms of religious mania went commonly enough with reforming ideas in church and commonwealth.

[5] Above, pp. 182-3.

only a statesman could frame a draft satisfying to so many interests[1] is in conflict with the evidence of private excellence provided, for instance, by document (3) above; moreover, the desire to see the monasteries north of the Trent saved and to keep the dispossessed monks from contact with the world by reconstituting a propertyless monasticism went clean contrary to express government policy. On the other hand, that the dissolution had bad social consequences became one of the commonplaces of the Latimer group of reformers.[2] Especially noticeable is the reference to monks 'accomptyd ded persons in the law',[3] correct enough but never allowed to interfere with the dissolution and in fact irrelevant to it; it recalls the juristic philosophizing of draft (3). To Mr. Stone, the petitionary phrase with which the document opens is categorical proof that it was 'either drawn up by the same hand as' the second act of succession, 'or was based upon it'. 'As such', he goes on, 'it must be the work of a lawyer, and one in the employ of the government.'[4] The deduction hardly follows; moreover, it is wise to avoid all dogmatism where the petitionary or enacting clause is concerned. There was little regularity or definition about the practice in such matters, except that there had to be a mention of king, lords, and commons. Remarks in the preamble about the hurt to the realm which the suppression of the monasteries had caused would read most surprisingly if they had been drafted by the government. The concern with husbandry, hospitality, unemployment and old age was at least as marked among the social theorists of the time as in Henry VIII's government; most people would say the former cared more. The sum of £1,000 allocated to the upkeep of fortifications is absurdly small when compared with the actual expenditure on such items in these years.[5] The choice of Coventry as the seat of the court—because it is 'not farre from the mydell of the realme'—provides the sort of fanciful touch one would expect in a private plan. All government was being more and more concentrated at Westminster, and no responsible statesman would have dreamt of sending so important a department as a virtual war office half way across the country. The further argument that the decay of Coventry might thereby be arrested recalls the reformers' concern with towns.[6]

[1] Stone, *op. cit.*, p. 4. His reference to 'a crank reformer' shows his misapprehension of the true position: the more far-reaching and complicated a suggested piece of legislation is, the less likely it is to have originated with the government. Those who had to carry laws into effect knew well the possible limits of the bureaucracy at their disposal.

[2] Cf. R. W. Chambers, *Thomas More* (1948), p. 261.

[3] Stone, *op. cit.*, p. 14.

[4] *Ibid.*, p. 4. The form of a petition by both houses also occurs in the attainder of Elizabeth Barton, the act confiscating the property of the knights of St. John and the Cleves divorce (23 Henry VIII c. 12; 32 Henry VIII cc. 24, 25; the last two are referred to by Mr. Stone). It proves nothing.

[5] E.g.: between September 1532 and June 1533 the treasurer of Berwick alone received £23,368 (*L.P.*, vi. 664); in 1538, financial assistance to be given to 'certain garrisons' if some plans were followed was put at 20,000 marks (*L.P.*, xiii. II. 1).

[6] In draft (2) above; and there too the name Gibson appears.

It is impossible to recite all the detail here: if the draft stood by itself, it could not seriously be thought to have been a plan devised by the government.

But Mr. Stone has argued that it was meant to provide the coping-stone in a system of despotism, and if his view that Cromwell was planning a despotism were tenable the draft would indeed fill that place well. This is not the place to enter into a consideration of Cromwell's real plans, though one may remark in passing that it was a strange despotism that relied so largely on the legislative supremacy of parliament. But Mr. Stone's own arguments in favour of his thesis must be rapidly reviewed.[1] Maitland's suggestion that in the 1530's the common law was nearly displaced by the civil law, and liberty therefore by despotism,[2] was long ago severely modified by Holdsworth:[3] the supremacy of the common law itself was never threatened by the conciliar courts, though these looked likely to become permanent rivals to the common law *courts*. The court of commonweal was not a government project, and if it had been it would not have threatened the common (and statute) law whose enforcement it was meant to secure; no basis for a 'Renaissance despotism' there.[4] Treason by words was recognized by the common law in the fifteenth century and only reduced to statute in 1534, not invented then.[5] The supposed nation-wide network of informers is a myth; men who wrote delating offenders were either magistrates whose ordinary duty it was to do so, or—very occasionally—men with a grudge; there is no trace of evidence for a government-organized system.[6] Cromwell's attempts to influence elections to parliament are not to be properly described as packing, being but mild precursors of the ordinary policy of the next 300 years and certainly not 'dictatorial' except perhaps in the one known case of Canterbury in 1536—and even there we are not familiar with the circumstances.[7] Whatever the purpose of the lost original draft of the Act of Proclamations may have been, no argument can rest on it *in absentia*; it is certain that the act as it stands only provides machinery for the enforcement of proclamations and it is at least likely that its first form was designed to do the same thing, though probably by less palatable methods.[8] In fact, there is not one piece of genuine

---

[1] Stone, *op. cit.*, p. 2.   [2] Maitland, *English Law and the Renaissance*.

[3] Holdsworth, *Hist. of Eng. Law*, iv. 252 ff., esp. 283–5.

[4] Cf. Plucknett, *op. cit.*, p. 130.

[5] I. D. Thornley, 'Treason by Words in the Fifteenth Century', *Eng. Hist. Rev.*, xxxii (1917), 556 ff.

[6] The argument (which is not peculiar to Mr. Stone) for this network relies on R. B. Merriman, *Life and Letters of Thomas Cromwell*, esp. pp. 116 ff. That book is marked by an unfounded over-emphasis on the supposed sinister and terrorizing activities of Cromwell. From it an idea seems to have arisen of Cromwell as a sort of premature Metternich organizing a police state.

[7] Cf. my remarks on the question of elections and Cromwell, *Camb. Hist. Journal*, x. 160 ff.

[8] Cf. Stone, *op. cit.*, p. 2, n. 11. E. R. Adair's discussion of this act (*Eng. Hist. Rev.*, xxxii. 24 ff.) must stand. Cromwell's letter of 1535 (*L.P.*, viii. 1042; Merriman, *op. cit.*, i. 409 f.) only proves that the judges held sound views on proclamations; he himself was so far from wishing to replace statute by proclamation that he doubted whether proclamations not grounded upon a specific statute were

evidence to suggest that Cromwell planned a despotism, 'Renaissance' or other-wise; the casual remarks of opponents like Chapuys or the virulence of personal enemies like Cardinal Pole are hardly worth calling evidence. No one can doubt that his government was vigorous, direct and often ruthless, employing the legitimate and constitutional means to hand; but that is a very different thing.

Mr. Stone sees the 'key to the whole of this elaborate programme' in the need for financial and military power, to be supplied from the wealth of the church and its suitable employment. Since there was no such elaborate pro-gramme it is the less necessary to look for a key. Nor were such far-reaching ambitions required to make Henry and Cromwell look to the Church for the filling of coffers left empty by Wolsey. Mr. Stone argues that the employment of clerical wealth for the creation of an army was much mooted; if he were right, one would indeed have to think differently of the draft under discussion. He prints a document which, he says, contains 'the basis of the government's policy' for a decade from 1533 onwards.[1] Perhaps so—but about as many of its sugges-tions as were adopted were never put through, and there is in it no trace of a plan for an army.[2] Where indeed is the 'considerable other evidence that the need for a standing army was preoccupying the government through those years'?[3] Chapuys said in 1535 that the king had enough money to equip a force of 1,000 men 'as they have sometimes said';[4] does this prove any intention to create a large army, or is it not rather in line with the setting up of the bodyguard of 200 (ultimately 50) gentlemen-pensioners, much discussed before it was established in 1539,[5] an altogether tamer affair? As for the projected garrisons in the north, the document quoted by Mr. Stone shows that Cromwell did not plan them so much as express doubts whether they would not lead to more trouble than they would cure,[6] while the plan of 1538 referred to a slight reinforcement for existing garrisons (probably those of Berwick and Carlisle).[7] Mr. Stone himself admits that attacks on episcopal wealth did not necessarily come from the government;

---

legal. Marillac's letter (*L.P.*, xiv. I. 1207) shows that, as so often, he had only heard an inaccurate rumour. Much of the 'despotic' flavour given to this period comes from excessive reliance on the hostile and ill-informed reports of ambassadors. The argument cannot be saved by what King James said seventy years after.•

[1] Stone, *op. cit.*, pp. 3, 9 ff. This paper was probably, though not certainly, produced by the govern-ment.

[2] The confiscation of episcopal lands and the payment of salaries to bishops did occupy the govern-ment's attention; Mr. Stone could have found better proof in a document written by Thomas Wrio-thesley and therefore certainly coming from the government (*L.P.*, vii. 1356).

[3] Stone, *op. cit.*, p. 5. His arguments are taken in turn.

[4] *L.P.*, viii. 121.

[5] *L.P.*, xii. I. 237; xiii. I. 503, 510; II. 1, 111; xiv. I. 29, 719, 745–6.

[6] *L.P.*, xi. 1410: 'If the King will have garrisons planted they should be thought of in time and so ordered as not to offend the people. . . .'

[7] *L.P.*, xiii. II. 1. The sum to be allotted was the same as that to be reserved for the upkeep of 200 gentlemen-at-arms.

his example—John Parkyns's scheme—is, within its narrower field, as detailed
as the plans for the court of centeners.[1] Not all devices to increase government
revenue at the expense of the Church arose in government circles; one of the
most extraordinary, advocating the confiscation of all church property down to
parish glebes, was certainly a private extravaganza.[2] Mere elaboration of im-
practicable ideas does not mark them as coming from the government. Mr.
Stone does not improve one's trust in his conclusions when—to prove that the
government contemplated the seizure of church ornaments and chantries—he
quotes a list of Cromwell's notes in which nothing of the sort occurs and a vague
view of the government's possible intentions expressed by the imperial ambassador.[3] There is practically no sign that Cromwell's government ever seriously
intended to proceed further with the confiscation of church revenues than the
dissolution of the monasteries and Order of St. John. What matters more here,
there is no sign at all that a standing army was ever contemplated. In 1539,
when the government was faced with the danger of invasion, it worked hard to
bring the militia up to strength, as plentiful muster rolls evidence,[4] but no army
of mercenaries was hired or even considered. What Sir Edward Coke said in
the reign of James I is hardly evidence; he may well have seen some such paper
as that under discussion here and also have thought it a government project.
His summary reads as though something like this document, or perhaps the
Lansdowne MS. quoted above, had been the basis of it, and even Coke could err.[5]

The conclusion must therefore be that Mr. Stone has failed to prove any
'despotic' intentions on the part of Cromwell's administration.[6] We repeat that
we cannot here join issue on the larger aspects of his paper, we cannot enter
our plea for a true view of the 1530's; what matters is that the draft for the
court of centeners—which in itself is about as sure not to have originated with
the government as any draft of this period—cannot be made part of a 'political
programme of Thomas Cromwell' which never existed. It follows that nothing
stands in the way to seeing in this document a private plan, communicated and
perhaps thought up by Thomas Gibson.

[1] L.P., xii. I. 261.
[2] Brit. Mus., Lansd. MS. 1, fos. 215–16.
[3] L.P., viii. 475; x. 282. Stone, op. cit., p. 5, n. 5.
[4] L.P., xiv. I. 652.
[5] Stone, op. cit., pp. 17 f. Mr. Stone says (p. 17) that Coke must either have seen such a plan or
simply invented it. Of course he did not invent it; the point is rather whether the plan he saw really
emanated from the government. That he said it did proves nothing at all.
[6] For a warning against Mr. Stone's too definite assertions cf. his statement that Chapuys reported
Cromwell to be in favour of slowing down the dissolution, but was opposed by the king (p. 8). The
letter he cites (L.P., x. 601) only shows that Chapuys was relating the merest rumour (even he said he
had only been told); yet this unreliable rumour becomes the basis for a confident assertion on Cromwell's
attitude to the dissolution, to be followed by a quite unsupported and equally confident allegation about
his attitude to bishops.

(8) A draft bill for abolishing some liberties enjoyed by the Church.[1] On both sides of small sheets, in an individual hand and with no spacings; therefore probably a private draft. As it is endorsed by a Cromwellian clerk with a rather lengthy title ('of grauntes by the noble prynces of this Realme for good intent yoven to spirituall men, nowe abused'), it may again have been sent to Cromwell for consideration. The fact that the bill would have subjected the inhabitants of these liberties to municipal and not to royal jurisdiction supports the view that the draft did not emanate from the government.

(9) A very long draft bill for a poor law.[2]* A 'proper' draft, except that it was written on both sides of small sheets; it seems to be in the hand of a government clerk. Its provisions were to come into operation on 1 March 1536-7, so that it may have been planned to take the place of the act of 27 Henry VIII c. 25 (passed in the spring of 1536). Its vast scope, general scale, and great administrative difficulties—it is a real though short-term poor law code, envisaging a system of public works paid for out of a general graduated income tax and complete with a health service for the labourers—would have caused it to be dropped in favour of a stop-gap measure when the government found itself confronted with the work caused by the dissolution of the monasteries. The draft deserves a detailed study which the present writer hopes to devote to it some time; in the meantime he can only give it as his opinion, for what it is worth, that it represents a plan drawn up not by the government but on its initiative. Possibly several ideas for a poor law were commissioned and collected, and the simplest put through.

That concludes the discussion of parliamentary drafts in the 1530's. Some represent the early stages of enacted legislation, some are government plans which came to nothing, some—and they include the most interesting—are the fruit of private labour, the work of men interested in social, economic and religious reforms who sent their ideas to Cromwell as their best hope, and at times prepared them in the form of parliamentary bills so that the minister might the more readily adopt them. About a few of the documents we cannot be sure. A list of the extant drafts classified accordingly is appended.

APPENDIX

This list does not claim to be beyond cavil, but it is hoped that at least it may be exhaustive. A number of documents described as drafts in the calendar are not included because they are in fact not drafts but later copies, or not parliamentary material at all. Two drafts listed in

[1] *L.P.*, xv. 501. *L.P.* refer to 32 Henry VIII c. 12 (concerning sanctuaries) but I can see little connexion between the two.

[2] Brit. Mus., Royal MS. 18. C. vi. (not calendared in *L.P.*).

L.P., v. 50 and vii. 1380 (2) cannot now be traced at the Public Record Office and have been omitted. All references but the last in the list are to volumes of the *Letters and Papers*.

Drafts for acts passed, originating with the government.
    iv. 6043 (6); v. 52 (1, 2), 721 (1, 4, 8, 9, 11), 1016 (1, 2); vi. 120 (3–8); vii. 57 (2), 62, 1381 (1–5); x. 246 (1, 2, 4–6, 8, 11, 14), 1090; xiv. I. 868 (9, 12); xv. 499 (1–3).

Drafts for acts passed, originating outside the government.
    iv. 6043 (7); v. 1016 (3, 4); vii. 1382 (1).

Abortive government drafts.
    v. 721 (10, 12); vii. 66 (2), 1611 (1, 2); x. 246 (18); xiv. I. 872, 876; xv. 502 (1); *Add.*, 663, 824, 899, 1453, 1480.

Abortive drafts from outside the government.
    vi. 120 (2); vii. 67, 1611 (4); x. 246 (16); xi. 204; xiv. I. 871; xv. 501.

Abortive drafts possibly commissioned by the government but drafted outside it.
    xiv. I. 868 (15); Brit. Mus., Royal MS. 18 C. vi.

7

THE POLITICAL CREED OF
THOMAS CROMWELL*

by G. R. Elton

TWO views are current concerning the political views of
Thomas Cromwell. One—the more common—holds that
he believed in absolute monarchy and desired to establish it
in England. The Abbé Constant, summarizing (as was his wont)
other people's views in language free from other people's reservations, stated it most starkly: he thought that Cromwell aimed at
making Henry 'tout-puissant' and that his ministry was the golden
age of Tudor despotism.[1] Quite recently, an ingenious theory,
buttressed with a misunderstood document, based itself on this
general conviction.[2] This view has suffered curiously little from
the growing realization that the Henrician Reformation rested on
conscious co-operation with Parliament and that the propagandists of the time never produced a theory of absolute monarchy.[3] Pollard, the defender of Henry VIII's constitutionalism,
seems to have held that, though the king had no ambitions for a
genuine despotism, Cromwell certainly harboured such ideas.[4]
The other view, recently given support by Dr. Parker,[5] holds
that Cromwell did not bother at all about theoretical issues, that
his 'resolutely Philistine type of mind' despised political theory,
and that he never thought beyond the establishment of a sovereign

[1] G. Constant, *La Réforme en Angleterre: Henri VIII* (1930), pp. 179 f,
Cf. R. B. Merriman, *Life and Letters of Thomas Cromwell* (1902) (hereafter
cited as *Cromwell's Letters*), i. 112; K. Pickthorn, *Early Tudor Government:
Henry VIII* (1934), p. 203, and J. B. Mackie, *The Early Tudors* (1952),
p. 417 (with reservations); P. Hughes, *The Reformation in England: The
King's Proceedings* (1950), p. 225.
[2] L. Stone, 'Thomas Cromwell's Political Programme', *Bull. Inst. Hist.
Res.*, xxiv (1951), 1 ff.; and cf. my reply, *ibid.*, xxv (1952), 126 ff.
[3] F. Baumer, *Early Tudor Theory of Kingship* (1940); W. G. Zeeveld,
Foundations of Tudor Policy (1948).
[4] A. F. Pollard, *Henry VIII* (1905), p. 323.
[5] T. M. Parker, 'Was Thomas Cromwell a Machiavellian?', *Journal of
Eccl. Hist.*, i (1950), 63 ff.

monarchy. Thus, too, Mr. Baumer thought that Cromwell saw in Parliament 'only a means of executing the royal will', but also that he 'had no theoretical views whatever about the relation of the king to the law'—passages hard to reconcile but suggestive of Dr. Parker's views rather than M. Constant's.[1]

In opposition to these views I should like to put forward an interpretation which, starting from the supposition that Cromwell was greatly interested in theories of the state and of law, arrives at the conclusion that his political creed centred on the legal supremacy of the king in Parliament and included no ambitions for a purely royal despotism. Admittedly, the attempt will encounter formidable difficulties. Interested in theory or not, Cromwell was certainly no writer of theory, and the only direct testimony to his political views is that on which rests the opinion that he favoured despotism. He is that bane of the historian—a man whose awareness of theory and capacity for real thought cannot be doubted, but whose tenets have to be laboriously extracted from his deeds. Yet, as Dr. Parker has recognized,[2] Cromwell's mind matters because it was he who directed the Henrician Reformation and in all probability determined its 'unique and peculiar course'. I have offered proof of this elsewhere[3]; here I must content myself with asserting that the ideas underlying the Reformation emanated from Cromwell rather than the king, and that the Reformation legislation embodies his views of Church and State. Furthermore, difficult though it is to maintain the distinction, I have time on this occasion only to discuss Cromwell's theory of the State; his attitude to Church and religion must on the whole be left out. In any case, he was notoriously secular in his thought, and an understanding of what he held about the nature of the State he was reconstructing is the first essential for an understanding of the man.

I

It is first necessary to dispose of the two established views just outlined. The notion that Cromwell had no time for theories is easily disproved. Whatever the value of Reginald Pole's famous account of his conversation with Cromwell on the State

[1] Baumer, *op. cit.*, pp. 152, 169.   [2] *Op. cit.*, p. 63.
[3] 'King or Minister? The Man behind the Henrician Reformation', *History*, Oct. 1954.

and the duty of a councillor (and it must engage our attention in a moment), it shows plainly that Cromwell, though he thought little of Plato, was well acquainted with writings on the State.[1] There are traces of a lively concern with ideas in his letters. An interest in theology appears in such remarks as his refutation of Fisher's citation of Amos or his reproof to Shaxton, whose scriptural quotations he confidently asserted were out of context.[2] A real acquaintance with legal theory is argued by his bold claim that the law divine is irrelevant to affairs in England.[3] Most conclusively, there is the testimony of Thomas Starkey, himself an undoubted theorist. He had, says he, many a talk with Cromwell 'of god, of nature & of other polytyke & wordly thyngys' from which he had 'geddryd more frute of truth then I haue downe of any other man lyuyng syth I cam here to my cuntrey'.[4] The praise may mean little, but the fact of those discourses cannot be ignored. On one such occasion Cromwell asked Starkey 'what thyng hyt ys aftur the sentence of aristotyl & the ancyent perypatetykys that commynly among them ys callyd pollycy', to be answered with a little pamphlet on the subject.[5] Clearly, Cromwell devoted time to enquiry about fundamentals; the assumption that he was capable, even avid, of genuine political speculation needs no further proof.

The other view, that Cromwell wished to establish a 'Machiavellian' despotism, is much more firmly entrenched and harder to shake. Its strength derives from its being based on the only detailed account of Cromwell's views which has survived. This is Reginald Pole's description, written a few months after

---

[1] Reginald Pole, 'Apologia ad Carolum Quintum Caesarem', *Epistolarum etc. Pars Prima* (ed. Quirini, Brescia, 1744), pp. 133 ff.

[2] *Cromwell's Letters*, i. 376; ii. 128 f.

[3] *Ibid.*, i. 376: anticipating Fisher's argument that one line of thought agreed with the law of God and another did not, Cromwell supposed that 'this had been no greate cause more to reiect the one than thother, for ye know by histories of the bible that god may by his reuelation dispense with his owne Law'. Dr. Parker's comment on this passage (*op. cit.*, pp. 73 f.) seems to me entirely tendentious. Cromwell here came as near to denying the place of the law divine in matters affected by the positive law of the realm as a man could who wished to avoid a charge of heresy.

[4] P.R.O. State Papers Henry VIII, vol. 89, fo. 138; *England in the Reign of King Henry the Eighth* (ed. S. J. Herrtage and J. M. Cowper, E.E.T.S., 1878; hereafter cited as *Starkey's England*), p. lxxi.

[5] Zeeveld, *op. cit.*, p. 143.

Cromwell had assisted in wiping out Pole's family. The general unreliability of his *Apologia*, with its delineation of the satanic disciple of Machiavelli fouling the pure spring of Catholic doctrine, was exposed a half-century ago by Van Dyke[1]; nevertheless his picture, etched with the acid of personal hatred, continues to be accepted. For while Van Dyke showed that Pole's general story will not stand up to examination, he failed to shake Pole's account of Cromwell's credo, and it is this that matters.

In the speech which Pole puts into Cromwell's mouth at his alleged (and mythical)[2] first interview with the king, he elaborated these arguments: a prince, being above the law, can alter the laws and give them to others; the distinction between right and wrong is relative and does not apply to kings in the same way as to lesser mortals—that is, political morality differs from abstract ethics; no realm can have two masters and the king must not be deprived of 'maximum auctoritatis nomen . . . Caput Ecclesiae'.[3] To this may be added the points which Pole says Cromwell made in conversation when they discussed the proper duty of a councillor.[4] In reply to Pole's view that a councillor's first concern was to serve the honour and advantage of his prince and to his academic citation of authorities, Cromwell replied that that was all very well for the schools and for popular consumption but of little use in practice. Advice must be suited to the time, the place, and the audience. A minister must study 'quo tendit voluntas principis', taking into account even unspoken desires. If he does his work well he will achieve the prince's ambitions without any appearance of disaffection or religious schism.[5] A show of moral virtue must be maintained. He rallied Pole on his inexperience of public life which made him feel shocked by these sentiments, and finished by recommending a book which Pole says he later found to be Machiavelli's *Prince*.

This description of a worldly-wise politician, concerned only with serving the powers that be and with saving face, is superficially credible enough. Whether it represents anything like

---

[1] P. Van Dyke, *Renascence Portraits* (1906), App., pp. 377 ff.

[2] G. R. Elton, *The Tudor Revolution in Government* (1953), pp. 73 f.

[3] Pole, 'Apologia', pp. 118 ff.*

[4] *Ibid.*, pp. 133 ff.

[5] '. . . ut et Princeps sua desideria consequatur nec tamen defectio ulla vel schisma in religione appareat.'

Cromwell's true opinion, or more than the passing mood of an argument in which Cromwell grew more cynical as Pole grew more priggish, is quite another matter. It is important to know whether Pole had good warrant for ascribing such views to Cromwell. He himself admitted that he could not report accurately a speech whose delivery he had not attended, and that he had never heard Cromwell make public statements of this kind.[1] But, he claimed, he had put nothing into Cromwell's mouth 'quod non vel ab eodem ... eo narrante intellexi, vel ab illis qui eius consilii fuerunt participes'.* The sayings which he had collected into one speech he had not spun out of his own mind but in effect had taken from Cromwell's own lips.[2] This seems an impressive voucher, until one looks at the facts. By his own admission, Pole had met Cromwell only once in his life;[3] in 1535, Starkey, who knew them both well, said they were 'almost vnacquaynted & of smal famylyaryte'.[4] Pole also admitted that he was never sufficiently familiar with Cromwell's circle to have been made privy to their inmost thoughts, a reservation which must be taken in conjunction with his statement that Cromwell never put forward his blasphemous ideas in public where he always appeared as a good Christian.[5] Nor will Pole deny that a man's actions may be variously interpreted and cannot afford an absolute insight into his mind; only God will see there. What then is left as the source of Pole's account of Cromwell's opinions? After all these concessions it is certainly surprising to find him offer these foundations: the single conversation about a councillor's duty, and those very actions whose utility for this purpose he had just queried.[6] Since his own report of his talk with Cromwell shows that they spoke of nothing except the office of a councillor and did not stray into such large fields as the king's relation to the law or the impossibility of two rulers in one realm, it follows that Pole had nothing to show for all his argument except his own prejudiced

[1] Pole, 'Apologia', pp. 123, 127.
[2] Ibid., pp. 123 f.
[3] Ibid., p. 132: 'semel et iterum, numquam amplius', which means twice. As Van Dyke has pointed out (op. cit., p. 393 n.), this conflicts with Pole's repeated mention of one conversation; it can only be reconciled on the likely supposition that the editor's comma ought to be shifted after 'semel'.
[4] Starkey's England, p. xv.
[5] Pole, 'Apologia', pp. 131 f.
[6] Ibid., p. 132.

interpretation of events, which he had himself agreed to be an unsafe guide.[1]

Pole is thus not to be relied on, but it is of course possible that, blinded by personal hatred though he was, he may yet have hit upon the truth. His accusation that Cromwell wished to elevate the king above the law has found the readier credence because there appears to be confirmatory evidence. In 1547 Stephen Gardiner wrote to the Protector Somerset a letter of self-defence in which he told how Cromwell had once, in Henry's presence, challenged him with the words: 'Come on, my Lord of Winchester . . . is not that that pleaseth the King, a lawe? Have ye not ther in the Civill Lawe . . . *quod principi placuit*, and so fourth? . . . I have somwhat forgotten it now.'[2] Gardiner, of course, gave the king much better and more constitutional advice. Once again, a leading enemy's word is taken without question. Gardiner himself admits that Cromwell 'turned the cat in the panne afore company' and pretended their parts had been reversed. Can we be sure that 'Wily Winchester' was telling the story the right way round? And even if he was, have we here more than an example of Cromwell's well-known lively conversation and sharp wit?[3] He had 'somwhat forgotten'. Indeed, he might easily have done so, for unlike Gardiner (who prided himself on his knowledge and—in Dr. Parker's words[4]—showed a 'donnish contempt for the unlearned Cromwell') he had never studied the civil law. Such casual talk should no more form the basis for an estimate of Cromwell's views than should another oft-quoted remark reported by Chapuys: Cromwell allegedly said that the Turk

[1] Having found Pole out in so much question-begging and feeble argument, one might be tempted to doubt the whole story of the conversation. Pole certainly did not think Cromwell so satanic as early as Wolsey's last year of office, for he later corresponded with him and had proof of potential favour (Van Dyke, *op. cit.*, pp. 406 ff.). Moreover, the whole argument about the schools and life—academic and political employment—sounds suspiciously like the points which in 1535 Cromwell told Starkey to put to Pole in an effort to win his services for the king's cause (*Starkey's England*, pp. xxii–xxiii). But we may let the interview stand, so graphically described by Pole, who did not seem to realize what a poor figure he cut in his own account—priggish, narrow-minded, inexperienced, and humourless.

[2] *Letters of Stephen Gardiner* (ed. J. A. Muller, 1933), p. 399.

[3] Van Dyke (*op. cit.*, p. 144) rightly speaks of Cromwell's 'habit of not taking himself too seriously'.

[4] Parker, *op. cit.*, p. 73.

might well be called king and prince 'for the absolute authority he exercises over his subjects'.[1] To read into this more than the momentary exasperation of a minister overwhelmed with the labour of governing a litigious and recalcitrant people is to use evidence by quantity instead of quality.

Cromwell's supposed liking for a true despotism—as distinct from strong and energetic rule—thus rests on quite insufficient foundations. What, then, can be made of the Machiavellian label stuck on him by Pole? Van Dyke argued that in 1528 Cromwell could not have recommended the *Prince*, not printed until 1532, and suggested that he was thinking of Castiglione's *Courtier*.[2] This idea found favour with L. A. Weisberger, who held that no Tudor statesman can be shown to have been a disciple of Machiavelli even if his actions agreed with the precepts of the *Prince*.[3] Of course, since Machiavelli did not so much teach new maxims of statecraft as summarize recognized and necessary practice, a touch of 'Machiavellianism' will be noticeable in every competent politician's actions as long as circumstances are as they are. Nevertheless, it would be interesting to know whether Cromwell did or did not read the book. Independently, Mr. Zeeveld and Dr. Parker have rejected Van Dyke's attempt to substitute the *Courtier* for the *Prince*;[4] the sentiments expressed by Castiglione certainly bear no relation to the points which Cromwell apparently made in his conversation with Pole.[5] On the other hand, Machiavelli's treatise also contains nothing about the duties of a councillor. Cromwell cannot be saved for Machiavelli's school by Mr. Zeeveld's argument that his mouthpiece Richard Morison knew the Florentine's works in 1535, immediately after his return from Italy; the question is whether Cromwell knew the *Prince* much earlier. One must in general agree with Dr. Parker that it cannot be shown whether Cromwell ever studied Machiavelli, while reserving judgment on his unsupported conclusion

[1] *Letters and Papers of Henry VIII* (hereafter cited as *L. & P.*), vii. 1554.

[2] *Op. cit.*, pp. 400 ff.

[3] 'Machiavelli and Tudor England', *Political Science Quart.*, xlii (1927), 589 ff.

[4] Zeeveld, *op. cit.*, pp. 184 ff.; Parker, *op. cit.*, pp. 67 ff.

[5] The *Cortegiano* (trs. Thomas Hoby, 1561; L. E. Opdycke, 1902) does not deal with ministerial duties, but only with the ceremonial, athletic, and artistic performances of the courtier.

that Cromwell was in any case 'Machiavellian' in the sense that he shared his 'drab outlook upon the world'.[1]

II

So much for the received notions; now to turn to Cromwell himself. His letters are those of a practical man; they stick to the point and rarely indulge in those generalizations which give an insight into a man's mind and of which even the few examples extant show him to have been perfectly capable. 'My prayer is', he wrote in March 1538, 'that God gyue me no longer lyfe than I shall be gladde to vse myn office in edificatione, and not in destruction.'[2] As it turned out, he was to be cut off in the middle of vigorous activity and yet full of plans for the better organizing of the realm.[3] It is usual to speak of him as a radical, and inasmuch as his work involved much sweeping away of men and institutions, and a cold-blooded disregard of obstacles, he deserves that name. But his positive notions seem to have been less radical than is supposed: he preached moderation, especially in innovation, though admittedly for a good practical reason. The bishops were warned to avoid extremes in enforcing the new teaching, so as not to 'brede contention Deuision and contrariety in opinion in the vnlerned multitude'.[4] He made much the same point in the debates preceding the publication, in 1537, of the *Institution of a Christian Man*, when he demanded unity on a basis of moderation, avoiding both popery and sacramentarianism.[5] Very nearly

---

[1] *Op. cit.*, pp. 74 f.

[2] *Cromwell's Letters*, ii. 129.

[3] Elton, *Tudor Rev.*, pp. 416 f., and 'Thomas Cromwell's Decline and Fall', *Cambridge Historical Journal*, x (1951), pp. 150 ff.

[4] *Cromwell's Letters*, ii. 112.

[5] A. Alesius, *Of the auctorite of the word of god agaynst the bisshop of London* (?1540; cf. *L. & P.* xii. I. 790). The occasion and date of the speech there reported are conjectural. Since the number of sacraments was the main topic of debate, 1536–7 is presumably right, though I had a passing thought of identifying this speech with that made in 1540 (next note). The difficulty is that Alesius speaks very definitely of the Parliament House as the stage of the disputation. The Parliament of 1536 cannot be meant because Cromwell did not attend the Upper House until the last day of that session (*Lords' Journals*, i. 101); the next Parliament met in 1539. Nor did Convocation meet in the interval. Perhaps one may guess at an informal meeting of the bishops, early in 1537, which happened to be held in the 'Parliament House';

the same words recur in his address to the House of Lords in 1540 when once more he insisted on the need for moderation and unity in religion.[1] In 1539 he wished to treat the Calais sacramentarians with 'charyte and myld handeling . . . without Rigour or extreame dealing',[2] and this should not be put down to his reformed sympathies which stopped well short of sacramentarianism and nonconformity. Though pressure from the king induced him to think them more dangerous than he had at first believed, he adhered to a preference for relative gentleness, if only because public and extreme measures would advertise disunion in the realm.[3]

Another important strand in his thought must be looked for in the idea of law. Like all Tudor councillors, Cromwell devoted much time to sifting petitions and adjudicating upon claims, though he showed no liking for the formal duties of a judge.[4] But if, unlike Wolsey, he did not wish to preside in a court, he seems nevertheless to have cultivated a reputation for strict 'indifference' or judicial fairness.[5] Several times he expressed specific respect for the law, telling Fisher that 'your thinking shal not be your triall, but the Law must diffine' his guilt,[6] or admitting even in his extremity that he was 'A Subiect and boorn to obbey lawse'.[7] 'The tryall of all lawse', he wrote in the same letter, 'only consystethe in honest and probable wytnes'—an interesting comment in itself as showing him capable of philosophizing about the law, but particularly interesting from one who is commonly charged with condemning men on slender grounds and even unheard. Whether, in fact, Cromwell was as black in these respects as he is painted it is outside the scope of this paper to enquire; in passing we may note that the point has

this is supported by Cromwell's reported thanks to the prelates for turning up and by the informality of his introducing Alesius, whom he happened to run across on his way to the discussion, into the meeting.

[1] *Lords' Journals*, i. 128 f.
[2] *Cromwell's Letters*, ii. 223 f.
[3] *Ibid.*, pp. 139 f., 142, 148 f., 226 ff.
[4] Elton, *Tudor Rev.*, pp. 132 f., 139.
[5] Cf. Van Dyke, *op. cit.*, pp. 163 f. There are many references to this 'indifference' in his correspondence, and not all of them can be put down to an interested party's attempt to flatter him.
[6] *Cromwell's Letters*, i. 377.
[7] *Ibid.*, ii. 273.

never been proved, being merely repeated by one writer after another.[1]

Cromwell, then, regarded the law with theoretical respect, and the respect was that of the common lawyer. Maitland's thesis that in the 1530's the fate of the common law hung in the balance—that England nearly had a 'Reception' of Roman law—has been laboriously and successfully overthrown by Holdsworth.[2] At most we can speak of danger to the old courts of the common law, which were being rivalled by new courts where the common law, augmented by statutes, was enforced more efficiently. The law itself never budged before the civil law, confined from the first to those spheres which the common law did not touch. It is, however, still supposed that it triumphed despite the intentions of the government. But was it the government who favoured a 'Reception'? Wolsey may have been influenced by civil-law principles, and in the 1530's many of Henry VIII's lesser servants were civilians. So were some bishops of the conservative party—Gardiner, Tunstall, Sampson, Clerk. If Starkey may be believed, Pole strongly favoured the sweeping away of the barbaric common law and its replacement by the enlightenment of Rome.[3] But all these supporters of the civil law were either subordinates, or in exile like Pole, or virtually excluded from a share in shaping policy.

Cromwell dominated the king's counsels, and his party included no civilians of note. The more or less radical bishops who looked to him—Cranmer, Foxe, Latimer, Shaxton—were theologians, not lawyers, and his leading professional assistants—

---

[1] The whole notion of Cromwell's 'terror', spy-system, and extra-legal practices rests, so it seems to me, partly on ancient misunderstandings (first created by Henry VIII's desire to throw all the blame for his vengeful deeds on others) and partly on Merriman's astonishing readiness to blow up every stray suspicion into fact. The strength of his argument may be gauged from one quotation: 'The punishments in these cases were very severe: there are almost no records of penalties inflicted on those against whom the depositions were brought, but there is reason to believe that comparatively slight misdemeanours were not seldom rewarded with death' (*op. cit.*, i. 118). Comment is superfluous on this cavalier treatment of one of the most difficult sixteenth-century problems: what happened when a man was denounced, and how far were laws effective?

[2] F. W. Maitland, *English Law and the Renaissance* (1901); W. S. Holdsworth, *History of English Law*, iv. 217 ff.

[3] *Starkey's England*, pp. 192 ff.

Audley, the lord chancellor, or Rich, the chancellor of Augmentations—were common lawyers tried and trained. It was during his tenure of office that the Court of Requests, a stronghold of civilians, acquired a common lawyer as a member of its permanent staff.[1] And he himself had long practised in the common law. His earlier correspondence abounds with notes of such work; he held powers of attorney, represented in suits, acted in cases of debt.[2] Even after he had entered the king's service he did not surrender his private practice;[3] later, legal work on the king's behalf occupied much of his time. He was a member of Gray's Inn.[4] The man who knew his Bracton well enough to recommend him to others for giving the king the title of *vicarius Christi* is at least as likely to have remembered that 'rex debet esse sub lege'* as the civilian principle to which Gardiner (as we have seen) said he appealed.[5] All we have heard about the 'toughness' of the common law and the unshakable devotion of its devotees applies also to Thomas Cromwell. Small wonder that the common law regained much ground during his ministry.**

But Cromwell was more than just another common lawyer, and nowhere is this seen more clearly than in his attitude to Parliament. He took an early opportunity to familiarize himself with its workings, sitting in the tumultuous assembly of 1523 which Wolsey found so intractable. Cromwell himself described in a letter how in that Parliament members had talked for sixteen weeks of

> warre pease Stryffe contencyon debatte murmure grudge Riches pouerte penurye trowth falshode Iustyce equyte discayte opprescyon Magnanymyte actyuyte force attempraunce Treason murder Felonye consyli[ation] and also how a commune welth myght be ediffyed,

and how in the end they had done as their predecessors, 'that ys to say, as well as we myght and lefte wher we begann'.[6] It is a little difficult to understand why writer after writer has taken this

[1] Elton, *Tudor Rev.*, p. 136, n. 11.
[2] E.g. *L. & P.*, iii. 2441, 2445, 2557, 2754, 3530.
[3] Elton, *Tudor Rev.*, p. 87.
[4] *D.N.B.*
[5] *L. & P.*, xiii. I. 120. Cf. F. Schulz, 'Bracton on Kingship', *Eng. Hist. Rev.*, lx (1945), 136 ff., for a citation of the relevant passages in Bracton.
[6] *Cromwell's Letters*, i. 313.

amusing note to show contempt for Parliament. Since one cannot wish to accuse so many acute historians of collectively failing in humour,[1] one must suppose that they found in the letter something which they sought. But the long recital of absurdities should have put them on their guard: this is no weighty and pompous judgment, but a man of affairs laughing at himself and his fellows. We might suspect even from this letter that Cromwell was fascinated by the work and potentialities of Parliament.

Six years later, in 1529, he found himself at a crisis in his career and perhaps even in danger of his life. Significantly enough he solved the problem by entering Parliament. That he meant to get in by hook or by crook is plain from the letter in which Ralph Sadler reported the negotiations to him.[2] He may have hoped to hide from his enemies under the cloak of parliamentary immunity, but there is fortunately quite conclusive evidence that he meant to do more. Parliament was to be the means to make him great—the scene and agent of his career. When he was in very low spirits, in October 1529, he wondered what to do; then, shaking off this uncharacteristic mood of indecision, he determined to ride to Court and either 'make or mar'. On his return he told Cavendish 'that he once adventured to put in his foot, where he trusted shortly to be better regarded or [before] all was done': he had got into Parliament.[3] How well he succeeded in his aim it is both unnecessary and here irrelevant to elaborate. By the middle of 1531 rumours of his activity in the House were spreading far and wide,[4] and the lists of matters to be done, letters of contemporaries, many corrected drafts, and entries in the *Lords' Journals* of bills brought by him from the lower house all indicate the hard work put in and the great influence gained. Entering Parliament to make a career, unprecedently active in it,

---

[1] E.g. Merriman, *op. cit.*, i. 27; H. A. L. Fisher, *Political History of England 1485–1547*, p. 247 ('cynical view'); H. Maynard Smith, *Henry VIII and the Reformation* (1948), p. 49 ('Cromwell no doubt continued to despise parliaments'); A. D. Innes, *Ten Tudor Statesmen* (1906), p. 119; Parker, *op. cit.*, pp. 70 f. (though he qualified his statement).

[2] *L. & P.*, iv, App. 238. For Cromwell's entry into the 1529 Parliament, cf. my *Tudor Rev.*, pp. 77 ff., where the whole question is discussed at length. *

[3] G. Cavendish, *Life of Cardinal Wolsey* (Singer's ed., repr. in Morley's Universal Library, 1887), pp. 149 f., 156, 159 f.

[4] *L. & P.*, v. 628.

using it to a degree which was novel and remained unrivalled for a long time, he well deserves the name of England's first parliamentary statesman.

His belief in Parliament appears most clearly in a striking devotion to statute. His papers are full of draft acts, and his memoranda suggest others.[1] The numbers of statutes passed during his ascendancy were prodigious.[2] The first nine sessions of Henry VIII's reign, spread over 22 years,[3] produced 203 acts of which 148 can be called public. Cromwell's eight sessions in eight years resulted in a total of 333, or at least 200 of general importance on which he exercised the influence of a chief minister. This average of about 25 public acts per session was maintained in Henry VIII's last years and under Edward VI, but declined under Mary and Elizabeth to about 20. In the 45 years of Elizabeth's reign only 79 more public acts were passed than in the eight years of Cromwell's ministry. More significant still is the space taken up by the acts, for this reflects the relative importance of legislation. From 1509 to 1531, 416 pages (in the *Statutes of the Realm*) were filled, and of these 135 resulted from the first two sessions of the Reformation Parliament. Cromwell's eight years produced 409 pages, and the consolidation of his work in 1540–7 another 207. Edward's six years can show only 196 pages, Mary's five 152, and the 45 years, 13 sessions, and 444 acts of Elizabeth's reign only 666. The figures demonstrate how much weighty legislation was crowded into Cromwell's years of power. There are obvious reasons for these differences—the demands of the break with Rome, Mary's lengthy repeals, Elizabeth's difficulties with her Parliaments—but they do not detract from the evident liking for statute and the amazing productivity displayed by Cromwell.

There are sufficient signs that Cromwell preferred statute to any other form of law-making, distrusting both the slow operation of judge-made law and the dubious authority of proclamations. He deliberately saw to the inclusion of treason by words in the 1534 Treason Act, although the principle had already earned recognition at common law in the 'constructive' treasons created

[1] E.g. *L. & P.*, vi. 299 (ix. D, xi), 1381 (1); ix. 725 (ii). *
[2] All the following facts and figures are derived from *Statutes of the Realm* (1810–28), vols. iii and iv.
[3] 1510, Feb. 1512, Nov. 1512, 1513, Feb. 1515, Nov. 1515, 1523, 1529, 1531.

by judges in the preceding century.[1] In 1535, the Council debated
whether the new ordinances for Calais should be enacted by Parliament or by proclamation;[2] Parliament won, and we cannot
doubt that in that year, when his power in the Council was at its
highest, Cromwell must have spoken a decisive word. The best
example of all is provided by the Act of Proclamations, still
wrongly regarded as an attempt to supersede statute. The act's
chief practical purpose was undoubtedly to create machinery to
enforce proclamations.[3] But further, it placed the powers of proclamations on the authority of statute by stating that the king
with his Council 'may set forthe at all tymes by auctoritie of this
Acte his proclamacions'.[4] The point assumes its full significance
when it is compared with Cromwell's known attitude to proclamations. In July 1535, at a time when Parliament was not sitting, it became necessary to prohibit the export of coin, a common
administrative measure and the sort of thing for which proclamations were specifically designed. Nevertheless, Cromwell thought
it desirable to consult the judges, and a search of the statutes discovered an act of Richard II on which the relevant proclamation
could be grounded. In the discussion Cromwell asked what the
king could do if 'ther wer no law nor statute made alreadye for
any suche purpose'. The lord chief justice replied, quite correctly,
that this would not prevent the issue of a proclamation 'of as good
effecte as Any law made by parlyament', an opinion which Cromwell was 'veray gladde to here'.[5] It appears then, that Cromwell—
far from wishing to supersede statute—did not feel sure whether
proclamations were ever effective unless specifically based upon
it, and though he was delighted to have his doubts resolved it
appears more than probable that the act of 1539 was designed to
put the matter beyond question by securing the authority of
Parliament for all future proclamations.

[1] Cf. I. D. Thornley, 'The Treason Legislation of Henry VIII', *Trans.
R. Hist. Soc.*, 3rd Ser., xi (1917), 87 ff., esp. p. 111.*

[2] *L. & P.*, ix. 766.

[3] Cf. E. R. Adair, 'The Statute of Proclamations', *Eng. Hist. Rev.*,
xxxii (1917), 34 ff., and my *Tudor Rev.*, pp. 343 f. **

[4] 31 Henry VIII c. 8 (*Stat. of the Realm*, iii. 726).

[5] *Cromwell's Letters*, i. 409 f.   This letter has been taken to prove that
Cromwell wished to use proclamations in order to avoid statutes; it seems
to me to prove just about the opposite.

III

This picture of Cromwell as a moderate whose ideas in the last resort derived from his training in the common law and in Parliament, is supported by some evidence of more theoretical views. Twice during his ministry Cromwell was closely associated with the publication of treatises on the State. The lesser instance is Thomas Starkey's *Exhortation to the people instructynge theym to unitie and obedience* (1535), a book which has been identified as the first exposition of the Anglican *via media*.[1] Starkey was promptly criticized for attacking both extremes, for being 'of nother parte but betwyx both indyfferent'.[2] Cromwell thought otherwise: to him the author had to apologize because 'thys mean ys not put out at large wych you requyre'. Starkey acknowledged the fault but doubted his capacity:

> for this mean in al thyng ys a strange stryng, hard to stryke apon & wysely to touch, for by thys the armony of thys hole world ys conteynyd in hys natural course & bewty.

Cromwell, who thought Starkey more of a philosopher than a theologian,[3] may have been more interested in a *via media* in England than in the harmony of the universe, but it is highly significant that he should have insisted on it before the book was written, and that when all men faulted a book for taking its stand in the middle he should have thought the middle position insufficiently stressed. We have already noticed his moderation in practice, which now looks to have been based on a theoretical belief in a 'middle way'. So far from being the violent revolutionary radical of tradition Cromwell now appears as the promoter of a successful compromise—the first exponent and perhaps the maker of that specific compromise on which the Church of England rests.[4]

---

[1] Zeeveld, 'Thomas Starkey and the Cromwellian Polity', *Journ. of Mod. Hist.*, xv (1943), 177 ff. (repr., with some cuts, in *Foundations*, pp. 128 ff.).

[2] *Starkey's England*, p. lxxi.

[3] *Ibid.*, p. xliii: 'you juge me more to be traynyd in phylosophye than in the trade of scripture'.

[4] On the whole subject cf. Zeeveld's article, above, n. 1. It is interesting to remark that Henry VIII could say about the *Exhortation* only that it was insufficiently drawn from Scripture (*ibid.*, p. 187). This throws

A greater thinker than Starkey was also called upon to support the Henrician Reformation. This was Marsiglio of Padua, the fourteenth-century protagonist of the secular State against the papal claim to *plenitudo potestatis*. Starkey himself derived some of his most striking ideas from Marsiglio.[1] More significant for the present purpose is the publication, in 1535, of a translation of Marsiglio's *Defensor Pacis* by William Marshall. Marshall was one of Cromwell's team of propagandists, and Cromwell advanced him the money for this particular publication, a debt he seems later to have cancelled.[2] He welcomed this ready-made piece of propaganda which he encouraged Starkey to use on Pole and Marshall on the recalcitrant Carthusians, in neither case with any success.[3] In other words, he sponsored the book, and it is a reasonable conclusion that he read it. The immediate usefulness of a work which attacked the papal position on the ground that 'in . . . regno unico esse oportet unicum tantummodo principatum'[4] needs no underlining; but it is worth recalling that one of the sentiments ascribed to Cromwell by Pole concerned the monstrosity of two heads in one realm.[5] Pole never mentions Marsiglio, a fact which suggests that he may have been unconscious of the source of the saying and really for once quoting Cromwell correctly. Another tenuous link is provided by Cromwell's enquiry after Aristotle's views on the State; it is at least not impossible that this question should have been suggested to him by a study of Marsiglio, 'un aristotélicien positiviste.'[6]

Certainly there are some points to suggest that Marsiglio directly influenced Cromwell's thought. Marsiglio held that the

much light on the king's indifference to 'philosophy' and preference for theology—which again indicates where we must look for the leadership in the political revolution.

[1] Baumer, 'Thomas Starkey and Marsiglio of Padua', *Politica*, ii (1936), 188 ff. Mr. Baumer displays much wonderment at Starkey's courage and revolutionary wisdom in putting forward constitutionalist notions 'at a time when Tudor despotism was at its peak'. The truth is that no one at the time put forward absolutist theories: constitutionalism was the thing.

[2] *L. & P.*, vii. 422–3; xi. 1355.

[3] *Ibid.*, viii. 1156; ix. 523.

[4] *Defensor Pacis* (ed. C. W. Previté-Orton, Cambridge, 1928), I. 17. 1.*

[5] 'Apologia', p. 121.

[6] G. de Lagarde, *La Naissance de l'esprit laique au declin du moyen âge*, ii. 155. On this point cf. also Previté-Orton's ed. of the *Defensor Pacis*, p. xiv.

State is autonomous and the Church subject to it; it has rightly been pointed out that the nearest realization of his views was achieved in the established Protestant Churches—that is, in Cromwell's Anglican Church.[1] Marsiglio, declaring the divine law irrelevant and ignoring the law of nature, held that only the positive law of the realm matters in human affairs;[2] we recall Cromwell's casual dismissal of the law of God in his letter to Fisher. On the positive law Marsiglio has much to say; his most lucid definition of it is 'regula . . . praeceptiva et transgressorum coactiva',[3] a view to which Cromwell, the maker of much penal legislation and the believer in statute, gave frequent practical expression. Marsiglio saw the essence of the State in its legislative activity, so that more than any other pre-Reformation thinker he approached the full modern notion of sovereignty;[4] as we shall see, legislative sovereignty was at the heart of Cromwell's thought. Though perfect proof is necessarily lacking, it does not seem too much to claim that as far as Cromwell was a theorist he was a conscious follower of Marsiglio.

As a practical statesman, however, Cromwell would have had to admit that Marsiglio's teaching, derived from observation of an Italian city-state, could not simply be applied to the kingdom of England. In this connection Marshall's translation deserves attention. The translator made some omissions and additions which, since he published under Cromwell's patronage, may safely be taken as consonant with Cromwell's views. For his omissions he has had much blame and scorn.[5] It is true that he transformed Marsiglio's preference for an elective monarchy into praise of one based on inheritance, that he omitted his author's insistence on the powers of the community to control and correct the ruler, and that he toned down Marsiglio's ascription of all ecclesiastical authority to the *legislator humanus*. But these changes were all demanded by the English conditions for which he wrote. That Marshall had no intention of doctoring Marsiglio's

[1] Ewart Lewis, *Medieval Political Ideas* (1954), p. 543.

[2] Lagarde, *op. cit.*, ii. 167 f.

[3] *Defensor Pacis*, II. 8. 5. *

[4] Lewis, *op. cit.*, p. 256. Lagarde (*op. cit.*, ii. 265) argues that Marsiglio came nearer a theory of sovereignty than Mrs. Lewis will admit.

[5] P. Janelle, *L'Angleterre catholique à la veille du schisme* (1935), pp. 252 ff.; Hughes, *op. cit.*, i. 332. The omissions are listed in Previté-Orton's edition of the *Defensor Pacis*, p. xl.

thought for the benefit of despotic theories is evident from the striking way in which his explanatory notes insist on bringing in Parliament. Marsiglio, the Italian, stressed the practice of the commune where the whole body of citizens, or at least its greater part (in quantity or quality), made the laws, a repetition of the impossible (for England) that drove Marshall to distraction. The notes abound: 'He meaneth here of those lawes which do passe by acte of parlyament'; 'In all this longe tale he speaketh not of the rascall multytude but of the parlyament'; 'where soeuer he speketh of such multytude he meneth when it is assembled in ye perlyamente, remembre this to auoyde captyousness'.[1] He inserted Parliament in the text in a manner highly reprehensible in a translator, but also highly significant in one of Cromwell's propagandists.[2] The book confirms that Cromwell's mind was concentrating on the law-making power of Parliament, seeing here the essential core of the State demanded by Marsiglio.

Cromwell, then, was a common lawyer and parliamentarian who believed in moderation and the middle way, trusted in statute, and is likely to have learned from Marsiglio certain theoretical views on the character of the independent State and the nature of legislative supremacy within it. These last two points underlie the acts of Parliament in which the reconstruction of the English State was embodied.

IV

It is because the preambles of the Reformation statutes were propaganda that they offer a clue to the political doctrines held by the government. That the acts exemplify Cromwell's policy and thought is patent from his work on them; especially is this true of the fundamental statute, the Act in Restraint of Appeals to Rome, which contained the clearest piece of political theory.[3] At the same time, there are fewer such theoretical pronounce-

[1] *The Defence of Peace* (1535), fos. 27v, 28v, 35.

[2] E.g. in the fourth conclusion (*ibid.*, fo. 138): the only law-maker is 'the prynce or his parlyament, or (where it is so vsed) hole vnyuersyte and congregacyon of Cytezens'—a paraphrase rather than a translation of the text. Also in I. 12. 5 (fo. 28) where 'valentiorem partem' is rendered as 'ye bygger parte of them assembled in the parlyament'.

[3] Cf. Elton, 'Evolution of a Reformation Statute', *Eng. Hist. Rev.*, lxiv (1949), esp. 196 f.

ments than one could have wished; to the last, Cromwell's mind remains half-hidden behind the deeds to which it gave birth.

The proper starting-point is the preamble to the Act of Appeals.

> Where by dyvers sundrie old autentike histories and cronicles it is manifestly declared and expressed that this Realm of Eng-lond is an Impire ... governed by oon Supreme heede and King having the Dignitie and Roiall Estate of the Imperiall Crowne of the same, unto whome a Body politike compacte of all sortes and degrees of people, devided in termes and by names of Spiritualtie and Temporaltie, ben bounden and owen to bere nexte to God a naturall and humble obedience.[1]*

These few words summarize the essence of the revolution. Eng-land, the act asserts, is a sovereign state, a political unit within which one authority only has the right to rule. The term used is 'empire' which here means simply national sovereignty: the king of England is an emperor, rules an empire, and wears an imperial crown because he has no superior on earth. The concept had a respectable and not unfamiliar history behind it. As early as 1208 the English canonist Alan stated that every prince owning no superior has as much power in his realm 'quantum imperator in imperio'.[2]** Later, in the fourteenth century, French lawyers developed these gropings into the principle that 'rex superiorem non recognoscens est imperator in regno suo'.† Cromwell may well have been familiar with this dictum, as Henry himself seems to have been when he said in 1515 that kings of England had never recognized any superiors on earth.[3] But in two ways the idea was here given a novel interpretation. While kings had called themselves emperors before, the Act of Appeals spoke of a sovereign territorial State, not only of a ruler with no superior. This change of a personal claim into a significant concept of political doctrine can, with some confidence, be ascribed to Crom-well, for the first mention of the term empire occurs in his corrections of the first draft of the 'Supplication against the

---

[1] 24 Henry VIII c. 12 (*Stat. of the Realm*, iii. 427).

[2] Cited Schulz, *op. cit.*, p. 150, n. 8. The whole problem is well sum-marized in Lewis, *op. cit.*, pp. 430 ff.

[3] Cf. J. Gairdner, *Lollardy and the Reformation* (1908), i. 283.

Ordinaries', made in 1529, before he was even in the king's service.[1]
Secondly, the notion of empire existing in all free monarchies had
been developed against the claims of the Holy Roman Emperor;
it had never been used to justify denial of the papal headship in
the Church and the total subjection of matters spiritual to the lay
ruler. Never before had the self-contained sovereignty of the
national State been so fully realized or so bluntly stated.*

Thus the basis of Cromwell's thought was a firm grasp of the
principle of national sovereignty. He was clear, too, about the
nature of the State so set apart. It was to be an organic unit consisting of the ruler and the body of subjects, both related to and
dependent on each other. The apparent dualism of clergy and laity
did not represent (as Mr. Baumer has argued)[2] a revival of
Gelasian doctrine; it simply reflects the particular preoccupations
of an act concerned with the administration of law, which had to
take cognizance of the double system of law and courts actually
in operation in the realm. This would have been clearer if motives
of policy had not urged the government to abandon some rather
extravagant theoretical claims: almost to the last, the act meant to
allege that all jurisdiction, both lay and clerical, proceeded from
the imperial crown of the realm, a claim which opposition from
the Church forced out of the statute.[3] The unitary character of
Cromwell's 'empire' was not affected by the existence of the
church courts with their canon law, any more than it was affected
by the existence of other courts administering another law, such
as Chancery with its equity.

However, this might suggest that the Cromwellian State was
seen as a despotism centred in the 'Supreme heede and King'.
In order to understand Cromwell's mind on this we must turn
to the question of law. That Cromwell saw the essence of a state
in its law is shown by the Act of Dispensations (1534) which
implies such a legal criterion in the definition of a political organization when it states that England, 'recognysyng noo superior
under God but only your Grace', is free from subjection to any

[1] P.R.O., State Papers Henry VIII, vol. 50, fo. 203. For the date cf. my
article 'The Commons' Supplication against the Ordinaries', *Eng. Hist. Rev.*,
lxvi (1951), 507 ff.

[2] *Op. cit.*, pp. 28 f.

[3] Cf. my article in *Eng. Hist. Rev.*, 1949, esp. pp. 184, 192. All the drafts,
down to and including A and D, contained the claim, which was only
abandoned after the conference on 5 Feb. 1533.

laws except such 'as have bene devysed made and ordyned within this Realme'.[1] It makes an exception for laws introduced from abroad which have received the consent of the people and the sufferance of the crown, but of course the condition renders such foreign laws equivalent to native ones. By simply ignoring them, this view removes all those laws other than human—the law of God, the law of nature—of which both philosophy and jurisprudence were so fond, an interpretation expressly stressed in the Act for the Punishment of Heresy (1534) in which canonical sanctions are declared insufficient because they

> be but humayne, being mere repugnaunte and contrarious to the prerogatyve of your ymperyall Crowne regal jurisdiccion lawes statutes and ordynaunces of this your Realme.[2]

The summary disposal of canon law as merely human can be linked with Cromwell not only because (as we have seen) he expressed similar views elsewhere, but also because the same denunciation of it as repugnant to the laws of the realm occurs in the draft of the 'Supplication' which he prepared for the 1532 session of Parliament.[3] His test for the validity of a law was thus not some extra-human body of rules, but the positive law of the realm, which means that he grasped the importance of legislative sovereignty within the sovereign State. A thoroughly Marsilian position, but it is likely that the views of a practising lawyer and statesman, concerned with this world only, simply found agreeable confirmation in the *Defensor Pacis*.

We now come to the crux of the matter: where, in Cromwell's view, lay the authority behind the positive law of the realm? Free enough though he was with deferential remarks about the imperial crown, it was not in a despotic king that he saw the lawgiver. Once more we refer to the Dispensations Act:

> In all and everey suche lawes humayne made within this Realme ... your Royall Majestie and your Lordes Spirituall and temporall and Commons, representyng the holle state of your Realme in this your most high Courte of Parliament, have full power and auctoritie ... the seid lawes ... to abrogate adnull amplyfie or dymynyshe ...

---

[1] 25 Henry VIII c. 21 (*Stat. of the Realm*, iii. 464).
[2] 25 Henry VIII c. 14 (*ibid.*, 454).
[3] P.R.O., State Papers Henry VIII, vol. 50, fo. 194.

The legislative supremacy lies in the High Court of Parliament; it is exercised by king, lords, and commons, and therefore expresses itself in statute. This is precisely the doctrine which Cromwell's practice would lead one to expect, but it is gratifying to have it explicitly stated. The doctrine here expressed involves (in legal terms) the supremacy and omnicompetence of statute, or (in terms of political philosophy) the existence of constitutional or limited monarchy. There can be no talk of despotism while the highest expression of the State's activity is seen as the work of an assembly joining together the Head and the Body Politic of which the Empire of England is comprised. It was only after Cromwell had taught him this lesson that Henry could make his famous pronouncement of 1543, to the effect that 'we at no time stand so highly in our estate royal as in the time of Parliament' in which the king as head and the nation as members 'are conjoint and knit together'.[1]

As Cromwell freed the notion of empire from the encumbrances of the past and gave it full practical expression, so he freed statute from the limitations which had clung to it. That statute was the highest form of law-making in the realm had long been recognized. But so far all doctrine asserted the existence of a higher law with which statute must be consonant. Fortescue had seen this higher law in the law of nature: he held that statute could be unjust and would then be properly disregarded.[2] Even on the eve of the Reformation, St. Germain, who ascribed overriding powers to statute, demanded that it should conform with the laws of God and of reason.[3] Though the judges of the fifteenth century admitted that statute could defeat canon law, they carefully excluded the field of *spiritualia*: statute could not make the king a parson, give laymen the rights of spiritual jurisdiction, or usurp the powers of the supreme head of the Church (that is, the pope).[4] Thus statute was not thought of as omnicompetent before the Reformation, simply because no human law was conceived of as possessing that quality. When the acts of the 1530's

[1] J. R. Tanner, *Tudor Constitutional Documents*, p. 582.
[2] Cf. S. B. Chrimes, *English Constitutional Ideas in the XV Century* (1936), pp. 201 ff.; E. F. Jacob, 'Sir John Fortescue and the Law of Nature', *Essays in the Conciliar Epoch* (1943), pp. 106 ff. (esp. p. 119).
[3] Chrimes, *op. cit.*, pp. 209 ff.
[4] *Ibid.*, p. 286.

invaded the prohibited field of *spiritualia* (though statute did not in fact create but merely accepted the royal supremacy), they asserted the nullity of all those limitations. In the works of theorists, especially in Hooker, the law of nature was to stage a come-back, but some men grasped the point which Cromwell had made: as Burghley said, there was nothing that an act of Parliament could not do in England.[1] Thomas More showed that he understood the issue perfectly:

> As this Inditement is grounded vpon an Acte of Parliament directly repugnant to the lawes of God and his holye Churche, the supreme Gouernment of which ... may no temporall Prince presume by any lawe to take vpon him ... it is therefore in lawe, amongest christen men, insufficient to charge any christian man.[2]

With the precision to be expected of a man of his stamp, he put his finger on the point that mattered; but his death demonstrated that in upholding a doctrine which certainly had age to recommend it he was wrong—wrong in law. However, his words will serve to remind us that the break with Rome and the emancipation of statute, which between them made up Cromwell's creation of true political and legislative sovereignty, did mark a break with the past that was revolutionary.

Thus, the sovereign nation state erected by Thomas Cromwell rested on the legislative supremacy of the king in Parliament, all imperfections and reservations disappearing as later developments subjected the Church, too, to that body instead of a personal royal supremacy. I suspect, though I cannot prove it, that Cromwell foresaw this change which the inevitable calling-in of Parliament was sure to bring about, but this whole question of the Henrician Church—vitally important though it is and often (as it seems to me) misinterpreted—cannot be discussed here. We merely wished to discover Cromwell's political ideas. We have seen that he had no intention of building a despotism. What he envisaged was the modern mixed sovereign, the king in Parliament, created by the deliberate infusion of the modern principle of sovereignty into those two great achievements of the middle

[1] Quoted Holdsworth, *op. cit.*, iv. 186, n. 2.
[2] N. Harpsfield, *Life and Death of Sir Thomas Moore* (ed. E. V. Hitchcock and R. W. Chambers, E.E.T.S., 1932), p. 193.

ages—the assembly of king, lords and commons, and the common law of the realm. So far from attacking either, Cromwell gave greater authority to both by destroying the rivals who had limited them. Cold-blooded and ruthless though he was, he was also a constitutionalist who realized the potentialities of common law and parliament, and who elaborated and employed the equipment of constitutional monarchy. There was no nemesis in the victorious struggle of the commons in the seventeenth century, but only the lamentable failure of later statesmen and king's ministers to preserve the harmony between king and Parliament —natural or contrived—which Cromwell had made the basis of England's State and government.

8

The Elizabethan Acts of Supremacy and Uniformity *

by J. E. Neale

'IT may seem rash to suppose that about those two famous statutes of the first year of Elizabeth anything remains to be said. They have been approached by innumerable writers from almost every conceivable point.' The quotation is from a brilliant excursion into Elizabethan history made by F. W. Maitland in this REVIEW[1] in 1903 ; and the passage of nearly fifty years might be thought to have added force to his words. Maitland himself investigated what 'diplomatic' could contribute to the subject, leaving, as I can vouch, scarcely an 'i' to be dotted. Characteristically, he perceived that parliamentary procedure might have something to add, but he left this approach more or less unexplored.

The problem that has baffled everyone is what happened in and out of parliament before Easter 1559, after which date the passage of these two acts can be satisfactorily followed by means of Maitland's 'diplomatic'. The evidence is tantalizingly inadequate : it is also very puzzling. The Commons Journals, on which attention must be centred, were still primitive. To anyone unaware of their informality they are a snare rather than an aid. No member of parliament kept a diary of the session ; and of this parliament alone in Elizabeth's reign it seems that there is nothing more we can know. Even the famous Zurich Letters, where a single document of the right date might solve our problem, fail us ; and the supplementary volume of letters of this character, recently acquired by St. Paul's Cathedral, contains no correspondence for the crucial period. Let me say at once that I have failed to find any new evidence to bring to the inquiry. It still remains a task—and how fascinating a task !—for the detective rather than the researcher. About the solution of the problem I would lay down two propositions : it must not do violence to such evidence as exists ; and it must be 'in period' with the way parliament then worked. Those qualified to judge would probably agree that no solution hitherto propounded satisfies these conditions.

[1] *E.H.R.*, xviii. 517 *seqq.* reprinted in *Collected Papers*, ed. Fisher, iii. 185 *seqq.***

Every writer, from Camden down to our own day, has started his story or argument from an anonymous document known as ' The device for alteration of religion in the first year of queen Elizabeth.'[1]   Written certainly before 27 December 1558 and possibly several weeks earlier,[2] it opens with the recommendation that ' the alteration ' should be attempted ' at the next parliament ', and goes on, with a recourse to detail that lends a specious air of authority, to advise the appointment of certain learned men—whom it names—' to review the Book of Common Prayer ' and prepare ' a plat or book ' for submission to the queen and afterwards to parliament.   No evidence exists to show that this advice was followed.   But the religious settlement, with its acts of supremacy and uniformity, fits so well into the general scheme of the Device, and seems in retrospect so natural an outcome of Elizabeth's first parliament, that we can readily understand why, in the silence that surrounds the question, it has been assumed that a committee substantially the same as the one recommended did meet and that the Elizabethan prayer-book was the result of its deliberations.

My first suggestion is that, instead of allowing this document to dominate our approach to the subject, we should adopt an alternative explanation and regard it as merely one of those political programmes or papers of advice inspired by a new and revolutionary regime.   There were others : indeed, as the recently published ' Remembrances ' of Sir Nicholas Throckmorton suggest, there were probably more than we know.[3]   I would couple the Device, so far as its authority and perhaps even its date are concerned, with two other well-known papers of this character, Richard Goodrich's ' Divers points of religion ' and Armagil Waad's ' The distresses of the commonwealth '.[4]   There can be no doubt that we are entitled to proceed on this hypothesis. Its great merit is to open the way to a new interpretation of events, before which the Device will wither away like the state in Marxist theory.

---

[1] Cf. Henry Gee, *The Elizabethan Prayer-Book*, pp. 14 *seqq.*   Dr. Gee's statement (p. 19) that part of the entry on the last page of the Cotton MS. copy ' is almost certainly in Cecil's handwriting ', proves on examination of the manuscript to be wrong.

[2] The paragraph urging prohibition of innovations (Gee, p. 201) must surely have been written before the proclamation of 27 December on this subject (Steele, *Tudor and Stuart Proclamations*, i. 52).   The advice ' to practise a peace ' with France (Gee, p. 197) might indicate a date fairly near to 23 November, when the queen issued instructions to commissioners to do this (*Foreign Cal. Eliz.* i. 10), and the phrases about Marian officials (Gee, pp. 198–9) are compatible with (though do not necessarily imply) an early date.   M. M. Knappen's argument (*Tudor Puritanism*, p. 169, n. 1) that the inclusion of exiles in the committee must date the document seems to me quite unconvincing. Gee's argument (p. 67 n.) based on the title ' *Marquess* of Northampton' is invalid. Throckmorton used this title in November (cf. *E.H.R.*, lxv. 96).

[3] *E.H.R.*, lxv. 93-98.   [4] Printed, Gee, *op. cit.* pp. 202 *seqq.*

There is one other document which, since Strype brought it to light, has been the twin support of the conventional theory. It is Edmund Guest's letter. Dr. Gee in his *Elizabethan Prayer-Book* [1] was baffled by it and tried to fit it into Edward VI's reign. I do not think that his suggestion can be sustained. As we shall see, I find a place for it later in our story.

The writs for Elizabeth's first parliament were dated 5 December 1558, and on 23 December the privy council appointed a committee 'for consideracion of all thinges necessary for the parlyamente', among the members of which were Sir Thomas Smith and Richard Goodrich, both capable of dealing with ecclesiastical matters. [2] I do not think that we need invent any second committee. Goodrich, in his 'Divers points of religion', written before he knew when parliament was to be summoned and therefore presumably before 5 December, had already expressed his opinion on the pace at which ecclesiastical change should proceed. If parliament were to be held 'before or in March next', he wrote, the pope's authority should 'not be touched, nor anything to be attempted there of matters in religion, except the repeal of the statutes of Henry IV and V', whereby 'quiet persons may live safely'. [3] His judgement was clearly at variance with that of the author of the Device. Nor was he alone in this respect. Armagil Waad, in his 'Distresses of the commonwealth'—probably written about the same time and probably addressed to Cecil—touched on the same subject, though in more general phrases :

> So would I wish that you would proceed to the reformation having respect to quiet at home, the affairs you have in hand with foreign princes, the greatness of the Pope, and how dangerous it is to make alteration in religion, specially in the beginning of a prince's reign. Glasses with small necks, if you pour into them any liquor suddenly or violently, will not be so filled, but refuse to receive that same that you would pour into them. Howbeit, if you instil water into them by a little and little they are soon replenished. [4]

Or take Sir Nicholas Throckmorton at the opening of the reign : the burden of his advice had been 'to succeed happily through a discreet beginning '. [5] Even in the Device there is a question which the author, at least in our copies of the document, did not answer : 'If the alteration must tarry longer, what order be fit to be in the whole realm, as an *interim*?' [6] It is a question which, in the light of the thesis to be developed in this article, is worth remembering. Nor should we forget that gradualness had been

[1] Gee, *op. cit.* pp. 31 *seqq.*   [2] Dasent, *Acts of Privy Council*, vii. 28.
[3] Gee, *op. cit.* p. 205.   [4] *Ibid.* p. 210.
[5] *E.H.R.*, lxv. 93.   [6] Gee, *op. cit.* p. 201.

the initial theme of the Edwardian reformation, while even
Mary Tudor had accomplished her counter-reformation in
stages.

This recurrent note of caution was clearly occasioned by the
dangerous international situation and by the paramount need
to establish the new queen securely on the throne. Presumably,
if the privy council committee on which Goodrich and Sir Thomas
Smith sat were allowed to deal with the subject, they heard
Goodrich's advice ; and since one copy of the Device is said to
have come ' out of a book of Sir Thomas Smith ',[1] it may well be
that they also heard the rival argument. At court the queen
must have listened to a babel of conflicting advice ; and this
crucial battle, fought as it were off-stage, must never be forgotten,
though little can be known of it. If the policy finally decided
upon by the government was neither as timid as Goodrich's
nor as venturesome as that of the Device ; if—as my thesis will
maintain—an *interim* was planned, with royal supremacy but
no prayer-book, need we be greatly surprised ?

Parliament met on 25 January 1559. The first of the government's ecclesiastical measures put before it was a bill to restore
to the crown first fruits and tenths. It was introduced into the
lords, which we must regard as deliberate policy, indicating that
the government was quite confident of the result and saw no
occasion to add momentum by passing it first through the commons. On the third reading all the spiritual peers voted against
it, as in conscience they were bound to do ;[2] but there was
no lay opposition. 'The queen', declared Philip II's special
ambassador, the Count de Feria, writing on 20 February, ' has
entire disposal of the upper chamber in a way never seen before
in previous parliaments ' ;[3] and while we need not, indeed must
not, endorse all that Philip's envoys wrote in their recurrent
moods of depression and elation, we should be extremely chary
of assuming that any appreciable number of lay peers would go
the length of rejecting or drastically amending a government bill.
The assumption that they would not—which I regard as sound—
becomes an important element in my argument.

Meanwhile, the house of commons, which, as Mary's parliaments had demonstrated and all subsequent Elizabethan parliaments were to confirm, could not be so easily kept to heel, had
discovered a way of starting up the hunt on their own initiative
when they discussed whether the omission of the words *supremum
caput* from the writs—what Maitland so felicitously called the
etceteration of Elizabeth's title—invalidated the parliament.
They appointed a large committee of twenty-four to investigate

---

[1] Gee, *op. cit.* p. 17.   [2] *Lords Journals*, i. 544–6.
[3] *Spanish Calendar, Elizabeth*, i. 32.

the point.[1] 'There was great talk about giving the title of
Supreme Head of the Anglican Church . . . to the queen',
reported the Mantuan, Il Schifanoya, 'much being said against
the church [of Rome]'.[2] It is the first hint we receive that the
protestants were in control of this assembly and had astute
leaders. But action waited on the government's initiative.
With the Marian bishops—such as were left of them—entrenched
in the upper house, where the lay peers could not match them in
theological debate, and with convocation firmly reflecting the
views of the episcopacy, the main assault on the catholic church
was bound to be opened in the commons.   There, on 9 February,
the clerk entered in his Journal the first reading of a bill 'to
restore the supremacy of the church of England, &c. to the crown
of the realm'.[3] It was the first of three bills of supremacy,
the last of which, introduced into the commons after Easter,
became the statute as we know it.

That this first bill was a government measure, no one familiar
with contemporary parliamentary procedure is likely to doubt.
Consequently, if we can guess its contents we shall gain some
knowledge—as it happens, quite decisive knowledge—of the
government's ecclesiastical policy at this juncture. I need
hardly say that no text of the bill is known. However, in a
very critical and independent house of commons the third
supremacy bill—our statute—was not committed, which is a
fairly sure sign that, save for the new title it gave to the queen,
the text had already been passed by them. This takes us back
to the second bill, in the form in which it passed both houses ; and
since I shall later show reason for thinking that the house of
lords had stripped this bill of the crucial amendments made by
the commons, thus restoring its main text to that of the initial
government bill, we arrive at the proposition that the first bill
was substantially the same as the third.   True, this third bill was
amended and extended during its passage, but as the changes
were made after ingrossing, we can, with the aid of Maitland's
'diplomatic', discover what they were and so arrive at the
substance of the first bill. For the time being, all this must
seem involved. Stated more precisely, it amounts to this : the
first supremacy bill consisted of the first eighteen sections of our
statute, though section xv concluded with a clause which in the
third bill was cancelled by the lords and replaced by a proviso
known to us as section xxi, while section xviii similarly incorporated the proviso which we know as section xxii.[4] There was
indeed one important difference from our statute. The title

---

[1] *Commons Journals*, i. 53 ; Maitland, *op. cit.* iii. 159.
[2] *Venetian Calendar*, vii. 26, 28.   [3] *Commons Journals*, i. 54.
[4] Maitland, *op. cit.* iii. 192.

assigned to the queen was that of her father and brother—
'supreme head' of the church. The fact is notorious and needs
no labouring, though it is by no means superfluous to add that
the first bill, like the final one, contained an oath in which the
title occurred.[1]

And now we come to the vital clue in this detective story.
Embedded in our act of supremacy, like a fossil in stone, and seen
but not perceived by those who have read the statute, is a clause
which preserves the history of the Elizabethan religious settlement. The act is hybrid. Though its long text is almost
entirely concerned with supremacy and the ramifications thereof,
one short section is not. It is section v, reviving the statute
1 Edward VI, c. i. 'an act against such persons as shall unreverently
speak against the sacrament . . . and for the receiving thereof
under [in] both kinds'. The point—who can doubt it ?—
was communion in both kinds ; which in fact was the statute's
purpose when enacted in 1547. But when embodied in a supremacy act and accompanied by an act of uniformity imposing a
prayer-book which itself prescribed communion in both kinds,
this provision was clearly redundant as well as anomalous.

There can be hardly any doubt that our anomalous section v
was taken over from the first and second bills of supremacy. The
government left it in the third bill, perhaps through oversight,
perhaps—for the second bill had passed both houses and been
ready for the royal assent before Easter—because they did
not wish to re-open the whole bill for debate when modifying
'supreme head' to 'supreme governor', which was the occasion
for having a third bill ; or it may be—and we shall later see
reason for preferring this explanation—that at the moment when
the third bill was introduced into the commons, the queen and the
protestant divines were having difficulty in agreeing on the
prayer-book, so that the government, being uncertain of the fate
of a bill of uniformity, wished to make sure of its initial policy
of communion in both kinds should the new and more radical
policy founder. As it happens, the Irish religious settlement
offers a striking contribution to this argument. Its act of
supremacy omitted the section concerning communion in both
kinds, thus tacitly acknowledging the incongruity ; but a separate
bill was made of it, which, together with the act of uniformity, was
certified by the English government in the preliminary letters
patent of October 1559. Now, the Irish bill on communion in
both kinds did not become a statute, though the bill of uniformity
did. The explanation, as Professor Dudley Edwards suggests,
must be that the bill ' was framed, evidently with the idea that

---

[1] Cf. *Spanish Cal. Eliz.* i. 33 ; *Venetian Cal.* vii. 52–3.

if the opposition were too strong for the uniformity bill, an alternative might be at hand '.[1]

The first supremacy bill, introduced into the commons on 9 February, provided for communion in both kinds. It is from this assumption that our story takes its shape. Dealing both with the government of the church and the character of its service, the bill was in itself a complete, if temporary programme ; and we may conclude that for the time being the government did not intend to go further. There was to be no prayer-book and no act of uniformity ; which, if true, incidentally disposes of ' The device for alteration of religion ', relegating it to the class of rejected addresses. Our surprise will be the less if we recollect that communion in both kinds was the first stage in the Edwardian reformation. Intended as an *interim*, it was on that occasion followed in the next parliamentary session by the first Edwardian prayer-book. The precedent must surely have been in the minds of Elizabeth's advisers : indeed, let us recall our earlier mention of that unanswered question in the Device, with its use of the word *interim*. Thus we may suppose that if the Elizabethan government's policy had prevailed, a prayer-book would have come in the second parliament of the reign : that is to say, it would probably have waited until the autumn of 1559. As already suggested, the international situation offers an explanation of this caution. So does what Armagil Waad described as ' quiet at home '. ' It requireth great cunning and circumspection ', he wrote, ' both to reform religion and to make unity between the subjects '.[2] Elizabeth may have hoped to carry the more moderate Marian bishops with her in her religious settlement. It is a point to which we shall return later. But quite apart from these cautionary reasons for the government's policy, there was a cogent procedural or constitutional argument in its favour. If the settlement had gone as planned, then the act of supremacy would have been employed to get rid of recalcitrant bishops, replacing them with protestants ; subsequently, a new parliament would have been summoned in order to obtain a new convocation, reflecting the protestantism of the new episcopacy ; and the prayer-book could then have come before parliament with the approval of convocation, the appropriate body for tendering advice on doctrinal matters. Moreover, its passage through the lords would have met with the unanimous support instead of the unanimous opposition of the spiritual peers. In brief, constitutional, not revolutionary procedure would have been possible. Elizabeth

---

[1] *Statutes at Large, Ireland* (1765), i. 275 *seqq.* ; Dudley Edwards, *Church and State in Tudor Ireland*, p. 177.

[2] Gee, *op. cit.* p. 210.

lived to regret, or at least to have reason for regretting, an unfortunate precedent. Her struggle later on with the puritans in parliament centred on this very point of procedure.

When Elizabeth told Feria in March that she was ' resolved to restore religion as her father left it ',[1] she was, we must now conclude, nearer the truth than has hitherto been thought. But even in Tudor politics schemes did not always go as planned. Caution may have been the watchword in official circles ; but ' Haste, post haste, haste for life ! ' reflected the mood of the Marian exiles, hurrying home to build the New Jerusalem in England. Whatever her expectations, Elizabeth could not repeat her father's exploit and carry the episcopacy with her in another break from Rome. The Marian reaction ensured that ; the first Elizabethan parliament confirmed it. Consequently, if the new regime was to be protestant—of which there was not the slightest doubt—it would have to take its church leaders, to a significant extent, from the Marian exiles. A number of prominent councillors were in sympathy with these men, and so were some eminent divines who had not been abroad. If they could display the necessary unity, resolution, and political skill, they might be able to force the pace of government policy. We know from the Zurich Letters that the leading protestant divines remained in London during the parliament. We can infer that they kept in touch with the left-wing leaders of the house of commons, some of whom had actually been fellow-exiles. But let our story demonstrate.

Against the entry of the first reading of the initial supremacy bill on 9 February, the clerk of the house wrote the name ' Mr. Coke '—Sir Anthony Cooke, father-in-law of Cecil and Bacon, and a returned exile. Usually such a note indicates a committal. But we must remember that the Commons Journal was as yet a personal *aide-memoire* of the clerk's, and that his chief concern in making these entries was to keep track of a bill. I am inclined to think that he jotted down the name of anyone who took a bill off and was responsible for returning it ; and I am therefore not disposed to see a formal committing for the purpose of amendment behind this entry. Possibly the house entrusted the bill to Cooke for perusal between the first and second readings, he being a leader of those who were discontented with its limitations. The bill reappeared for a second reading on 13 February. It was the last of three bills read that morning, and an appreciable time was perhaps spent in debate. In those days it was unusual for a debate to spill over into the second day ; but on this extraordinary occasion there was also debate on the second and third

[1] *Spanish Cal. Eliz.* i. 37.

days, the whole of the second morning being given to the discussion, except for the opening period when an unimportant bill was given a first reading while the house filled. Dr. Gee saw in this prolonged discussion ' hints at strenuous opposition ': ' convocation took heart at the resistance of the commons '.[1] He utterly misjudged the tone of the house. There was indeed ' strenuous opposition ', but, as our narrative will make abundantly clear, it was to the government's timidity.

Early on the third morning, 15 February, the bill was ' committed to Mr. Knolles, Mr. Cooke '—evidently Sir Francis Knollys and Sir Anthony Cooke.[2] This was a real committal, in all likelihood to more than the two members mentioned. Perhaps, being a long and important bill, it was divided into two for scrutiny, Knollys taking one part and Cooke the other. Like Sir Anthony Cooke, Sir Francis Knollys was recently back from exile. His later career, both in and out of parliament, showed that, though a privy councillor and related to the queen through his wife, he could be strikingly independent over matters of conscience. Cooke, too, was the type of man impatient of playing politics over religious causes. ' We are moving far too slowly ', he wrote to Peter Martyr on 12 February ; ' but the result of this meeting of parliament will, as far as I can judge, confirm my hope '.[3] He must have based his hope on the mood of the house of commons and on the activities of divines such as Grindal, Sandys, and others out of parliament ; perhaps, too, on the sympathy of such keen protestant councillors as Bacon, Bedford, and Cecil, though it seems impossible to discover what these men were thinking, especially Cecil, whose views may or may not have coincided for a time with the caution of his mistress. Sir Nicholas Throckmorton had named Sir Anthony Cooke to Elizabeth as a possible lord chancellor : ' all Israel ', so Jewel wrote, expected as much, though Jewel himself thought his capacities unequal to the post.[4]

The same day that the government's supremacy bill was committed, the clerk entered in his Journal the first reading of ' The bill for order of service and ministers in the church ', and the next day a first reading of ' The book for common prayer and ministration of sacraments '.[5] Here indeed is a mystery. Nothing more is heard of these items. Moreover, judging by the amount of other business got through at that sitting, it is most unlikely that the reading was followed by any debate. Now, government measures were not treated in this cavalier way : unless, of course, the government underwent a sudden change of

---

[1] Gee, *op. cit.* p. 81.

[2] *Commons Journals*, i. 54.

[3] *Zurich Letters* (Parker Soc.), ii. 13–14.

[4] *E.H.R.*, lxv. 95 *Zurich Letters*, i. 8, 53.

[5] *Commons Journals*, i. 54.

mind, a contingency which on this occasion seems out of the question. I have therefore no misgivings in regarding these two entries as the result of an independent move by the commons —not the last move of the kind, as we shall see. What, then, were the bill and the book ? And why their single appearance ? Until some evidence is forthcoming, it is anyone's guess. So let us try.

Much later in the reign the puritans attempted to presbyterianize the church by introducing into the commons a bill and a book—the Genevan book. I do not think there is the slightest possibility that this book was in question in 1559. The 'troubles at Frankfort' among the Marian exiles had decided that ; and the divines in London—Cox, Sandys, Grindal, and others—who were probably behind this move in the commons, would, I think, have opposed any such proposal. Nor does the title given in the clerk's Journal suggest the Genevan book. It would suit Edward VI's first prayer-book. But this was too conservative ; and—not to mention other difficulties—it is unlikely that any of the agitators in or out of parliament would willingly have gone back so far. A reasonable case could be made for the liturgy drawn up by Cox and others at Frankfort in 1555 [1]—a simplified version of the second Edwardian book, which, in the interests of harmony, laid aside certain practices ' in their own nature indifferent '.[2] If we were to argue this case, then we should presumably have to assume that the reform party also drew up a bill of uniformity, which either, like Edward VI's second act of uniformity, gave statutory sanction to an ordinal—for the bill read on 15 February was for an order of ministers as well as an order of service—or else incorporated the sections relating to the ministry in the ' discipline ' used at Frankfort. Though we can place little faith in reminiscences reaching back more than twenty-seven years, we may note that in a ' general supplication ' prepared by the puritans for the parliament of 1586, there are some seemingly relevant remarks. ' In the beginning of her Maties raigne, a number of worthie men . . . desired such a booke and such order for the discipline of the Church as thei had seene in the best reformed Churches abroad '.[3] It may be that some of the returned exiles were ready with what we may term a Frankfort programme, and that the commons were willing to listen to this as an epilogue to the debate on the supremacy bill or even as an extreme policy for their committee to consider.

---

[1] Miss C. H. Garrett evidently takes this view. Cf. her *Marian Exiles*, p. 58.
[2] Letter of Cox and others to Calvin, 5 April, 1555, in *Troubles at Frankfort*, ed. Arber, p. 77.
[3] *Seconde Parte of a Register*, ed. A. Peel, ii. 84.

However, this does not seem to me a likely solution of the problem. I am not inclined to interpret the clerk's entries of this bill and book in too formal a manner. The titles he gave to bills were sometimes descriptive, differing, for example, from those in the Lords Journals, which were official. Again, a ' 1 ' against an entry, though usually indicating a first reading, may on this particular occasion simply signify that something was read, without implying a legislative first reading. Even the word ' bill ' may have a general instead of a technical meaning. With such thoughts in mind, I ask myself how the clerk would have noted the items in his Journal if, after debates indicating that the committee should so amend the supremacy bill as to bring about a revival of the religious situation at the end of Edward VI's reign, it was then decided to have, say, parts of the act of uniformity of 1552 and parts of the second Edwardian prayer-book read as a reminder to the house. If one could believe that in such circumstances the clerk might make the two entries we are discussing, this would fit in with what I am disposed to think happened in committee. But, until further evidence turns up, we must leave this section of our inquiry with a heavy mark of interrogation.

In committee the government's supremacy bill was fundamentally altered ; which can be inferred from the mere fact that it emerged as a new bill. This second supremacy bill was given a first reading on 21 February, appearing as the last item of business ; and since five other bills were read that morning we may conclude that there was little or no debate. It was read a second time the next day, when nearly all the morning must have been given to the debate ; but as it was sent to ingrossing without a further committee, a majority of the house clearly approved of the committee's work. It passed the house, with the addition of two personal provisos, on 25 February, the title now given to it by the clerk being, 'The bill for the supremacy of the churches of England and Ireland, and abolishing of the bishop of Rome. . .'[1] The record of business that morning suggests that there was another, though briefer debate. Our task is to discover, if we can, what were the contents of the bill at this stage in its history ; in other words, what changes the commons had made.

The most reliable clue is found in a speech by Scot, bishop of Carlisle, which must have been delivered on the report stage after the committing of the bill in the house of lords. He praised the members of the lords' committee for two amendments that they had made in the bill.

First . . . they will not suffer the service of the churche, and the dew admynistration of the holie sacraments therof, to be disanulled or all reddye altered, but to be contened [retained] as they have ben heretofore.   And secondlye, for that their charitie and pittie towards the poor clargie of this realme dothe appeare in mytygatinge th' extreme penalties mentioned in this bill for the gayne-sayers of the contents of the same.[1]

The second of these two points is the simpler.   Let us deal with it first.   Writing about the bill the day after it passed the commons, Feria reported that ' they seek to bring it to pass that the entire kingdom shall swear to observe ' the royal supremacy, ' and that those who refuse to do so shall be accounted traitors, as in the time of King Henry '.[2]   If we were to accept his report as reliable we might assume that the commons' committee, comparing the government bill with the statute of 28 Henry VIII, c. x., 'extinguishing the authority of the bishop of Rome '— the first section of which was obviously the model for section xiv of the Elizabethan supremacy act—decided to adopt the extreme penalty for refusing the oath of supremacy imposed by section viii of the Henrician statute.[3]   However, I am inclined to believe that Feria was writing loosely or in partial ignorance; and, following a lead given in a letter dated 21 March from Il Schifanoya,[4] I would conclude that the committee added a clause to the bill, making a second refusal of the oath treason.   This, in fact, was ultimately done in 1563 by 5 Elizabeth, c. 1, section ix. In either case, what emerges from our evidence is that the commons, in this matter of penalties, were dissatisfied with the government's moderation, and that the conservative house of lords deleted the amendment, restoring the bill to its original form.   In doing this, the lords were simply preventing the commons from materially altering a government measure.   It is a useful clue for the next, and more important, stage in our argument.

We learn from Bishop Scot's speech that the commons had managed in their amendments to alter the church service.   How was this done, and what was the new service ?   I think the answer is that they revived the second Edwardian prayer-book : in fact, I cannot imagine how to make a plausible case for anything else.   Let us consider an alternative.   Let us suppose, for the sake of argument, that the ' book ' read on 16 February was a purified version of the Edwardian book—the Frankfort liturgy, shall we say ?—and that Bishop Scot was referring to this.   We must then suppose that it was accompanied by a new bill of

---

[1] Strype, *Annals*, I. ii, 408–9.   I have failed to discover the original manuscript of this speech, which one would have expected to be among the Foxe MSS. in the British Museum.

[2] H. N. Birt, *Elizabethan Religious Settlement*, p. 75.   Cf. *Spanish Cal. Eliz.* i. 33.

[3] *Statutes of the Realm*, iii. 665.   [4] *Venetian Cal.* vii. 52–3.

uniformity : indeed, anyone arguing along this line would point to the 'bill' read on 15 February as the very bill. Presumably the book would have been attached to it. But are we to believe that the commons incorporated into the government's supremacy bill, or tacked on to it, a new bill of uniformity, with a prayer-book attached ? It is perhaps not inconceivable, but it is certainly not plausible. The evidence does not suggest it. Moreover, as will gradually be borne in on us, the leaders of the commons were astute tacticians as well as keen protestants. Their activities were unofficial and in flagrant opposition to government policy. Their only hope was to appear conservative, to be restoring, not innovating ; and as nothing less than the second Edwardian book would have come voluntarily from them, this I think it must have been.[1]

Now, Il Schifanoya tells us that the commons also made the marriage of clergy permissible ;[2] which was so emphatic a desire of the protestant divines that we may readily accept the statement. Adding this to my suggestion about the second Edwardian prayer-book, I think we have the lead we require for visualizing the operation of the commons' committee. The government, in drafting its supremacy bill, had centred attention on nullifying Mary Tudor's second statute of repeal, passed in 1555 (1 and 2 Philip and Mary, c. 8), the purpose of which was to undo the Henrician reformation ; and, incidentally, if we view the government's action from this angle, how true becomes Elizabeth's claim that she was re-establishing religion as her father left it. The Edwardian reformation had been swept away by Mary earlier—in 1553, by her first statute of repeal (1 Mary, st. 2, c. 2). This statute Elizabeth's act of supremacy ignored ; except that it revived the Edwardian act concerning communion in both kinds, though even in doing this it ignored Mary's repeal of the act. Dare we infer from this strange silence that the government foresaw the danger of directing attention to the first Marian statute of repeal ? At any rate, what the government so deliberately ignored, the commons took to heart. Their committee based its amendments on a scrutiny of this 1553 statute : or so I infer, and the simplicity of the thesis is an argument in its favour. If we in turn make a scrutiny of Mary's first statute of repeal, attempting to imagine what the committee may have done about

---

[1] As a matter of interest, though I am not inclined to attach much weight to it, let us note the following passage from the puritan ' supplication ' of 1586 (*Seconde Part of a Register*, ii. 84). ' But anie chaunge from that [service which] was used concerning religion in Queen Maries daies being then thought by such as ruled the state as daungerous, as it was pretended, that either that which was then used must be retained still, or the former order of King Edward receaved, a number were wrought diverslie to yeild therunto. . . .'

[2] *Venetian Cal.* vii. 52.

it, we shall, I think, conclude that they revived four of the Edwardian acts there repealed, including the second act of uniformity, and possibly revived part of a fifth.[1] And how easy the process ! They had only to redraft section v of our supremacy act so that it repealed Mary's statute, though without reviving all the Edwardian acts. They even had a model before them, in the way the government bill handled Mary's second repeal act. When the bill, as amended by the commons, got to the house of lords, where we may suppose that the clerk entered the official title in his Journal, it was described as ' An act for restoring the supremacy to the imperial crown of this realm, and repealing divers acts of parliament made to the contrary '.[2] With its deliberate mention of ' repealing ', the title was not too flagrant a misdescription—certainly less flagrant than if a new act of uniformity and a new prayer-book had been incorporated in the bill.

If we now turn to what little contemporary evidence there is on this matter, we shall see that it favours our thesis, or at least is not incompatible with it. Il Schifanoya referred to the commons as ' forbidding the mass to be said or the communion to be administered except at the table in the manner of Edward VI ; nor were the divine offices to be performed in church ; priests likewise being allowed to marry, and the Christian religion and the sacraments being absolutely abolished '.[3] The passage is not precise enough to be decisive, but there is much clearer evidence in the postscript to a letter of 28 February written to Bullinger by Richard Hilles, who was one of the members for London in this parliament [4] and therefore must have known what was happening. Parliament, he wrote,

> has now been sitting nearly six weeks. Nothing however has yet been publicly determined with respect to the abolishing popish superstition, and the re-establishment of the christian religion. There is however a general expectation, that all rites and ceremonies will shortly be reformed by our faithful citizens, and other godly men, in the afore-mentioned parliament, either after the pattern which was lately in use in the time of king Edward the sixth, or which is set forth by the protestant princes of Germany, in the above-mentioned Confession of Augsburg.[5]

[1] Namely : 1 Edw. VI, c. i (concerning the sacrament of the altar) ; 2 and 3 Edw. VI, c. 21 (concerning the marriage of priests) ; 5 and 6 Edw. VI, c. 1 (the second act of uniformity) ; 5 and 6 Edw. VI, c. 12 (a declaratory act concerning the marriage of priests). The act which may have been partially revived is 3 and 4 Edw. VI, c. 10 (concerning images).

[2] *Lords Journals*, i. 555.

[3] *Venetian Cal.* vii. 52. The word ' book ' preceding the quoted passage should clearly be ' bill '.

[4] Browne Willis, *Notitia Parliamentaria*, iii. 65. Willis gives ' Rich. Halls ', an obvious misreading for ' Hills '.

[5] *Zurich Letters*, ii. 17.

The postscript must have been added between the 1st and the 8th of March ; that is, after the bill had received its first reading in the lords.

In 1549 Hilles had likened the first Edwardian prayer-book to ' the manner of the Nuremberg churches and some of those in Saxony ' ; [1] and for this reason, if no other, we may equate the ' Confession of Augsburg ' with the 1549 book. It looks as if the postscript confirms my conjecture that the commons had revived the second Edwardian prayer-book, and also indicates that Hilles had reason to anticipate opposition, resulting in a compromise on the basis of the first prayer-book. He was wrong if he thought that the next stage in events would shape that way : the queen was not yet prepared to allow doctrinal change. But we must not think him ill-informed. A doctrinal settlement acceptable to the Lutheran princes appeared to have immense diplomatic value for Elizabeth at this juncture. Indeed, on 6 February she had sent the following message to an agent of the duke of Wurtemberg : ' As to the request of those persons who wished that the Confession of Augsburg should be received and approved by her, she informs them that she has certainly no intention of departing from that mutual agreement of Christian churches, amongst which that of Augsburg appears to be the most weighty '.[2] Even in the following July she was harping upon the same string.[3] It was diplomacy, of course ; but instead of assuming that she was answering fools according to their folly,[4] may we not ask whether she herself preferred the 1549 prayer-book ? We shall return to this point. In the meanwhile, what matters is that Richard Hilles had reason for inserting the alternative in his postscript.

He may also have had the debates of the commons in mind. There had evidently been divergent views : ' some spoke in favour of moderation ', Feria reported.[5] In such a large assembly there were presumably some who would have preferred the 1549 prayer-book ; and if the queen's theological leanings were known to be that way, then a number of privy councillors must have found their position even more difficult. The Commons Journals contain the following entry :

Mr Chancellor of the Duchy [Sir Ambrose Cave] complained that Sir T. White [M.P. for Hampshire] had called him a witness, not to like the book of service : Mr. White answered, that Mr. Chancellor said, he wished the book to be well considered : but, for that the house

[1] *Original Letters* (Parker Soc.), i. 266.   Cf. A. F. Pollard, *Cranmer*, p. 220.
[2] *Foreign Cal. Eliz.* i. 115-16, and cf. p. 112.
[3] *Ibid.* pp. 353, 354, and cf. p. 218.   [4] Cf. *Ibid.* ii. lxiii.
[5] H. N. Birt, *op. cit.* p. 75.

doth take that Mr. White did mistake him, therefore Mr. White, standing, asked him forgiveness ; which Mr. Chancellor did take thankfully.[1]

Probably Cave, as a councillor, had been hovering between his official misgivings about the tactics of the house and his reluctance to seem an opponent of reform. Had he also doubts between the 1549 and the 1552 prayer-books ? Whether Cecil thought his protestant friends theologically too radical or politically too hasty, or alternatively was urging them on, we do not know. Feria has an obscure passage on the subject. Alluding to the third reading debate, he remarks 'that it was necessary . . . for secretary Cecil to throw the matter into confusion, and so passed it ' : [2] as though, without appearing to support the reformers, he nevertheless abetted them. One or two councillors may have openly urged caution. On the other hand, we can be fairly confident that Sir Francis Knollys, though a councillor, strenuously supported the amendments. Such divergence of opinion and action among councillors in the house of commons was a feature of high Elizabethan days and need not surprise us in the first parliament of the reign.

From the commons the bill went up to the lords on 27 February. It was read a first time on the 28th and then, as Il Schifanoya says, was consigned to silence, 'the court preachers in the presence of her majesty and the people ' meanwhile ' doing their utmost to convert the latter, seeking to prove by their false arguments that the pope has no authority, and uttering the most base and abominable things that were ever heard against the apostolic see '.[3] Perhaps, during this interval, there was a tussle at court while the government—which in effect was the queen— decided what its attitude should be towards the commons' amendments. On 13 March the bill was read a second time, was obviously the subject of debate, and was committed to thirteen temporal peers and two bishops. Six of these peers and the two bishops were later to vote against the government's bill of uniformity. On the other hand, only one of the temporal peers dissented at the passing of both the second and the third supremacy bills.[4] Clearly, so long as official policy refrained from changes in the liturgy, it was a safe committee. And surely the government was shrewd enough to make skilful use of its supporters in the upper house.

But let us not treat this question of opposition in the lords too seriously, as though we were writing about a modern legislative chamber with the party whips off. When Bishop Scot made

---

[1] *Commons Journals*, i. 56.   [2] *Birt*, p. 75.
[3] *Lords Journals*, i. 555 ; *Venetian Cal.* vii. 46.
[4] *Lords Journals*, i. 563; *E.H.R.*, xxviii. 537.

his speech on the bill, he prefaced his criticism of the royal supremacy by saying :

> Ther be two thinges that do much move me, and, as it were, pull me backe from speaking any thinge in this matter. The first is, that I perceave the quene's highness . . . is, as it were, a partie therin unto whom I do acknowledge that I owe obedience. . . .[1]

In voting against a government bill, and even in speaking, some at least of the peers must have considered that they were indulging in a harmless form of conscientious objection. Surely that pliant nobleman, the marquis of Winchester, who as lord treasurer set a precedent for the vicar of Bray, would have been shocked if, later on in the session, his vote against the act of uniformity had lost the government its bill. Winchester was a member of the committee on the supremacy bill. He must have known the government's plans. Indeed, for him, as for certain other members of the upper house, the real battle was being fought at court, perhaps also in council ; and it was probably from the court that instructions, or at any rate the broadest hint, came to the committee to purge the bill of the commons' amendments. Writing his first letter to Peter Martyr after returning to England, John Jewel, who now took his place in London with the other divines interested in guiding the work of parliament, and regarded the catholic bishops as their greatest obstacle, explained that the queen

> though she openly favours our cause, yet is wonderfully afraid of allowing any innovations : this is owing partly to her own friends, by whose advice every thing is carried on, and partly to the influence of Count Feria. . . . She is however prudently, and firmly, and piously following up her purpose, though somewhat more slowly than we could wish. And though the beginnings have hitherto seemed somewhat unfavourable, there is nevertheless reason to hope that all will be well at last.[2]

This was written on 20 March, two days after the lords had passed the amended supremacy bill. Il Schifanoya wrote a dispatch on the following day which alludes to the amendments made by the lords' committee. After referring to the liturgical and other points in the bill as it came from the commons, he declared that ' by a majority of votes ' the lords ' have decided that the aforesaid things shall be expunged from the book [i.e. bill] and that the masses, sacraments, and the rest of the divine offices shall be performed as hitherto '.[3]

Broadly speaking, the lords' committee had restored the supremacy bill to its original form. Their proposals, consisting of ' provisos and amendments ', written on paper—in the clerk's

---

[1] Strype, *Annals*, I. ii. 408.   [2] *Zurich Letters*, i. 10.   [3] *Venetian Cal.* vii. 52.

terminology ' *quedam billa* '—were read the first time on 15 March and a second time on 17 March, when the ' bill ' was committed for ingrossing : that is to say, the provisos were to be ingrossed, the amendments to remain on paper for the clerk of the lower house to effect the necessary alterations in the original bill if the commons approved of them. Then the whole bill, ' with certain provisos added thereunto by the lords, and sundry other amendments ', was read a third time on 18 March and passed with twelve dissentients out of an attendance of forty-five—two temporal peers and all the spiritual peers present.[1] It was perhaps on this occasion—at any rate, he made no reference to liturgical changes still being in the bill—that Archbishop Heath, ' for the dyscharge of my conscience ', made his dignified criticism of ' the body of this acte ' and of the title, ' supream head of the churche of England, ymmediat and next under God ', which it contained. In the course of his speech he touched on Elizabeth's sex—a stumbling block to radicals as well as conservatives. ' Her highness ', he declared, ' beyinge a woman by birthe and nature, is not qualyfied by God's worde to feed the flock of Chryst ' ; and he went on, like Knox in his *Monstrous Regiment of Women*, to quote St. Paul for confirmation.[2]

Now, Feria made an interesting remark in a dispatch written at this time. He states that ' on Wednesday the 15th of this month '—the day the committee reported back to the house— ' they proposed what had been introduced at the opening of parliament, but in more moderate terms, so that as regards the supremacy she [the queen] might take the title if she wished to, in any case rejecting the pope's authority '. Moreover, in the same dispatch he declared that Elizabeth had told him ' she would not take the title of head of the church ' ; and she said the same in a later interview on 20 March.[3] Since, as we shall see, she was prepared as late as 23-24 March to give the royal assent to this second supremacy bill, it seems as if Feria, our sole source on the point, might be right, and that the lords' committee— briefed from the court, as I have suggested that it was for its other amendments—provided an escape clause, possibly in a proviso, by which Elizabeth could renounce the title of supreme head if she wished. The question is perhaps best left open ; but, as we all know, the queen did ultimately give way to con- servative and radical prejudice against a woman being head of the church, and as a compromise took the title of supreme governor in the final statute.

We may begin our account of the commons' reaction to these events with a report from Il Schifanoya.

[1] *Lords Journals*, i. 563, 564, 565.   [2] Strype, *Annals*, i. ii. 399–407.
[3] Birt, *op. cit.* pp. 78–9 ; *Spanish Cal. Eliz.* i. 37, 43.

'The members of the lower house', he wrote, 'seeing that the lords passed this article [i.e. bill] of the queen's supremacy of the church, but not as the commons drew it up . . . grew angry, and would consent to nothing, but are in very great controversy, as they must of necessity ratify what the lords have done in the upper house. . . . [The bishops] are . . . attacked by the modern preachers, one of whom, who is their scribe, and a member of parliament, threatened that if things do not pass according to their will, he and his brethren, who call themselves ministers of Christ, will return to Geneva.'[1]

Il Schifanoya was right : unless the commons were prepared to forgo the destruction of papal supremacy, they had to accept the bill as amended by the lords.   They were in a quandary, but they were defiant ; and they expressed their defiance by action which deserves our closest attention.   On 17 March, two days after the lords' committee had presented their amendments to the upper house and a day before that house finally passed the supremacy bill, a bill was introduced into the commons which the clerk, with his propensity to describe rather than entitle a bill—this time bringing clarity to our puzzled minds—entered as a measure 'that no persons shall be punished for using the religion used in king E.'s last year'.[2]   We might paraphrase this by saying that if uniformity on the basis of Edward VI's second prayer-book was not to be permitted, then a qualified non-conformity should be tolerated.   In framing the bill the commons dared not wait until their mangled supremacy bill was returned to them.   Haste was essential, for Easter Day was only nine days off, and it was intended to close the parliament before then.   The sense of urgency is eloquently conveyed by their treatment of the measure. It was read twice and sent for ingrossment in a single morning, 17 March, and was read a third time and passed the next day. Such precipitate action violated the conventions of procedure, especially in a bill of this nature.   There could be no more glaring proof that the reform party dominated this house of commons.   As eight other bills were read on 17 March and six others on the 18th, there can have been little or no debate on the measure.   Opposition must have been negligible.   The commons had risen as a body in a gesture of open defiance.

Their leaders can surely have been under no illusions about the fate of the bill in the upper house.   They were really fighting in the off-stage battle going on at court for the soul, or rather the political mind, of their queen ; it was a propaganda demonstration, such as we have seen in revolutionary movements of our own day.   The bill was brought into the lords on Monday, 20 March ; and there, we may presume, the clerk gave it its

[1] *Venetian Cal.* vii. 52–3.   I cannot identify 'the scribe'.
[2] *Commons Journals*, i. 58.

formal title. This was ' An act to take away all pains and penalties made for religion in queen Mary's time ' : [1] a clever and politic camouflage of its purpose. The bill was read a first time by their lordships on the same day ; and that was the end of it.

Meanwhile, the reformed supremacy bill had gone back to the lower house on 18 March. The commons added a proviso of their own—we have no hint as to its nature, but it cannot have been controversial—passed this and the lord's amendments on 22 March, and on the same day the lords passed the new proviso through all its stages so that the bill was now ready for the royal assent.[2] The queen intended to give her assent. Fortunately the evidence is decisive on this important point, for a proclamation was printed, dated that very day, 22 March, the opening words of which are as follows : ' Whereas the Queen's Majesty hath in the present last session of Parliament, with the assent and consent of the Lords spiritual and temporal and the Commons in the same assembled, made amongst others one statute [the act of supremacy] . . ..' In passing, let us note that unless the conciliar ·convention of ' *nolens volens* ' was held to apply in the house of lords—and we may also have in mind the ' ancient order ' of the lower house by which a division, when in favour of a bill, was thereupon converted into unanimous approval [3]—the ' consent of the Lords spiritual ' was a fiction. The proclamation went on to say that Easter being at hand, and ' great numbers, not only of the nobility and gentlemen, but also of the common people ' being unwilling to receive the sacrament except under both kinds, ' according to the first institution, and to the common use both of the Apostles and the Primitive Church ' (significant phrases, these) ; and since the supremacy act is too long to be printed and published in time, and no ' other manner of divine service for the communion of the said holy Sacrament (than that which is now used in the Church) can presently be established by any law until further time therefor may be had ' ; therefore the statute of Edward VI for communion in both kinds, revived in the supremacy act, is declared to be revived and in force.[4] In brief, the people were to have their Easter communion in both kinds, either at their own parish church, or elsewhere if the priest proved obstinate.

---

[1] *Lords Journals*, i. 566. [2] *Commons Journals*, i. 58 ; *Lords Journals*, i. 568.
[3] Cf. my *Elizabethan House of Commons*, pp. 397–8.
[4] Gee, *op. cit.* pp. 255-7. The proclamation, we should note, proves that the section concerning communion in both kinds was in the second supremacy bill. My assumption, earlier in this article, that it was also in the first, rests on two arguments : (i) that the lords' amendments to the second bill were based on the principle of restoring the bill to its original form, and it is most unlikely that they would have added such a section on their own initiative ; (ii) that the appearance of this provision in the government's later programme for the Irish parliament suggests a government origin for it.

With the close of parliament at hand—in all likelihood a dissolution—and with nothing to boast of but the royal supremacy
and this sop of communion in both kinds, no wonder that
Feria, on 24 March, was able to remark : ' I see that the heretics
are very downcast in the last few days '.[1] We can determine,
with welcome precision, the time at which Elizabeth changed her
mind. On the night of 23 March, she sent to Feria to fix an
audience for 9 a.m. the next day. He was about to set out for the
court to keep this appointment when a message reached him
postponing the visit because the queen was very busy. She had
resolved, he reported, to go to parliament at 1 p.m., after dinner
that day to give the royal assent to bills—that is, to close the
session.[2] She did not go. Perhaps over night, perhaps that very
morning of Good Friday, 24 March—certainly one or the other—
she reversed her policy, and parliament was simply adjourned
over Easter to 3 April. In these few hours the pattern of the
Elizabethan religious settlement was altered. Three centuries
and more of the old, familiar story make it hard to realize that,
if it had not been for that change of mind, no prayer-book would
have come from the first parliamentary session of the reign.

What had happened ? I have little doubt that the principal
reason for the new policy was the news, which reached England
on Palm Sunday, 19 March,[3] that peace had been concluded with
the French at Cateau Cambrésis. Elizabeth could now feel
secure enough on the throne to take the second step in her religious settlement. But would that step have been taken so soon
if the house of commons, inspired by the protestant divines—who
might almost be likened to an unofficial convocation assembled
in London—had not fought so remarkable a battle ? ' We were
indeed urgent from the very first ', wrote one of these divines,
Edmund Grindal, two months later, ' that a general reformation
should take place. But the parliament long delayed the matter,
and made no change whatever, until a peace had been concluded
between the sovereigns, Philip, the French king, and ourselves '.[4]

In the new situation the government again followed the precedent of Edward VI's reign. His first bill of uniformity had
been preceded by a disputation of the bishops in the parliament
house, with the commons as onlookers.[5] A similar overture was
to precede the Elizabethan act of uniformity. Such colloquies
were becoming a sixteenth-century theological habit. We

---

[1] *Spanish Cal. Eliz.* i. 44.   [2] *Ibid.*   [3] *Ibid.* p. 42.
[4] *Zurich Letters*, ii. 19.
[5] A contemporary report or journal of this disputation is printed in Gasquet and
Bishop, *Edward VI and the Book of Common Prayer* app. v. 397 seqq. Cf. *Original
Letters* (Parker Soc.) i. 322–3, 469. To term this disputation a ' debate in parliament '
or ' in the house of lords ' is misleading, and can lead to erroneous deductions since,
for example, Sir Thomas Smith spoke.

know that this particular one had been decided upon by 20 March, for Jewel, writing his first letter to Peter Martyr on that day, told him of the news. The first discussion, he wrote, was to take place on 31 March, when nine catholic leaders were to confront nine 'on our side '—Scory, Cox, Whitehead, Sandys, Grindal, Horne, Aylmer, Guest and Jewel himself.[1] With the exception of Guest, all the protestant protagonists had been in exile during Mary's reign, and six [2] of them—seven including Guest—were soon to be bishops ; which is striking proof of the new government's dependence upon them, and therefore of the pressure which potentially they could exercise.

Now, as we have seen, as late as the night of 23 March or the early morning following, Elizabeth intended to close the session of parliament ; and unless she had in mind a very brief prorogation, which does not seem probable, a second parliament was not likely before October or November. On the other hand, the proposed disputation was obviously planned as the forerunner of liturgical and doctrinal reform. We have only to consider the three subjects of debate to realize this : the use of the vulgar tongue in church services ; the right of every provincial church to establish its own liturgy ; the lack of scriptural justification for the propitiatory sacrifices in the mass. As Jewel declared, the catholic bishops were to be deprived of any excuse that they had been put down only by power and the authority of the law.[3] But why, for three days or more, was Elizabeth pursuing two different policies ? The answer is inherent in personal rule : uncertainty of mind. The illogical situation probably reflected the battle that was going on at court. As we have noted, there was much to be said for the original policy. It offered a sound constitutional solution of the problem ; it might be thought to offer a chance of weaning some of the Marian bishops and clergy from catholicism, so making the queen less dependent on the radically-minded protestant exiles and opening the way to a broad church establishment. Even the author of the Device was not unaware of this latter point, as witness his recommendation of the stern hand for left-wing extremists.[4] Nor is it altogether irrelevant to recall Catherine de Medici's well-meant but misguided efforts at compromise in France. The consistent and unanimous opposition of the spiritual peers to all ecclesiastical bills in parliament, combined with the skilful use of their power by the protestant exiles, must have undermined the policy of gradualness. When news arrived that the peace with France was safe,

---

[1] *Zurich Letters*, i. 10–11.
[2] I have included Horne as successor to a Marian bishop, though he was not consecrated till February 1561. Aylmer is excluded.
[3] *Zurich Letters*, i. 10–11.   [4] Gee, *op. cit.* p. 200.

its last justification was gone ; and it was presumably then that the queen allowed the reform party to go ahead with plans for a disputation. However, it was not until the decisive morning of 24 March that she really surrendered to the new policy ; though even then, as we shall see, it was not total surrender.

There is no need to describe the disputation. It did not modify the convictions of the protagonists, any more than the Colloquy of Poissy was to do two years later. Elizabeth can have had no illusions on this score, for, unlike Catherine de Medici, she did know what the word ' dogma ' meant. What was wanted was propaganda to launch the religious settlement : we recognize the revolutionary technique. The disputation broke up in disorder at its second meeting on Monday, 3 April. This was the day to which parliament stood adjourned ; and the clerk of the house of commons on that day made only one entry in his Journal :

> This day Mr. Speaker, with few of this house, were here ; and part of the bill for scaling of cloths was read : but for that this day was appointed to have disputation before the council and lords in Westminster quire, between the bishops and Mr. Horne, Mr. Cocks, and other Englishmen, that came from Geneva ; and for that it was meet, that they of this house should be there present to hear ; this court was continued until the morrow following.[1]

Though the Lords' Journals contain no similar entry, it is clear that the upper house did the same.

This surely must be the time at which a ' committee ', if there really was one, undertook the revision of the prayer-book : not in January-February as writers have usually assumed, but after 3 April. In considering its composition we need not pay any attention to ' The device for alteration of religion '. Events had passed this by. We are now in April : the Device has been left high and dry in December, when, if our argument be sound, the policy it advocated must have been rejected. Instead, a new prominence has been given to those nine—if that was the number—protestant divines of the Westminster disputation : ' the Englishmen that came from Geneva ', as the clerk of the lower house so erroneously, and yet, in a way, so significantly described them. That some, if not all, of them were involved in the revision seems a reasonable assumption. The situation demanded it : could the government deny it ? I am inclined to view the revision as a tussle between this group and the queen.

It is here that I would place that other central document, the letter from Edmund Guest.[2] The letter is without date. As Dr. Gee says, Cecil came across it among his papers in 1566.

---

[1] *Commons Journals*, i. 59.   [2] The text is in Gee, *op. cit.* pp. 215-24.

I see no reason to doubt that it was addressed to Cecil.[1] Assuming this, Guest had obviously been in communication with Cecil and had undertaken the revision of the prayer-book along certain lines. The letter appears to indicate that he, or his group, had been instructed to work on the basis of the first Edwardian prayer-book, not the second. This is the point which troubled Dr. Gee and led to his rather desperate conjecture that the document might belong to Edward VI's reign. But if we are interpreting Elizabeth's views correctly in assuming that she preferred the 1549 book, it is a sign that the letter is correctly placed here. As we should expect in any revision sponsored by the émigré divines, Guest's proposals went somewhat beyond even the second book. That his enterprise had official backing and was not free-lance in character may be inferred from the fact that he expected the revised book to go before parliament : ' God for His mercy in Christ, cause the Parliament with one voice to enact it, and the realm with true heart to use it '.[2]

The letter begins :

> That you might well understand, that I have neither ungodly allowed anything against the Scripture, neither unsteadfastly done anything contrary to my writing, neither rashly without just cause put away that which might be well suffered, nor indiscreetly for novelty brought in that which might be better left out, I am so bold to write to your honour some causes of the order taken in the new service.[3]

This use of the first person is puzzling. Guest writes as if the revision were his own work. Did he act as secretary of the group of Westminster disputants ? The phrasing hardly suggests this. Or did the queen place the onus of revision on the one divine among these disputants who had not been an exile and who might therefore be thought to be more in sympathy with her conservatism ? If so, we may be fairly certain that Guest used his fellow-disputants as collaborators, for a letter from Sandys to Parker, written on 30 April, suggests that he was one of a group behind the revised prayer-book. Referring to criticism by Dr. Boxall and others of the prayer of consecration in the communion service, and to Boxall's attempt through ' the Treasurer ' and Feria to dissuade the queen from giving her consent to the act of uniformity, Sandys wrote : ' Mr. Secretary is earnest with the book and we have ministered reasons to maintain that part '.[4] Though Guest's letter must have been written two to three

---

[1] Dr. Gee's suggestion (p. 45, n. 4) that the mode of address, ' right honourable ', may indicate ' some member of the House of Lords other than Cecil ', is a bad slip. It indicates a privy councillor who was not a peer.

[2] Gee, p. 224.   [3] *Ibid.* pp. 215–16.

[4] *Correspondence of Abp. Parker* (Parker Soc.), pp. 65–6.

weeks before the letter from Sandys, may it not be Guest's comment on this prayer to which Sandys was referring ? [1]

It will be noticed that Matthew Parker does not come into the picture : he was at Cambridge at the time. I do not think this is perplexing. Owing to the false lead given by the ' Device ' we seem to have made far too precise and administrative a business of this prayer-book revision. It looks to me as if the queen had been moved from her initial and purely political predilection for things as her father left them, as far as the first Edwardian prayer-book, where both theological and political predilections would possibly have halted her ; and it was just a question whether left-wing pressure could move her forward another stage or more. The 1549 book, which Stephen Gardiner had declared 'he could with his conscience keep',[2] might even yet offer hope of some degree of unity at home. Indeed, as late as September 1559, when a more radical prayer-book was an accomplished fact, Elizabeth still retained a little optimism, demonstrating her hope of winning over the venerable Tunstal of Durham and the Marian bishops of Bath and Wells and of Peterborough by including them in her abortive commission to consecrate Matthew Parker.[3] Though there is no need to import political stratagem into an explanation of the reform party's desire for the 1552 prayer-book, may they not have perceived that it made compromise impossible and so would place the church in their hands ? ' I cannot agree myself to be a Sacramentary ', wrote Tunstal in August 1559 ; [4] which indicates his attitude to the 1552 book. As for the queen herself, on the day that the bill of uniformity finally passed in the lords, she told Feria ' that she wished the Augustanean confession to be maintained in her realm ' ; which we may equate with the first Edwardian prayer-book. And then she added that ' it would not be the Augustanean confession, but something else like it, and that she differed very little from us as she believed that God was in the sacrament of the Eucharist, and only dissented from three or four things in the Mass '.[5] May we not see in these remarks that preference in high quarters for the first Edwardian book, which is so evident in Guest's apologetic letter ? And may we not also see in them the reason for adding in the Elizabethan prayer-book those famous ' two sentences ' in the delivery of the sacrament to communicants,

---

[1] Cf. Gee, pp. 221–2. It is just possible, however, that Sandys was referring to the ' Declaration of doctrine ' which, in a letter of 28 April (*Zurich Letters*, i. 21) Jewel says they had ' exhibited to the queen ', and which Dixon prints in his *Hist. of the Church of England*, v. 107 n.

[2] Muller, *Stephen Gardiner*, p. 188.

[3] *Cal. Patent Rolls, Eliz.* i. 28. I owe the suggestion to Professor Norman Sykes, who very kindly read this article.

[4] Sturge, *Cuthbert Tunstal*, p. 323.   [5] *Spanish Cal. Eliz.* i. 61–2.

borrowed from the 1549 book : 'The body of our Lord Jesus
Christ, which was given for thee, preserve thy body and soul into
everlasting life' ; and 'The blood of our Lord Jesus Christ. . . .' ?

There was obviously a battle at court after Guest and his
collaborators had finished their revision ; and—as we have seen
from Sandys's letter of 30 April—there was a final skirmish
between the passage of the uniformity bill through parliament
and the royal assent. Sandys was not too confident of victory :
'I trust they cannot prevail', he wrote.[1] Perhaps the retention
in the third supremacy bill of that extraordinary and illogical
section v, granting communion in both kinds, is an indication
of the uncertainty in government circles whether there would
in fact be any prayer-book or act of uniformity this parliament.
For, to secure a prayer-book there had to be agreement between
two parties : let us grasp that point clearly.   One party was the
queen, the other the protestant divines and a house of commons
overwhelmingly on their side.   And it is evident that neither
the divines nor the house of commons would consent to a return
to 1549.   Politically, they held the trump cards ; and surely the
most important and fascinating revelation of this whole story
is the consummate way in which they played them.   Our prayer-
book, it seems, was a compromise, with the queen conceding
most.   We are afforded a glimpse of this from both sides.   In
1571 Parker recalled how the queen, talking to him once or twice
on a certain point, had told him that she 'would not have agreed
to divers orders of the book' had it not been for the notorious
proviso about ornaments in the act of uniformity (section xiii).[2]
Now it happens that Sandys wrote to Parker about this very
proviso, just after the bill had passed the lords : 'our gloss upon
this text', he declared, 'is that we shall not be forced to use'
the ornaments.[3] How characteristic of a compromise : each
party reading its own meaning into it !

Before leaving this theme, we may indulge in a guess about
the date of Guest's letter.   If Jewel co-operated with him in the
revision of the prayer-book, then it is probable that the letter was
not written much earlier than 14 April, for on that day—which
was four days before the bill of uniformity was introduced into
parliament—Jewel still retained confidence in the queen :

> This woman, excellent as she is, and earnest in the cause of true
> religion, notwithstanding she desires a thorough change as early
> as possible, cannot however be induced to effect such change without
> the sanction of law; lest the matter should seem to have been
> accomplished, not so much by the judgment of discreet men, as in
> compliance with the impulse of a furious multitude.

[1] *Parker Correspondence*, p. 66.   [2] *Ibid.* p. 375.   [3] *Ibid.* p. 65.

Perhaps by ' discreet men ' he meant those divines, of whom he said later in his letter : ' Sandys, Grindal, Sampson, Scory (and why should I particularize these?), all of us remain still in London '. Jewel chafed at the delay, so different from the precipitancy of the Marian reaction : ' We manage every thing with so much deliberation, and prudence, and wariness, and circumspection. . . .' [1] When all was over, he was a disillusioned man. He scoffed at the retention of ' the scenic apparatus of divine worship ' : ' *we* are not consulted '. ' Others ', he added, ' are seeking after a *golden*, or as it rather seems to me, a *leaden* mediocrity ; and are crying out, that the half is better than the whole '.[2]

The rest of the story can be quickly told. Parliament resumed its sitting on 3 April, and on the 10th a new bill of supremacy—the third—was read a first time. Feria reported that Cecil went that day ' to the lower house and told them from the queen that she thanked them greatly for their goodwill in offering her the title of supreme head . . . , which out of humility she was unwilling to accept, and asked them to devise some other form. . . . He was answered that it was against the word of God and the scripture, and they were surprised at his coming to them every day with new proposals and objections.' [3] Perhaps critics did say something of the sort ; perhaps they did not. Feria took credit to himself for the queen's scruples ; the reformers gave it to one of themselves, Mr. Lever ; and as for Jewel, he was ' not much displeased '.[4] Cecil no doubt was ready with the new bill embodying the new title of supreme governor. Technically there had to be a new bill, for although it presumably differed little from the one passed before Easter, the old one could no longer be amended. We need not follow it through the two houses.[5] Though all the spiritual peers and one temporal

---

[1] *Zurich Letters*, i. 17–18.   [2] *Ibid*, p. 23.
[3] *Commons Journals*, i. 59 ; *Spanish Cal. Eliz.* i. 52.   [4] *Zurich Letters*, i. 24.
[5] The subsequent discovery of Bowyer's abridgement of the Lords Journals enables us to add a footnote to Maitland's analysis of the original bill. Bowyer (*E.H.R.*, xxviii. 537) reveals that the lords added a ' proviso ' to the bill. This was obviously what Maitland (*Collected Papers*, iii. 191) describes as ' the second schedule ', containing three provisos, printed as sections xx, xxi, xxii. The bill and ' proviso ', or schedule was sent to the commons on 26 April ; and, though the clerk there made no entries for it in his Journal—an omission which warns us to be careful in interpreting the evidence of the Journal—the commons added a proviso of their own, which was passed by the lords on 29 April (*E.H.R.*, xxviii. 539). This second proviso was obviously Maitland's ' first schedule ', containing the proviso printed as section xix. Let us note that the order in which a group of schedules—placed one on top of the other—are stitched to the parchment bill is clearly haphazard. In this particular instance, the wrong ' historical ' order obscures a very interesting point, for section xix of our statute was the retort of the protestant house of commons to section xx, devised by the lords ; and I am inclined to guess that it was the commons who inserted in section xx that passage about the canonical scriptures and the first four general councils which so interested Maitland (*op. cit.* iii. 191-2, and cf. *Parker Correspondence*, p. 66). A

peer, Viscount Montague, voted against it, the government can have been in no doubt of it passing.

As for the bill of uniformity, though the off-stage battle delayed its introduction into the commons until 18 April, it had a rapid passage there. It was read a second time on the next day, 19 April. From the brief agenda that morning we may infer that there was debate, but the bill was not committed : indeed, we might almost describe the process of compromise between the queen and Guest's group as an informal committee-stage. It was passed on the third day, 20 April.[1] In the lords it had as rapid a passage. It was not committed. Queen and government, not to mention the commons, were behind it. For staunch catholics there was no compromise possible, but simply that freedom of speech which in 1593 the queen was to define as : ' To say yea or no to bills, God forbid that any man should be restrained or afraid to answer according to his best liking, with some short declaration of his reason therein '.[2] Some did make their declarations, though not short : we know that Abbot Feckenham, Bishop Thirlby and Bishop Scot spoke against the bill.[3] On the third day, 28 April, it passed the lords with eighteen dissenting voices—nine prelates and nine temporal peers. Feckenham's name is missing.[4] Presumably he was absent that day, though if the speech that we possess was his and was delivered—which I see no reason to doubt—then he had been present the previous day. It seems odd.

Feria reported that the bill was carried by only three votes.[5] The relevant page of the Lords Journals, by which we might check this, is lost ; but if it means that thirty-nine peers were present that day and that proxies were not invoked, it is quite likely correct. If proxies had been used, then the majority would have been substantial, if entirely lay. In other words, the bill was as safe as its very rapid progress through the house suggests ; and the two privy councillors among the dissentients, the marquis of Winchester and the earl of Shrewsbury—perhaps some of the others as well—could indulge their consciences without fear of jeopardizing a government bill. In the light of our revised version of an old story, the formal dissent of some of

---

final point : the provisos for Chetwood and Harecourt, which are sections xxiii and xxiv of our statute, must have been annexed to the bill when it first went to the lords ; and since their initial appearance was as an addition to the first bill, we may presume that they were either already attached to the third bill when it was introduced into the commons, or were immediately and automatically added. Historically they are the first and second schedules, not the third and fourth, as the haphazard stitching has placed them.

[1] *Commons Journals*, i. 60.　　　　　　　　　　[2] *E.H.R.*, xxxi. 136.

[3] Feckenham's and Scot's speeches are printed in Strype, *Annals*, i. ii. 431, 438. For Thirlby, see *Spanish Cal. Eliz.* i. 64 ; *Zurich Letters*, i. 20.

[4] *E.H.R.*, xxviii. 538.　　　　　　　　　　[5] *Spanish Cal. Eliz.* i. 67.

these nine temporal peers may indicate, not a catholic vote but
the disgust of moderate men at the queen surrendering so much
to the protestant left wing.   It may have been a demonstration
aimed at strengthening the final conservative move—which,
be it noted, was not necessarily or exclusively catholic—to
persuade Elizabeth to veto the bill.[1]   At any rate, these noblemen
must have known that their vote could do no harm.   One wonders
if a similar knowledge kept Abbot Feckenham away that day :
he was in the house on 1 May.[2]

A final point calls for brief comment.   From Bowyer's
abridgement of the Lords Journals, made before the missing
pages were lost, we learn that on 29 April the clerk again entered
the bill of uniformity, this time as received back from the commons,
once more writing the word ' *conclusa* ' against it.   If correct,
this would indicate that the lords, without a commitment,
had made some small alteration or alterations in the text, which
required and received the approval of the commons.   And yet
there is no corresponding entry in the Commons Journals.   Unfortunately, it is equally possible that the clerk of the lower house
was at fault or that the higher clerk was.   Bowyer assumed the
latter.   Maitland's analysis of the scribal corrections in the
parchment text of the bill would suit either thesis.[3]

[1] Cf. *Parker Correspondence*, p. 66.   [2] *Lords Journals*, i. 576.
[3] *E.H.R.*, xxviii. 539; Maitland, *Collected Papers*, iii. 204 *seqq.*

9

Peter Wentworth*

by J. E. Neale

PART I

F EW English parliamentarians before the age of the Stuarts have left behind them any substantial memory of their parliamentary achievements, and of these few Peter Wentworth is probably the first, certainly the most attractive. So slight is our acquaintance with his forerunners, that were we to attempt, even in a single article, to fashion an earlier parliamentary biography than his, the person and his works would inevitably be lost in the historical setting that we should have to provide. Wentworth thus owes some of his fame as a pioneer to the accident of historical knowledge ; but it would be an error to suppose that our dim perception of earlier parliamentarians and our growing familiarity with later can be explained by time's ravages amongst documents. They are explained by a notable feature in the evolution of parliament. Before the accession of Elizabeth the corporate spirit of the commons was but dawning, prolonged and concerted opposition to the Crown was hardly known, and the story of parliament therefore lacked that significance and fascination for contemporaries that might have immortalized it in abundant historical sources. Early in Elizabeth's reign severe strife with the Crown began, and enlivened debate gave incentive to the curious ; parliamentary diaries appeared, speeches were written and preserved, and public interest broadened to sweep parliament within it. But the fitful keeping of diaries and writing of speeches had to be transformed into habit, and parliament to be converted by public curiosity into a stage whose drama was worth retelling, before the flood of historical sources under the Stuarts became such that historians might plan a parliamentary biography upon the scale of a book. Of the Elizabethan age it is enough to say that two articles will exhaust our knowledge of the most courageous, and perhaps the most prophetic, parliamentarian of his time.

Of Wentworth's career we possess two accounts, apart from the comments in the histories of the period. The one is by W. L. Rutton in his *Three Branches of the Family of Wentworth*, the other by Sir Charles Wentworth Dilke in the *Dictionary of National Biography*. Neither, however, is much more than a sketch, and no apology need be offered for a third biography, especially as the new documents which have come to light, more in number than those already known, amend and amplify the accepted story at its most important points. Little need be said here of genealogical facts : they are Rutton's province and are fully dealt with by him. Wentworth was a gentleman 'of a good house and of good breeding '.[1] His grandfather, the founder of a new line of Wentworths in Essex, was a younger son of the Nettlestead Wentworths, the first branch of the family to settle out of Yorkshire ; whilst his father, Sir Nicholas, who was chief porter of Calais under Henry VIII and Edward VI, acquired as his principal estate the manor of Lillingstone Lovell, then in Oxfordshire, and held property in addition in Essex, Oxfordshire, Northamptonshire, Buckinghamshire, and London. As the eldest son, Peter succeeded to the lands at Lillingstone. He married twice, his first wife being a daughter of Sir Ralph Lane of Horton, Northamptonshire, first cousin of Queen Katharine Parr ; his second, a sister of Sir Francis Walsingham. Sir Walter Mildmay also married a sister of Walsingham's, so that Wentworth was brought into relationship with another of Elizabeth's councillors ; and his connexion with the court was further strengthened by the tragically short marriage of Burghley's daughter with the eldest son of Lord Wentworth of Nettlestead. In addition, he may have been related to the St. Johns of Bletsoe,[2] whilst his parliamentary friendship with Walter Strickland of Yorkshire was cemented by the marriage of his daughter to Strickland's son.[3]

Of Wentworth's early life very little is known. He was born about 1524,[4] and, according to the fashion of his day, rounded off his education by a legal training, entering Lincoln's Inn in 1542.[5] He did not begin his parliamentary career until 1571, when he was forty-seven, and he was probably prompted to it, not so much by a desire for public life and experience, as by an urgent sense of duty. 'I was first stirred vpp to deale ' in the succession question, he wrote in 1593, ' xxxi yeares past, by godes good motion : then, by sundry graue and wise menn vnknowne vnto mee ; and allso by lamentable messages sent vnto mee, by men likewise vnknowne vnto mee.'[6] This was

---

[1] Sir John Harington, *A Tract on the Succession to the Crown (1602)*, ed. by C. R. Markham (1880).

[2] Oliver, brother of Lord St. John, referred to Wentworth as his cousin : at least so Humphrey Winch states in his confession (Brit. Mus., Harleian MS. 6846, fo. 83 b).

[3] *Dict. of Nat. Biog.* (orig. ed.), lv. 54.

[4] On 18 September 1595 Wentworth wrote that he was over seventy-one years old (Brit. Mus. Add. MS. 24664, fo. 50 b).

[5] *Records of Lincoln's Inn. Admissions*, i. 53. I am assuming that his is the name that appears upon the register. The date agrees with his age, and his children and grandchildren went to the same inn.

[6] Brit. Mus. Add. MS. 24664, fo. 44 b.

probably at the time of parliament's great campaign in 1562–3 and 1566. Of its frustrated hopes he must have heard from his brother. Paul, and hearing, perhaps was persuaded to strengthen the puritan ranks in parliament by seeking election to the next parliament, that of 1571. He sat for the borough of Barnstaple, and as we do not know that he owned property in the west country, he probably owed his election there, and for the borough of Tregony later, to the patronage of puritan friends.

It was an eventful session in which he first sat. In the previous parliament of 1566 the attention of the commons had been so centred upon the question of the succession, that only towards the close of the session had they been able to turn to that other great cause, which, with the succession, was the object of their most intimate concern, the reform of the church. It had then been too late. A bill to give statutory authority to the articles of 1562 had indeed reached a first reading in the lords, but it had lapsed because of the queen's intervention ; and five other bills had got no further than a first reading in the commons when the parliament was dissolved.[1] Already, however, parliamentary policy was achieving a continuity that defied the accident of dissolutions and long recesses. The succession agitation of 1562–3 had been revived in 1566.[2] The campaign for ecclesiastical reform was to be reopened in 1571.

No sooner was the parliament in session than Walter Strickland caught up the threads that had been dropped in 1566. He secured the appointment of a committee, the bills of the last session were revived, and to them a new bill was added.[3] Strickland was a zealous but intemperate man, who took no thought for the Crown's rights ; and he would have proceeded with the bills, had the house not shown greater tact and withheld them from a formal reading until it had consulted the bishops.[4] The bishops do not appear to have been particularly obstructive. One bill, it is true, that for pensions out of benefices, must have succumbed immediately to their opposition, if indeed it had been revived in this session ; but otherwise only one bill seems to have aroused controversy. That was the bill concerning the articles ; and Wentworth's first known speech was made when he and other members were sent to discuss it with the archbishop of Canterbury.[5] The commons had struck out certain of the articles, perhaps only retaining those which concerned ' the confession of the true Christian faith and the doctrine of the sacraments ' : [6]

---

[1] *Spanish Cal., Eliz.,* i. 605–6 ; *Commons' Journals,* i. 79.

[2] Cf. *E.H.R.,* xxxvi. 502–3.

[3] *Commons' Journals.* i, 83 ; D'Ewes's *Journals,* pp. 156–7, 184–5.

[4] *Commons' Journals,* i. 83.   [5] *Ibid.* p. 86 a.

[6] See the act 13 Eliz., cap. xii, *Statutes of the Realm,* IV. i. 546.

certainly they had deleted articles 35 and 36 on the homilies and on the consecration of bishops and ministers. Their action surprised the archbishop, but his surprise was greater when Wentworth explained that they had had no time to see how the missing articles agreed with the word of God. 'What, said he, surely you mistook the matter, you will refer your selves wholly to us therein ? No, by the Faith I bear to God,' said Wentworth, ' we will pass nothing before we understand what it is ; for that were but to make you Popes ; make you Popes who list, . . . we will make you none.' [1] The bill was proceeded with, passed by the commons in two days, and sent to the lords. There it was read once, when the queen intervened.[2] Although statutory authority had been given to the six articles of Henry VIII's reign, Elizabeth was loath to encourage the puritans in their belief that parliament ought to legislate for the church. The bill was not a government measure, even though the bishops were privy to it ; and if it emasculated the articles her interference was doubly justified. She was tactful, however, and promised to publish and execute the articles by virtue of her royal supremacy ; only, parliament was not to deal with them.

Strickland's zeal still remained unsatisfied. He was not content with a confession of faith. He wanted the prayer book purged of needless ceremonial as well, and introduced a bill for this purpose. He had neither obtained the queen's consent nor proposed to obtain it ; and as the lord keeper had explicitly charged the commons at the opening of the parliament to meddle with no matters of state save such as should be propounded unto them, his action was a serious infringement of the royal prerogative for which there could be no excuse. Once more, however, the commons tempered his rash designs by their tact, and after a first reading held up the bill until they had petitioned the queen for her licence to proceed.[3] But their action could not clear Strickland of blame. During the Easter recess he was summoned before the privy council, confined to his house, and prevented from returning to the parliament when it reassembled. There was nothing unconstitutional in what the government had done, but puritan members were not to be stayed by any such argument. They regarded Strickland's restraint as an affront to their privileges, and when feelings were running high over a speech of Wentworth's upon another incident, a member called attention to Strickland's absence, and a debate followed, remarkable for its daring, and reminiscent of the spirited speeches made

---

[1] D'Ewes, pp. 239–40.

[2] The bill was entitled, ' for Conservation of Order and Uniformity in the Church ' (Commons' Journals, i. 86–7 ; Lords' Journals, i. 678).

[3] D'Ewes, pp. 141–2, 157 a, 166–7 ; Commons' Journals, i. 84 b.

in 1566. Passions were so vehement that in prudence the council sent Strickland back to the house the next day : whereby a victory was won which must have confirmed Wentworth's exalted notions of parliamentary privilege.[1]

But open interference with personal liberty, a crude device, and one apt to defeat its object by exciting resentment in the house, was not the sole restraint upon freedom of speech and action. Intimidation and rumours of the queen's displeasure were subtler and surer in their effects, especially if offenders were lawyers of promise, dependent upon the favour of the court for their careers. It was against these devices that Wentworth had reason to fulminate in this parliament, as he had later in 1575/6. The occasion arose out of the subsidy bill which on 7 April was proposed by a private member, who suggested that the house should anticipate the motion customarily made by a privy councillor. His speech seemed a rather artless attempt to curry favour, and was resented. It was an unpropitious opening for the government, and when the debate developed, Robert Bell, a prominent lawyer,[2] started an avalanche by linking the redress of grievances with supply and inveighing against licences and the abuse of promoters. Not only was he responsible for a debate which was unpleasant for the government and resulted in the appointment of a committee for griefs and petitions along with that for supply, but his complaint indirectly touched the Crown, and the cry of prerogative might therefore be raised. Said Wentworth, his speech was so disliked by some of the council that he was sent for and so hardly dealt with that he came into the house with an amazed countenance, which daunted all in such sort that for ten, twelve, or sixteen days not one in the house durst deal in any matter of importance. And in simple matters they spent more words and time in their preamble, requiring that they might not be mistaken, than in the matter they spake unto. So that this rumour grew in the house : ' Sirs, you may not speak against Licences, the Queens Majesty will be angry, the Councel will be . . . angry.'

The intimidation of Bell was a warning to the commons, and was followed by a command from the queen ' to spend little time in Motions, and to avoid long Speeches '. Moreover, on the day on which parliament rose for the Easter recess, Sir Humphrey Gilbert prompted the revival of Bell's motion with the object of attacking it as a violation of the royal prerogative. His speech was disliked, but the adjournment stopped members from answering it. Against Wentworth's resentment, however, time

[1] Trans. Devon. Assoc. (1879), xi. 479 ; D'Ewes, pp. 175–6.
[2] Bell was Speaker in 1572 and 1575/6, and chief baron of the exchequer later. Cf. D'Ewes, pp. 205, 277.

did not run. He nursed his wrath during the recess, and when
the house met again retorted upon Gilbert. He likened him to
the chameleon which could change itself into all colours save
white : even so could he change himself to all fashions but
honesty. He denounced his speech as tending ' to no other end
than to inculcate fear into those which should be free ', and
' requested care for the credit of the House, and for the maintenance of free Speech '. Bell's speech, he said, had been misreported
to the queen, and he would reprove the guilty person in the
words of David : ' Thou O Lord shalt destroy Lyers.' The
Speaker tried to calm the feelings of the house, and poured the
oil of royal flattery upon them ; but the only result of his intervention was that the storm passed into the debate upon Strickland's restraint.[1] At length the session closed, and the lord
keeper conveyed the queen's thanks to her parliament. They
were tendered unalloyed to the lords, but for the commons they
were mixed with the chastening of those few who ' have shewed
themselves audacious, arrogant and presumptuous, calling her
Majesties Grants and Prerogatives . . . in question, contrary to
their Duty and place that they be called unto '.[2] It was a
troublesome house and it was dissolved.

The next parliament met on 8 May 1572. Wentworth was
returned for Tregony and his brother Paul, who had not sat
in the last parliament, for another Cornish borough, Liskeard.[3]
It was the Ridolfi plot that caused the early summons of a new
parliament, and the independence of the house of commons,
which was nourished by opposition to the Crown, drew strength
from the vigorous pressure which all agreed to exert upon
Elizabeth, in the hope of inducing her to execute Norfolk and
either to attaint Mary or at least to deprive her of her right to
the succession. Unfortunately we are no longer served by the
anonymous diarist whose delightful reports give an accidental
prominence to the events of the previous session : and it has
hitherto been supposed that Wentworth played no very noteworthy part in this, his second parliament. It was known only
that he was a member of the grand committee for Mary's cause.[4]
However, when the manuscripts of Mr. Ralph Bankes of Kingston
Lacy were calendared for the Historical Manuscripts Commission,
a speech of Wentworth's was discovered. Unfortunately only
the description, which is in Wentworth's words, was quoted.
This I repeat here :

Speech uttered by me the Weddensdaye, Thursdaye, and Saterdaye in
the Whitson Weeke, and in the 14th yeare the Queene's Maty's raygne,

[1] *Commons' Journals*, i. 83 ; D'Ewes, pp. 158–9, 167–8, 175, 242 ; *Trans. Devon.
Assoc.*, xi. 479.   [2] D'Ewes, p. 151.
[3] *Official Return*, part i, p. 408.   [4] *Commons' Journals*, i. 95.

1572, upon a message sente by her Matie in the parliament house, whereupon two of the house made a motion that the speaker and certen of the house shoulde goe to her Matie and give her thankes in the behalf of the whole House for the good opinions conceaved of us, the which for my part I did not think her Matie had deserved, soe that my speech was to staye thankes, and to other ends, as shall appear hereafter when the effect of her Matie's message shall be declared. The speech uttered on the Wednesday.[1]

The days referred to were 28, 29, and 31 May. Already the lords and commons had agreed to proceed against Mary in the highest degree of treason, touching her in life, in title, and in dignity ; and they had persisted in their decision even after a message had come from the queen stating her preference for delaying the attainder, and for proceeding immediately only against her title to the succession. As a consequence the committees of both houses had been summoned to the court on the morning of Wednesday, 28 May, and there Elizabeth had repeated her wishes.[2] Perhaps in her isolation she had resorted to flattery, a weapon she wielded with much skill, and the report of the committee had so charmed two members that they had made the motion which drew from Wentworth his speech. It is a cause of great regret to me that I have not succeeded in seeing this manuscript. But that Wentworth did not mince his words is clear from the meagre quotation that I have given and from a reference to a speech of his this session which he made when a committee of the commons was examining him in 1575/6. ' Did I not ', said he, publish Mary ' openly in the last Parliament to be the most notorious whore in all the world and wherefore should I then be afraid to call her soe nowe againe ? ' [3] Parliament's campaign against Mary failed. Even the bill against her title was denied the royal assent. Elizabeth tried to sweeten the bitterness of her decision by asking her subjects to construe *la royne s'advisera* literally ; but to allow her to be advised, as they well knew, was to give her leave to forget altogether.[4]

Adjournment instead of dissolution was a reward that might follow the good behaviour of the commons ; and as the queen hoped by graciousness to hold the affections which her championship of Mary threatened to estrange—for to the people, as Sir John Hayward remarked, ' no musicke is soe sweete as the affability of ther Prince ' [5]—the parliament of 1572 was granted a new lease of life and met again on 8 February 1575/6. Wentworth

---

[1] *Hist. MSS. Comm. Rep.*, viii. 212 b.

[2] *Commons' Journals*, i. 95 f.

[3] Inner Temple, Petyt MSS. 538, vol. xvii, fo. 254. I am indebted to the Benchers of the Inner Temple for permission to inspect and to quote from this manuscript.

[4] La Mothe Fénelon, *Correspondance Diplomatique*, v. 42 ; Digges, *The Compleat Ambassador* (1655), p. 219.

[5] Hayward, *Annals of Elizabeth*, ed. Bruce (Camden Soc.), p. 18.

had now sat through two sessions : he had seen Robert Bell coerced for talking of abuses in high places, and members intimidated by the mere rumour of the queen's displeasure ; he had watched members sit at a division [1] ' in an evil matter against which they had most earnestly spoken ', and had found ' that it was a common Policy . . . to mark the best sort '—privy councillors and courtiers—' and either to sit or arise with them ' ; [2] he had seen Strickland confined to his house, and the queen's inhibition placed upon the unauthorized introduction of bills concerning religion, both in 1571 and 1572 ; and he had noted in the last session the impotence of parliament to force upon the queen a decision which all thought to be essential for the safety of the realm. Upon this experience he brooded during the interval at home, and taking as his text the words of Elihu,[3] ' Behold, I am as the new Wine which hath no vent and bursteth the new Vessels in sunder, therefore I will speak that I may have a vent, . . . I will regard no manner of Person, no man will I spare,' he prepared a remarkable indictment of queen, council, and parliament, to be spoken when next the house met. Twenty times and more as he walked in his grounds, his own fearful conceit warned him that the speech would surely lead him into prison ; but where personal safety was to be won only, as he thought, at the expense of danger to queen and country, his conscience was ever clamant enough to outcry his fears.

One bill had been read in the new session when he rose and astounded the house. He began, as he was to begin other speeches of his, by expounding the commodities that grow to the prince and whole state by free speech, ' the only Salve to heal all the Sores of this Common-Wealth ' ; and, by claiming for parliament the right to remedy all ills and to avert all perils, to advance God's honour and to offer means for the profit of the state, he asserted its right to freedom of speech and conscience. Even if the envious should offer anything hurtful in parliament, no incommodity, nay much good, would grow thereby, ' for by the darkness of the Night the brightness of the Sun sheweth more excellent and clear ', and a wicked purpose may the easier be prevented when it is known. Free speech, he argued, was granted to parliament by a special law, ' as that without the which the Prince and State cannot be preserved or maintained ', and therefore was the queen subject to it, for though she had no peer or equal, yet she was subject to the law. As his speech was born of his experience in the two last sessions, so was it illustrated by it. Rumours and messages, of which the Devil was the first

---

[1] i. e. vote against a motion. In a division those in favour of a motion, as innovators, went out of the house : their opponents remained seated.
[2] D'Ewes, pp. 240–1. [3] Job xxxii. 19 f.

author, he would have buried in Hell. Hate all messengers and
tale-carriers, was his cry ; yea, hate them as venomous and poison
to the commonwealth : spare none, for the higher place he hath
the more harm he may do. Then, like a father over his child,
he took the queen to task. It was a dangerous thing in a prince
to oppose herself against her nobility and people. No doubt
but that some of her council had dealt plainly and faithfully
with her for her refusal of the bill against Mary in the last parliament. Let her know such for approved subjects, and those
who had supported her refusal, let her know them for traitors
and underminers of her life. He opened his criticism of the
queen with the words, ' none is without fault, no not our Noble
Queen ', and as he uttered them he paused at the amazement
on the countenances of his hearers. ' Then ', said he to the
committee which examined him upon the speech, ' I was afraid
with you for Company and fear bad me to put out those words
that followed, for your Countenances did assure me that not one
of you would stay me of my Journey ; yet the consideration of
a good Conscience and of a faithful Subject did make me bold to
utter it . . . and I praise God for it, and if it were to do again
I would with the same mind speak it again.' [1]

How much further than those unpardonable words he got,
we do not know ; but the house stopped him ' out of a reverend
regard of her Majesty's Honour ' before he had completed his
speech, and having sequestered him, committed him to the
serjeant's ward and appointed a committee to examine him
' for the extenuating of his fault '. The report of the examination
portrays Wentworth's character admirably. It is of course his
own version of what was said, but there is no reason to doubt
its substantial accuracy, even though one may suspect that the
dialogue proceeds too rapidly in his favour. The committee
were evidently anxious to extenuate his fault as they were
charged to do. But when they wished to take cognizance only
of what had been spoken, characteristically he insisted upon the
whole speech being shown to the queen. When they endeavoured
to draw an apology from him which would mitigate his offence,
he obstinately persisted in justifying himself. ' Mr. Wentworth ',
said Seckford, ' will never acknowledge himself to make a fault,
nor say that he is sorry for anything that he doth speak.' At
the opening of the examination Wentworth seized upon the
presence of privy councillors on the committee as an excuse
for reasserting his theories of privilege.

If your Honours ask me as Councellors to her Majesty [he said in reply to
a question] you shall pardon me ; I will make you no Answer : I will
do no such injury to the place from whence I came ; for I am now no private

<hr>

[1] D'Ewes, pp. 236–43 ; *Commons' Journals*, i. 104 ; *Spanish Cal., Eliz.*, ii. 524.

Person, I am a publick, and a Councellor to the whole State in that place where it is lawful for me to speak my mind freely, and not for you as Councellors to call me to account for anything that I do speak in the House. . . . But if you ask me as Committees from the House, I will make you the best Answer I can.

And again, later, he was unduly sensitive. ' If you offer me an Oath of your Authorities, I will refuse it, because I will do nothing to infringe the Liberties of the House.' One of his replies when two or three precedents were quoted to justify the queen's messages to the house is thoroughly worthy of the Stuart period. ' Sirs,' said he, ' you ought to alledge good Precedents to comfort and embolden men in good doing, and not [1] evil Precedents to discourage and terrifie men to do evil.' There is a version of the examination in the Petyt manuscripts at the Inner Temple which contains a passage not in that made familiar by D'Ewes. According to this the committee remarked, ' You called the Scottish Queen Isabelle. What meant you by that ? Did I not ', answered Wentworth, ' publish her openly in the last Parliament to be the most notorious whore in all the world and wherefore should I then be afraid to call her soe nowe againe ? She is a Queen ', he was told, ' you ought to speake reverently of her. Let him take her parte that list,' retorted he, ' I will speake the truth boldly.' [2]

The committee made its report to the house, and on the motion of the treasurer Wentworth was committed to the Tower. There he remained for just over a month, when the queen intervened and the house released him after he had made his submission and craved her pardon. Mildmay seized the occasion to preach a homily upon the queen's good and clement nature, her respect for the house, and its duty towards her. He acknowledged their right to liberty of speech, but drew a distinction between liberty and licence ; pertinence, modesty, reverence, and discretion in speech marking the one as the opposite qualities marked the other. Elizabeth's act was gracious, and she deserved the credit that Mildmay took care to claim ; but the session was then two days from its close, and it is doubtful if she appreciably lessened Wentworth's confinement. The government must have rejoiced that such a nuisance had during a whole session been kept suppressed.[3]

[1] This word is omitted in D'Ewes, p. 242, clearly by error. It occurs in the Petyt MSS. 538, vol. xvii, fo. 253 b.

[2] Petyt MSS. 538, vol. xvii, fo. 254. In Brit. Mus., Harleian MS. 161, fo. 30, which is the manuscript of Wentworth's examination that D'Ewes owned, there are fragments of these passages about Mary. So there are in Harleian MS. 1877, fo. 29 b. It is hardly likely that the parent manuscript of these two was difficult to read at one point only, and therefore it looks as though the passages were censored. They are senseless in the mutilated form and so were omitted by D'Ewes.

[3] *Commons' Journals*, i. 104, 114 ; D'Ewes, pp. 258–60.

In the interval before the next parliament Wentworth was again in trouble. The privy council was informed by the bishop of Peterborough that there was great resort of people out of their own parish to Wentworth's house at Lillingstone Lovell, there to receive the communion. Accordingly in May 1579 he was summoned before the council, and at the same time the bishop and other high commissioners were ordered to go to Northampton and inquire into the disorders. Their report is entered in the council register. Divers of the townspeople, they discovered, refusing to conform in religion, repaired to Lillingstone, and there received the sacrament after another sort.[1] Unfortunately our information goes no further, and we do not know how the council treated Wentworth. The incident is interesting as an isolated illustration of his prominence among the puritans of his district : he was, said Sir John Harington,[2] ' a man of great accompt with all of that profession '.

On 16 January 1580/1 the old parliament met for its third and last session. When in its early days Paul Wentworth proposed the ordering of a public fast and preaching, it looked as though there was to be another stormy session. The motion was carried by 115 to 100 after a debate in which official opinion was divided ; and the preaching was arranged to be in the Temple church. Once more the religious zeal of the puritans had encroached upon the queen's ecclesiastical powers, and she met the incursion with a message that blended wrath with clemency and laid the blame for their rashness chiefly upon her own lenity to Paul's brother in the previous session. The commons submitted, and when religious grievances reappeared this session the queen's ruling that they should act through the bishops was faithfully complied with, both the speaker and the house showing great anxiety to avoid offence.[3] The session continued tranquilly, and, unless our authorities deceive us, Peter Wentworth held his peace. His brother sat in no more parliaments, and he himself, for what reason we do not know, was not a member in the next parliament of 1584/5.

The Babington plot necessitated the calling of a new parliament in October 1586, and Wentworth was then elected for the city of Northampton, a constituency where his own influence was strong.[4] The autumn meeting was an extraordinary one. Normal business, if not entirely set aside as the government would have wished, was completely subordinated to the task of pressing remorselessly for the death of Mary ; and not until after the Christmas recess, by which time Mary had been executed, was

---

[1] Dasent, *Acts of the Privy Council*, xi. 132, 133, 218, 219.
[2] *Op. cit.* pp. 6–7.
[3] *Commons' Journals*, i. 118 f.   [4] *Official Return*, part i, p. 419.

it possible to renew old controversies. Then, however, a new
campaign for the puritan reformation of the church was opened
by Anthony Cope,[1] a neighbour of Wentworth's and member for
Banbury. He offered a bill and a book to the house which
aimed at a drastic reconstruction of the church upon a presbyterian basis ; and although the speaker reminded members of
the queen's former inhibitions, they persisted in reading them.
The cue of the official party was to play for time. Therefore,
before the decision could be put into effect, Dalton interfered
to oppose it, drawing Lewknor, Hurlston, and Bainbrigg in its
support ; the morning was talked away, and the queen was given
her chance to act. According to D'Ewes, whose authority is the
clerk's rough draft of the journal, Elizabeth not only sent a
message to the speaker on 27 February, the day of the debate,
but she summoned him before her on the following day, and in
consequence the house did not sit.[2] On the other hand, an
anonymous member's diary [3] reports proceedings on 28 February
and does not suggest that the speaker actually saw the queen.
According to this account, which I think the more reliable, the
speaker announced on that day that he had sent the bill and
book to Elizabeth, and at once a debate followed in which
Dounlee, Topcliffe, Bainbrigg, Hastings, Aldred, and Alforth all
spoke on church abuses. Hastings's speech was in some respects
a prelude to the action which Wentworth took on the following
day. He had been at strife with himself, he said, whether to
speak or to hold his peace ; but considering his duty to God,
loyalty to the queen, and love to his country he could not be
silent, but in a place of free speech must be willing and ready to
deliver his conscience. Whatever the cost, they must not turn
God out of doors.[4]

By 1 March, then, an attempt had once more been made to
reform the church, and had failed because the queen would not
tolerate it. Her interference was in Wentworth's eyes a derogation
from parliament's rights, and with the refractory spirit manifest
in the house to encourage him, he determined to strike at the root
of all their troubles and to obtain from the commons rulings on
their privileges. That is to say, the commons were not to leave
it to the queen to define freedom of speech, but were to confront
the interpretation put upon it by the lord keeper and enforced
by the queen's rulings, with a decision of their own. It was

---

[1] Of Hanwell, near Banbury. Cf. *Dict. of Nat. Biog.* ; *Official Return*, part i,
p. 419.

[2] D'Ewes, p. 410.

[3] Harleian MS. 7188, fos. 88 f. This and other new parliamentary journals and
speeches of the reign I hope ultimately to publish as a supplement to D'Ewes's *Journals*.

[4] *Ibid.* fos. 93 b–94. For the constituencies which these members represent see
the *Official Return*.

a fundamental move, in extension of the tactics adopted by his brother in 1566,[1] and had the temper and courage of Elizabethan parliamentarians equalled Wentworth's, might have precipitated the constitutional crisis that came under the Stuarts. He proposed to propound a series of questions, the replies to which would stand as rulings of the house. The questions are well known : at least the version printed in D'Ewes's *Journals* is.[2] A second version, however, exists amongst the Burghley papers in the Lansdowne collection, containing ten questions in place of the usual eight. They are as follows : [3]

1. First, whether the Prince and state cann be mainteyned without this court of parliament.

2. Item, whether there be any counsell that cann make or abrogate lawes ? but only this court of parliament.

3. Item, whether free speache and free doinges, or dealinges be not graunted to euerye on of the parliament howse by lawe.

4. Item, whether that greate honor to god and those greate benefits may be doon vnto the prince and state without free speache and doyngs in this place, that may be donn with them.

5. Item, whether it be not an Iniurye to the whole state, and against the law, that the prince or priuie councell should send for any membre of this howse in the parliament tyme, or aftre the end of the parliament, and to checke, blame or punishe them for any speache used in this place, except it be for trayterous wourds.

6. Item, whether this be a place to receyue supplications of the greues and sores of the common wealth, and ether that we should be humble suters vnto the Quene her maiestye for releffe, or els to releue them here as the case requireth.

7. Item, whether yt be not against the orders and liberties of this howse to receyue messages ether of commaundinge or prohibiting, and whether the messenger be not to be reputed as an enemye to god, the prince and state.

8. Item, whether it be not against the orders and liberties of this howse to make any thinge known vnto the prince that is here in hand to the hurte of the howse, and whether the tale carriar be not to be punisshed by the howse and reputed as an enymye vnto god, the prince and state.

9. Item, whether we doo shewe our selues faithfull vnto god, the prince and state in receyuing suche messages, and in takinge such tales in good parte, without punisshing of the messenger and tale carriar by the order and discretion of this howse.

10. Item, whether he or they may be not to be estemed reputed and used as enemyes vnto god, the prince and state that should doo any thing to infringe the liberties of this honorable councell.

Both texts are no doubt genuine. They are perhaps an earlier

---

[1] Cf. *E.H.R.*, xxxvi. 506.   [2] D'Ewes, pp. 410–11.
[3] Lansdowne MS. 105, fo. 182.

and a later draft, though which is the later it is extremely difficult to say. I incline towards the opinion that the Burghley paper is a copy of that which Wentworth had in the house.

For the course of events on 1 March, the day on which Wentworth made his speech, we are dependent upon D'Ewes, our anonymous diarist on this of all days, having gone off to hear a sermon at the court. Wentworth evidently delivered his introductory speech and then handed the questions to the Speaker to be put to the house. He was asked to spare his motion until the queen's pleasure was further known concerning Cope's bill and book ; but as he refused, the Speaker declared that he would first peruse the questions and then do what was fit. The story is continued in a note appended to the version of the questions used by D'Ewes. ' These questions ', it states, ' Mr. Puckering pocketted up and shewed Sir Thomas Heneage, who so handled the matter, that Mr. Wentworth went to the Tower, and the questions not at all moved. Mr. Buckler of Essex herein brake his faith in forsaking the matter, and no more was done.' The Speaker was sent for before the day's business was ended, and the house therefore rose. It was most unusual for the queen to terminate the sitting of the house in this way, and although it is not a necessary assumption that Wentworth's action was the cause of it, yet if it was, one can only conclude that the privy councillors who were watching the proceedings felt that a crisis was at hand and took extraordinary steps to avoid it. Wentworth was sent to the Tower, perhaps that day. The next day Cope, Lewknor, Hurlston, and Bainbrigg were sent there also.[1]

It has always been supposed that these members were imprisoned for the speeches that they delivered in parliament. Were it true, and were there no modifications to be made in the history of other incidents in the reign, then there would perhaps be some excuse for regarding freedom of speech in the Elizabethan age as a sorry fiction. But the assumption has its difficulties. Strickland had been confined to his house in 1571 for introducing a bill on church reform, and Cope might on this occasion have been justly imprisoned for a similar violation of the royal supremacy : although it must be borne in mind that Strickland's confinement had been tacitly admitted by the council to be a false move. But why, we must ask, were Lewknor, Hurlston, and Bainbrigg sent to the Tower, whereas Throgmorton, Dounlee, Topcliffe, Hastings, and others were not, although they also, as the anonymous diary shows, urged the reform of the church ? [2] The difficulty is not insuperable, but

[1] D'Ewes, pp. 410–11.   [2] Harleian MS. 7188, fos. 93 b–94.

fresh doubts appear when we turn to the official reply vouchsafed to a motion of Sir John Higham's on 4 March. He had said

that he would not nor thought none of the howse would once open his mouth for any disloyal subiect such as Parry was that was taken out from amongst them and worthily committed. but incoraged by the liberties of the howse, he was more bold to beseach the howse to ioyn with him as humble sutors to her maiesty for the inlargment of some of the howse he herd to be latly committed to the Tower for speaking of ther conscience. not well seinge how the howse could further procead well in matters of so great importance without his members.[1]

To this the vice-chamberlain replied by protesting his concern for the liberties of the house and admitting the wisdom of petitioning the queen if the commitment were for matter within the compass of their privileges ; yet suggesting that it might be strange from them and appertaining to the queen's justice.[2] D'Ewes and all his successors have regarded the reply as a subterfuge. If it was a subterfuge, then it was an extraordinarily clumsy one, and could not have deceived the house had parliamentary speeches been the cause of imprisonment. Yet the commons were apparently satisfied that they could not even sue for the release of their fellow members.

Clearly some other explanation of the imprisonment should be sought : and it is supplied by a comment of William Lambert's, who was a leader of the agitation in parliament in 1566, and was, I think, Lambarde the antiquary. He compiled a small volume of parliamentary precedents in which the following passage occurs :

Mr. Cope Lewknor Hurlstone Baynbridge &c were comitted to the Tower by the Queene for that before the parliament they had sundry conuencions for the preferring in parliament a booke touching the rites of the church and a forme of an Acte for establishing of the same, which also they did printe preferre and urge in parliament. But it seemed if they had treated thereof only in tyme of parliament being Burgessees they should not haue bynne ympeached. Feb. 28 Eliz.[3]

---

[1] i. e. members of the house (Harleian MS. 7188, fos. 95 b–96).

[2] *Ibid.*, fo. 96 ; D'Ewes, p. 412 a.

[3] Brit. Mus., Add. MS. 5123, fo. 18 b. The manuscript is entitled, ' Some certaine notes of the Order, Proceedings, punishments, and priuiledges of the lower howse of Parliament '. The reasons for attributing it to Lambarde are the following. On fo. 10 b, in referring to the suit to the queen concerning the succession in 1566, the author states that the suit ' was in a sorte moued to bee yntreated by the speeche of this writer W: L: . . . We know from the *Commons' Journals* (i. 76) that this person was named Lambert. Further, the tract is prefaced with a bibliography, item 4 of which is ' The fragments of my writinge ' : and no contemporary writer on constitutional subjects is known with a similar name, other than Lambarde. Two objections are easily met. The first is the form of the name. But I have noted several contemporary instances where the antiquary's name is spelt Lambert (Dasent, *Acts of the Privy Council*, xxiii. 258 ; Harleian MSS. 539, fo. 100, 1877, fo. 58, 5141, fo. 45 b ; Cotton MS. Titus, B. ii, fo. 263 ; Stowe MS. 415, fos. 1, 30 b, &c.). Probably

We need not, however, rely solely upon Lambert, for in an interview between Wentworth and James Morice, attorney of the court of wards, in 1592/3, Morice offered this significant advice : 'And you Mr. Wentworth . . . should beware of conferences for if you remember you and others weare committed to the Tower for your conference in matters of religion the last parleament.' [1]

If we are to appreciate the full significance of this new evidence we must look back a little. The puritan agitation in the country had reached a climax at the time of the last parliament in 1584–5. Petitions had been sent up to parliament by organized effort, members had been canvassed and stirred into activity, and a false impression of spontaneous and general discontent had been created which temporarily deceived both council and queen.[2] The restrictions imposed and gradually acquiesced in during the course of previous sessions ultimately broke down before passions so cleverly stimulated, and bills for ecclesiastical reform were set on their way through the house, unsanctioned, until the queen reprimanded the commons and forbade further proceedings. Elizabeth judged the temper of members, however, and though firm was conciliatory. At the close of the session she sought to assuage their discontent by assuring them personally of her concern for the reform of abuses.[3]

Organization had therefore justified itself if it had not triumphed ; and Cope's action in 1586/7 was evidently the opening of a renewed parliamentary attack which was to be pressed forward by a group of members who had previously prepared their campaign. Perhaps we should associate it with the puritan synod that was held in London at the same time.[4]

they are phonetic spellings. The second objection is that we should have to assume that a southerner sat for a Yorkshire borough in parliament (*Official Return*, part i, p. 406). That, however, is by no means strange in the Elizabethan age. If Lambarde be accepted as the author, then his parliamentary experience is an extremely interesting addition to our slight knowledge of his life. Furthermore, Lambarde is then the author of the first parliamentary precedent book that I at any rate know of ; and May's *Parliamentary Practice* therefore comes down in a long line of descent from it on the one side and the medieval ' Modus ' on the other. Other copies of the pamphlet are Harleian MSS. 2234, fos. 1 f., 4619, fos. 1 f. It was published in 1641 with the title The | Orders | Proceedings, Punishments, | and | Priviledges of the Commons | House of Parliament in | England. | It was also included in the *Harleian Miscellany*. But both these printed texts are incomplete and corrupt.

[1] Harleian MS. 6846, fo. 108. Morice is clearly referring to 1586/7, although ' the last parleament ' was really 1588/9.

[2] See Usher, *Reconstruction of the English Church*, i. 39 f., and *Presbyterian Movement* (Camden Soc.), pp. xix, 40 ; also Fuller, *Church History* (1845), v. 83.

[3] Neal, *Hist. of the Puritans* (1822), i. 364–6 ; D'Ewes, pp. 328, 329. Unfortunately we cannot follow properly the progress of the puritan bills this session. The *Commons' Journals* are lost, and D'Ewes's habit of citing the readings of only a proportion of the bills leaves several points obscure.

[4] Usher, *Presbyterian Movement* (Camden Soc.), p. 98. Cf. Fuller's statement about the connexion of the synod in 1584/5 with parliament (*Church History*, v. 83).

Cope, Lewknor, Hurlston, and Bainbrigg had therefore discussed matters of state outside parliament where there could be no question of privilege, and their imprisonment concerns, not the liberty of speech of members in the house of commons, but the liberty of speech of the general public outside.   This, which may seem a quibble, is really an important distinction.   Ultimately the wider freedom had to reveal itself as a necessary corollary to the narrower, even for the conduct of parliament ; but though it be assumed that the real object of the imprisonment of these members was to frustrate their agitation in parliament, yet the choice of the ground of attack was a tacit acknowledgement that it was inadvisable—we cannot say illegal—to imprison members for speeches in parliament, even when they were upon forbidden topics.

The connexion of Wentworth with Cope and the other imprisoned members is not clear.   Morice says that he took part in their conferences ; and so far as we know he is the *et cetera* of Lambert's note.   If so, then his speech and questions were a move in their common tactics, a move no doubt of his invention.   I think we can be sure that he was at some conference. The note at the end of his questions is significant : ' Mr. Buckler of Essex herein brake his faith in forsaking the matter.' [1]   And an echo of the incident probably comes to us from 1592/3, when, as we shall see, similar tactics were tried : Mr. Wentworth, wrote one who then met in conference, told us ' how diuers old parliament men had failed him in former tymes, some of them haueinge promised to second him, and back him in a motion to be made by him, neuer speakinge a word therein : others vndertakinge to beginne the motion neuer openinge their lippes in the same '.[2]   Moreover, there is in a Harleian volume of miscellaneous papers, in close proximity to other speeches of Wentworth's, a long speech headed simply, ' Freedome of Speech ', which was obviously intended to support Wentworth's motion and questions this session.   The same ideas, the same outspoken manner, often the same phraseology characterize it as characterize his other writings.

The speech opens as the speech of 1575/6 opened : ' Mr. Speaker sweet (indeed) is the name of libertie but libertie yt selfe is (indeed) and (indeed) a value beyond all inestimable treasure.' Thereafter it describes the powers of parliament :

This Honourable house and assembly is termed a Counsell, yea . . . the great Counsell of England, and highest Court of this Realme. . . . All Courtes ar here to be controlled : here may and ought to be made such lawes as god is honoured by : heare ought to be reuoked and frustrated

---

[1] *Supra*, p. 259.
[2] Harleian MS. 6846, fo. 97 b.   The confession of Richard Stephens.

all such lawes as god is dishonoured by : here we ought to counsell with
the wise men of this Realme for the maintenance of the Queens maiestes
estate : here lawes ar to be deuised for the preseruacion of her maiestes
person and this noble common wheale and punishment of any traytors or
treason therunto : and if it may be knowene that any persons, within
the realme or without, intend any perill either to her maiestes estate or
person, or to this noble Common wealth, here must be deuised how to
cutt of such ill reedes and how to withstand their traiterous purpose :
here must be studied and foreseene that if any charge do come vpon her
maiestie and this her Realme, how it may be honourably sustained . . . :
here ought to be deuised how her maiestie may be inriched and made
strong [against her enemies] . . . : here lawes ar to be made for the common
weale, to be frustrated, to be added vnto, to be deminished or taken
from . . . : here that offence and person which law cannot punish, this
honourable Counsell and high Court may : . . . [yea, it] may iudge of all
titles, euen the highest, and may also take away liffe, lyme and inheri-
taunce, and he is a traytor that saieth it wanteth power ; . . . and to conclude no other Counsell or Court hath authoritie to doe all those waightie
bussinesses. . . .

With biblical and classical quotations the writer enumerates the
benefits that flow from taking counsel. As it is a certain thing
that unto every council free speech is due, so *a maiore* is it due
to this, the highest court and greatest council. He describes the
duties of those trusted to give counsel. To withhold it is treason
to God, the prince and the realm, and the divine punishment
such an offence incurs is to be cast into outer darkness. All who
bring in doubt or question whether free speech is due to this
council or not are guilty of the crime in the highest degree ;
and, moreover, he adds, Christ said ' he that is not with me is
against me '. Evidently anticipating that Wentworth's motion
would be opposed as an innovation, the writer asserts that the
liberty of the house

seemeth in my simple iudgment greatly weakenned and preiudiced by the
last speech . . . in that it is obiected that the Queens maiestie liketh not
of innouacions. I answer . . . this is no innouacion, but rather a renouacion.
. . . And who [he continues] dare tell her maiestie what we ar in hand withall
in this high Counsell without the consent of the house . . . for that warr
a betraying of the secretes . . . and . . . an intollerable fault ? . . . to conclude
I am in humble harty and feruent manner to require euery one of this
honourable Counsell to stick earnestly to the former motion, to wit, that
the house may answer these questions, by question. . . .[1]

In all probability it was Wentworth who composed the speech.
Elizabeth once said that he had an opinion of his own wit.[2] He
certainly did not hesitate to compose speeches for others ; and

[1] Harleian MS. 1877, fos. 55–7.
[2] Add. MS. 24664, fo. 45 a.

this may well be the speech which he expected Buckler to deliver. If Buckler's part was arranged at a conference, he was not to our knowledge imprisoned for his share in the conspiracy, although it is quite possible that he and others were examined by the privy council and escaped punishment because they had deserted the cause. We have no idea how long the imprisoned members remained in the Tower. Apparently they did not return to the house that session.

Peter Wentworth

PART II

AFTER the parliament of 1586–7 the interest of Wentworth's career changes. Hitherto he has appeared as the most insistent and courageous champion of freedom of speech, showing a profound sense of realities in perceiving that the way to victory in the puritan cause lay through a struggle for parliamentary privilege. Such freedom as he sought would, if won, have unmasked the queen's resistance to reform, and would have left her with her veto alone to oppose a massed sentiment in parliament and the clamour of puritan opinion in the country. Even in 1586–7, when he co-operated in the campaign for a presbyterian church, his part was not to lead the assault, but, when that failed, to convert the contest into one for privilege. With the year 1587, however, privilege ceased to be uppermost in his mind, and he became absorbed in the problem of the succession. It may be that as he grew old in a seemingly forlorn enterprise impatience of delay seized him : or perhaps the perilous condition of the succession cause operated as a call to strike directly for his goal. For whereas that cause had once been so vigorously supported as to leave the queen isolated in her resistance, in 1587 it was devoid of open supporters and lay lifeless for lack of a leader brave and tenacious enough to revive it. No action of Wentworth's more became his character than the endeavour to resuscitate the succession agitation which filled the remaining years of his life. If we preface our story of it with a review of the agitation in earlier years, it is because such a review seems to be an essential prologue, as yet never adequately presented, without which the qualities of mind that Wentworth's action called for are not to be appreciated ; and again because Wentworth sat in all but one of the parliaments from 1571 to 1587. He witnessed and perhaps helped—though he did not lead—the agitation during those years. His mind was certainly informed by it : his campaign is hardly to be understood without knowledge of it.

Men were first troubled about the succession in the early years of Elizabeth's reign as her reluctance to marry became evident ; and in October 1562, when she was taken seriously ill

and the country realized that its sovereign was mortal, all other
interests were dwarfed.   There were many claimants to the
throne, against all of whom some legal bar could be urged ;
and where no certainty was, there was abundant hope and fear.
Partisans schemed and spread their propaganda ; others urged
the settlement of the succession or opposed it according as they
dreaded more the prospect of civil war at the queen's death,
or the plots that gather round an heir and the desperation
of competitors balked in their play for the highest of stakes.
Elizabeth remained resolute throughout, fortified by precedents
from David and Absalom to Queen Mary and herself.   At first
she was almost alone in defence of her policy of inaction.   Yet
by a masterly adroitness she turned that policy to account in
diplomacy, and compensated herself for the anxiety which
parliament's clamour for a settlement caused, by the use she made
of it, first to checkmate Mary of Scotland and later to restrain
James.[1] She had always to be vigilant, for whilst in parliament
members strained at the leash by which she sought to hold them,
outside parliament a battle of pamphlets was waged.

The parliamentary agitation opened in 1562/3 and reached
its climax in 1566.   Of those sessions the story has already been
told.[2] Before a new parliament met the troubles of the reign
had begun, and that unity of sentiment which had been so
formidable to the queen in 1566 was shattered.   Many, however,
were still intransigeant, and when the government introduced its
treason bill[3] into the commons in 1571 they saw their chance
and seized it.   At the first reading Thomas Norton proposed
that an act of his own drafting should be incorporated in the
official bill.   Norton had already shown where his sympathies
lay.   A vigorous puritan, he had been joint author with Sackville
of the play *Gorboduc*, the fifth act of which was little more than
a tract for the times and contained a thinly veiled attack upon
the Scottish claim to the succession.[4]   The bill which he now

---

[1] *Scottish Cal.* v. 497, 597, 660 ; vi. 76, 81, 423.   *Despatches of the Marquis de Cour-
celles* (Bannatyne Club, 1828), p. 29.   A veiled use of this weapon can be seen throughout the *Letters of Q. Eliz. and Jas. VI* (Camden Soc.), e. g. pp. 30, 32, 34, 42, 44, 46,
49, 87.

[2] *E.H.R.*, xxxvi. 497 f.

[3] Its provisions are represented by the first section of the printed act (*Statutes
of the Realm*, iv. i. 526).

[4] Cf. *The Tragidie of Ferrex and Porrex* (1570), Act V, Scene ii.

> Right meane I his or hers upon whose name
> The people rest by meane of natiue line,
>
> •   •   •   •   •
>
> Such one so borne within your natiue land,
> Such one preferre, and in no wise admitte
> The heauie yoke of forreine gouernance :
> Let forreine titles yelde to publike wealth.

presented to the house renewed the attack. Its purport was given by an anonymous diarist of the session as follows :

First that whosoeuer in her lyfe tyme [i.e. Elizabeth's] hath doone or shall make claime to the imperiall crowne of this Realme, that hee or they or their heires shalbe forebarred of any clayme, challenge or Title to be made to that crowne at anie tyme heereafter, and euery person who shall mainteyne that Tifle to be accompted a Traitor. And further that whosoeuer shall saie the court of parliament hath not auctoritie to enacte and to bynde the Title of the crowne, to be adiudged a Traitor.[1]

The intention is clear enough. The retrospective force of the act was meant to be fatal to the claims of Mary and her successors.

It was a clever device to suggest the incorporation of the bill in the government's. It solved the difficulty of introducing it in face of the 'queen's opposition, and placed the government in a dilemma. But success was by no means assured. Legal minds stuck at retrospective laws, and though some let their zeal for the cause silence their scruples, there was weighty support for the privy councillors who urged that the bills should be kept separate, thinking probably that Norton's could be defeated in one house or the other, or at the worst that Elizabeth could quash it. Their counter-manœuvre failed, however. Both bills were entrusted to a committee with orders to join them, and when they reappeared in the house the essential character of Norton's was unchanged.[2] A last effort was made to disjoin them, but failed again, this time by thirty-six voices only, and the next day the expanded bill was through the commons and the government was compelled to turn for help to the more pliant upper house.[3] Here they succeeded. The lords drew the sting of the bill for them. But the small majority in the commons was stubborn, and stomached the changes only after delay and conference. At length the bill was enacted as we now know it. Its retrospective force was taken away and the loss of a claimant's title to the succession no longer involved the heir's. Even so, one suspects that Elizabeth disliked it, and swallowed the diluted dose of Norton's medicine only under compulsion.[4]

One thing the session of 1571 made clear ; the queen was not

---

[1] Cotton MS. Titus F.i, fo. 138 b; D'Ewes, p. 159 b. Froude's account of the events is in his *History of England*, ix. 437 f.

[2] *Commons' Journals*, i. 84; D'Ewes, pp. 162–5; Cotton MS. Titus F.i, fos. 142 a–143 a; Fénelon, *Correspondance diplomatique*, iv. 57.

[3] *Commons' Journals*, i. 86 ; *Trans. Devon Assoc.* (1879), xi. 480.

[4] *Lords' Journals*, i. 683, 686, 688 ; *Commons' Journals*, i. 88–90 ; *Statutes of the Realm*, iv. i. 526–8. In his journal of this session (*Trans. Devon. Assoc.* xi. 490) Hooker gives an interesting account of Elizabeth's intervention at the moment of passing the bill, and of a speech which she made. Constitutionally the incident may be regarded as an impotent survival from the days before the Crown's response was limited to aye or no. Also cf. Fénelon, *op. cit.*, iv. 136.

likely to succeed in suppressing the succession agitation whilst
the catholic Mary lived or retained her claims to the throne :
and though Norton's proposals were shorn of their real purpose,
his assertion of parliament's right to settle the succession survived in the act, and doubtless seemed to his supporters to bring
their goal nearer.

On the eve of the new parliament, which met in May 1572,
the Spanish and French ambassadors both noted a general
expectation that the succession question would be dealt with
in the coming assembly. In March Elizabeth had suffered from
what Fénelon described as a great tortion of the stomach after
eating fish. During three nights Leicester and Burghley had
watched by her bed ; and, as in 1562, her illness had caused the
first stirrings of parties which, had she died, would probably have
heralded civil strife. Fénelon thought that the queen had in
consequence been reconciled to some manner of settling the
succession.[1] In this he was deceived. It was not the queen's
conversion but the Ridolfi plot that brought the question before
parliament. Members' passions were aroused, and as the least
concession to their demands, they expected that Mary would be
deprived of her title to the succession. Hence instead of a covert
attack such as Norton's had been, supported by a small majority
in the commons and easily checkmated in the lords, there was now
an open assault. The Hertford claim to the crown, so the
Spanish ambassador said, was discussed in the commons—a bold
act, if true, and one only to be explained by the nature of the
crisis and Elizabeth's delicate position.[2] Both houses and her
principal advisers were in favour of the bill against Mary, and
she could no longer defend the Scottish queen from behind the
scenes. She trod warily, but even so had openly to veto the bill,
for her quibble about *la royne s'advisera* deceived no one. Wentworth had his share in these events, but unfortunately we know
too little about it.

Elizabeth's vigilance was matched against the tenacity of the
commons. In 1575/6 the Spanish ambassador reported that
those who had wished to revive the succession question that
session had been silenced, and in 1580/1 that the lord keeper had
forbidden its discussion in his opening speech.[3] But the fever of
anxiety continued to possess people and was aggravated by an
atmosphere of plots. In July 1584 William of Orange was
assassinated : the nerves even of statesmen were shattered ;
and the bond of association was circulated about the country,
pledging all who signed it to pursue to the death any one in
favour of whose title to the crown the death of Elizabeth might

---

[1] Fénelon, iv. 411, 426 ; *Span. Cal., Eliz.,* ii. 390.
[2] *Span. Cal., Eliz.,* ii. 393.   [3] *Ibid.* ii. 529 ; iii. 81.

be plotted. Its spirit was the spirit of lynch law. The wrath against Mary which Elizabeth had successfully quenched in the parliaments of 1571 and 1572 burst forth anew, and when parliament met in November a bill for the queen's safety was framed with the same passionate disregard of justice that the bond of association had revealed. It disabled from their right to the throne any by whom or for whom an attempt was made against the queen's life. Probably it disabled their heirs also, and contained a section giving statutory approval to the bond of association.[1] For the substance of the bill the council seems to have been responsible ; although it was framed, or at least sponsored, by a committee of the lower house. But there were many people who had refused to sign the bond of association, and there were many members of the house of commons who, having signed, had repented upon reflexion. Its obligations were not consonant with God's laws, nor yet with statute law, and when they heard its echo in the new bill they listened in sad silence.[2] Their passive resistance may have rallied Elizabeth to an assertion of her own wishes, and on 18 December she interfered tactfully in the interests of justice. She thanked the house for its care for her and approved of its proposals, but would have those touched by the act heard in their own defence before they were deprived of their titles ; and further, would ease the conscience of any who had signed the bond of association, by taking away, presumably, the proviso which gave statutory approval to it.[3]

The bill was dropped and a new one framed by a committee of the house. An outline of a bill has survived which actually follows the queen's suggestions.[4] By its provisions loss of title

[1] The contents of the bill as first put forward are probably given in State Papers, Dom., Eliz., clxxvi, no. 34. This paper is in the attorney-general Popham's hand, and I take it to be an outline of the various acts which the government proposed to initiate this session. *Ibid.* no. 11 is a proviso giving statutory approval to the bond of association. Burghley's endorsement on it, ' xv Janu.', must be wrong, for this is clearly the proviso which on 18 December Elizabeth said she would take away.

[2] Lansdowne MS. 98, fo. 14. This is endorsed by Burghley, ' Janu. 1584. Mr. Digges discourse uppon the association '. There is a copy in State Papers, Dom., Eliz., clxxvi, no. 26, which Froude used, but it contains no clue to the author's identity. The author was a member of parliament, but the omission of Digges's name from the *Official Return* may be due to the *Return* being defective.

[3] D'Ewes, p. 341 b. Digges gives the following summary of the queen's message : ' hir Maiestie would not consent that eny one should be poonished for the faulte of an other, but every one beare the burden of their owen faulte, Nor that eny thinge should passe in that Acte that should be repugnant to the Lawe of God or the Lawe of Natuer, Or greevouse to the conscience of eny of hir good subiectes. Or that should not abyde the viewe of the worlde aswell enemyes as frendes, aswell in forraine Nations as at home. That hir maiesties confydence was in God onely for hir safetie, And singularly well lyked of the zeale of any such hir Maiesties faithfull subiectes as desired with upright conscience to serve hir and God together ' (Lansdowne MS. 98, fo. 15). [4] State Papers, Dom., Eliz., clxxvi, no. 24.

was to be suffered only if those on whose behalf any attempt was made against the Crown had assented to it, and the accused were to be heard in their defence either personally or by deputy ; no mention was made of pursuing them to the death, and the titles of their heirs were not specifically involved. The full story of the new bill we do not know. The committee was a long time framing it. But as it finally passed into law it did not fully reflect the queen's wishes, for the clause in the outline which definitely conceded to the accused the right to defend themselves was omitted. Nevertheless, if I construe it aright, it did get rid of the objectionable character of the earlier bill, and only those were to lose their titles to the throne ' by whom or by whose means assent or privity ' any invasion or rebellion or attempt against the queen's life should be made.[1] Moreover, the bond of association was stripped of its most objectionable features, for it was not to be construed except in conformity with the act. Unfortunately the act is badly worded, and with the bond of association in their minds, rather than the trial of Mary Queen of Scots, historians have usually assumed—erroneously I think—that it nullified the title of any one in whose favour, merely, plots were hatched.[2]

We cannot leave this act without telling the interesting history that lies behind its second clause, for it brings out most forcibly the fear of the future which possessed even Burghley's mind and which we shall see was the spring of Wentworth's activity. The second clause, setting up a tribunal to discover and punish the guilty in the event of the queen's death by violence, is only a remnant of a larger scheme. Burghley was tormented by the thought that under the usual constitutional procedure anarchy must follow the murder of the queen, for with her death all appointments to office would lapse, and the collapse of government would play into the hands of the murderers. To guard against this he devised a scheme for an organized interregnum, which he proposed to embody in the act for the queen's safety. Two outlines of his proposals exist in his own handwriting, and

---

[1] *Statutes of the Realm*, IV. i. 705. This passage, which I have abbreviated, states, so I think, the intention of the whole of the first clause. The clause goes on to provide that if the queen's death results from any attempt against her life ' then every such person by or for whom any such act shall be executed and their issues *being any wise assenting or privy to the same* ' shall be excluded from their title to the crown. In the *Statutes of the Realm* the passage is so punctuated as to make the words that I have italicized refer only to ' their issues '. Statutes, however, are without punctuation, and the qualification surely applies also to the words ' every such person '. If it applies in the case of the greatest crime, then *a maiore* it applies in the case of the lesser crimes. As a matter of fact the act was interpreted as I have interpreted it at the trial of Mary Queen of Scots.

[2] Cf. Pollard, *Political Hist.*, 1547–1603, p. 387 ; Creighton, *Queen Elizabeth* (new ed.), p. 214 : Pollen, *Queen Mary and the Babington Plot*, p. cxciii.

a full draft with his revisions.[1]   All persons in authority at the time of the queen's murder were to retain their offices ; a grand council was to come into being which would govern the realm and punish those responsible for the assassination ; parliament and convocation were to be summoned in order to settle the succession, and, that the danger of elections might be avoided, their membership was to be the same as in the last assemblies held during the queen's life.   The rôle allotted to parliament is striking.   For a time it was to act virtually as a sovereign body.   Members of the grand council were to appear before it, make report of all their proceedings, and submit the continuance, cessation, or alteration of their authority or of their numbers and the ratification of their acts to its judgement.   Each house, moreover, was to appoint ten of its members to take over control of the finances, and the council was empowered to conclude treaties and utilize the forces of the realm only until the parliament should declare otherwise.   Had the scheme prospered the act would have been one of our most significant constitutional documents.   Unfortunately it foundered, and only a miserable wreck survived.   The grand council was converted into a tribunal. All else was swept away.   There can be little doubt that Elizabeth would not tolerate such vulgar prying into the mysteries of government.   The estate of monarchy could not but have been prejudiced by the scheme.   It savoured of popularity and must have violated her regal sense.

With the parliament of 1586–7 we come to the end of our introduction.   Hitherto there had been no lack of members only too eager to raise the question of the succession.   Baffled in their attempts to persuade Elizabeth to name her heir, they had fallen back upon the alternative of destroying Mary's title to the throne, by which means they would have rid themselves of their worst fears.   With great courage Elizabeth had consistently withstood them, but the torrent of public wrath at last became too strong for her and Mary was executed.   That unhappy event solved the acutest of the succession problems, and though uncertainty still reigned many people were now content to let time work out its own solution.   Even those who still remained faithful to the cause found their passion dulled by the passing of a great fear, and were the more easily cowed into silence by the well-known opposition of the queen.   Save in the secrets of men's minds the cause was dead, unless some leader of outstanding courage and

[1] State Papers, Dom., Eliz., clxxvi, nos. 22, 30, 39. Also cf. no. 28. Burghley may have partly derived his ideas from a discourse, probably written by Digges (*ibid.* no. 32). I impute the authorship of the discourse to Digges because in his other discourse upon the association to which I have already referred, he mentions ' this other short treatise ', which I take to be this.

pertinacity would dare to breathe new life into it. Such a leader was Peter Wentworth.

Wentworth had been interested in the succession question since about 1563, and had played some part—though what, we are hardly aware—in the parliamentary agitation against Mary. It was some time in the eighties, however, that he seriously devoted himself to the cause, and his first concern was to write a pamphlet for which he had long been gathering material. This was his *Pithie Exhortation to her Maiestie for Establishing her Succession to the Crown*. It was written probably in 1587 [1] and later handed to Dr. Thomas Sparke, a Buckinghamshire minister, to be reviewed. Sparke professed to have set its arguments in better order and to have mollified its harsh phrases, but whether in revising it Wentworth undid much of his pruning, or not, the work is remarkably outspoken. [2]

As its title implies, the pamphlet is addressed to the queen, and its object is to urge her speedily to summon a parliament, there to have all titles and claims to the succession examined, and then forthwith by its authority to make known the rightful heir. The exhortation is supported by arguments, some characteristic of the whole succession agitation, others of Wentworth himself; and biblical, classical, and historical allusions abound to give point and weight to them. It is usual, says Wentworth, early in the pamphlet, for the Holy Ghost to call princes ' Gods and nursing Fathers and nursing mothers vnto his Church '. These titles ' proue the honorablenesse and lawfulnesse of your high callings, against all Anabaptisticall spirites '; but they also ' teache you your duties ', which include provision for the future. An uncertain succession can only result in extreme confusion and the subversion of the realm, and if you would not have God regard you as ' one that had denied the faith, and so worse than an infidell ', you must perform this Christian duty of settling the succession. Moses, David, and Hezekiah, the Medes, Persians, and Romans, Henry VIII, all furnish him with quotations or stories to intensify the obloquy which a refusal would merit. Drawing upon his imagination and echoing the fears of his contemporaries he gives a harrowing picture of the state of England if Elizabeth should die and no successor be known. Competitors and their supporters will be up in arms; common people, unacquainted with their titles, will be at their wits' end, not knowing what part to take and yet driven to take some;

---

[1] Wentworth said that he wrote the pamphlet six years before the parliament of 1592/3 (Add. MS. 24664, fo. 44 b). It was published surreptitiously by his friends in 1598, after his death.

[2] Sparke's confession, Harleian MS. 6846, fo. 101. Also see his tract, *A Brotherly Persuasion to Unitie* . . . (1607), pref. There is an account of Sparke in the *Dict. of Nat. Biog.*

and soon the whole realm will be rent into as many shivers as
there be competitors.   Party will consume and devour party,
and the land be so weakened that it will become an easy prey
to foreign enemies.   The strong will be slain in the field, children
and infants murdered in every town ; the rich will not be able
to say, ' This is mine ', but they, as well as the poor, will think
themselves happy if they may have their lives for a prey ;
religion will be laid in the dust, and neither God nor man will be
regarded.[1]

But the interests of the queen no less demand the settlement
of the succession, says Wentworth ; for the strength of princes
and the safety of their thrones depend principally upon this,
' that they alienate not the hearts of their subiectes from them,
by their vnkinde and mercielesse dealing towardes them '.   The
story of Rehoboam drives his point home.   What arguments
he can conceive might be advanced against a settlement, these
he answers.   The more difficult the elucidation of the titles, the
more dangerous is delay ; and as for the supposed danger to
Elizabeth's person in naming a successor, even supposing the
fears to be well grounded, yet the perils of the realm are great
and palpable and duty is to be preferred to our own safety.
With shrewdness he reminds the queen that Esther did not shrink
from entering Ahasuerus's presence to save her people.

Towards the close of the pamphlet comes a passage of amazing
daring :

True and vnfained loue doeth euen force vs to vtter vnto you (our most
deare and natural Soueraigne) that when soeuer it sall please God to
touche you with the pangs of death (as die most certainlie you shall,
and howe soone is knowne to none but to the Lord onlie) if your Maiestie
doe not settle the succession in your life-time, which God for his mercies
sake long prolong, we do greatlie feare, that your grace shall, then, finde
such a troubled soule and conscience, yea, ten thousand helles in your
soule, euen such bitter vexation of soulè and hart for the perilling of the
Church of God, and of your naturall countrie, as to be released therof,
you would giue the whole world, if you had it. . . . Wee beseeche your
Maiestie to consider, whither your noble person is like to come to that
honorable burial, that your honorable progenitours haue had . . . if your
successor be not setled before your death. . . . Wee doe assure our selues,
that the breath shall be no sooner out of your body . . . but that al your
nobility, counsellours, and whole people will be vp in armes . . . and then it
is to be feared . . . that your noble person shall lye vpon the earth vnburied,
as a dolefull spectacle to the worlde. . . . Againe, we feare . . . that . . .
you shall leaue behind you such a name of infamie throughout the whole
world . . . that the forethinking therof, cannot . . . but deepelie grieue
and wound your honorable, pitifull and tender heart.[2]

[1] Cf. the closing speech in *Gorboduc*, Act V.
[2] *Pithie Exhortation* . . (1598).

About three months before the parliament of 1588/9 Went-worth handed his pamphlet to John Blundeville of Banbury, a schoolmaster, to be written out in a fair hand, telling him that it was ' a supplicacion to be deliuered by the Courte of Parliament vnto her Maiestie '.[1] He was intending to revive the succession agitation. Unfortunately for his plans parliament met shortly after the defeat of the Armada, and the time could hardly have been less propitious for stirring up controversies. Perhaps he recognized this, but he was much too conscious of the urgency of his suit to abandon it altogether, and as an alternative to parliamentary action he tried to see Burghley and induce him personally to prevail upon the queen to settle the succession. It was of no use. Burghley simply denied him his presence, though he made three or four attempts to see him during the session. Wentworth, however, was not a man who readily forsook his plans, and in the spring of 1590 he came to London again and renewed his approaches. It may have been then, or perhaps it was in the previous year in parliament time, that he wrote him a ' sharpe, yet trew louinge letter '. Whichever it was, the honourable and gentle reply that he received gave Wentworth an opening for a further letter on 9 May, in which he chided the statesman for the long-continued displeasure and heavy counte-nance he had shown towards him ; as though he had given cause for offence when in reality he had sought to load him with the greatest honour and benefits that could be wished, to win him the favour of God, the queen, and the whole realm, great love, a good name, an easy conscience ; and these by persuading him to perform a service which his place, his honour, and his duty bade him perform. Burghley answered with a courteous letter reassuring Wentworth of his good opinion of him.[2] Nothing more was to be expected, for, whatever his personal views, he was too wise a man to venture further. Wentworth now forsook Burghley and pinned his faith on a Dr. Moffat, to whom he gave his *Pithie Exhortation* so that he might move the earl of Essex and have it presented to the queen. Unfortunately Moffat sent it to a tailor's shop to be copied, copies got abroad, and the secret being out, Wentworth was sent for by the privy council.[3] This was in August 1591, and on the fifteenth his appearance was entered in the council register. He was committed a close prisoner to the Gatehouse, and an order was issued for the search of his house and of Mr. Anthony Cope's where last he abode, ' for all letters, bookes, or writinges whatsoever that may concern . . .

---

[1] Blundeville's confession, Harleian MS. 6846, fo. 92.
[2] State Papers, Dom., Eliz., ccxxxii, nos. 16, 19.
[3] *Ibid.* ccxl, no. 21¹. ' owte of cobblers and taylors shoppes ', is misread in the *Calendar.* Also cf. Harleian MS. 6846, fos. 90, 92.

matter that hath bene or may be intended to be moved in Parliament, and especially suche notes, collections, books or papers as conteine matter towchinge the establishing of the succession '.[1]

Wentworth was incorrigible. Whilst under restraint he turned his mind, not to submission and apology which might have reduced his term of imprisonment, but to the old plan of winning Burghley over to his cause. Two letters of his are extant, written from the Gatehouse.[2] The one is a private note, without address or date, which was enclosed with a more formal letter. There can be little doubt that it was written to Burghley, and probably the enclosure to which it refers is the other surviving letter, addressed to him : although the date of this—27 September— is rather longer after his committal than one might have expected. In the private note Wentworth explains why he said so little at his examination in defence of his pamphlet. The copy the councillors had was not made with his consent or knowledge ; in naming it ' A booke of the heyre apparante ' the lord chancellor so misdescribed it that he thought it could not be his, and it would have been the height of folly to justify anything the nature of which he was not sure of. However, he is prepared to acknowledge and justify his own work. Then he turns to entreat Burghley's help in persuading the queen to settle the succession; and asks him to alter the more formal letter that he encloses, if he thinks fit, that he may rewrite it. For he presumes that the statesman will show it to the queen and in that way will be able to urge her to give heed to it without risking her wrath by raising the question himself. The enclosed letter is a lengthy epitome of Wentworth's arguments for the naming of an heir, and is also an appeal to Burghley to induce the queen to adopt that policy. It is likely, Wentworth admits, that she will be offended when first she reads his *Pithie Exhortation*, but he is convinced that her rare wisdom and deep judgement will soon show her the force of his reasons. And though she be displeased, that would not trouble him, for the spirit of God in Solomon had said, ' The woundes of a louer are faythefull : and the kisses of an enemye are deceytfulle ' ; and he preferred ' to wounde her maiestie faythefully, thereby seekinge her preservation '.

On 21 November Wentworth was set free from the Gatehouse upon his own bonds and confined to the house of one unnamed in Whitechapel. In all he was under restraint twenty-five weeks and five days, and his final release therefore came on or about 11 February 1591/2.[3] It was lenient treatment, compared at least with that meted out to Roger Edwards, who had written

---

[1] Dasent, *Acts of the Privy Council*, xxi. 392–3.
[2] State Papers, Dom., Eliz., ccxl, nos. 21, 21¹.
[3] Add. MS. 24664, fo. 51 a.

a tract, *Castra Regis*, in 1567/8, opposing a settlement of the
succession, and, when copies of the tract got abroad, had been
fined £500 and imprisoned in the Tower for fifteen months,
despite the fact that he had advocated what was the queen's
policy.[1] Wentworth's impression that Burghley looked upon
his cause with favour may therefore have been correct. At the
council table, so he said, Burghley affirmed that he had thrice
read his pamphlet and was assured that its arguments were
true ; the queen, however, had determined ' that that question
should be suppressed so long as euer she liued '.[2] With whatever
justification, Wentworth was coming to believe that his campaign
might be permitted. In prison he had written his short treatise,
afterwards appended to the *Pithie Exhortation*, answering the
objection that the king of Scots would become an enemy of
England if a settlement of the succession were arrived at and
proved unfavourable to him ; and he declared that he wrote
it at the instance of privy councillors. His strong imagination
led him on to conceive that the queen had seen and approved
of his book, and when a parliament was called for February
1592/3, he assured himself for a time—or at any rate he assured
others—that it was called to discuss the settlement of the
succession.[3]

The parliament of 1592/3 has had an ill fame in the history
of parliamentary liberties, what with its cryptic definition of
free speech, ' your privilege is aye or no ', and the savage punishment that befell Wentworth for meddling with the succession
question. But constitutional history, above all, has been rich
in fiction, and that ill fame has little more substance than a
myth. As the ' aye or no ' speech has been corrected,[4] so now
must we discard the conventional explanation of Wentworth's
imprisonment : and for the same reason, namely, that we have
sounder authorities than D'Ewes's *Journals*. Not indeed that
D'Ewes's account is so lamentably wrong over Wentworth's
activities : we must determine later what reliance can be placed
upon it. But instead of depending upon a partial and misleading
narrative, we can now reconstruct our story from the original
depositions and confessions of Wentworth and his associates,
which were preserved by the lord keeper, Puckering, and after
passing into the Baker collection of manuscripts, found their
way through the Harleian library into the British Museum.[5]
The story they present is a very detailed and surprising one.

---

[1] See the edition of the tract by the Roxburghe Club (1846).
[2] *Pithie Exhortation* (1598), the ' Discourse ', p. 3.
[3] Cf. the various confessions and depositions of 1592/3, Harleian MS. 6846, fos. 88,
92, 94, 96, 97.   [4] *E.H.R.*, xxxi. 128.
[5] Harleian MS. 6846, fo. 65 f. There are transcripts, *ibid.* 7042, fo. 171 f.

As we have seen, Wentworth seems to have persuaded himself, at least momentarily, that the opportunity which he had been seeking for some time was to be afforded him in the coming parliament. He was determined that it should not be lost ; indeed, that it should be forced, if it was not afforded : and so he set to work with his preparations before the assembly met. He talked to his friends in the country ; evidently he busied himself also in the parliamentary elections, for he told a friend that ' he had travayled into dyuerse places and laboured to procure such Burgesses as might fauour the . . . cause '.[1] Finally he brought with him to London all the papers necessary for his campaign : a speech with which he was to introduce the succession question in the commons ; a bill ready drafted with blanks to be filled in after parliament had determined the order of the succession ; perhaps a petition to the house of lords for its co-operation, although here Wentworth differed from other deponents in asserting that it was not written out ; a petition of both houses to the queen ; a thanksgiving to be offered if she acceded to their request, and a rejoinder for a possible refusal ; his *Pithie Exhortation*, written out anew by Blundeville ; and perhaps notes of objections that might be raised against his plans, and answers to them.[2]

Parliament was opened on Monday, 19 February, and then adjourned until the Thursday. On Tuesday, 20 February, Wentworth met a friend, Black Oliver St. John, cousin to Oliver St. John of Bedfordshire, the brother of Lord St. John.[3] He asked him to come to Lincoln's Inn the next day to the chambers of Humphrey Winch, member for Bedford, and to bring any honest gentlemen with him whom he knew, for he meant ' to acquaynte certeyne with some things he had donne and purposed to deale in this parlement that if they dislyked anye thinge the same mighte be corrected by them, if theye lyked it that then they might promise to further the same in the best sort theye mighte '. So far as we know, this St. John was not a member of parliament.[4] Perhaps he had sought election but had been defeated. In any event he appears to have been in close collaboration with Wentworth and to have acted as his lieutenant in the campaign, an undertaking doubly dangerous for a private person. He had been at Wentworth's house the previous summer and

[1] Robert Lynford's deposition, Harleian MS. 6846, fo. 96.

[2] Harleian MS. 6846, fos. 65–108, *passim*.

[3] See *Dict. of Nat. Biog.* (orig. ed.), l. 150 b; *Notes and Queries*, 2nd ser., vii. 27; *Letters of Lord Carew to Sir Thomas Rowe* (Camden Soc.), pp. 140–3.

[4] An Oliver St. John was member for Cirencester in 1592/3, but he is usually said to have been the Wiltshire St. John, afterwards Viscount Grandison, and I assume this to be correct since Winch was doubtful whether Black Oliver was a member (Harleian MS. 6846, fo. 81). The writ and return for the borough are missing.

K

had talked with him about the succession, and had then spread amongst country gentlemen Wentworth's belief that the question would be dealt with in the next parliament. He had spoken to Sir John and Oliver St. John of Wiltshire, to a Mr. Butler who had been with him at Wentworth's house, and to two Sussex gentlemen, Mr. Hobson and Mr. White ; and since the meeting of parliament he had spoken to his cousin Oliver and to a member named Peck.[1] Probably these are only a few of the people he approached, for he was not likely to expose the full measure of his activities to the privy council. On the Tuesday night after meeting Wentworth he saw Richard Blount of Sussex, son-in-law of Lord Delaware and member for Lymington, with whom he had already spoken about the matter, and invited him to the meeting. Similarly he invited Henry Apsley of Gray's Inn, one of the members for Hastings, a man, he said, fearful to offend and of good judgement in the laws of the land. Wentworth for his part called on Richard Stephens of the Middle Temple, a member for Newport in Cornwall, left his *Pithie Exhortation* and another of the papers with him for perusal, and coming for them the next morning told him of the meeting and persuaded him to attend.

On the Wednesday morning these five, along with Oliver St. John of Bedfordshire, and Winch, met at the latter's chambers. Blount was uneasy about the legality of the meeting and the trustworthiness of those present—an ominous sign ; but he was reassured. The morning was spent in reading and discussing some of the papers which Wentworth had brought to town with him, and after dinner two more hours were passed in reviewing the others. Knowing how downright was Wentworth's language, we are not surprised that the tone of his writings was generally disliked. The speech was especially offensive, for Wentworth had let his homilies upon the duties of the queen and councillors run without restraint. Altogether, his lack of moderation was not likely to stay the fears of men who had but little experience of parliament, and most of whom were more diffident, or certainly more cautious than himself. Consequently it was proposed by some that the campaign in parliament should be opened with the petition to the queen, and that the bill should be proceeded with only after receiving her sanction. To this Wentworth was opposed. He feared, as Blount said, ' lest if her Maiesty once misliked it and reiect it, in duty then it could not be offred ' ; and he advanced the argument that the house was not possessed of the matter nor would meddle therein without a bill. The

---

[1] St. John's confession, Harleian MS. 6846, fo. 88. Probably Wentworth's other friends talked also, and one is reminded of Doleman's statement that in Amsterdam it was presumed the succession question would be discussed this session (*A Conference about the next Succession . . .*, by R. Doleman, 1594, pref.).

uneasiness was not dispelled by this argument, and Wentworth
was urged to consult some old, discreet, and grave parliament
men, James Morice and Serjeant Yelverton being mentioned
amongst others. To Yelverton Wentworth would not agree,
because he was too timid ; and he went on to justify his lack of
trust in great parliament men by telling of their breach of faith
in earlier undertakings of his. To consult Morice, however, he
readily agreed. The papers were then handed to Winch, Stephens,
and Apsley to be looked over at their leisure, and the meeting
broke up.[1]

The following morning, Thursday, Wentworth went to see
Morice according to his promise. Of the interview we have
Morice's account, which reflects very well the change that had
taken place in the attitude of many prominent men towards the
problem of the succession. The old certainty of the need for
a settlement had weakened, doubtless in consequence of Mary's
death ; in some minds, as in Morice's, it had vanished ; and the
dominant feeling was one of fear to touch the subject. When
Wentworth told him that he wished to consult him about moving
the succession in parliament, ' Succession ! ' was his comment,
' what is he that dare meddle with it ? ' He reminded Wentworth
of his late trouble over the same cause, and tried to dissuade
him from his plans. When Wentworth came to see him the next
day for his opinion on the speech that had been left with him,
Morice's attitude was unchanged. He disapproved uncompromis-
ingly of the whole scheme, pouring scorn on Wentworth's writings,
refused to be a party to a conference on this or any other parliamentary subject, and recalled Wentworth's imprisonment for the
conference on religious questions in 1586/7. He was sceptical of
the other's optimism, and prophesied an instant inhibition from
the queen. Moreover, he confessed that he himself had been
converted by Dr. Wotton to the view that it was neither safe
for the queen nor good for the realm to deal in the matter. In
high dudgeon Wentworth left him.[2]

That afternoon, Friday, there was to have been a further
conference at Winch's chambers. Black Oliver St. John met
Blount in the morning and invited him to attend. He refused.
From the first he had been uneasy in his mind, and was not
reassured when on the Wednesday, after the conference, he had

---

[1] This account is pieced together from the various papers in Harleian MS. 6846,
fo. 65 f. For the parliamentary seats of the members named, see the *Official Return*.
[2] Morice's confession, Harleian MS. 6846, fo. 108. Morice inserted this confession
in his account of his imprisonment—or rather, restraint—this session. That account
is in the Baker MSS. at Cambridge (vol. xl) and is entitled, ' A Remembrance of certein
matters concerninge the Clergye and theire Jurisdiccion '. I am indebted to Miss
M. B. Hume of Radcliffe College, U.S.A., for calling my attention to the references
to Wentworth and for lending me her transcript of the document.

met Sir Thomas West and been advised not to proceed any
farther unless it was agreed to open the campaign by petitioning
the queen. The lord keeper's speech on the Thursday had
confirmed his fears.[1] What was the attitude of the others, or
who were invited to the second conference, we do not know,
for it was never held. News of Wentworth's scheming had
leaked out, and within an hour or two of seeing Morice he was
summoned before a number of privy councillors and committed
to prison.[2]

For reasons which we shall examine later it seems probable
that the council did not immediately learn of the conference at
Winch's chambers, but when they did, all who were implicated
were summoned before Lord Keeper Puckering, Lord Buckhurst,
and Sir Robert Cecil, and examined. Notes were taken of the
examinations, and these, along with a number of the confessions
written by the accused, form the body of papers from which our
narrative has been constructed. The first in date is Apsley's
confession on 10 March. Stephens's, which bears no date, may
have been as early or earlier. The next is the first of two sets of
questions submitted to Wentworth, along with his replies : the
date is 12 March, just over a fortnight, be it noted, after his first
summons before the council. On the same day or the following
Winch was examined, and on the 13th and 14th he wrote out
two confessions. Blount was examined on 13 March, and Black
Oliver St. John wrote a deposition on the 14th. With further
details in their hands the councillors re-examined Wentworth
on the 14th, and on the 17th Morice was before them and wrote
an account of his interview with Wentworth. Blundeville and
Sparke were sent for and examined on 22 and 27 March respectively, and one Robert Lynford added some details of a conversation which Wentworth had with Mr. Bulkley before coming
to the parliament. From a memorandum of Puckering's we
learn that Oliver St. John of Bedfordshire, and Wentworth's son,
who had handled his father's papers, were also examined. But
their depositions have not survived.

Wentworth showed something of the old stubbornness in his
examinations. Some questions he had to be charged upon his
allegiance to answer ; others he refused to answer. At first he
was apparently unaware that the council had knowledge of the
conference at Lincoln's Inn. His early answers in the first
examination avoided any mention of the conference or of any
actions since the summoning of parliament. The government
wanted information about all his activities since the parliament
of 1588/9, evidently suspecting that he had conducted propaganda

---

[1] Blount's confession, Harleian MS. 6846, fo. 75.
[2] *Ibid.* fo. 108 ; Baker MSS. (Cambridge), xl. 31.

and organized a party in the country; and Wentworth seized upon the range of time in their questions to conceal what he had done since 1592. As the questions succeeded one another, however, he must have realized that the secret was out. The fifth cornered him, and he was compelled upon his allegiance to divulge the names of Stephens and Winch. Even so, one would be unaware from his answers that a conference had been held or a parliamentary campaign planned. It was the others who gave the council its material evidence. Between this first examination on 12 March and the second surviving one on the 14th, there may have been an intermediate examination, the details of which have not come down to us. On 14 March the council merely 'wished to discover where the papers were that he had had at Winch's chambers, and how far Morice and Yelverton were implicated in his schemes. One answer of Wentworth's on this occasion deserves notice : he would not, he said, give up the draft of his speech, since it was to have been delivered in parliament, where speech was free, and he claimed the privilege of parliament in refusing to show it.[1]

As a result of the inquiry Wentworth remained in the Tower and Stephens in the Fleet. Winch, Apsley, Blount, and Oliver St. John of Bedfordshire do not appear to have been imprisoned nor to have been stayed from attending the parliament.[2] They were merely bound over by recognizances on 14 March not to leave London or Westminster without licence, and to appear when summoned; and all save St. John, and perhaps even he, had to sign an agreement not to disclose the proceedings at the inquiry, nor to confer with any one about the succession, but to report any news of such a conference that they might hear.[3] What happened to Black Oliver St. John we do not know. He can hardly have escaped punishment. It looks as though a number of succession pamphlets were found in his rooms, judging from the questions put to Wentworth; and no doubt his offence was exaggerated by his not being a member of parliament. Morice was already under restraint at the house of Sir John Fortescue for delivering two bills into the commons which entrenched upon the queen's ecclesiastical supremacy; and his association with Wentworth, innocent though it was of real offence, simply deepened Elizabeth's displeasure with him.[4]

So far we have proceeded with our narrative entirely from the new sources. They leave a gap in the story, however, and we must now turn to D'Ewes's account of what happened this session.

[1] Harleian MS. 6846, fos. 67 f.
[2] Reference to one or other of these members this session will be found in D'Ewes, pp. 474 a, 475 b, 489 b, 501 b, 512 b.
[3] Harleian MS. 6846, fos. 73, 77 ; Birch, *Memoirs of Queen Elizabeth*, i. 96.
[4] Baker MSS. xl. 128.

It is taken from an anonymous member's diary of the parliament, and the important passages, which appear under Saturday, 24 February, are the following :

This day Mr. Peter Wentworth and Sir Henry Bromley delivered a Petition unto the Lord Keeper, therein desiring the Lords of the Upper House to be suppliants with them of the lower House unto her Majesty for Entailing the Succession of the Crown, whereof a Bill was readily drawn by them. . . .

The day after . . . they were called before the Lord Treasurer, the Lord Buckhurst and Sir Thomas Heneage. The Lords intreated them favourably and with good Speeches ; But so highly was her Majesty offended that they must needs commit them, and so they told them. Whereupon Mr. Peter Wentworth was sent Prisoner unto the Tower ; Sir Henry Bromley and one Mr. Richard Stevens, to whom Sir Henry Bromley had imparted the matter, were sent to the Fleet, as also Mr. Welch the other Knight for Worcestershire.

About this matter in the beginning of the Parliament was appointed a Committee to be had of many grave, wise and ancient Parliament men, which were of the House, but at this time few met at the place appointed, at least not such as were expected.

It was appointed also at this time to Mr. Stevens to peruse the penning of the Petition that should have been delivered to that House, and to have provided a Speech upon the delivery of it. . . . What other things were done or spoken in that Conference, were, as I heard, confessed to some of the Privy-Council by some of those Parties that were present at that Conference. All that were there, except those before-named, went free and were never called in question that I heard of.[1]

In the first place it will be noticed that the last two paragraphs read like a postscript giving later information, and that they are a fairly accurate, if only partial account of the events which I have described. Their chief error lies in the words ' was appointed a Committee ' ; but even here it may only be a supposition of ours that the phrase refers to any action taken in parliament. The first paragraph, which is the one usually quoted, is at first sight perplexing. It is strange that no one has yet ventured to doubt the conventional interpretation of it. The Speaker was ill on the Saturday, no business was transacted in the lower house, and therefore any action taken by Wentworth and Bromley could only have been by way of a private venture. That in fact it is inaccurate we now know, since Wentworth was first summoned before the council on the Friday and not on the Saturday. But admitting that anything which these two members did was extra-parliamentary,[2] we have yet to probe the truth that may lie in the paragraph.

[1] D'Ewes, pp. 470–1.
[2] If further proof were needed that no parliamentary action was taken, Wentworth

So far Bromley has been deliberately excluded from our narrative. We do not possess his depositions, nor do we possess Walshe's, though no doubt these and others once existed ; and only in Stephens's confession is there a reference to him. The reference is as follows :

It is allreadie confessed and knowen, what I said to Sir Henry Bromley knight. The said Sir Henrie meetinge me in Fleete streate in the eueninge on the friday night, told me,. that he had bene examined before some of the Lords of the counsell touchinge this matter, and had forborne to shew their Lordshippes, that he heard thereof by me, vntill he might haue my consent so to doe. I then answeared him, that I was lothe, that he should abide trouble through me, and had rather it lighted on my selfe ; and so consented, that he might discouer my name to their honors.[1]

This and the entry of the anonymous diarist given by D'Ewes furnish the only positive evidence about Bromley's actions that I know of, except that Morice confirms the fact of his imprison- ment as an accomplice of Wentworth's.[2] But the evidence will carry us a fair way if it is carefully reviewed. Wentworth and Bromley were first examined by a group of councillors on Friday, 23 February. Bromley was not committed after this preliminary inquiry, although Wentworth was, if we may believe Morice. On the Saturday or Sunday a further examination took place which implicated Stephens, and probably Walshe also, unless he had likewise been before the council on the Friday. According to the anonymous diarist all four were thereupon committed. A fortnight elapsed and then came Apsley's confession, which, if we omit Stephens's undated confession, was the first of a series relating to the conference at Winch's chambers on 21 February. We cannot, I think, regard these later examinations merely as a continuance of the earlier. The group of councillors was different, and the questions put to Wentworth on 12 March were not supplementary ones. they suggest rather the opening of a new inquiry ; and Wentworth, as I have already pointed out, appears to have been unaware beforehand that the secret of the conference was known. If Wentworth did not disclose the secret, there was no need for Bromley or Walshe to have done so, for neither were parties to the conference ; and as for Stephens, his remark, 'It is allreadie confessed and knowen, what I said to Sir Henry Bromley ', which comes in his later confession, may be taken to imply that when he was first examined on Saturday or Sunday, 24 or 25 February, he, like Wentworth, maintained a

himself might be cited. In a letter to the council, written on 11 November 1593, he states: 'And the bill and Petition the which I intended to preferr into the howse . . . I preferred them not into the howse ; but am punished for that I intended to preferr them ' (Add. MS. 24664, fo. 44 b).

[1] Harleian MS. 6846, fo. 98 b.   [2] Baker MSS. xl. 131.

discreet silence. However, if we infer that the government was ignorant of the conference when Wentworth, Stephens, Bromley, and Walshe were committed, we must postulate some other offence to account for their imprisonment, and so assume a widening of the earlier conspiracy. The connecting link is Stephens. It was he who involved Bromley in Wentworth's schemes, and Bromley probably who involved Walshe.

The difficulty, however, is to discover what these four did, our only evidence being the anonymous diarist's statement that Wentworth and Bromley presented a petition to the lord keeper; but, as we have already accepted so much of this writer's narrative, we may as well see what can be made of the statement. If we remember that at the last parliament Wentworth tried to use Burghley as an agent, it is not altogether incredible that this session he tried to use Puckering. For such an attempt Bromley would have been useful, since he was the son and heir of the late lord keeper; and it is possible that he and Wentworth approached Puckering in the hope of winning him over to support their cause, and either facilitate in some way or other the joint action of the two houses of parliament, or intervene for them with the queen. If the lord keeper was informed of their plans, then, whatever his own sympathies, as a privy councillor he was bound to disclose them; and perhaps in this way Wentworth and Bromley came to be summoned before the council. Walshe was implicated, though how we do not know.

However, the factor of probability is soon exhausted in this sort of speculation, and my suggestions are lame enough already. I find it difficult to believe that if Wentworth distrusted Yelverton he trusted Puckering, and on the whole I think it safer to query the story of the petition and to leave the precise nature of Bromley and Walshe's co-operation with Wentworth an unsolved problem. All we can say with assurance is that they must have been active in some way, news of which leaked out; Stephens was involved as the link between Wentworth and Bromley; and these four managed to confine their revelations to their own group, so that at first the council was unaware of the real extent of Wentworth's actions. Our first-hand authorities tell us no more. Says Stephens,

On the friday ... Mr. Wentworth tolde me, that it was knowen abroad, that he meant to make the motion for the succession, and that he was sent for by the right honourable Mr. Vicechamberlein, but said he I will not hurt any of those, whose aduise I vse in this matter.[1]

Here, where we might have expected it, there is no hint of the petition. It does not necessarily follow, because most of those

---

[1] Harleian MS. 6846, fo. 98 b.

who met at Winch's chambers went free whereas Bromley and
Walshe were imprisoned, that these two members had committed a more heinous offence than the former. They were
imprisoned before the council learnt of the conference, and since
Winch, Apsley, and the rest showed in their confessions that
without vigorous leadership they would have feared to do anything, Bromley and Walshe were sufficient scapegoats and their
punishment a salutary lesson to the others. By silencing Wentworth the council had effectually scotched the succession agitation. No doubt, had that conference taken place which was
intended on the Friday afternoon, Bromley and Walshe, and
perhaps other new adherents, would have attended, and a conspiracy which was marred at first by the timidity and inexperience of its members might have become formidable.

One point, however, we must make perfectly clear. None of
these members of parliament were imprisoned for anything that
they had said or done in parliament ; and when on 10 March
Mr. Wroth moved in the commons that the house should sue to
the queen for the release of its members, the privy councillors
replied very much as they had done in 1586/7 : ' her Majesty had
Committed them for Causes best known to her self, and for us to
press her Majesty with this Suit, we should but hinder them whose
good we seek.' [1]

Here we may conveniently turn aside to examine two manuscripts in the British Museum.[2] The one is headed ' Peter Wentworth speech when the Queen would dissolue the parlament ' ;
the other, ' A speech by him deliuered for the Speaker to say
vnto the Queene '. The first is a brief speech moving the Speaker
to entreat the lords that they join in a message which he is to
read to the queen. The second is the message. They assume
a situation in which a bill has been introduced into the commons
to settle the succession, a supplication sent to the queen for
permission to proceed with it, and a subsidy and two-fifteenths
offered to procure her approval. In reply the queen has intimated
that on a certain day—so uncertain that blank spaces are left
where the date should be—she will dissolve the parliament ;
and she has therefore preferred to lose her supplies rather than
settle the succession. At first sight the documents are puzzling.
So far as we know there never was such a situation in Elizabeth's
reign. But the mystery vanishes when one recollects the various
papers which Wentworth brought with him to the parliament
of 1592/3. Among them was a reply written lest Elizabeth
should deny parliament's suit ; and one might suspect that the
new manuscripts are transcripts of two of the very papers read
at Winch's chambers. But they are not. The threatened

¹ D'Ewes, p. 497.   ² Harleian MS. 1877, fos. 37 b–39.

dissolution is a frill not alluded to in the 1592/3 depositions, and what meagre internal evidence there is suggests an earlier date. Wentworth remarked once that he had rough-hewed the bill and petition of 1592/3 twenty years before,[1] and this speech and message therefore were probably discarded drafts, written some time in the eighties, out of which grew the reply to the queen's possible refusal which he took to London with him in 1592/3.

They are remarkable speeches, as bold in expression as anything of Wentworth's that we know ; and it is easy to imagine from them what was the tone of some of the papers to which Winch and others took exception at their conference in Lincoln's Inn. The first speech opens thus :

Ah Mr. Speaker ther was neuer so dolefull a message sent by any Prince nor receaued by any Subiectes. See theffect therof and ponder grauely what it importeth. It is as much to say as her maiestie had rather refuse our reliefe of mony for the which (wee doubt the parlament was assembled) then her maiestie would see the state preserued. Is this loue (Mr. Speaker) no surely : I cannot so take it, neither can I hold my peace for any displeasure, but I must needes earnestly require you, and the whole house presently to goe to the Quenes Maiestie with this message. . . . And albeit the speech (Mr. Speaker) wilbe iudged (of some here) to be ouer sharp I shall require them to consider that it is the opinions of the best surgeons, that dead flesh must haue sharpe corseyes to eat it out, it may otherwise perill the whole body. . . .

The second speech, or message, first refers to the notice of parliament's imminent dissolution, and then continues :

[The nobles and commons] loue, they protest, your maiesties soule and body in most dutifull wise. And therfore they haue willed me to shew your maiestie that they tremble lest that your maiestie should iustly deserue god his euerlasting wrath through wilfull and most lamentable and vnnaturall murther, they do meane the murther of an infinite number of your owne people and innocentes and that not for the sheding of one drop of blood only ; but for making riuers to run therof, and that, that is also most greuious vtterly to subuert the whole state. . . . And would not your maiestie haue the state preserued : but rather vtterly subuerted, with the mercilesse blood shedding of many bloody battailes, is this loue, ys this the loue that should be in your maiestie to your people. Art thou a king (saieth Seneca) and hast no time to be a king the which is as much to say as Bishopp Tunstall did interprett yt in his oration before your noble father. Art thou a king and dost nothing profitable for thy people. Art thou a king and seest thy people to haue vnsufficient law. Art thou a king and wilt not prouide a remedy for the mischeife of thy people. O England England how great ar thy sines towardes thy mercifull god, that he hath so alienated the harte of her that he hath sett ouer thee to be thy nource, that she should withold nourishing milk from thee, and force thee to

---

[1] Add. MS. 24664, fo. 44 b.

drinke thyne one distruction. . . . Thes vngodly and vnnaturall euills they
cannot thinke or iudg to be in your maiestie as of your self and of your
owne nature, but that your maiestie is drawen vnto it by some wicked
charming spiritt of traiterous persuasion, or that your maiestie is ouercome
by some feminine conceipt. . . . They say, that they dare not depart the
house without making knowne vnto your maiestie that when the knightes
and burgesses of this house be retourned home into their seueral countries
the question wilbe demaunded of them of the sodaine breaking vpp of the
parlament. . . . [And when they explain the reason will it not] plainely shew
in your maiestie a want of loue, and a carelesse regard vnto the state, will
not this be perill to your person, will not this giue iust cause to coole
or vtterly to alienate the mindes of the people from your maiestie, who
(in reason) loue you : as they be beloued : let wise heades gesse, and faythfull tounges vtter their hartes plainely. . . . They assure your maiestie
[and here Wentworth is clearly making a personal confession] that
they haue ben soundry times moued to deale in this matter by sondry
people as gentlemen, preachers and countrye men : with some acquainted
with some neuer seene before. But foolish feare so ouercame them that
they durst not deale in it. Foolish feare (they say) because they feared
your maiesties displeasure more then they right feared, wayed or considered, your maiesties great and iminent daunger of god his high indignation. . . . And they praise their god from the botome of their hartes, that
he hath made them now so strong to deale therin : and they beseech the
same good god to make them all as earnest with your maiestie, as the
matter is earnest, for it importeth more (they say) then all ther heads ;
and ten thouzand more be worth and therfore they ar not much to account
of your maiesties present displeasure espetially sithence the sequell must
needes bee, that nothing can or will please your maiestie so much as this
their faythfull dealing with your maiestie for when your maiestie shall
tourne vnto god with a broken harte and see your one daunger through
your slacknes want of loue and dutifull consideracion to god and your
people. . . . O what comfort of conscyence, what quietnes of mind and
assurance of your person shall your maiestie be then in. . .

After referring to the rumour of the queen's displeasure with
the speech last used in the house, this being obviously the speech
with which Wentworth intended to have opened the campaign,
the message comments upon David's reference to a prince as
a god, but adds,

[They think it good to remind your majesty] of the wordes of the heathen
and noble Emperor, Tyberius, vnto Maritus his successor, Nature hath
giuen vnto bees (said he) rulors or heades and hath armed their king with
a sting, as with a naturall rodd of power to thend that he may sting those
that do not yeld vnto him their dutifull obedience : but this Master bee
may not use his sting like vnto a tyrant. But wher it is deserued, and to
a common benefitt and commoditie. . . .[1]

Wentworth was still in the Tower when in 1594 Doleman's

---

[1] Harleian MS. 1877, fos. 37 b–39.

tract on the succession was published ; and with his usual
temerity he acceded to the request of some friends and replied
to it.[1] His reply was published along with the *Pithie Exhortation*
after his death, as *A Discourse containing the Authors opinion
of the true and lawful successor to her Maiestie*,[2] and took the form
of a letter to one of his friends maintaining the right of James
of Scotland. In writing it Wentworth made himself liable under
the act of 13 Elizabeth, cap. 1, to a year's imprisonment and forfeiture of half his goods ; and his rashness was justified only by
the importance of the pamphlet which he was refuting. It was
in fact a departure from the policy which he had hitherto followed.
Both in 1591 and in 1592/3 the privy councillors who examined
him had tried to convict him of plotting on behalf of some
particular candidate for the throne ; but in vain.[3] He had denied
the charge, and all the evidence that we possess justifies his denial.
Nevertheless, it does not follow that he was not privately a
partisan. As a puritan he probably hoped for the succession of
the earl of Hertford's children or the earl of Huntingdon, whilst
Mary lived ; but her death cleared the way for that change
of opinion to which he himself confessed. His friends, the editors
of the *Pithie Exhortation*, imply that Wentworth already thought
James the rightful heir when he wrote that pamphlet.[4] One
cannot be sure. But it can hardly be doubted that such was his
conviction in 1591–2 when he composed the brief tract showing
that the king of Scots would not object to the settlement of
the succession. At any rate, his conversion was complete by
1594. It follows, therefore, that Sir Charles Dilke was wrong
when in the *Dictionary of National Biography* he suggested that
Elizabeth was embittered against Wentworth during his final
imprisonment because he supported the Hertford claim. His
authority is a letter of November 1595 in Strype's *Annals*[5] concerning an alleged plot by Sir Michael Blount, lieutenant of the
Tower. Strype's mispunctuation obscures the meaning of the
letter, and so I quote the passage here from the original manuscript, my punctuation being enclosed in square brackets.[6]

[Blount's] speche to me touchinge the Earle of Hertforde was, that
M[r] Wenteworthe his standinge for to haue a successour established was
onelye in the fauor of his Lo: children wherof when I spoke vnto M[r] Wenteworthe he answered he dothe me wronge for he himselfe is of that faction
which he hathe playnelye discouered vnto me (saith he) and shewde me
reasons to strengthen his opynyon[.] for his speache to M[rs] Wenteworthe,

---

[1] *A Pithie Exhortation* . . . (1598), pref.
[2] On the separate title-page of the Discourse the title is differently worded.
[3] Cf. p. 1 of the *Discourse* ; Harleian MS. 6846, fo. 68.
[4] *A Pithie Exhortation*, p. 37, marginal comment.
[5] iv. 334–5.   [6] Lansdowne MS. 79, fo. 10.

that if the gentlemen of Englande wer honest, ther woulde be fiue hundred in prison for her husbandes opinyon, ere it wer longe[,] bothe Mr Wenteworthe and his wife doe affirme it and haue done before captaine Wanema and my selfe. . . .

The political theories which Wentworth was compelled to expound in answering Doleman's tract make his *Discourse* an interesting pamphlet. Doleman had ridiculed the idea that the succession of princes by nearness of blood was determined by divine or natural law. In every commonwealth, he wrote, human and positive law regulates the succession. Therefore for just cause the commonwealth may alter it. And so alongside birth he placed election, and utterly repudiated the doctrine of divine hereditary right. Wentworth directs his reply to the implied argument of Doleman that parliament can take away the king of Scots' right to the English throne ; and in consequence is led to define the power of parliament. ' It is ', he writes, ' most sacred, most ample and large and hath prerogatiues and preheminences farre aboue anie Court whatsoeuer, which is established by God under the heauens.' Yet its power is not unlimited. It ' is straightlie stinted and defined with the limites and meeres of iustice and equitie : and is appointed by God, as the power next to himself to reforme and redresse wrongs and outrages which can not be holpen by any other means, and by good and wholesome lawes to procure the peace and wealth of the Realme '. Parliament is ' the Court of most pure and exquisite iudgement '. If by presumption of its power it do injury to any man or transgress the bounds of right, this transgression ' is accounted of before God ', and the iniquity is the iniquity of the whole land.

He then proceeds to expound the doctrine of divine hereditary right. The right, however, is conditional. ' A Prince which hath the right (as we speake) of God, he is the ordinance, not of anie man, but of God, appointed and substituted by God himselfe, as his deputy for the maintenance of his truth, and to minister Iustice according to the good and wholesome lawes of that land ouer which he doeth place him.' Therefore if the king of Scots, having the right of God, ' be willing to gouerne vs according to our owne lawes (as no question he will) ', it were the highest injustice to deprive him of his ' right anointed '. To this, he states, some have answered that parliament ' hath taken the rightfull lands and liuings of men, and hath repealed the acts and statutes of former Parliaments '. For his own part, he is prepared to admit that as a limb may wisely and rightly be amputated from a natural body when without such remedy the rest may be endangered, so in the body politic any subject may be deprived of lands, livings, or life. But he hastens to escape

from the full implications of the argument. First there is no
danger from the king of Scots, for he will preserve ' our religion
and lawes ' ; then although the power is undoubted over subjects,
yet the king of Scots is not a member incorporated of our body
politic, and it is doubtful if it holds against him. Moreover,
such acts of parliament must be understood as concerning private
men and not princes ; and whatsoever has been given to princes
and their heirs by a free and lawful parliament has not, he thinks,
been taken away by another free parliament save with the
consent of those princes or their heirs.

This leads him to conceive of the institution of kingship as
an act of contract ; but the devolution of power is conditional.

If all the people . . . by common and voluntarie consent, for themselues
and their posteritie, do transferre and surrender the gouernment of themselues and their state into the hands of some chosen man, to bee gouerned
by him and his heires for euer, according to such and such lawes, as they
shall agree vppon, or haue alreadie established,

then ' if he be willing to preserue their lawes ', that power which
they formerly surrendered cannot still rest with them. The
judgement of parliament itself, he argues, proves his case. For
in the coronation of a king it is not claimed that it seemed good
to the nobles and commons so to advance him : on the contrary
the reason given is that he is next heir to a certain prince. And
making a point from historical experience, he asserts that in the
conceit of the usurpers themselves, amongst whom he instances
Henry IV and Richard III, ' the moste lying, infamous and falsely
forged pretence of next and most lawful blood is to be preferred
before any Parliament '.

It may seem strange that the most radical parliamentarian of
his age should be refuting a pamphlet that exalted parliament's
powers. But Wentworth's pamphlet is a *livre de circonstance*,
not a systematically developed political philosophy. His theory
of divine hereditary right, tempered as it is by a half-veiled right
of deprivation, inevitable to a puritan who could not possibly
contemplate the accession of a papist, is as frankly utilitarian
as Doleman's theory of popular rights ; and the shrewd blow
which he aims at Doleman recoils upon himself when he writes,
' I pray you thinke with your self if it should fall out that the
Parliament . . . should bestow the crown quite contrary to the
expectation of these men, who stand so precisely for the absolute
power and soueraignetie of it . . . do not you think that the case
would be altered with them ? '

Wentworth was in the Tower when he wrote his *Discourse*,
and there he remained for nearly five years. It was an inordinate
punishment and in marked contrast with the lenity shown

towards Sir Henry Bromley, who was released after only seven
or eight weeks' restraint.[1] In part it was his own choice. He
refused to purchase liberty at the price of confessing his fault
and of renouncing all desire to hasten a settlement of the succession. This we can see very clearly in three letters of his to the
council, for although he wrote petitioning for release, he yet
maintained an unbending attitude.[2] The first was written on
7 November 1593 and contained a review of his actions and an
earnest justification of them.

My very good Lords [he wrote] I doe perceaue that no submission
wilbee accepted vnless I acknowledg my selfe to commit a faulte. . . .
I protest before god yf her highnes would make mee a duke and giue mee
twenty thousand pounds a yeare of her best land to haue my consent
to forbeare the setling of the succession for the space of one quarter of
a yeare longer then it might conuenientlye bee effected . . . I would denye
and defye that honnour and inheritaince as bastardly poysonfull and
mysbegotten.

The boast was not lightly uttered : rather it was the considered
judgement of an old and sickly man after nine months' confinement in a city, plague-stricken in summer ; and Wentworth
well knew that its probable effect would be to prolong his
imprisonment. 'Such sutes', wrote Cecil of Arundel's, in 1564,
'are heard slowly, because he doth not knowledg himself a
fawlter' : [3] and for Wentworth death was speedier than the
passing of the queen's wrath.

At no time was he so indomitable in spirit as in these last
years of imprisonment and broken health. 'The case is very
hard with us poore parlament men', he once said summing up
the tragedy of his own life, ' when we deserue to hang in hell
(by the iustice of god) if we neglect his seruice or the seruice of
our prince or state . . . and may neither serue god or prince or
state truely nor faithfully . . . but ar sure of displeasure and
punishment therefore.' [4] The queen, as Burghley remarked,
was determined that the question of the succession should be
suppressed as long as ever she lived : inevitably the suppression
of Wentworth followed. In a second letter to the council, written
on 10 August 1595, and in a third, written a month later, he
was still resolute. No doubt when his name recurred in connexion with the succession, in November 1595, in the stories told
of the plotting of Sir Michael Blount, lieutenant of the Tower,[5]
the queen's heart hardened towards him, and it did again in

[1] Baker MSS. xl. 131.
[2] Add. MS. 24664, fos. 43 f.
[3] Wright, *Queen Elizabeth and Her Times*, i. 180.   Also cf. *Hatfield MSS.* xiv. 69.
[4] Harleian MS. 1877, fo. 56 b.   [5] *Supra*, p. 288.

July 1596 when it was found that he still had copies of his
Pithie Exhortation about him.[1] But if we may judge from his
letters to the council, it is likely that at any time after November
1593 he could have had his liberty, only the price demanded
of him was too high. At last in July 1597 arrangements were
actually afoot to free him, on conditions that closely regulated
his movements. But not yet was his spirit broken, and in the
last glimpse of him that we are afforded we find him demanding
to see the conditions of his release, for otherwise he cannot with
honesty entreat any sureties to enter into the bonds.[2] Whether
he refused the terms when all was ready, or whether his ' oftener
than weekly sicknes ' took a critical turn that forbade his
removal, we do not know. Little more than three months later
he was dead, a prisoner. He was then over seventy-three years old.

To appraise Wentworth's career at all adequately would
plunge us into a long argument upon the history of freedom of
speech in parliament. We must, therefore, begin with a conclusion for which justification will be offered elsewhere,[3] namely,
that the construction which Wentworth put upon the privilege
of free speech was without historical warrant. Despite his own
and later beliefs he was aiming not at renovation but at innovation. From the point of view of parliamentary liberties, the
importance of Elizabeth's reign was that it began with free speech
a vague and narrow privilege, and closed with two widely divergent interpretations of it. On the one hand was the Crown's,
sound in its conservatism, on the other Wentworth's, highly
novel, reaching out towards the fact, if not towards the theory,
of parliamentary sovereignty.

Wentworth was no mere theorist, for though he dressed his
claims in theories they subserved practical aims. He appears
to have grasped more clearly than the fellow agitators of his day
that reform of the church and even the settlement of the succession, which were the ultimate objects of his and of their
endeavours, were dependent upon the solution of a profounder
problem, and that if only freedom of speech as he conceived it
were secured, then all else might follow. He did not justify
himself so much by an appeal to precedents, as the gathering flood
of antiquarian research enabled his Stuart successors to do.
To him parliament was the organ of the commonwealth where
all grievances might be expressed, the highest council of the
realm whose business was to offer advice upon all matters.
By its nature a plenitude of freedom was due to it, for otherwise

---

[1] *Hist. MSS. Com., Hatfield MSS.*, vi. 284, 288, 289.

[2] *Ibid.* vii. 286, 303, 324.

[3] See my essay, ' The Commons' Privilege of Free Speech in Parliament ', in
Tudor Studies, ed. by R. W. Seton-Watson, *supra*, chapter 5, pp. 147-76.

counsel would be hindered and God, the prince, and the common-wealth betrayed and endangered. The crucial question of the Crown's right to withhold any subject from discussion he solved by reposing the obligation to give counsel upon a councillor's duty to God, and he tried to set his far-reaching notions of free speech beyond legitimate challenge by incorporating them in the fundamental laws of society. Without this privilege the preserva-tion of prince and realm could not be assured : hence it existed by virtue of a law superior to the Crown.

Whilst not depreciating the ultimate value of such thorough-going descriptions of freedom as Wentworth's, we should beware of giving his mind too modern a cast or thinking it too logical. If pressed, he would in all likelihood, as a matter of constitu-tional theory, have admitted the Crown's contention for a division of power, for distinct spheres of action in which the Crown by its prerogative might alone determine certain things, and the Crown in parliament others. But a written constitution was then an unknown aid to divided sovereignty, and facts and the passions of the time, as Wentworth felt them, were against nice con-stitutional distinctions. Turning a blind eye to these, he came very near, if he did not come completely, to asserting that the will of the nation in all matters should express itself in parliament, unrestrained except by the royal veto. From this position to a practical extinction of the veto and to parliamentary sovereignty was but an easy journey, which time and a quickening national opinion would inevitably take, and were indeed taking under Elizabeth. If few in his days went so far as he in their conception of free speech, yet in minor matters of privilege all displayed a jealousy that wasted hours of time in comparatively short and congested sessions ; and it was no accident that the first standing committee for privileges was established in Elizabeth's reign.

If Wentworth fanned the flame of liberty with such success, in the mechanism of politics his achievements were no less great. His experiments in party organization are the most significant revelations of our new sources. They carry us back to the Elizabethan age for origins we have hitherto sought under the Stuarts. Indeed, we must go back earlier. Interchange of ideas and co-operation among members of the lower house were no doubt old practices. Under Henry VIII we find members discussing parliamentary business—to their imminent danger—over dinner at an inn.[1] In 1555 there was some arrangement amongst a group which secured the rejection of the bill to recall absentees ;[2] and perhaps the able manœuvres in the

---

[1] State Papers, Henry VIII, cxxv, fo. 248 (*Letters and Papers*, XII. ii, no. 952).
[2] Peck, *Desiderata Curiosa*, i. 9 ; Dasent, *Acts of Privy Council*, v. 202-8

parliament of 1566 were successfully executed because a few members had agreed to work together. Moreover, in Elizabeth's reign the radical section of the commons took to sitting at one end of the house, which must have given physical solidarity to their group, and, since courage consorts with numbers, must have made considerable difference to the voting upon measures that privy councillors, courtiers, and staid lawyers condemned ; for fear, as the bitter complaints of Wentworth show, too easily overcame men's consciences.

But if already there was this feeling after party organization, greater deliberateness was needed for its consummation ; and it was just that quality that Wentworth possessed. He was gifted with courage and pertinacity ; for years he would brood upon his parliamentary programme ; and at home, where he was respected as a leader of the puritans, he used his leisure to propagate his political doctrines. The immediate stimulus to party organization probably came from the ' classical ' movement amongst puritan ministers.[1] To it was due the parliamentary agitation of 1584/5, and an extension of its methods to the puritan section in parliament was carried out in 1586/7, if not earlier, when Cope and Wentworth and three other members planned to carry through a reform of the church. Of this group Wentworth was probably not the leader, but in 1592/3 he confirmed the experiment by repeating it, and went further, so it seems, by conducting an election campaign to ensure support in the house. His conference at Lincoln's Inn was not a complete success, it is true ; although there may have been ramifications to his plans of which we are ignorant. Says the anonymous journalist of that session, ' few met at the place appointed, at least not such as were expected ' ;[2] and he is probably right. But the conspiracy was nipped in the bud, and the group might have become formidable but for the intervention of the government. Inevitably it must have remained small in numbers. Matters of state might be discussed in the house of commons by presuming upon the queen's reluctance to punish offenders : nothing could shield members who discussed them out of parliament. Elizabeth was wise to swoop down upon Wentworth. One imagines that there was a large section of the house which would have voted for the settlement of the succession :[3] a few only were needed, strong in the consciousness of mutual support, to open the campaign and mass the sentiment of the house behind them.

[1] For an account of this movement, see Usher, *Presbyterian Movement* (Camden Soc.).

[2] D'Ewes, pp. 470–1.

[3] Cf. Sir Michael Blount's supposed remarks, quoted *supra*, p. 288.

And yet Wentworth was not a great parliamentarian. His language was often immoderate, his outlook unbalanced, his temper unaccommodating. He was too set upon certain objects. The frequency with which a member in the Elizabethan house of commons was placed upon committees is some indication of his interests and his prestige. Of this William Fleetwood is a good example. In his later life he was the Nestor of parliament. He could always win the ear of the house, and it appreciated his jokes and reminiscences even when they were not to the point. He and men like Dalton served on innumerable committees, and even Cope and Strickland were appointed to many. With Wentworth it was different. Our sources are deficient, but they record only three committees upon which he served. In a sheet of alliterative bombast called 'A Rayling libell against those of the parliament house', a member described Paul Wentworth as Wentworth ' the wrangler ' ; [1] and perhaps many in the house, certainly the more sober, regarded Peter in the same light. He was a man, wrote Sir John Harington, ' of a whett and vehement spirit '.[2]

To Wentworth himself his career must have appeared a failure. The church remained unreformed, the succession unsettled, his conception of free speech unrealized. That his mantle had fallen upon the group he had gathered about him,[3] that parliamentary tradition had put on immortality as country gentlemen and lawyers made membership the hobby of a life-time, and that his own experience and experiments were in consequence not lost, this he could not have known. The splendour of his ideal and the passion that had urged him forward as a pioneer left him blind to his achievements ; and in those last years of imprisonment, the future, hidden from him, had no solace to offer but an epitaph.[4]

---

[1] Brit. Mus. Stowe MS. 354, fo. 18.

[2] *A Tract on the Succession to the Crown* (*1602*), ed. by C. R. Markham (1880), p. 33.

[3] In 1598 his disciples published his succession tracts, the privy council in 1600/1 taking steps to suppress an edition printed at Middelburg in the Netherlands (Dasent, xxxi. 216). Under James I his son Thomas emulated him in parliament (cf. account in *Dict. of Nat. Biog.*). In 1614 Black Oliver St. John suffered fine and imprisonment for opposing a benevolence (cf. *ibid.* orig. ed. l. 150 b, and authorities cited there). In the Stuart struggle the St. Johns of Bedfordshire were found on the popular side.

That this was his feeling on the eve of his death appears from a poem he wrote, entitled, 'The Causes of my Longe Imprisonmente', which survives amongst the manuscripts of H. G. Gurney, Esq., at Keswick Hall, Norfolk (cf. *Hist. MSS. Com.*, Rep. xii, app. ix, p. 143). The verse is such hopeless doggerel that I refrain from quotations, but I wish to thank Mr. Gurney for permission to use the poem, and Mr. Wallace Notestein for securing me a transcript of it.

PERSPECTIVES IN ENGLISH PARLIAMENTARY HISTORY[1]*

By J. S. ROSKELL

THE reaction, mainly exemplified in the work of A. F. Pollard,[2] H. G. Richardson and G. O. Sayles,[3] against William Stubbs's interpretation of the development of the English parliament in the Middle Ages, has in some ways been very salutary. The medieval constitution was a " king-spun " constitution. And it was important to emphasize the authoritarian origin of parliament ; to realize that every time the king summoned a general parliament he was exacting a response to his own power of command and seeking his own ends, rather than consciously providing a channel of communication for the nation's will in answer to a demand from below which it would have been imprudent to resist. For, although the representative parliaments of the fourteenth and fifteenth centuries met even frequently, they met intermittently and by no stable rule binding upon the king. It was also necessary to realize that the growing complexity of the royal government and administration demanded a " clearing-house " for difficult questions which parliament could best provide, especially when, with the king and his council at its centre, it was attended by the prelates, lay magnates, and commons ; and that parliament was, in this sense, a necessary complement to the normal administrative machinery. For Mr. Richardson and Dr. Sayles, parliament was " the child of the monarchy and reared by the civil service " as an instrument

[1] A lecture delivered in the Library series of public lectures.

[2] *The Evolution of Parliament* (2nd edn., London, 1926).

[3] H. G. Richardson and G. O. Sayles, " The Early Records of the English Parliaments ", *Bulletin of the Institute of Historical Research (B.I.H.R.)*, v (1927-8), vi (1928-9) ; " The Parliaments of Edward III," *ibid.* viii (1930-1), ix (1931-2) ; " The King's Ministers in Parliament ", *English Historical Review (E.H.R.)*, vols. xlvi-vii (1931-2).

H. G. Richardson, " The Origins of Parliament ", *Transactions of the Royal Historical Society (T.R.H.S.)*, 4th ser., vol. xi (1928) ; " The Commons and Medieval Politics ", *ibid.* 4th ser., vol. xxviii (1946).

G. O. Sayles, *The Medieval Foundations of England* (London, 1948), chap. 27.

of the king's administrative authority.[1]   These critics of Stubbs would seem, however, to have erred in being too eager to define with exactness and precision what, originally, parliament was, especially by insisting that down to Edward III its judicial function was all-important and quite essential, this deduction supplying the chief clue to any proper understanding of its early character. Despite T. F. T. Plucknett's warning of the danger of making any rigid distinction between early parliaments and great councils,[2] and despite Sir J. Goronwy Edwards's demonstration that the essence of parliament's functions was " not specifically judicial . . . or specifically anything " but rather " consisted in being *unspecific* ",[3] Mr. Richardson and Dr. Sayles have, nonetheless, very recently re-asserted their views.[4]

Mr. Richardson and Dr. Sayles have also consistently " written down " or " disparaged " the rôle of the Commons in medieval parliaments both early and late.   They tell us that in early times the Commons were politically ineffective, this notion being a natural inference from the theory that what then really mattered in parliament was " justice " and not " politics ".   Subsequently, we are told that in later times (when " politics " had become more important than " justice ") the Commons continued to be politically ineffective, this notion being a natural inference from the theory that they had now become subservient to the Lords.   Dr. Sayles has insisted that " the facts point to the subservience rather than the independence of the Commons "[5] ; Mr. Richardson, that " the position occupied by the baronage in parliament . . . largely determined the part played by the Commons ".[6] According to this school of thought, the dominance of the Lords pre-ordained the dependence of the Commons : unless directed

[1] The quotation, from Sayles, *The Medieval Foundations of England*, p. 449, is cited by Edward Miller in *The Origins of Parliament* (Historical Association, Pamphlet, General Series, no. 44), and the words that follow it are his.

[2] T. F. T. Plucknett, " Parliament " in *The English Government at Work, 1327-1337*, vol. 1, ed. J. F. Willard and W. A. Morris (1940).

[3] *Historians and the Medieval English Parliament* (David Murray Foundation Lecture in the University of Glasgow, 1955 ; Glasgow, 1960), pp. 23-24.

[4] " Parliaments and Great Councils in Medieval England ", *The Law Quarterly Review*, vol. lxxvii (1961).

[5] *The Medieval Foundations of England*, p. 464.

[6] *T.R.H.S.*, 4th ser., xxviii. 21.

from above, the Commons were politically of little account. As Mr. Edward Miller has summarized their doctrine, the Commons " long remained in the outer darkness of inessentials ; and even when they emerged into the parliamentary light they were scarcely capable of positive attitudes and soon fell victims to the power of the lords, their masters ".[1]   The possibility of the Commons being sometimes " prompted " by the Lords was conceded by Stubbs.   But, of course, the views of Mr. Richardson and Dr. Sayles are diametrically opposed to Stubbs's assertion that "under Edward II, Edward III, and Richard II, the third estate claimed and won its place as the foremost of the three".[2]   Stubbs's view, at any rate as expressed in these terms, contains an exaggeration. But must we go to the other extreme of accepting the theory of Mr. Richardson and Dr. Sayles?

Their assertion that the medieval Commons were generally subservient to the Upper House was based upon the frequent connection between individual lords and knights of the shire and also the procedure of joint discussion between the Houses by delegations drawn from each. K. B. McFarlane once objected to the theory that subservience was inevitable because of the existence of personal ties between M.P.s and peers, even though there is evidence of aristocratic influence on shire elections in the fifteenth century.[3]   And Sir J. Goronwy Edwards has shown that the procedure of joint discussions by delegations (" inter-communing "), far from assisting the Lords to direct the Commons, is more liable to have had an opposite effect, especially regarding that most important concern of parliaments, the voting of taxes.[4] Political ineffectiveness, indeed, seems to consort ill with the Commons' vital right to withhold assent to taxation (secured well before the end of the fourteenth century), the right to appropriate supplies, and the claim (only spasmodically made but, when made, not infrequently recognized) to exercise an audit of accounts of expenditure of taxes.   Nor does it seem easy to recon-

[1] Miller, op. cit. p. 7.

[2] Stubbs, *The Constitutional History of England* (Library edn., 1880), ii. 332.

[3] K. B. McFarlane, " Parliament and Bastard Feudalism ", *T.R.H.S.*, 4th ser., vol. xxvi (1944).

[4] J. G. Edwards, *The Commons in Medieval English Parliaments* (The Creighton Lecture in History, 1957), pp. 5 ff.

cile political ineffectiveness with the Commons' capacity for initiating legislation by common petition. Mr. Richardson admitted this capacity in his statement that in the fourteenth century the Commons' petitions became " the normal basis of legislation ".[1] He and Dr. Sayles even went so far as to draw attention to the way in which this development resulted under Edward III in unprecedentedly "repetitive and ill-digested statutes".[2] It appears, however, that they have failed to notice that the royal judges (provided that their professional ability to produce a tidy draft was no less than their predecessors') must therefore have been forced to adhere closely to, and therefore hold in proper respect, the verbal form of the petitions receiving engrossment at their hands. Such a gloss hardly suits Mr. Richardson's suggestion (on another occasion) that " if the king declared that their [the Commons'] advice and assent was to be sought in the making of statutes, we must not read too much into words such as these ".[3] Is there not some danger that we may read too little or, much more, nothing at all? Nor is the theory that the Commons were politically insignificant consistent with what we know of the social standing and administrative importance of many of the medieval knights of the shire and not a few of the burgesses, the frequently long and sometimes intensive parliamentary experience of members, and the onset of the momentous invasion of borough seats by the gentry before the middle of the fifteenth century.[4]

How come about these contradictory interpretations of the rôle of the medieval Commons? Undoubtedly, one reason is to be sought in the defects of the evidence relating to the medieval parliament in general and to the Commons in particular, not least the sheer paucity of that evidence. *The Anonimalle Chronicle* provides a narrative account of some of the Commons' own sessions in the Good Parliament of 1376[5]; but it is a brief account, a unique disclosure, and relates to an unusual session. That central source, the *Rotuli Parliamentorum*, records no more of the

---

[1] *T.R.H.S.*, 4th ser., xxviii. 27.　　　[2] *B.I.H.R.*, ix. 13.
[3] *T.R.H.S.*, 4th ser., xxviii. 32.
[4] J. S. Roskell, *The Commons in the Parliament of 1422* (Manchester, 1953).
[5] *The Anonimalle Chronicle*, ed. V. H. Galbraith (Manchester, 1927), pp. 80-83, 85, 88.

Commons' doings than their formally stated results and does not
record how those results were arrived at in the Commons' own
house of assembly.   Moreover, as Sir J. Goronwy Edwards has
stated, the evidence of the parliament-rolls has " a certain quality
of fortuitousness ",[1] reducing the value of original finds and
making any arguments *ex silentio* very precarious and even dangerous.   Even regarding what parliament did as a whole, the rolls
provide inadequate information : regarding the internal proceedings of the Commons, virtually nothing at all.   What would
be needed to appraise the Commons' rôle in " ordinary politics "
(to say nothing of " high politics ")—records of their debates,
diaries, letters, such as appear in Elizabethan times in all their
dazzling irridescence—is absent from what evidence there is of
how the medieval parliament worked and of what it did.

Original sources apart, my feeling is that contradictory interpretations and therefore contradictory estimations of the rôle of the
medieval Commons have arisen, at least in part, out of an unreal
distinction in the treatment of the history of parliament between
the medieval and modern periods.   Or perhaps I should say, as a
result of a misplacing of the frontier between the modern constitution, of which parliament is an indispensable, inevitable and
permanent part, and the pre-modern (including medieval) constitution, in which parliament, being dependent directly upon the
king's will for its meetings, was an extraordinary and occasional
event and not a regular part of the constitution.   The eventual
achievement of constitutional and political independence by the
Lower House has to be examined against the background of
parliament's emergence as an essential and regular part of the
constitution.   If parliament is to control government in a really
effective manner, the control applied must be the opposite of
intermittent, spasmodic and uncertain.   But especially must
this be the case if that control is to be effectively exercised by the
elected Commons, for whenever the king dissolved parliament
the life of the Lower House was *pro hac vice* extinguished, whereas
the House of Lords was, in a sense, only adjourned, albeit indefinitely.[2]   However the Commons are elected, however com-

---

[1] *The Commons in Medieval English Parliaments*, p. 4.
[2] Betty Kemp, *King and Commons, 1660-1832* (London, 1957), p. 51.

posed, however privileged, however aggressive, so long as they are dependent upon the king's volition or discretion for their very existence, their control will fall short of reality.[1] The basic precondition of control of government by the Commons is that parliament should meet regularly. Not until the end of the seventeenth century was this requirement conclusively admitted.

A limitation of the royal prerogative of summons had soon been recognized as a practical necessity by the Long Parliament of Charles I. Or rather this parliament had recognized the need to limit the abuse of that prerogative by omission. And so the Triennial Act of 1641 (signed on the same day as the bill of attainder against Strafford) provided for the meeting of parliament if the king, within three years of dissolving this or any future parliament, failed to summon a new parliament : in this event, if the Lord Chancellor defaulted, the peers were to meet and twelve or more of them might issue the writs ; failing action on the part of the peers, the sheriffs and other returning officers were to hold elections ; failing action on *their* part, the electors were to meet as if the writs had been regularly issued ; and no parliament so unusually convened was to be dissolved without its own consent before fifty days had elapsed from the date appointed for its meeting. This Act of 1641 was repealed in 1664, and, although a new statute re-declared the principle of triennial parliaments, no machinery, alternative to that provided for in 1641, was introduced, so that, although Charles II went on to fulfil the intention of the Statute of 1664 in a general sense, he was able to break it in the last years of his reign. So, too, James II. All that was demanded on this subject in the Declaration of Right was that parliament should meet frequently. And it was left to the Triennial Act of 1694 to provide a solution to the problem of a statutory interval between parliaments which lasted until 1887. In practice, the annual need to pass the Mutiny Act (from 1689) and also to make appropriation of supply ensured that parliament would meet every year. This in itself ended the possibility of long intervals between parliaments.

But if parliament, and especially the Lower House, was to be a vital part of the constitution, this would not only depend upon a

[1] Ibid. p. 16.

limitation of the royal prerogative of summons[1] : it would also depend upon a limitation of the king's right to dissolve parliament at his discretion ; there would need to be a rule controlling the duration of parliaments. Before 1641, the king's right to end a parliament at will, even after only a brief session, had never been effectively disputed,[2] and the Long Parliament's early insistence on a minimum life of fifty days (unless it consented to an earlier dissolution) was conditioned by its memory of the eleven years' tyranny and of Charles I's previous use of his prerogative of dissolution to escape from demands for redress of grievance. After the Restoration, however, and the experience of the Cavalier Parliament, with its sixteen sessions extending over a period of eighteen years, it began to be felt not only that intervals between parliaments should be curtailed, but that the maximum life of parliament should be regulated: " a standing parliament ", resulting from the king's indefinite continuance of parliament, would render the Commons more susceptible to corruption and, therefore, more liable to royal control. The Declaration of Right made no reference to this question of duration of parliaments. The Triennial Act of 1694, however, as well as requiring that not more than three years should elapse between parliaments, also stipulated that no parliament should last longer than three years. The maximum life of parliament was extended to seven years by the Septennial Act of 1716. But this so much longer term soon came to be regarded by the Commons as the principal guarantee of their independence of the king and the House of Lords, with the result that the Act of 1716 was interpreted in the eighteenth cen-

---

[1] Mr. R. W. K. Hinton, when discussing, in his valuable article " English Constitutional Doctrines from the Fifteenth Century to the Seventeenth "(*E.H.R.*, lxxv. 410-25), the early seventeenth-century problem whether the " good of the commonwealth ", which was the object of legislation, could best be provided by parliament as the highest court of the realm, stressed the effect on this capacity of the king's right to determine when parliament met and how long it sat.

[2] One of the ten questions put to Richard II's judges at Nottingham in 1387 was : " Numquid Rex quandocumque sibi placuerit poterit dissolvere Parliamentum, et suis Dominis et Communibus precipere quod ab inde recedant, An non? "* Their answer was in the affirmative and that if anyone proceeded against the king's will " ut in Parliamento ", he stood to be punished as a traitor (*Rot. Parl.* iii. 233). It would appear that the royal right to dissolve parliament at will had been challenged in the parliament of 1386.

tury as if it prescribed not the maximum but the normal duration of a parliament, a span of life to which every parliament was conventionally entitled.[1]

It is chiefly because of the practical necessity since 1689 for parliament to meet each year and the statutes controlling the use of the royal prerogatives of summons and dissolution that, roughly, the turn of the seventeenth century constitutes the main line of demarcation between modern and earlier parliamentary history. Only then did parliament become a really regular part of the constitution.

Now, there has been no shortage of eloquent advocacy of the theory that parliament, and especially the House of Commons, was set upon a new career in the sixteenth century. For this theory we are mainly indebted to specialists in Tudor history, principally to A. F. Pollard, Sir John Neale, and G. R. Elton ; and it is perhaps not unfair to ask whether these historians may not have been moved unconsciously to exaggerate the significance, for the history of parliament, of the period upon which they chose to concentrate so devotedly. To help substantiate the responsibility of the Tudors for the emergence of parliament in the modern, say, " historic " phase, may they not have run the risk of depreciating the significance of parliament, especially its Lower House, in the medieval, say, " pre-historic " phase? Pollard regarded Henry VIII as having "magnified" parliament,[2] spoke of its being " Henry's extension and not his restraint of parliament that makes his rule unprecedented ",[3] and described the sixteenth century as " the great period of the consolidation of the house of commons ", the time in which it " acquires a weight which makes it the centre of parliamentary gravity ".[4] But parliament's influence upon the course of events was bound to be conditioned and affected by the intermittent character of its meetings. And that the meetings of the Tudor parliament were only occasional, there is no question. They were far less frequent than in pre-Tudor times. Between 1327 and 1485 only forty-two individual years went by in which parliament did not meet. We can count as many such years (43) between 1509 and 1603 ; and of the forty-four years of Elizabeth

[1] Kemp, op. cit. p. 34.   [2] *The Evolution of Parliament*, p. 215.
[3] Ibid. p. 277.   [4] Ibid. p. 160.

I's reign no fewer than twenty-six were quite uninterrupted by any parliamentary session. To apply the test of the medieval suggestion that parliament should meet at least once a year (to do justice to petitioners for grace) would obviously be unrealistic, since this suggestion was only very occasionally made even in the fourteenth century (when the dispensing of " justice " was still a significant function of parliament) and in any case was ineffectual.*
But if, solely for purposes of comparison between pre-Tudor and Tudor times, we apply the criterion of frequency thought proper or adequate in the seventeenth century, we find (*a*) that between 1327 and 1485 only twice did three years and more elapse without parliament meeting, and that these two occasions fell very late in that period (namely, in 1456-9 and 1478-83), and (*b*) that in the Tudor period, during which thirty-three parliaments met, such an interval occurred no fewer than ten times, half of these under Elizabeth I. Meeting at well-spaced intervals, Elizabeth's parliaments in fact were few. As her Lord Keeper explained as late as 1593, " Her maiestie hath euermore been most loth to call for the assemblie of her people in parlement, and hath done the same but rarely ".[1] And clearly some of her subjects must have readily sympathized : as Sir Thomas Smith had put it in 1560, " What can a commonwealth desire more than peace, liberty, quietness, little taking of base money, few parliaments. . .?"[2]

But, of course, we must ask whether, if Tudor parliaments were fewer than those of the medieval period, this was compensated by a tendency for parliament to run to a plurality of sessions and/or to enjoy a longer life. In the medieval period, down to the end of Henry V's reign in 1422, a single session had sufficed for all save nine parliaments (1328-9, 1332-3, 1371, 1381-2, 1388, 1397-8, 1406, 1410, and 1416), of which only one (1406) ran to three sessions. But under Henry VI and the Yorkists two out of every three parliaments had two or more sessions (four in 1445-6, seven in 1472-5), whereas under Tudor rule barely half sat for more than a single session. (The eight sessions of the Reformation Parliament of 1529-36, the four sessions of the parliament of

[1] J. E. Neale, " The Lord Keeper's Speech to the Parliament of 1592-3 ", *E.H.R.*, xxxi (1916), 130.
[2] J Strype, *The Life of Sir Thomas Smith* (Oxford, 1820), p. 192.

1547-52, and the three sessions of the parliament of 1572-83, were quite exceptional.) Turning to the question of mere duration, we find that a parliament under Edward III lasted on average for three weeks, during the following half-century for twice as long, and under Henry VI for more than twice as long again : and this average duration of about three months under Henry VI is characteristic of the sixteenth century (provided we exclude the quite unusually long Reformation Parliament with its eight sessions totalling the equivalent of ten months). Less frequent and fewer in number though they were, Tudor parliaments did not as a general rule last longer, in terms of time spent in actual session, than Henry VI's and other later medieval parliaments.

But it is on more immediate grounds than these that we should perhaps be wary of accepting Pollard's estimate of the significance of the Tudor period in the history of parliament, especially of the Lower House, and particularly his emphasis on the partnership between king and Commons as a great landmark. Dr. Elton subscribes to Pollard's view that parliament entered upon its proper career in the sixteenth century.[1] He, however, is evidently uneasy about this ascription of novelty to the community of interests between king and parliament, even especially when he is concerned with the effect on the Commons of their share in promoting the ecclesiastical changes made by the Reformation Parliament. Speaking of Henry VIII and Cromwell's employment of parliament and statute to make their revolution legally enforceable, he suggests that we waste no time " in admiring their penetration in choosing parliament as a partner, because in fact they never had any choice ".[2] And that the implicit meaning of these words is that the medieval development of parliament holds at least some importance for Dr. Elton is brought out in a subsequent remark of his : " the polity which Cromwell wanted rested not on the supremacy of the king, but on the supremacy of king in parliament. Of course this was not totally new; all medieval development stood behind this flowering of parliamentary monarchy."[3] Nevertheless, Dr. Elton holds by Pollard's main thesis that parliament underwent a species of conversion in

[1] G. R. Elton, *England under the Tudors* (London, 1955 [reprinted 1959]), p. 14.   [2] Ibid. p. 167.   [3] Ibid. p. 168.

the sixteenth century. But if, as Dr. Elton says, the principal achievement of Henry VIII's reign, the supremacy of the king in parliament, was " *not totally* new " [my italics[1]] this is hardly to say that, although the achievement might owe something to the medieval parliament, this something amounted to very much. In fact, Dr. Elton expresses himself more succinctly, if not very much more helpfully : " building upon the medieval foundations but erecting *something quite new* on them [my italics again], the Tudors and their ministers produced the composite sovereign body of the king in parliament."[2] It all depends on how important to a structure you regard its foundations. Personally, I would prefer (supposing I trusted the metaphor) not to discriminate too positively between these parts of the edifice. We may, however, quote against Dr. Elton the judgement of Pollard that the effect of the Act of Proclamations of 1539 was to free the supreme head of the church from subjection to parliamentary conditions in the exercise of his supremacy.[3] And also (and with no less conviction) we may quote against Pollard, Dr. Elton's estimate of the effect of the Commons' participation in the ecclesiastical work of the Reformation Parliament : from 1529 " the Commons ", says Dr. Elton, " experienced a few short and rather spurious years of primacy, at first (1529-31) because they were the natural mouthpiece of anti-clericalism, but then simply because Cromwell sat there. . . . In 1539 when he sat in the Lords, all the important bills were introduced there first."[4] None the less, in general Dr. Elton holds by Pollard's main thesis that it was in the sixteenth century that parliament entered upon its proper career. So, in his great trilogy, does Sir John Neale.[5]

What is basically important to Sir John Neale is (1) to dis-

[1] G. R. Elton, *England under the Tudors* (London, 1955 [reprinted 1959]), p. 168.   [2] Ibid. p. 14.

[3] *The Evolution of Parliament*, p. 268. Dr. Elton's objection to this view of the Act seems to depend upon his deduction that, because the Act was seldom used for the purpose mentioned, it was not intended to be so used (" Henry VIII's Act of Proclamations ", *E.H.R.*, lxxv (1960), 213, n. 2).   [4] Op. cit., pp. 174-5.

[5] J. E. Neale, *The Elizabethan House of Commons* (London, 1949) ; *Elizabeth I and her Parliaments, 1559-1581* (London, 1953) ; *Elizabeth I and her Parliaments, 1584-1601* (London, 1957).

pose of the legend of Tudor despotism, (2) " to banish the old illusion that early Stuart parliaments had few roots in the six-teenth century ",[1] and (3) to establish that by the end of that cen-tury " parliament had become a political force with which the Crown and government had to reckon ", this being " a change . . . brought about by developments in the power, position and prestige of the House of Commons ".[2] But Sir John Neale's more particular task is to elucidate these problems by discovering the " vital significance ", for the growth of parliament, of the reign of Elizabeth I.[3] Well aware of the fewness of her parlia-ments and the brevity of their sessions—only ten parliaments, comprising thirteen sessions averaging less than ten weeks each in duration, and with an average gap of over three years between each session[4] —he makes it abundantly clear that the age was still one of personal monarchy and rightly insists that parliament was not an ordinary but an extraordinary part of the constitution, and that it was none of its business to exercise supervision over the government of the country. But he achieves the first of his basic aims.* And if we treat as Elizabethan anticipations of early Stuart conditions the conversion of patronage into " a political weapon ",[5] " the growing disputatiousness of the Commons "[6] who were learning " the ineradicable lesson of defying their Sovereign "[7] (partly through the medium of " the concerted preparation behind many of the agitations "),[8] and the desire of the " opposition " members to initiate bills and to frame the agenda of parliament,[9] we may concede that Sir John Neale achieves even the second of his basic aims. But what of the third?

At least some historians would take the view that not later than the end of the fourteenth century parliament " had become a force with which the Crown and government had to reckon ", and that this was so from then on. We may therefore concentrate

---

[1] *Elizabeth I and her Parliaments, 1559-1581*, p. 11.   [2] Ibid. p. 16.
[3] *The Elizabethan House of Commons*, p. 12.
[4] Ibid. p. 381.   [5] Ibid. p. 241.   [6] Ibid. p. 382.
[7] *Elizabeth I and her Parliaments, 1559-1581*, p. 421.
[8] Ibid.   [9] Ibid. p. 28.

rather on the statement that whatever " change " took place had been " brought about by developments in the power, position and prestige of the House of Commons ". Sir John Neale has himself summarized developments in the position of the Commons between Henry VIII's accession and Elizabeth I's : " the House of Commons had acquired the right—not the exclusive right—to control the attendance of its Members ; it had created for itself the right to enforce its privilege of freedom from arrest ; it had invented a power to imprison offenders against its privileges and its dignity ; it had converted an uncertain prescriptive enjoyment of free speech into a formal privilege possessing revolutionary possibilities ; it had even established precedents for punishing licentious speech by Members, thus covertly encroaching on the jurisdiction of the Crown, though on each occasion it took care to recognize that discipline in such matters belonged to the Sovereign. In brief, it had arrogated to itself the functions of a court ".[1] This is a fair statement. But it cannot be overemphasized that its validity depends upon the qualifications and reservations, the language of scholarly caution, with which the writer has wisely tempered his assertions. Moreover, it is of first-rate importance to recognize a distinction between privileges which affected the power of the Lower House over its own members and towards the public, and those which affected its power to control or influence the government.

Of all these privileges mentioned by Sir John Neale the most important was the privilege of free speech. That, following Sir Thomas More's claim for freedom of speech in 1523, Henry VIII " had allowed opposition in parliament " (Elton[2]), is a statement which would have been more meaningful and conclusive had there not existed a " natural community of interests between him and his parliaments " (Elton[3]), and had the Commons done more than "exploit More's conception of the privilege as licence to oppose any bill or motion " (Neale[4]). The Commons' right to speak and vote against government measures, won by the time of Elizabeth I's accession, was something negative. What Elizabeth's

---

[1] *Elizabeth I and her Parliaments, 1559-1581*, p. 19.
[2] *England under the Tudors*, p. 171.   [3] Ibid.
[4] *Elizabeth I and her Parliaments, 1584-1601*, p. 435.

reign produced, says Sir John Neale, was an opposition which " wanted to initiate : to introduce bills and motions of their own, to frame the agenda of parliament ",[1] and needed freedom of speech in order to do so. But when we are considering the *power* of the Commons in that period, surely what we must ask is, first, whether the privilege upon which that desire depended for its realization was really enjoyed, and, second, whether that desire itself was actually fulfilled.

What chiefly upset the relations between Elizabeth and her Commons in the first half of her reign was the question of the royal succession and, more especially, religious and ecclesiastical issues. And " the conflicts and divergences " between them were such that " there was not a session free from collision of some sort ".[2] But there is no doubt that the Commons' enlarged claim to freedom of speech was contested. What is more, it was generally contested by the queen with success. Elizabeth, as Dr. Elton says, " put precisely those things out of bounds which the opposition wished to discuss ",[3] and the defence of freedom of speech itself in 1576 by Peter Wentworth only resulted in his imprisonment in the Tower (where he remained until, after a month, the queen remitted her displeasure). Admittedly, it was the Lower House itself which, startled by Wentworth's excessive use of what it was his aim to defend, appointed a committee of all the privy councillors who were M.P.s to decide his punishment.[4] But it can be of small comfort to the protagonists of the view that the Commons were developing political muscle at this time that, in this particular instance, the Commons were exercising their right of committal only to the detriment of their claim to freedom of speech. Wentworth's propensity to bold utterance again resulted in his committal in 1587. Then, at the outset of the parliament of 1593, Elizabeth defined liberty of speech in terms which went far to repudiate the Commons' claim. The Lord Keeper, having on the queen's behalf told the Speaker to suppress " any bill that passeth the Reach of a subiectes brayne to mencion", explained that what she would allow was "liberall but not licentious speech,

---

[1] *Elizabeth I and her Parliaments, 1559-1581*, p. 28.   [2] Ibid. p. 420.
[3] *England under the Tudors*, pp. 268-9.
[4] Neale, *Elizabeth I and her Parliaments, 1559-1581*, pp. 318-29.

libertie therefore but with dew limitacion ".   " The uerye trew libertie of the house ", went on the Lord Keeper, " was to say yea or no to Bills ": a member might briefly explain his reasons, but his freedom did not extend " to speak there of All causes . . . and to frame a forme of Relligion or a state of gouernment as to their idle braynes shall seem meetest ": no ruler " fitt for his state " would tolerate " such absurdities ".   Already, the Lord Keeper had made it clear that membership of the House would not pro-tect from punishment any M.P. who overstepped the bounds of " loyaltie and good discretion ": he ended his advice by saying that the queen hoped that " no man here longeth so much for his ruyne " or " to make such a perill to his own saffetye " as to offend, especially now that she had made the Commons "partakers of her entent and meaninge ".[1] Wentworth's third imprisonment, along with the imprisonment or sequestering of six other members,[2] for trespassing beyond the limits of discretion later in the same session, suitably enforced the queen's warnings.   What Went-worth's imprisonments for audacious speaking surely indicate is that the right he claimed was largely illusory in practice.   Evi-dently, such treatment did not succeed in gagging Wentworth, but the example made of him and others can only have had its effect on some less foolhardy than they.   Although parliament, by Sir John Neale's showing, was less tractable than used to be thought and " there was not a session free from collision of some sort ", that the queen was able to control her Commons and curb their fantasies is surely a tribute less to the growing power of the Lower House than to the continuing power of the sovereign.   In controlling her Commons Elizabeth sacrificed little if anything, certainly nothing vital, of her prerogative.   Restiveness in opposi-tion is not power, although it may lead to a claim to it.   A claim to power, important though it is, is not the same as power acquired and put to effective use.   Bickering, wrangling, petulance and

[1] Neale, *E.H.R.*, xxxi (1916), 136-7. This version of the speech is far superior to that of D'Ewes's *Journals* which included the following words: "Privi-ledge of Speech is granted, but you must know what priviledge you have, not to speak every one what he listeth, or what cometh in his brain to utter that ; but your priviledge is I or No." Another version has " your priuiledge is for such speech as shall be used with Iudgement and sobrietye " (ibid. p. 128).

[2] Neale, *Elizabeth I and her Parliaments, 1584-1601*, p. 278.

resentment are nothing of themselves. What counts is not the passion with which men create or enter into opposition, but that this opposition, whether passionate or not, should be successful in attaining its ends. Elizabeth's policy towards parliament was co-operation—and through members of her Privy Council in the Lower House she was in a fair way to obtain it—but, if she failed to obtain it, then mastery. In Sir John Neale's considered judgement, " from the constitutional point of view, the most important theme in our story is the relationship of the Puritan Movement to parliamentary development ".[1] We may use his own words as comment : that by 1601, " there was no longer a Puritan organization in the background, and the fanatical mentality of bygone assemblies was in disrepute ".[2] So much for the threat to personal monarchy and the preparation of the constitutional revolution of Stuart times.[3]

Elizabeth I's last parliament of 1601 witnessed no shortage of free speech, or of indignation, in the debates over royal monopolies. Indeed, there was a considerable amount of virulent abuse. But under the early Stuarts what the Commons conceived as their right to free speech was many times so honoured in the breach as to leave it at best precarious : illusory in practice. For those who spoke indiscreetly or intemperately were liable to be punished in some way. We may recall the imprisonment of Sir Thomas Wentworth and three other members after the Addled Parliament of 1614, when five more were forbidden to leave London and another four were dismissed from the commission of the peace. During the next parliament, in November 1621, occurred the arrest of Sandys along with Selden, James I himself explaining his reasons : " we think ourself very free and able to punish any man's misdemeanours in parliament, as well during their sitting as after ; which we mean not to spare hereafter, upon any occasion of any man's insolent behaviour there that shall be ministered unto us."[4] And this was no idle threat : the Commons'

---

[1] *Elizabeth I and her Parliaments, 1584-1601*, p. 436.
[2] Ibid. p. 437.
[3] Ibid. p. 435.
[4] *Select Statutes and other Constitutional Documents illustrative of the reigns of Elizabeth and James I*, ed. G. W. Prothero (Oxford, 1894), p. 310.

L*

protestation of 18 December, which included an assertion of their right to liberty of speech in discussing all questions of public concern, the king ripped out of their Journal with his own hands and, having dissolved parliament, imprisoned Sir Edward Coke and four other M.P.s (including Selden) and sent another four to act unwillingly as royal commissioners in Ireland. Charles I's second parliament (1626) witnessed the committal to the Tower of Eliot and Digges for alleged insolence of speech, and, following Charles's next parliament (1628-9), Eliot again and this time no fewer than eight other M.P.s were fined and sent to prison by the King's Bench, Eliot dying there in 1632, Valentine remaining in confinement until the Short Parliament of 1640. Their conduct stigmatized by the king himself as " disobedient and seditious ",[1] these M.P.s had been afforded no protection by privilege or right. Moreover, it was not until 1667 that these judgements were reversed as illegal and " against the freedom and privilege of Parliament ".[2] Meanwhile, several M.P.s had again been imprisoned after the Short Parliament. The famous attempted arrest of the Five Members for high treason in January 1642 was an infringement more dramatic, of course, but mainly because of Charles's personal intervention, his visit to the Lower House with an armed escort, and the escape of his intended victims with the connivance of the House. Not until the Bill of Rights was any constitutional safeguard found for freedom of speech, protection being then supplied by the reservation to parliament of all cases involving the privilege. Such privileges and rights as freedom from arrest at private suit, the right of the House to expel a member (exemplified in 1581 and 1585), the determination of contested elections and decisions upon the legality of returns (1604), are important evidence of the growing corporateness of the Commons, but, relative to the power of control of royal government by parliament, they are unsubstantial. Freedom of speech in the Commons, however, was a *sine qua non* of effective participation. Neither Tudor nor early Stuart parliaments enjoyed it without question and in comfort.

No one is likely to forget Professor Wallace Notestein's im-

[1] T. P. Taswell-Langmead, *English Constitutional History* (10th edn. by T. F. T. Plucknett), p. 422.   [2] Ibid. p. 424 n.

portant contribution in the Raleigh Lecture of 1924, entitled
" The Winning of the Initiative by the House of Commons ".[1]
What he most memorably demonstrated, in underlining the growing contentiousness of the Commons under James I, was how
much of this was due, negatively, to the king's failure (until 1614[2])
to influence elections with a view to enlisting a majority of supporters among the Commons, to the inadequacy in both number
and competence of the Privy Councillors in the House, and to the
king's inability to keep the Lords firmly on his side ; positively,
to the growth of " an entirely new Committee system " (especially
the growth of the Committee of the Whole House), by which
the Speaker's power was restricted and the power of the opposition leadership given greater scope. But, as in the struggle for
freedom of speech, so in these new developments, what was
being fashioned was the wherewithal to secure power, not power
itself. The new institutions, or rather practices, were means to
an end. Control ultimately depended on such, but by their invention and use control itself was not established.

One of the obvious ways of testing the control exercised by
parliament over the royal government and administration is to enquire (a) whether parliament could properly require the sovereign
to appoint important officials and councillors acceptable to it, (b)
whether, once so appointed, these were effectively made answerable to parliament, and (c) by what procedure parliament could,
if gravely dissatisfied with any aspect of their public conduct,
bring them to book.[3] During the medieval period, only in a

[1] *Proceedings of the British Academy*, vol. xi. This lecture was separately published by the Oxford University Press in 1924 and reprinted photographically in
1949.

[2] I regard Professor Notestein's opinion about royal interference in the 1614
elections as confirmed by the evidence contained in Chap. iii of Mr. T. L. Moir's
book, *The Addled Parliament of 1614* (Oxford, 1958). That there was " no great
conspiracy to pack the lower House " (ibid. p. 163) is not necessarily at variance
either with Mr. Moir's evidence in Chap. iii or the implication of his statement
that " the resentment of the gentry at ' interference ' in local elections found
tumultuous expression during the session " (ibid. p. 54).

[3] Cf. Charles I's definition of the rôle of the House of Commons : " an excellent Conserver of Liberty, but never intended for any share in Government, or
the chusing of them that should govern " (his answer to the Nineteen Propositions
composed by Sir John Colepeper, Chancellor of the Exchequer, and Viscount
Falkland, Secretary of State, 21 June 1642 [John Rushworth], *Historical Collections*

royal minority or when the affairs of the realm were so out of joint as to need drastic reforms requiring the appointment of officials and councillors whom parliament could trust, was the exclusive right of the Crown to appoint its own ministers at all disputed. This exclusive right to appoint was generally not disputed under either Tudors or Stuarts. But in the fourteenth and early fifteenth centuries there had been at least some occasions when parliament had felt moved to interfere. Moreover, on some of these and at other times the Commons had used the process of impeachment at the bar of the Upper House to secure the punishment of officials and others for crimes and misdemeanours offensive to the Crown and detrimental to the public weal. In the Good Parliament of 1376 the King's Chamberlain and the Steward of the Household (both of them peers), in 1386 the earl of Suffolk, the ex-Chancellor, in 1388 the royal judges, and in 1397 Archbishop Arundel, were all brought to trial in this way, in each case, save the last, in despite of the king and against his will. After Richard II's reign the procedure of impeachment was only once again used in the medieval period, namely, in 1450, when the duke of Suffolk was subjected to it. Thereafter it fell into abeyance until revived by the Commons in 1621. When seeking punishment for political offenders, the Tudors had in fact preferred to use Star Chamber or, if and when they used parliament, to initiate state trials by bills of attainder introduced in the Upper House. Whether or not the Tudor Commons were unequal to the strain of making impeachments, they did not in fact do so. It was, therefore, a medieval instrument which was revived in 1621 against the Lord Chancellor (Bacon) and was used again in 1624 against the Lord Treasurer (Cranfield), each of whom was condemned for bribery. Between then and 1688 there were about forty cases of impeachment. The Commons would have used it against Buckingham in 1626, had not Charles forestalled them by dissolving parliament. Early in the Long Parliament they put it to unprecedentedly extensive use against Strafford, Laud, Finch (the Lord Keeper), Windebank (Secretary of State), thirteen of the

(London, 1721), iv. 731). For a discussion of the general constitutional significance of Charles's statement, see C. C. Weston, " The Theory of Mixed Monarchy Under Charles I and After ", *E.H.R.*, lxxv. 429.

bishops, and six judges. And so on and so forth. To the last quarter of the seventeenth century, in the trial of Danby in 1679, belongs, however, the formulation of two very important problems in the history of the procedure, important for what their settlement would imply, namely, that impeachment, whatever it had been originally, was not now at the suit of the Crown. The two problems were : (a) was a royal pardon pleadable to an impeachment by the Commons that was depending? and (b) did impeachment abate if parliament were prorogued or dissolved? The first question, important because a royal pardon could be used to screen ministers of the Crown from parliamentary justice and so render entirely nugatory their pretended responsibility, was answered to the detriment of the prerogative in the Act of Settlement of 1701. The second was to be answered in the same spirit, but not until 1791 (during the impeachment of Warren Hastings), the reason for the long postponement of a settlement of this crucial issue of principle being that the procedure itself had become anachronistic and moribund " as the criminal law gradually embraced a wider variety of financial misdeeds, and as the growth of ministerial responsibility provided a sufficient sanction against ministers whose political conduct gave offence ".[1]

Earlier in this paper, I have referred to the importance, for parliamentary legislation by statute, of petitions promoted by the Commons. It was in the fourteenth century that these became " the normal basis of legislation " of this kind, provided they were agreed by the Lords and assented to by the king. Even though from the middle of the fifteenth century onwards parliamentary law-making became increasingly officially-inspired, the Lower House inevitably remained the source of origin of much of the legislation issued with parliamentary authority. Legislation by petition from below was, however, subject to a royal power to make amendments which seem not to have required " reference-back ", and in any case depended absolutely upon the royal assent. The sovereign's right to veto bills was unquestioned in both theory and practice, a vital and cherished part of the prerogative. In theory it still survives. But for how long did it survive in practice? When did the Crown effectively cease to

[1] Taswell-Langmead, op. cit. pp. 590-601.

reject what both Lords and Commons willed to have law? In the medieval period, the veto was freely used. Under Elizabeth I it could still be extensively used, at least on occasion.[1] It is true that its use became infrequent under the Stuarts, but this was because they preferred to use their dispensing power, Charles II and James II a suspending power as well. And the revival of the royal veto under William III can best be understood in the light of the recent declaration, in the Bill of Rights, that these special powers of dispensing and suspending were illegal except when used with parliamentary consent, which was virtually to vitiate their prerogatival character. William III's revival of the veto was a cause of disappointment, and it was short-lived.[2] Only once, in 1708, did Anne refuse her assent to a bill (the Scottish Militia Bill), since when that faintly derisive formula, *Le Roi s'advisera*, has never been used. As Miss Betty Kemp has said, " As far as legislation went, parliament seemed to have vindicated its supremacy and, in this sphere, not only to have deprived the King of independent power but also to have deprived him, in practice, of his position of equality with the other two parts of parliament ".[3] In future, the Crown, if opposed to a parliamentary bill, would need to defeat it in its earlier stages by political contrivance.

The question of parliamentary control of government sooner or later imposes an enquiry into taxation, to secure parliamentary sanction for which was the main single object of the summoning of most parliaments before this was made regular at the end of the seventeenth century. Upon direct taxation, subsidies levied throughout the land generally on men's lands or goods, and also upon the regular continuation of indirect taxation, the customs and subsidies on imports and exports, depended the royal administration, especially during an emergency or in the conduct of a foreign policy resulting in military enterprise abroad and entailing heavy expenditure. The acid test of the power of parliament lies in its control of these revenues.

---

[1] Cf. the message from the queen delivered by the Speaker to the Commons on 27 February 1593 : " it is in my power to assent or dissent to anything done in Parliament . . ." (Prothero, op. cit. p. 125).
[2] Kemp, op. cit. pp. 26-27.   [3] Ibid. p. 27.

Recognition of the need for the consent of parliament to both direct and indirect taxation had been secured in the medieval period. And that this consent was then a reality was, so far as direct taxation is concerned, sometimes convincingly demonstrated by a refusal by parliament to meet the demands of the Crown and, so far as indirect taxation is concerned, by changes in the rates of the customs, by variations in the period for which these grants were made available, and even, although only very occasionally, by dramatic token suspensions of the customs for brief intervals of time.[1] Let me hasten to add that under Edward III the consent of the Commons had become equally essential with that of the Lords, and that in 1407 it was established that the Lords should merely assent to what had been granted independently by the Commons who were, moreover, literally to be left with the last word, since the final declaration of a grant was then reserved for their Speaker[2]: by 1455 the Lords' power of amendment extended in practice only to a reduction of the amount of a grant, not to its enhancement.[3] In view of the assertions of historians of parliament in the Tudor period that the power of the Commons was perceptibly growing in that period, it is necessary to point out that even the long-established and elementary right of the Commons to initiate all money bills was jeopardized so late in Elizabeth I's reign as 1593. When, on this occasion, the Lower House had offered two subsidies, and the government had succeeded in getting the Upper House to make a bigger grant, the Lords demanded a conference with the Commons where Burghley stated that they insisted on *three* subsidies. Sir Francis Bacon objected that this amendment, as it stood, was a breach of the Commons' privilege. But apparently all that he could do to protect this privilege was to suggest that the Commons should themselves offer the three subsidies the Lords had already proposed : and it was this grant which finally passed.[4] " In this

---

[1] Such suspensions occurred in 1381 and 1385 (*Rot. Parl.* iii. 104b, 204b).

[2] *Rot. Parl.* iii. 611. Reference was expressly made to this precedent in the dispute over the subsidy in 1593 (Sir Simonds D'Ewes, *Journals of all the Parliaments during the Reign of Queen Elizabeth* [London, 1682], p. 485b).

[3] S. B. Chrimes, *English Constitutional Ideas in the Fifteenth Century* (Cambridge, 1936), p. 361.

[4] Neale, *Elizabeth I and her Parliaments, 1584-1601*, pp. 300-10.

serious clash between the houses—the first in the century—the
Commons ", says Dr. Elton, " had successfully protected their
right to initiate all money bills."[1] So, in a sense, they had. But we
can hardly fail to observe that the price of protection eventually
paid by the Commons was their acquiescence in the outcome of
the original offence. It was not until 1678 that the Commons
finally made good their claim that money bills must originate in
their House. But they were then able to add to this the stipul-
ation that, although the Lords might still reject their money bills,
they could not amend them, not even by reduction.

The power of parliament and especially of the Commons has
always depended in the last resort upon control of taxation.
This control underwent a contraction throughout the Tudor
period, partly because parliament was ready to allow all of the
Tudor monarchs at the beginning of each of their reigns and for
life the customs-dues and tonnage and poundage, which together
formed a very substantial and certainly highly necessary part of
the constant revenues of the Crown. The fact that these grants
were " in the bag " from the beginning of a reign meant that the
bargaining power of the Commons was reduced *pro tanto*. For
grants for the life of the king there were, it is true, medieval precedents (in 1398,[2] 1415, 1453, 1465, and 1484) : each one of the
successors of Edward III, save Henry IV, had enjoyed such a vote.
The grant made to Edward IV lasted eighteen years. The other
pre-Tudor grants, however, had been in the event short-lived, so
that all of them together accounted for no more than about a third
of the period involved. Moreover, of all the medieval kings who
received this mark of parliamentary approbation, only Richard III
did so in his first parliament, that is, as though it were a matter of
course. Then, however, the grant of the customs and tonnage
and poundage did become just that : from this time forward they
were never withheld until, in Charles I's first parliament, the
Commons refused to grant the subsidies for more than a year.
Charles, insisting that they should be voted him for life as before,
was therefore only claiming what each of his last seven predeces-

---

[1] Elton, *England under the Tudors*, p. 462.

[2] Richard II's grant extended only to the wool-subsidy, tonnage and poundage
not being included.   Later grants for life covered all of these subsidies.

sors had been allowed. Evidently the Lords felt much as the king did ; at least they rejected the limitation. Perhaps Charles had a right to *expect* a grant for life. But no more. And there is no doubt that the Commons, following medieval precedents, had every right not to make such a grant, unless their right of consent was to be set aside as unreal or negligible. We may admire the stubbornness of the Lower House over this issue, but we shall avoid any risk of exaggerating their power to enforce their right if we remember that Charles collected the taxes in question without any parliamentary authority, continuing to levy them even after 1629, when he actually renounced all right of his own conceiving. So long as the king was fully entitled to dissolve parliament at his pleasure and was able to use this prerogative to choke opposition when it became intolerable, it was next to impossible for the Commons to secure the abolition of levies collected by mere royal authority, especially if, as for example in the case of impositions under James I and ship-money under Charles I, there was current at the time some genuine doubt as to their illegality. The Commons' power was still permissive : in the last resort it depended, as their existence did, upon the king's will. It could be argued, of course, that Charles's wilful exaction of levies legally requiring the Commons' consent without that consent helped to produce the explosion which brought his system crashing to the ground and eventually cost him his head. But had the years made him wiser, more appreciative of the need for accommodation and compromise, and careful to avoid the appearance of duplicity, he might still have escaped the graver consequences of his financial, as well as other, policies.

The Tudor period witnessed a contraction in parliamentary control of taxation, not only because tonnage and poundage, etc., were granted for a reign once and for all at its outset, but also because the Tudors sometimes resorted to very profitable extra-parliamentary forms of financial levy, such as benevolences and forced loans (which parliament now and then abjectly sanctioned in retrospect, treating them as taxes or, in the case of loans, cancelling the king's indebtedness).[1] But not only for this reason.

[1] In 1495 parliament sanctioned the benevolence of 1491, and in 1529 and 1544 it released the king from any obligation to repay forced loans.

To be effective, parliamentary control of taxation must needs contain more than recognition of the elementary principle of simple consent. If parliament was really to control taxation, it was necessary that it should be able to make its grants conditional upon their appropriation to specific purposes, and to ensure that these appropriations were adhered to, either by the appointment of special treasurers supervising the receipt and expenditure of grants or simply by audit of accounts. Medieval parliamentary grants, from 1340[1] onwards, were with a fair constancy tied to expenditure in certain directions, mainly to finance war or measures for defence. The appointment of special treasurers or recei...ers in charge of tax-funds and the use of audit (or view) of accounts were also resorted to at the Commons' demand.[2] It is true that both these last devices were always precarious, were employed only spasmodically (and even then by royal condescension), and that after Henry IV's reign the first was hardly ever used and the second not at all (so far as the records show). But, under Yorkists and Tudors alike, *all* of these devices were in abeyance. In fact, appropriation to specific objects was not to be resurrected until 1624,[3] was then not again re-introduced until

[1] See G. L. Harriss, " The Commons' Petitions of 1340 ", *E.H.R.*, lxxviii (1963), 628, 642-3, 645-6.

[2] Special treasurers of moneys voted for the wars were in office in 1377-9, 1382, 1385-7, 1390-1, 1404-6, and 1450. Audits of their accounts were allowed to the Commons in 1378, 1379, 1404, and 1406.

[3] It was not as if the need for a clause of appropriation in the subsidy bill had never, in the meantime, entered the heads of M.P.s. At the beginning of the parliament of 1593 the Lord Keeper gave out that the principal reason of its meeting was " preparation of aid . . . against the mighty and great forces of the King of Spain, bent and intended against this Realm ", and the Commons' Committee for the aid soon advised a grant of two subsidies. According to D'Ewes's *Journal*, Nathaniel Bacon, himself one of the Committee, supplemented its report with a statement that some of the members had proposed that " the present necessity of the Causes moving them to offer the said double Subsidy " should be " set down and inserted in the Bill ". And the *Journal* then goes on to relate that Serjeant Harris desired " in the subsidies to have it set down, that those Subsidies be to maintain a War impulsive and defensive against the Spaniard ". The main point of this intervention (as the next speaker, Sir Walter Raleigh, made clear) was to ensure that a state of open war with Spain should be declared. Nonetheless, the wish that the grant should be specifically appropriated to such a war was itself so strongly felt as to result in a demand that this condition should be " inserted into the preamble of the said Bill " (op. cit. pp. 477-8). The burden of the long

1665, and was only made invariable after the Revolution of 1688. And audit, although revived in 1624 and 1641, was only indisputably re-established in 1667.

What I have been trying to do is to demonstrate that if we seek for " a great divide " in the history of parliament and especially of its eventually dominant House, we can best find it in the seventeenth century, in the late seventeenth century, or about the turn of the seventeenth century. And the so many convergent indications of a fundamental change in the position of the Commons appearing in the late seventeenth century may perhaps drive us to ask ourselves whether the Tudor period can have been so really important for the history of the development of the Lower House as is sometimes made out. And if we decide that that degree of importance is hard to substantiate, then perhaps we should ask, too, whether the medieval Commons can have been so immature and ineffective as is also sometimes made out, not least by those who exaggerate the importance of their Tudor successors. Now it would appear that the real break in the history of the Commons comes not with the Tudor period, even though it was then that the Reformation enlarged the scope of the intervention of parliament in public affairs, and that religious and ecclesiastical questions produced quite unprecedented states of emotional tension, especially among the Commons. Nor does this break come with the abolition by the Commons of

and eloquent preamble to the subsidy bill was, admittedly, the need to furnish the defence of the realm. But, although it was made evident that the King of Spain was the enemy meant, the object of the expenditure of the grant was given no greater particularity than " for our Defence " (*Statutes of the Realm*, vol. iv, part 2, p. 867). Specific appropriation had obviously been evaded in the drafting.

The appropriation of 1624 was of quite a different order : it was " for the defence of this your Realme of England, the securing of your Kingdom of Ireland, the assistance of your neighbours the States of the United Provinces and other your Majesties friends and allies, and for the setting forth of your Royall Navie ". Seven sworn treasurers were appointed, their expenditure to be controlled by warrant of the members of the Council of War. The treasurers were to account to the House of Commons which was empowered to commit offenders to the Tower, and these were to remain as close prisoners until delivered by the order of the House. The offences of peers were to be brought to the notice of the Lords, who were to have similar powers of committal (*Statutes of the Realm*, vol. iv, part 2, pp. 1247, 1261-2).

M

both the Monarchy and the House of Lords in 1649, because at
that point the old constitution was merely suspended for a time.
It comes, rather, with the end of the power of the Crown to govern
effectively without parliament.   And as soon as parliament has
made itself indispensable and even inevitable (but when the peers
have established their freedom to disobey the royal summons to
attend) we can say that parliament has moved into a significantly
new phase of its history.   The constitution of the *ancien régime* is
now really at an end : not moribund, but defunct.   What the
Tudor Commons had been creating by organizing their own self-
discipline, for example, controlling their own attendance, sending to prison offenders against their privileges, keeping their own
Journal, and so emphasizing their corporateness, was not power,
much less authority, but merely potentiality.   Or rather what they
had done was to add by these developments to an already existing
potentiality, the potentiality furnished by the medieval Commons,
at the same time allowing that medieval potentiality to be diminished or to lose some of its value by disuse, it being left to the
seventeenth-century Commons not only to exploit and fulfil that
Tudor potentiality but also to re-discover and salvage what had
been lost of the medieval potentiality, and to do the first of these
things all the more effectively by doing the second as well.   The
seventeenth-century lawyers, searching for precedents in the parliamentary records of the fourteenth and fifteenth centuries
appropriate and apposite to their own situation, mistakes of interpretation though they committed from time to time, suffered
from no delusions as to the importance and relevance of the work
of their medieval forebears.   What, in my opinion, actuated them
was a consciousness of continuing or recurrent constitutional and
political realities or situations.   The basic English constitutional
and political problem of what we call later medieval and early
modern times was how to control a monarchy which, though at no
time despotic, was never less than a monarchy.   The Tudors,
in taking into partnership the community of which parliament
was the microcosm, were using the familiar Plantagenet expedient:
participation in government at the sovereign's command.   But
if we regard parliament, as certainly some medieval Englishmen
were capable of doing, as a means of limiting monarchical author-

ity[1]—the expression of a *dominium politicum et regale*—the Tudor period was generally one in which the traditions of the medieval Commons were not, so far as the Commons' relations with the royal government are concerned, substantially extended ; and if in some respects they were expanded, we should recognize that in others they underwent a contraction. It was only in the seventeenth century, when the state of the monarchy prompted and the national situation permitted it, that such of those medieval traditions as had been in abeyance and yet were valuable, experienced a real and now revolutionary re-quickening.

[1] Hinton, op. cit. pp. 410-17.

EDITORIAL NOTES

1. The Commons and the Council in the Reign of Henry IV.

p. 31* Reprinted from *E.H.R.* LXXIX (1964), 1–30. J. L. Kirby covered some of the same ground in an essay published almost simultaneously: 'Councils and Councillors of Henry IV', *T.R.H.S.*, 5th ser., XIV (1964).

p. 31** See the critical assessment of Henry IV's parliamentary title by G. Lapsley, *E.H.R.* XLIX (1934), reprinted in his *Crown, Community and Parliament*, pp. 273 ff.

p. 33* The 'advice' is translated by B. Wilkinson, *Constitutional History of England in the Fifteenth Century*, pp. 237–8.

p. 39* Translated C. Stephenson and F. G. Marcham, *Sources of English Constitutional History*, p. 260.

p. 45* Translated Wilkinson, *op. cit.*, pp. 239–40.

p. 45** Translated Wilkinson, *op. cit.*, pp. 239–40.

p. 46* Subsequently published in *B.I.H.R.* XXXVII (1964).

p. 48* Translated B. Wilkinson, *Constitutional History of Medieval England, 1216–1399*, II, 224.

p. 51* All revenues arising from 'wardships, marriages, issues of the temporalities of vacant archbishoprics (and) bishoprics, escheats, forfeitures, alien priories, customs and all other commodities, profits, revenues and emoluments of the kingdom, both fixed and occasional'.

p. 53* 'And we further command you that against our coming to our city of London, which with God's help will be on Tuesday next, you will have a copy made of all the statutes and ordinances made in our last parliament to be kept continually by us.'

p. 59* 'Our redoubted and sovereign lord, we commend ourselves to your highness as humbly as we know how to do and can do. And most redoubted lord, be pleased to know that yesterday (Friday), after we had left your noble presence, we assembled at the Friars Preachers to discuss many important affairs and matters touching the honour, well-being and security of your royal person and the noble estate of yourself and your kingdom; and our purpose was to declare our intention and advice thereon on

Saturday morning about seven o'clock. And because we were then certified that you had left London early to go where it pleased you, we assembled afterwards at the said Friars and by common assent charged your faithful liegeman, John Dorewarde, a member of your council, to come to your most honourable presence to show and declare to you the said affairs and matters on our behalf in the presence of the Earl of Somerset, your chamberlain, and the Earl of Worcester, steward of your household, or one of them. May it please your royal highness to hear him graciously about these affairs and matters and to accord him firm faith and credence in this respect; and inform us by the said earls what your will and intention are, to the great comfort of your humble lieges and servants, who pray that the Blessed Trinity will grant you good and long life to the honour and satisfaction of God and for the good governance of your realm.'

To our most redoubted and   Your humble lieges and servants,
sovereign lord   all of your great council.

2. Acts of Resumption in the Lancastrian Parliaments, 1399-1456.

p. 61* Reprinted from *E.H.R.* LXXIII (1958), 583-613. Later Acts of Resumption between 1461 and 1495 are discussed by the same author in *E.H.R.* LXXI (1956) and LXXIX (1964).

p. 62* Only the Ancient Custom granted to Edward I in 1275 was recognized by the Lords Ordainers. They abolished the New Custom on alien merchants, instituted by Edward I in 1303.

p. 63* 'Be it noted that castles, cities and towns, vills, manors and hundreds which were held [through a royal grant] by diverse persons for life or a term of years had been recorded in the memoranda roll of 7 Edward III [under the heading of] the proffer of the Michaelmas term and [under the same heading] in the memoranda rolls of the preceding years. [But they had not been thus recorded since that date] and should not be mentioned unless they had reverted to the king, because previous to their reversion nothing can be exacted for the king's benefit. A similar memorandum should be inserted at the end of each proffer.'

p. 69* On this parliament and its reforming programme see A. L. Brown, *supra*, chapter 1 and J. L. Kirby, *T.R.H.S.*, 5th ser., XIV (1964), 54-6.

p. 77* 'By the lord cardinal on king's mandate under the signet issued during parliament' and 'by signet [warrant] issued in parliament, by testimony of J. Stanley, B. Hawley and others.'

p. 91* There is no evidence that Henry suffered from recurrent insanity after he had recovered from the first bout of this illness in 1454. *Cf.* J. R. Lander in *Bulletin of John Rylands Library*, XLIII (1960), 46–69.

3. Attainder and Forfeiture, 1453–1509.

p. 92* Reprinted from *Hist. J.* IV (1961), 119–51. See also M. H. Keen, 'Treason trials under the Law of Arms', *T.R.H.S.*, 5th ser., XII (1962).

p. 94* Similar conclusions are summarized by K. B. McFarlane, 'The Wars of the Roses', *P. Brit. Ac.* L (1964), 115–19.

p. 94** 67 per cent [instead of 76]. This correction has been requested by Professor Lander.

p. 94† For the background to Edward IV's use of attainders see J. R. Lander, 'Marriage and politics in the fifteenth century: the Nevilles and the Wydevilles', *B.I.H.R.* XXXVI (1963) and 'The treason and death of the duke of Clarence', *Canadian Journal of History*, II (1967).

p. 106* For the background to Henry VII's use of attainders see W. H. Dunham, *Lord Hastings' Indentured Retainers* (New Haven, 1955). pp. 90–116; G. R. Elton, 'Henry VII: rapacity and remorse', *Historical Journal* I (1958), J. P. Cooper's reply, *ibid.* II (1959) and Elton's counter-reply, *ibid.* IV (1961); B. P. Wolffe, 'Henry VII's land revenues and chamber finance', *E.H.R.* LXXIX (1964).

4. London and Parliament in the Reign on Henry VIII.

p. 125* Reprinted from *B.I.H.R.* XXXV (1962), 129–49.

5. The Commons' Privilege of Free Speech in Parliament.

p. 147* Reprinted from *Tudor Studies presented . . . to Albert Frederick Pollard* (ed. R. W. Seton-Watson, 1924), pp. 257–86. See also chapters 9 and 10 *infra*. Subsequent publications making further important contributions to this subject include J. S. Roskell, *The Commons and their Speakers in English Parliaments, 1376–1523* (1965); J. E. Neale, *Elizabeth I and her Parliaments*, 2 vols. (1953 and 1957); Conyers Read, *Mr. Secretary Cecil and Queen Elizabeth* (1955) and *Lord Burghley and Queen Elizabeth* (1960).

p. 147** For recent views on some aspects of parliamentary history under Henry IV see vol. I, chapter 13 and *supra*, chapters 1 and 2.

p. 147† Subsequently published as *The Anonimalle Chronicle, 1333-1381* (Manchester, 1927).

p. 150* 'That what he should thus say in this parliament on behalf of the said Commons should not be interpreted as coming from him personally or on his own individual initiative.'

p. 150** 'Firstly, on behalf of the commons. Should he happen to say anything which might sound as prejudicial, damaging, slanderous or evil towards our lord the king or towards his crown or as belittling the honour and estate of the great lords of the kingdom, this should be ignored by the king and the lords as if it had never been said. Because the commons are moved by nothing save an overriding desire to maintain and safeguard the honour and the estate of our lord the king and the rights of his crown in all things and [by a wish] to preserve the reverence due to the other lords in everything.' This motive may also help to explain the concern of the commons about tale-bearers who reported to the king what was said in their assembly: H. G. Richardson, *T.R.H.S.*, 4th ser., XXVIII (1946), 45, n. 1.

p. 152* 'Your humble son Henry, Prince of Wales and the lords spiritual and temporal beg . . .'

p. 152** This practice of 'intercommuning' is discussed more fully in J. G. Edwards, *The Commons in Medieval English Parliaments* (9th Creighton lecture of the University of London, 1958). For the most complete study of the commons as petitioners in the fifteenth century, see A. R. Myers, *E.H.R.* LII (1937), 385-404, 590-613.

p. 153* 'Because the matters submitted to them touch so highly and so nearly their liege lord they asked that certain prelates, earls and barons of the realm should be vouchsafed to them . . . to intercommune with them.'

p. 153** 'It would be neither profitable nor honourable to treat of such great things and grave matters without the counsel and aid of greater and wiser persons than we are ourselves and we should not begin this without the consent of the lords.'

p. 153† 'To aid and counsel us, to hear what we shall say and to bear testimony to this.'

p. 155* On this change see also T. F. T. Plucknett, 'Ellesmere on Statutes', *L.Q.R.* LX (1944), 247-9.

p. 162* 'The king's majesty will not deny honest freedom of speech.'

p. 165* 'That which is done in parliament by a statute shall not be annulled without parliament.'

p. 166* The evidence for this statement is discussed more fully in S. B. Chrimes, *English Constitutional Ideas in the Fifteenth Century* (Cambridge, 1936), pp. 231–3.

p. 166** *Cf. supra.*, chapter 4, p. 135 for other similar provisos added to enactments in this parliament.

6. Parliamentary Drafts, 1529–1540.

p. 177* Reprinted from *B.I.H.R.* XXV (1952), 117–32. A supplementary note was published *ibid.* XXVII (1954), 198–200.

p. 178* See also E. W. Ives, 'The genesis of the Statute of Uses', *E.H.R.* LXXXII (1967) and G. R. Elton 'The Law of Treason in the Early Reformation', *Historical Journal*, XI (1968).

p. 180* Subsequent publications include J. P. Cooper, 'The Supplication against the Ordinaries Reconsidered', *E.H.R.* LXXII (1957); M. J. Kelly, 'The Submission of the Clergy', *T.R.H.S.*, 5th ser., XV (1965); J. J. Scarisbrick, *Henry VIII* (1958), pp. 297–300.

p. 185* For the London tithes *cf. supra*, chapter 4, pp. 143–6.

p. 189* For a detailed reconsideration of the Act of Proclamations by Elton see *E.H.R.* LXXV (1960), 208–22.

p. 191* Elton subsequently discussed this draft in *Econ. H.R.*, 2nd ser., VI (1953), 55–67. For William Marshall, a possible author of this draft, see J. K. McConica, *English Humanists and Reformation Politics under Henry VIII and Edward VI* (Oxford, 1965), pp. 136–8 and *passim*.

7. The Political Creed of Thomas Cromwell.

p. 193* Reprinted from *T.R.H.S.*, 5th ser., VI (1956), 69–92. There was a lengthy debate on Dr. Elton's view of the 'revolution in government' in Henry VIII's reign in the pages of *Past and Present* nos. 25–6, 29, 31 (1963–5). Other recent works dealing with the problems discussed in this article include: A. G. Dickens, *Thomas Cromwell and the English Reformation* (1953); A. G. Dickens, *The English Reformation* (1964), especially chs. 5–8; J. K. McConica, *English Humanists and Reformation Politics under Henry VIII* (1965); S. E. Lehmberg, 'Supremacy and Viceregency: a Re-examination', *E.H.R.* LXXXI (1966); J. J. Scarisbrick, *Henry VIII* (1968).

p. 196* 'The highest title of authority . . . head of the church.'

p. 197* 'Which is not either what I understood him to say from his own mouth or from those who partook of his counsel.'

p. 203* 'The King ought to be under the law.'

p. 203** For one contribution by Cromwell to the growth of the jurisdiction of the common law courts, see E. W. Ives, 'The Genesis of the Statute of Uses', *E.H.R.* LXXXII (1967), 673 ff.

p. 204* See also A. J. Slavin, *Politics and Profit: a Study of Sir Ralph Sadler, 1507–47* (1966), 17–22, for a re-examination of the evidence.

p. 205* See also G. R. Elton, *supra*, ch. 6.

p. 206* See also G. R. Elton, 'The Law of Treason in the Early Reformation', *Historical Journal*, XI (1968), 211–36.

p. 206** See also G. R. Elton, *E.H.R.* LXXV (1960), 208 ff.

p. 208* 'In any one realm it is proper that there should be one ruling authority only.' There is a complete translation of this work by A. Gewirth, *Marsilius of Padua, 'Defender of the Peace'*, II (1956).

p. 209* 'A rule which commands and coerces transgressors.'

p. 211* Printed G. R. Elton, *The Tudor Constitution*, pp. 344–9.

p. 211** 'As the emperor in the empire.'

p. 211† 'The king recognizes no superior and is emperor within his kingdom.'

p. 212* See also R. Koebner, ' "The Imperial Crown of this Realm:" Henry VIII, Constantine and Polydore Vergil', *B.I.H.R.* XXVI (1953).

8. *The Elizabethan Acts of Supremacy and Uniformity.*

p. 217* Reprinted from *E.H.R.* LXV (1950), 304–32.

p. 217** For a commentary on Maitland's excursions into Tudor history, see H. E. Bell, *Maitland: a Critical Examination and Assessment*, pp. 124 ff. For a more extended treatment of the religious settlement in its parliamentary context, see J. E. Neale, *Queen Elizabeth and her Parliaments, 1559–1581*, pp. 51 ff. Conyers Read, *Mr. Secretary Cecil and Queen Elizabeth* (1955), pp. 126–33, substantially accepts Neale's conclusions. Extracts from the acts are conveniently available in G. R. Elton, *The Tudor Constitution*, pp. 363–8, 401–4 and fuller texts in G. W. Prothero, *Select Statutes and other Constitutional Documents illustrative of the Reigns of Elizabeth and James I*, pp. 1–20.

9. Peter Wentworth.

p. 246* Reprinted from *E.H.R.* XXXIX (1924), 36–54, 175–205. See also chapter 5, *supra*. Subsequent publications concerned with Peter Wentworth include J. E. Neale, *Elizabeth I and her Parliaments*, 2 vols., 1953 and 1957; Conyers Read, *Lord Burghley and Queen Elizabeth* (1960); P. Collinson, *The Elizabethan Puritan Movement* (1967).

10. Perspectives in English Parliamentary History.

p. 296* Reprinted from *Bulletin of the John Rylands Library*, XLVI (1964).

p. 302* 'Whether the king, whenever it pleased him, could dissolve parliament and command his lords and commons to depart therefrom, or not?'

p. 304* See J. G. Edwards in vol. I., ch. 10.

p. 307* But see J. Hurstfield, 'Was there a Tudor Despotism after all?' *T.R.H.S.* 5th ser., XVII (1967).

p. 309* On the whole question of free speech, see J. E. Neale, *supra*, ch. 5.

p. 317* On the other hand, the customs' accounts reveal that, on a number of occasions in the reigns of Richard II and Henry IV, the 'suspended' duties continued to be collected during periods when they were supposed to be in abeyance.

SELECT BIBLIOGRAPHY

I HANDBOOKS AND SOURCES

(a) *Lists of parliaments and related assemblies*

Handbook of British Chronology, ed. Powicke, F. M. and Fryde, E. B. (2nd ed., London, 1961).

(b) *Collections of sources in English (original or translated)*

Chrimes, S. B. and Brown, A. L., *Select Documents of English Constitutional History, 1307–1485* (London, 1961).

Elton, G. R., *The Tudor Constitution* (Cambridge, 1960).

Prothero, G. W. (ed.)., *Select Statutes and other Constitutional Documents illustrative of the Reigns of Elizabeth and James I* (Oxford, 1894).

Stephenson, C. and Marcham, F. G. (eds.), *Sources of English Constitutional History* (New York, 1938).

Tanner, J. R., *Tudor Constitutional Documents, 1485–1603* (2nd ed., Cambridge, 1951).

Wilkinson, B., *Constitutional History of England in the Fifteenth Century* (London, 1964).

(c) *Major collections of original sources*

D'Ewes, S., *The Journals of all the Parliaments during the Reign of Queen Elizabeth, both of the House of Lords and the House of Commons* (London, 1682; 1693).

Hughes, P. L. and Larkin, J. F., *Tudor Royal Proclamations, I, The Early Tudors, 1485–1553* (New Haven, 1964).

Journals of the House of Commons, I: 1547–1628 (London, 1803).

Journals of the House of Lords, I–II (London, 1846).

Rotuli Parliamentorum, III–VI (London, 1783).

Statutes of the Realm (11 vols., London, 1810–28), vols. II–IV.

(d) *Bibliographies and bibliographical studies*

Cuttino, G. P., 'Medieval Parliament Reinterpreted', *Speculum*, XLI (1966).

Edwards, J. G., *Historians and the Medieval English Parliament* (Glasgow, 1960).

Hoyt, R. S., 'Recent Publications in the United States and Canada on the History of Representative Institutions', *Speculum*, XXIX (1954).

Levine, M., *Tudor England, 1485–1603* (Cambridge, 1968: a Biblographical Handbook).

Read, C. (ed.), *Bibliography of British History, Tudor Period, 1485–1603* (2nd. ed., Oxford, 1959).

Wilkinson, B., 'Fact and Fancy in Fifteenth-Century English History', *Speculum*, XLII (1967).

II GENERAL STUDIES

(a) *General, constitutional and legal histories*

Chrimes, S. B., *English Constitutional Ideas in the XV Century* (Cambridge, 1936).

Chrimes, S. B., *Introduction to the Administrative History of Medieval England* (Oxford, 1952).

Dickens, A. G., *The English Reformation* (London, 1964).

Elton, G. R., *England under the Tudors* (London, 1955).

Elton, G. R., *The Tudor Revolution in Government* (Cambridge, 1953).

Holdsworth, W. S., *History of English Law*, vols. I–V (London, various editions; vol. I, 7th ed. revised by Chrimes, S. B., 1956; vols. II–V, 1936–45).

Hurstfield, J., 'Was there a Tudor Despotism after all?', *T.R.H.S.*, 5th ser., XVII (1967).

Jacob, E. F., *The Fifteenth Century, 1399–1485* (Oxford, 1961).

Jolliffe, J. E. A., *Constitutional History of Medieval England* (3rd ed., London, 1954).

Keir, D. L., *Constitutional History of Modern Britain since 1485* (7th ed., London, 1964).

Lyon, B., *Constitutional and Legal History of Medieval England* (New York, 1960).

Mackie, J. D., *The Earlier Tudors, 1485–1558* (Oxford, 1952).

Plucknett, T. F. T., *Concise History of the Common Law* (5th ed., London, 1956).

Stubbs, W., *Constitutional History of England*, III (5th ed., Oxford, 1903).

Zeeveld, W. G., *Foundations of Tudor Policy* (Cambridge, Mass., 1948).

(b) *Comparative studies of representative institutions*

Cam, H. M., Marongiu A. and Stökl, G., 'Recent work and Present views on the Origins and Development of Representative Assemblies', *Relazioni del X Congresso di Scienze Storiche*, I (Florence, 1955).

McIlwain, C. H., 'Medieval Estates', *Cambridge Medieval History*, VII (Cambridge, 1958).

Marongiu, A., *Medieval Parliaments: a Comparative Study* (London, 1968).

Myers, A. R., 'The English Parliament and the French Estates-General in the Middle Ages', *S.I.C.* XXIV (1961).

Richardson, H. G. and Sayles, G. O., *The Irish Parliament in the Middle Ages* (Philadelphia and London, 1952).

(c) *General Studies of English parliamentary history.*

Bindoff, S. T., 'Parliamentary History, 1529–1688', in *Victoria County History, Wiltshire*, V (1957).

McFarlane, K. B., 'Parliament and "Bastard Feudalism" ', *T.R.H.S.*, 4th ser., XXVI (1944).

McIlwain, C. H., *The High Court of Parliament and its Supremacy* (New Haven, 1910).

Pollard, A. F., *The Evolution of Parliament* (2nd ed., London, 1926).

Richardson, H. G. and Sayles, G. O., 'Parliaments and Great Councils in Medieval England', *L.Q.R.* LXXVII (1961).

Thompson, F., *A Short History of Parliament, 1295–1642* (Minneapolis, 1953).

Wedgwood, J. C., *History of Parliament, 1439–1509*, 2 vols. (London, 1936–38; partly unreliable).

(d) *Political theories*

Allen, J. W., *A History of Political Thought in the Sixteenth Century* (London, 1928).

Carlyle, R. W. and A. J., *History of Medieval Political Thought in the West*, VI (Edinburgh, 1936).

Elton, G. R. 'Constitutional Development and Political Thought in Western Europe' in *New Cambridge Modern History*, II (Cambridge, 1958: for the sixteenth century).

Hinton, W. K., 'English Constitutional Doctrine, from the Fifteenth Century to the Seventeenth', *E.H.R.* LXXV (1960).

McIlwain, C. H., *Constitutionalism Ancient and Modern* (Ithaca, N.Y., 1947).

Morris, C., *Political Thought in England: Tyndale to Hooker* (Oxford, 1954).

Pocock, G. A., *The Ancient Constitution and the Feudal Law* (Cambridge, 1957).

Smith, T., *De Republica Anglorum or a Discourse on the Commonwealth of England* (1583), ed. Alston, L. (Cambridge, 1906).

Ullmann, W., *Principles of Government and Politics in the Middle Ages* (London, 1961).

(e) *Taxation and representation*

Gray, H. L., 'The First Benevolence' in *Facts and Factors in Economic History: Essays presented to E. F. Gay* (Cambridge, Mass., 1932).

Harriss, G. L., 'Parliament and Taxation: The Middle Ages', *S.I.C.*, XXXI (1966).

Harriss, G. L., 'Aids, Loans and Benevolences', *Historical Journal*, VI (1963).

Kirby, J. L., 'The Issues of the Lancastrian Exchequer and Lord Cromwell's Estimates of 1433', *B.I.H.R.* XXIV (1951).

McFarlane, K. B., 'Loans to Lancastrian Kings: the Problem of Inducement', *Cambridge Hist. Journal*, IX (1947).

Pennington, D., 'Parliament and Taxation, 1485–1660', *S.I.C.* XXXI (1966).

Power, E., *The Wool Trade in English Medieval History* (Oxford, 1941).

Ramsay, G. D., 'Two Sixteenth Century Taxation Lists, 1545 and 1576', *Wiltshire Archaeological and Natural History Society, Records Branch*, X (1954: especially important for the benevolences under Henry VIII).

Schofield, R. S., 'The Geographical Distribution of Wealth in England, 1334–1649', *Econ. H.R.*, 2nd ser., XVIII (1965; important for the subsidies under the Tudors).

Stephenson, C., *Medieval Institutions: Selected Essays*, ed. Lyon, B. D. (Ithaca, N.Y., 1954).

Wolffe, B. P., 'The Management of English Royal Estates under the Yorkist Kings', *E.H.R.* LXXI (1956).
Wolffe, B. P., 'Henry VII's Land Revenues and Chamber Finance', *E.H.R.* LXXIX (1964).

(f) *The lords in parliament*

Harcourt, L. W. V., *His Grace the Steward and Trial of Peers* (London, 1907).
Miller, H., 'Subsidy Assessments of the Peerage in the Sixteenth Century', *B.I.H.R.* XXVIII (1955).
Miller, H., 'Attendance in the House of Lords in the Reign of Henry VIII', *Historical Journal*, X (1967).
Pike, L. O., *Constitutional History of the House of Lords* (London, 1894).
Powell, J. Enoch and Wallis, K., *The House of Lords in the Middle Ages* (London, 1968).
Pugh, T. B. and Ross, C. D., 'The English Baronage and the Income Tax of 1436', *B.I.H.R.* XXVI (1953).
Roskell, J. S., 'The Problem of the Attendance of the Lords in Medieval Parliaments', *B.I.H.R.* XXIX (1956).
Stone, L., 'The Inflation of Honours, 1558–1641', *Past and Present*, 14 (1958).
Stone, L., *The Crisis of the Aristocracy, 1558–1641* (Oxford, 1965).

(g) *The commons in parliament*

Bassett, M., *Knights of the Shire for Bedfordshire during the Middle Ages* (Bedfordshire Historical Record Society, XXIX, 1949).
Cam, H. M., 'The Community of the Shire and the Payment of its Representatives in Parliament', *Liberties and Communities in Medieval England* (Cambridge, 1944).
Cam, H. M., 'Medieval Representation in Theory and Practice', *Speculum*, XXIX (1954).
Cam, H. M., 'Theory and Practice of Representation in Medieval England', *History*, XXXVIII (1953), repr. *Law-Finders and Law Makers in Medieval England* (London, 1962).
Edwards, J. G., *The Commons in Medieval English Parliaments* (London, 1957).
Edwards, J. G., 'The Emergence of Majority Rule in English Parliamentary Elections', *T.R.H.S.*, 5th ser., XIV (1964).
Edwards, J. G., 'The Huntingdonshire Parliamentary Election of 1450' in *Essays in Medieval History presented to Bertie Wilkinson* (Toronto, 1969).
Edwards, J. G., 'The Emergence of Majority Rule in the Procedure of the House of Commons', *T.R.H.S.*, 5th Ser., XV (1965).
Gooder, A., *Parliamentary Representation of Yorkshire*, I (Yorkshire Arch. Society, Record Series, XCI, 1935).
Hornyold-Strickland, H., *Biographical Sketches of the Members of Parliament of Lancashire, 1290–1550* (Chetham Society, XCIII: Manchester, 1935).
Houghton, K. N., 'Theory and Practice in Borough Elections to Parliament during the Later Fifteenth Century', *B.I.H.R.* XXXIX (1966).

Latham, L. C., 'Collection of the Wages of the Knights of the Shire in the Fourteenth and Fifteenth Centuries', *E.H.R.* XLVIII (1933).

McKisack, M., *The Parliamentary Representation of the English Boroughs during the Middle Ages* (Oxford, 1932).

Mitchell, W. M., *The Rise of the Revolutionary Party in the English House of Commons, 1603–1629* (New York, 1957).

Notestein, W., *The Winning of the Initiative by the House of Commons* (Oxford, 1924).

Richardson, H. G., 'The Commons and Medieval Politics,' *T.R.H.S.*, 4th ter., XXVIII (1946).

Roskell, J. S., *Knights of the Shire for the County Palatine of Lancaster, 1377–1460* (Chetham Society, XCVI: Manchester, 1937).

Roskell, J. S., 'The Medieval Speakers for the Commons in Parliament', *B.I.H.R.* XXIII (1950).

Roskell, J. S., *The Commons in the Parliament of 1422* (Manchester, 1953).

Roskell, J. S. 'Parliamentary Representation of Lincolnshire', *Nottingham Mediaeval Studies*, III (1959).

Roskell, J. S., *The Commons and their Speakers in English Parliaments, 1376–1523* (Manchester, 1965).

(h) *The Organization of parliament*

Adair, E. R. and Evans, F. M., 'Writs of Assistance from 1558 to 1700', *E.H.R.* XXXVI (1921).

Neale, J. E., 'The Commons' Journals of the Tudor Period', *T.R.H.S.*, 4th ser., III (1920).

Pollard, A. F., 'The Authenticity of the Lords' Journals in the Sixteenth Century', *T.R.H.S.*, 3rd ser., VIII (1914).

Pollard, A. F., 'Fifteenth Century Clerks of Parliaments', *B.I.H.R.* XV (1938).

Pollard, A. F., 'The Under-Clerks and the Commons' Journals', *B.I.H.R.* XVI (1939).

Pollard, A. F., 'Queen Elizabeth's Under-Clerks and their Commons' Journals', *B.I.H.R.* XVII (1939).

Pollard, A. F., 'The Clerical Organization of Parliament', *E.H.R.* LVII (1942).

Pollard, A. F., 'Receivers of Petitions and Clerks of Parliament', *E.H.R.* LVII (1942).

(i) *Parliament, legislation and the Courts of law*

Adair, E. R., 'The Statute of Proclamations', *E.H.R.* XXXII (1917).

Baldwin, J. F., *The King's Council in England during the Middle Ages* (Oxford, 1913).

Bindoff, S. T., 'The Making of the Statute of Artificers', *Elizabethan Government and Society: Essays presented to Sir John Neale* (London 1961).

Elton, G. R., 'Henry VIII's Act of Proclamations', *E.H.R.* LXXV (1960).

Elton, G. R., 'Government by Edict?' *Historical Journal*, VIII (1965).

Gray, H. L., *The Influence of the Commons on Early Legislation: a Study of the Fourteenth and Fifteenth Centuries* (Cambridge, Mass., 1932).

335

Levine, M., 'A Parliamentary Title to the Crown in Tudor England', *Huntington Q.R.* xxv (1962).

Myers, A. R., 'Parliamentary Petitions in the Fifteenth Century', *E.H.R.* LII (1937).

Myers, A. R., 'Some Observations on the Procedure of the Commons in dealing with Bills in the Lancastrian Period', *Univ. of Toronto Law Journal*, III (1939).

(j) *Representation of the clergy*

Kemp, E. W., *Counsel and Consent: Aspects of the Government of the Church as exemplified in the History of the English Provincial Synods* (London, 1961).

Lunt, W. E., *Financial Relations of the Papacy with England, 1327-1534* (Cambridge, Mass., 1962).

Snow, V. F., 'Proctorial Representation and Conciliar Management during the Reign of Henry VIII', *Historical Journal*, IX (1966).

Weske, D. B., *Convocation of the Clergy* (London, 1937).

III WORKS PRINCIPALLY RELATING TO SPECIFIC PERIODS

(a) *The Lancastrian period*

Fraser, C. M., 'Some Documents relating to the Hilary Parliament of 1404,' *B.I.H.R.* xxxiv (1961).

Kirby, J. L., 'Councils and Councillors of Henry IV, 1399–1413', *T.R.H.S.*, 5th ser., XIV (1964).

Lander, J. R., 'Henry VI and the Duke of York's Second Protectorate, 1455 to 1456', *Bulletin of the John Rylands Library*, XLIII (1960).

McFarlane, K. B., 'The Lancastrian Kings', *Cambridge Medieval History*, VIII (1936).

Myers, A. R., 'A Parliamentary Debate in the Mid-Fifteenth Century', *Bulletin of the John Rylands Library*, XXII (1938).

Plucknett, T. F. T., 'The Place of the Council in the Fifteenth Century', *T.R.H.S.*, 4th ser., I (1918).

Plucknett, T. F. T., 'The Lancastrian Constitution', *Tudor Studies Presented to Albert Frederick Pollard* (London, 1924).

Rogers A., 'Henry IV, the Commons and Taxation', *Mediaeval Studies*, XXXI (Toronto, 1969).

Roskell, J. S., 'The Social Composition of the Commons in a Fifteenth-century Parliament', *B.I.H.R.*, XXIV (1951).

Virgoe, R., 'Three Suffolk Parliamentary Elections of the Mid-fifteenth Century', *B.I.H.R.* xxxIX (1966).

(b) *The Yorkist period and the reign of Henry VII*

Dunham, W. H., (ed.), *The Fane Fragment of the 1461 Lords' Journal* (New Haven, Conn., 1935).

Lander, J. R., 'Marriage and Politics in the Fifteenth Century: the Nevilles and the Wydevilles', *B.I.H.R.* xxxVI (1963).

Pickthorn, K., *Early Tudor Government: Henry VII* (Cambridge, 1934).

Pollard, A. F., 'The De Facto Act of Henry VII', *B.I.H.R.* VII (1929).
Williams, C. H., 'A Norfolk Parliamentary Election, 1461', *E.H.R.* XL (1925).

(c) *The reign of Henry VIII*

Cooper, J. P., 'The Supplication against the Ordinaries Reconsidered', *E.H.R.* LXXII (1957).
Dickens, A. G., *Thomas Cromwell and the English Reformation* (London, 1959).
Elton, G. R., 'Evolution of a Reformation Statute', *E.H.R.* LXIV (1949).
Elton, G. R., 'The Commons' Supplication of 1532', *E.H.R.* LXVI (1951).
Elton, G. R., 'The Law of Treason in the Early Reformation', *Historical Journal*, XI (1968).
Ives, E. W., 'The Genesis of the Statute of Uses', *E.H.R.* LXXXII (1967).
Kelly, M., 'The Submission of the Clergy' [*1532*], *T.R.H.S.* 5th ser., XV (1965).
Pickthorn, K., *Early Tudor Government: Henry VIII* (Cambridge, 1934).
Pollard, A. F., 'An Early Parliamentary Election Petition', *B.I.H.R.* VIII (1931).
Pollard, A. F., 'Thomas Cromwell's Parliamentary Lists', *B.I.H.R.* IX (1931).
Pollard, A. F., 'A Changeling Member of Parliament', *B.I.H.R.* X (1932).
Plucknett, T. F. T., 'Some proposed Legislation of Henry VIII', *T.R.H.S.* 4th ser., XIX (1936).
Scarisbrick, J. J., *Henry VIII* (London, 1968).
Stone, L., 'Thomas Cromwell's Political Programme', *B.I.H.R.* XXIV (1951).
Thornley, I. D., 'The Treason Legislation of Henry VIII', *T.R.H.S.*, 3rd ser., XI (1917).
Woodward, G. W. O., 'The Role of Parliament in the Henrician Revolution', *Schweizer Beiträge zur allgemeinen Geschichte*, XVI (1958). Reprinted in *S.I.C.* XX (1959).

(d) *The reign of Elizabeth*

Bayne, C. G., 'The First House of Commons of Queen Elizabeth', *E.H.R.* XXIII (1908).
Birt, H. N., *The Elizabethan Religious Settlement* (London, 1907).
Black, J. D., *The Reign of Elizabeth, 1558–1603* (Oxford 1949).
Collinson, P., *The Elizabethan Puritan Movement* (London, 1967).
Hinton, R. W. K., 'The Decline of Parliamentary Government under Elizabeth I and the Early Stuarts', *Cambridge Historical Journal*, XII (1957).
Levine, M., *The Early Elizabethan Succession Question, 1558–1568* (Stanford, 1966).
MacCaffrey, W. T., 'England: the Crown and the New Aristocracy, 1540–1600', *Past and Present*, No. 30 (1965).
Maitland, F. W., 'Elizabethan Gleanings', *Collected Papers*, III (Cambridge 1911).

BIBLIOGRAPHY

Neale, J. E., 'The Lord Keeper's Speech to the Parliament of 1592–3', *E.H.R.* XXXI (1916).

Neale, J. E., 'Queen Elizabeth's quashing of the Bills in 1597–8', *E.H.R.* XXXIV (1919).

Neale, J. E., 'Parliament and the Succession Question in 1562–3 and 1566', *E.H.R.* XXXVI (1921).

Neale, J. E., 'Three Elizabethan Elections', *E.H.R.* XLVI (1931).

Neale, J. E., 'Parliament and the Articles of Religion, 1571', *E.H.R.* LXVII (1952).

Neale, J. E., *Elizabeth I and her Parliaments*, 2 vols. (London, 1953–7) *The Elizabethan House of Commons* (London, 1949).

Pollard, A. F. and Blatcher, M., 'Hayward Townshend's Journals', *B.I.H.R.* XII–XV (1934–37).

Read, C., *Mr. Secretary Cecil and Queen Elizabeth* (London, 1955).

Read, C., *Lord Burghley and Queen Elizabeth* (London, 1960).

INDEX